Lesbian / Woman

by Del Martin & Phyllis Lyon

Twentieth Anniversary Edition

The people described in this book are real. The incidents and situations are true. However, we have changed most of the names and places to protect the innocent, lest they be punished for the infamous crime of being.

Library of Congress Cataloging-in-Publication Data

Martin, Del.
    Lesbian/Woman / by Del Martin and Phyllis Lyon. — Updated and expanded.
      p.   cm.
    ISBN 0-912078-91-X : $25.00
    1. Lesbianism—United States. I. Lyon, Phyllis. II. Title.
HQ75.6.U5M37   1991
306.76′63′0973—dc20   91-15045
                                          CIP

A condensation entitled "Lesbian Love & Sexuality" appeared in *Ms.* July 1972.

PRINTING HISTORY
Glide edition published July 1972
Bantam edition / November 1972
2nd printing . . . December 1972   4th printing . . . December 1977
3rd printing . . . June 1973   5th printing . . . April 1983
Revised Bantam edition . . . December 1983

Production by David Charlsen & Others
Printed in the United States of America

Please enclose $25.00 for each copy of **LESBIAN/WOMAN** ordered. For postage and handling, add $3.50 for the first book and $1.00 for each additional book. California residents add appropriate sales tax. Please contact Volcano Press for group discount prices.

Volcano Press, Inc. P.O. Box 270, Volcano CA 95689
PHONE   (209) 296-3445   FAX   (209) 296-4515

Hardcover Trade Edition   ISBN 0-912078-91-X
Special Limited Edition   ISBN 0-912078-93-6

Table of Contents

To the Daughters of Bilitis—
and to all the other daughters throughout the world
who are struggling with their identity
as Lesbian/Woman.

Introduction to
Twentieth Anniversary Edition

This edition of *Lesbian/Woman* is divided into two parts: the original book published by Glide Publications in 1972, and a twenty-year update. The ten-year update in the Bantam edition of 1983 has been revised, and a review of the 1980s and a projection for the 90s have been added in this Volcano Press volume.

In reviewing the two decades since the first printing of our book, we are impressed with how much change has occurred. Yet what we described twenty years ago is still true in many areas of the United States and the world.

For several years *Lesbian/Woman* has been out of print. We owe many thanks to Carol Seajay for her unrelenting campaign to get us to put together another updated edition. And we congratulate Carol and her *Feminist Bookstore News* for receiving the 1989 Publisher's Service Award sponsored by *Lambda Book Report*. We also thank Ruth Gottstein and David Charlsen of Volcano Press for their assistance, and for pinning us down to a deadline.

Introduction

A Lesbian is a woman whose primary erotic, psychological, emotional and social interest is in a member of her own sex, even though that interest may not be overtly expressed. At a time when women, the forgotten sex, are voicing their rage and demanding their personhood, it is fitting that a book on the Lesbian be written. Like her heterosexual sister, the Lesbian has been downtrodden, but doubly so: first, because she is a woman, and second, because she is a Lesbian.

Nonfiction books and articles are almost exclusively devoted to the male homosexual, with perhaps a chapter on or incidental mention of the Lesbian. The implication is either that what is said applies equally to female homosexuals or that the Lesbian, because she is a woman, is just not that important. It is true that the male homosexual and the Lesbian have many common concerns, and that her numbers probably equal that of the male—one in every ten women. It must be noted, however, that the Lesbian differs greatly from the male homosexual in attitudes, problems and life styles.

The lack of research and scientific knowledge on the Lesbian is due to a number of factors. By nature the Lesbian is a chameleon creature, having learned for her own protection to cover up. She is, therefore, not easily studied. Most researchers are men who are interested primarily in the enigma of male homosexuality. They are less likely to take the female homosexual seriously, and when they do decide to conduct a study on Lesbians, they find a great resistance from these women, because they are men. Women researchers (still very rare because of discrimination against women) who might meet with less reluctance from Lesbians are not likely to go into this particular field lest they themselves become suspect to their academic colleagues.

At the 1962 convention of the Daughters of Bilitis, an internationally known Lesbian organization, a panel discussion on Lesbian literature led to a debate between Jess Stearn and Tracy Laing, book reviewer, as to who could write the definitive book about the Lesbian—a man or a woman. Tracy said that what was needed was qualified writers who were Lesbians, that budding authors were often told to "write what you know about." Jess took the position that as a man he could be more objective because of his detachment. But even Jess would have to admit he was not altogether detached in his book, which was published subsequent to the debate. In the back of his heterosexual head there was always the unsaid thought, "Oh, what a waste," when he was forced to the realization that these women, many of whom he found attractive, were not attracted to him or to other men.

There have been other debates within the homosexual community as to the objectivity or bias of research when conducted by presumed heterosexuals. But where do the scientists gather their data? From whom? How do they measure the thoughts, feelings and attitudes of their subjects? Experience indicates that the questions are made up generally by heterosexuals and asked of homosexuals who very often find them irrelevant to their particular life style. The questions, for the most part, are unanswerable by the required yes or no or multiple choice, and their only virtue is that they are easily computerized into instant (misleading) statistics.

It is our contention that there can be no definitive book on the Lesbian, nor one which is wholly objective. We do feel, however, that the experience of Lesbians, expressed in their own terms and in the context of their own self awareness, has merit in and of itself. It is through such insights into others that understanding and acceptance of human beings comes about.

The particular expertise we bring to this book is that we are Lesbians and have lived together as lovers for nineteen years. We also helped to found the Daughters of Bilitis in 1955. Over the years in which we have been deeply involved in the homophile movement we have talked to, counseled, socialized with and been friends with thousands of Lesbians. The term *homophile* was put into usage by the Mattachine Society in the 1950s. Homosexual (using the Greek derivation of *homo* rather than the Latin) means sex with same, while homophile means love of same. Too often people think of homo*sex*uality only in terms of specific sexual acts instead of considering a person's sexuality as a single facet or characteristic of the whole being. We hope that this book will help to put that three-letter word *sex* in proper perspective with reference to the female homophile.

Because we are Lesbians we have lived the experiences that we are writing about. We have coped with the identity crisis, with the parent-child relationship both as child and as parent, and with the emotions of love and jealousy. We own our own home and have wrestled with plumbing problems, insurance, taxes and wills—not to mention gardening, for which we have no aptitude.

Our stance in the book is that of the everyday life experience of the Lesbian: how she views herself as a person; how she deals with the problems she encounters in her various roles as woman, worker, friend, parent, child, citizen, wife, employer, welfare recipient, home owner and taxpayer; and how she views other people and the world around her.

Admittedly, then, this is a subjective book. It is not a true confession. But it does not pretend to be scientific, either. It is written from experience—firsthand experience with the persons involved. It is partisan. But we hope it will be coolly, rationally, factually and heatedly partisan. For no book on the Lesbian can overlook the feelings, the thoughts, the self image, the *beingness* of the woman who has adopted this as her life style.

This isn't just "our" book. It is the story of the many Lesbians we have met over the years, without whom it could never have been written. We wish to acknowledge the invaluable contributions of particular individuals who helped us with some of the nitty-gritty details: Hy Cohen, Sally Gearhart, Emogene Kuhn, Kenneth Zwerin, Barbara Lucas and Linda Chaney. To Ruth Gottstein and the rest of the Glide Publications staff we express special thanks for keeping the faith after McCall Publishing turned us down because, among other things, we "apparently had no doubts about our life style, and that's impossible."

Of course, we had our doubts in the beginning—society saw to that. But over the years, as you will see, we learned many things that led us to self acceptance—and liberation.

1. The Lesbian — Myth & Reality

So little is known about the Lesbian that even Lesbians themselves are caught up in the myths and stereotypes so prevalent in our society.

When we first started living together as a couple we knew practically nothing about female homosexuality. We only knew that we loved each other and wanted to be together. Somehow that tagged us as Lesbians and bound us to some mysterious underground "gay" society of which we were only barely aware. That was back in the days when the term "gay" was an in-group password, a means of double talk in a hostile "straight" (heterosexual) society. It was a word you could use to let someone else know you were homosexual without the fear that anyone overhearing it would understand—unless, of course, they were in the know. With increased attention of the media to the subjects of homosexuality and Gay Liberation, the term is now popular in its usage.

Del had read a few books—that's all there were in earlier days. She had been to a number of gay bars, which was always a twitchy experience, since police raids were commonplace then. She had met a few Lesbians and had one previous affair.

Phyllis had been vaguely aware of homosexuality, but, like so many other women, never heard or thought of it in terms of the female, only in terms of the male. That the reason she and her roommate had been thrown out of their college dorm was undoubtedly due to implied homosexuality never occurred to her until years later. The dean of women and the housemother had charged that Phyllis and Jane were "too close," that they engaged in double talk at the dinner table, that they did not mix socially with the other girls in the dormitory, and that they had missed "lock out" a couple of times.

Although she liked men, dated them and even once went so far as to become engaged, Phyllis still had reservations about taking that final step down the aisle. She sought a career in journalism and enjoyed her independence. She had always maintained a number of close friendships with women and recalls feeling very resentful when one of them would call up and cancel a prior engagement to go to the movies with her, just because some man had asked for a date.

That's about where we were. Hardly the ideal background from which to launch a Lesbian "marriage," which is the way we thought of our relationship. The only model we knew, a pattern that also seemed to hold true for those few Lesbians we had met, was that of mom-and-dad or heterosexual marriage. So Del assumed the role of "butch" (she was working at the time) and Phyllis, being completely brainwashed in society's role of woman anyway, decided she must be the "femme." Like her mother before her, she got up every morning to make breakfast—at least for the first week.

The closest friends we had at the time were a newly married heterosexual couple. They, too, assumed that Lesbians would adopt butch-femme roles. Sam happily encouraged Del to be a male chauvinist, slapping her on the back and plying her with cigars, all the while telling her she had to keep Phyllis in her place and coaching her on maintaining the upper hand. Meanwhile Sue and Phyllis plotted the traditionally sneaky ways women devise to gain and maintain the upper hand. If this sounds like an arm-wrestling match, it was. Like so many heterosexual couples, we played the roles in public, and with Sue and Sam, and then we went home and fought about them. The only thing that saved our relationship was Phyllis's stubborn resolve that it would last at least a year. The fact we had known each other for more than three years and had established a basic friendship was the other thing we had going for us.

In the course of our nineteen years together we have learned that many Lesbians in our age group (late forties) went through the same kind of role playing. While a few become trapped in this butch-femme pattern, most come in time, as we did, to the realization that they are both women and that's why they are together.

Because the Lesbian is every woman. She is the college student preparing for a career that will make her economically independent and give her some measure of personal accomplishment. She is the dedicated nurse or the committed social worker. She works on the assembly line of an electronics plant, drives a taxicab, or goes to night school. The Lesbian is an attorney, an architect, or an engineer. She is the blind poet and songwriter. She serves on municipal commissions, is the author of a best seller, and is honored among the "Ten Most Distinguished Women of the Year." She is a welfare recipient, an auto mechanic, a veterinarian, an alcoholic, a telephone operator, a civil service or civil rights worker. She may be a lieutenant in the armed forces or a beauty operator. And, being a woman in western society, she is certainly a clerk-typist, secretary or bookkeeper.

The Lesbian is aboard ship traveling around the world. She resides in every country. She lives in an apartment or is paying for her own home in the city, in the suburbs, or in a small country town. She is raising goats on a farm in the Ozarks or is part of a harem in Saudi Arabia. She is in attendance at state social gatherings in the White House. She lives in the Orient, Australia, Germany. She is a Democrat in the United States or a Socialist in Italy. She is the cloistered young Catholic woman in Latin America or lives in a *kibbutz* in Israel. She is a geisha girl in Japan or a belly dancer in a night club in New York City. Or she may be the Jane Doe suicide in the city morgue.

However women are depicted in world society, so may the Lesbian be. For the Lesbian is *all* women. As you who read this have related to women personally and generally in your life, so have you become personally involved with Lesbians, whether you have been aware of it or not. For you have known, met and talked with Lesbians throughout your life—in your family, at school, on the job, at the corner cocktail lounge, at the neighborhood bowling alley, at your church. You may have known and loved a Lesbian dearly or been wary of her, sensing that, despite all appearances to the contrary, she is somehow different.

Most of you can probably recall a distant cousin or a maiden aunt about whom the family whispered vaguely. But few of you wish to admit that the Lesbian in your life was really much closer to home. For we are also your daughters, your sisters, even some-times your mothers. The Lesbian comes from all walks of society, every economic class, every educational level, every racial and eth-nic group, every religious background. She is in every type of work, of every political persuasion, and in every part of the world. The Lesbian is:

—The divorced mother, Inez, who places her child in a day care center while she commutes to her office job in the city, barely eking out a living despite the child support minimally and grudg-ingly paid by her ex-husband on order of the court. Underlying her daily routine is the constant fear that she will be discovered to be a Lesbian and lose not only her job, but her child as well.

—A teacher in specialized education working with the deaf, for whose services several school districts have been competing. Yet in spite of her known expertise and talent as a teacher, should it become known that she is a Lesbian, Olga would be unemploy-able.

—Natalie, a likeable, adequate, very average worker in a plastics factory making wastebaskets, fired when it was made known that she was a Lesbian.

—Betty, caught up in a raid on a gay bar some years ago, who lost her job as a civil service playground director even though the charges against her were dismissed. She spent more than ten years in meaningless jobs before she once again was accepted in the civil service in an area where her education and talents could be put to use.

—A Black teenager, Bea, three months away from high school graduation, who was literally thrown out of her home when she told her mother she was gay.

—The successful business woman and socialite, Constance, active in civic affairs, who is seldom seen with her "roommate" of ten years lest the finger be pointed at her, thus destroying her "image."

These are typical of the many Lesbians we have met over the years. We mention them to show how the preference for a member of her own sex as a love or life partner—which is all that sets the Lesbian apart from any other woman—can affect her entire life and inhibit or kill dreams, ambitions, creativity. Being a Lesbian makes her a misfit in American culture and sets up a barrier which prevents her from revealing herself to you. For her own protection, learned through painful experience, the Lesbian generally maintains a dual life—one that is visible and one that is kept secret. Understandably, this can lead to emotional conflicts, and time and energy wasted on weaving a web of lies. It can lead to a loss of self and potential in the process of face-saving conformity.

Understandably, too, since the Lesbian in our society is generally hidden, her existence has generated a great deal of conjecture and intrigue, out of which a whole body of folklore has been perpetrated on the public as fact.

Once aware of the Lesbian's existence, most people tend to view her solely as a sexual being. She is seen as a sad caricature of a male, trying to dress and act in the manner she deems "masculine," and generally aping some of men's worst characteristics. Or she is conceived of as a hard, sophisticated female who indiscriminately seduces innocent girls or women into the mysteries of some "perversion" they know little or nothing about. On the other hand, she is seen as an unfortunate, pitiable spinster, who, unable to catch a man, has settled for a less desirable substitute in another woman as her lover—whom, of course, she will immediately abandon when and if she meets "him." Some men fantasize the Lesbian as a voluptuous, sensuous mistress who is unscrupulous in her sexual tastes, insatiable in her sexual appetite and therefore indiscriminate in her choice of sexual partner.

These stereotypes are based upon the false assumption that the Lesbian is first and foremost *sexual* in all her thoughts, desires and actions. What people fail to realize is that being a Lesbian is not merely indulging in physical acts or lovemaking. For the woman involved it is a way of life, encompassing the structure of her whole personality, one facet of which is, of course, her sexuality. For her it is the expression of a way of feeling, of loving, of responding to other people.

Furthermore, Lesbians are no more preoccupied with sex than are other people. We don't spend all our time in bed—and neither does anyone else we know. We, too, go to work, clean house, do the shopping, watch television, go to the movies, work on hobbies, have guests in for dinner, visit friends, and do all the other ordinary humdrum things which make up life in America today.

Also contrary to popular belief, most Lesbians seek relationships with those in their own age bracket. They do not put a premium on youth, as do many male homosexuals, but prefer partners with whom they have something in common besides sex. They look for companionship, community of interests, and all those other ingredients necessary to make any relationship work over a period of time.

Yet one of the myths that seems to hang on in our society is that Lesbians molest little girls and seduce young women. In actuality, childhood homosexual experiences are usually episodes of experimentation between little girls of the same age. Del recalls engaging in such experimentation at the age of nine with a girl who may have been a year younger and who, incidentally, was the initiator. But the incident bore no particular significance for Del at the time, since most of the youngsters, male and female, were in the habit of "playing doctor" and examining each other's bodies and genitals. Instances of an adult woman molesting a small child are so rare that we have not run into even a single case.

We have known Lesbians who "came out" when they were teenagers, but their partners were schoolmates or youngsters in their peer group. We have also known eighteen- and nineteen-year olds who became involved with "older women" of twenty-two or so, above the legal age for marriage between members of the opposite sexes. But by and large, most older Lesbians, while appreciative of youthful good looks, are seeking someone more sophisticated and experienced. As forty-year-old Carmen put it, when she came to us hoping we might be able to introduce her to some older Lesbians: "What on earth would I do with a twenty-year-old? I'm not looking for a daughter to raise!"

A 1959 survey by the Daughters of Bilitis indicated a very high ratio of Lesbians in the teaching profession. In writing up the research, however, these women were lumped in with the "professional" classification which comprised 38 percent of the sampling. This particular point of information we purposely withheld at the time lest a witch hunt be initiated in the California school system. Discovery or even the mere accusation of a teacher's homosexual orientation was cause for immediate dismissal or request for one's resignation, along with revocation of one's teaching credential, until 1969. It was then that the California State Supreme Court ruled that teachers may not have their teaching credential taken away simply because they have engaged in homosexual acts not specifically spelled out in the criminal statutes.

Despite the large number of Lesbians who are teachers, there is no data available, other than in fiction, that they have seduced or become sexually intimate with their female students. Yet the myth persists. It has always mystified us that the public remains so fearful of Lesbian teachers when criminal statistics clearly indicate that young girls who are seduced or raped are invariably victimized by men. While men are increasingly taking over the elementary classroom, there is still only concern lest they be homosexuals. We can only suppose that parents and school administrators are concerned solely with preventing the possibility of a homosexual encounter—like those police officers from Northern Station in San Francisco during a 1970 police-community relations confrontation with members of the homophile community:

"Think what a traumatic effect it would have on a young boy!" the police lieutenant cried out.

"But what about the girls? What about rape?" a young Lesbian countered.

"That's different. That's 'normal'," two patrolmen replied in unison.

Before we lay the bugaboo of homosexual child-molesting to rest, we must note that women, having found each other in the women's liberation movement, are beginning to knock down this myth themselves. In New York City during their regular Saturday Women's Liberation meetings in 1970, the women asked the men to take on the responsibility for child care. The most reliable and dependable group of men to report regularly each week for such duty was from the Gay Liberation Front. Through a pact of mutual respect and trust, women learned to leave their young sons in the care of homosexual men without compunction, without hesitation. Some were even considering adding *"gay* care centers" to their demands.

Women have always been carefully warned to shun the Lesbian; after all, the sanctity of home and family must be protected. Men, on the other hand, become increasingly fascinated by the unattainable, independent woman who is not an adjunct or appendage to a man, who does not seek nor require his approval for her existence, who even dares to compete with him not only in the job market but for "his" women as well. The predatory male heterosexual can only imagine that the poor thing just hasn't met the "right man" and, of course, is eager to lay claim to the title.

At one point, Del thought she really knew the answer to discouraging unwanted male advances. She told her boss, who had been pestering her, that she was gay. But much to her dismay, instead of discouraging him, this bit of juicy information only enhanced his ardor. It seemed his wife wouldn't let him make love to her "that way." As time went on, we learned that many Lesbians have used the same spurning technique with the same burning results.

But this woman-to-woman relationship, because it is contrary to the accepted and expected man-woman relationship and because there is so little known about it, is regarded as something weird, mysterious—and downright "queer." By community standards anything that is different must also be wrong. Consequently some people's first reaction, on learning that someone is a Lesbian, is that there must be something wrong with her physically. She must be some kind of biological freak whose genitals are somehow malformed; or perhaps she is the unfortunate victim of some type of hormone imbalance.

Phyllis was left with her mouth hanging open in astonishment when, on a guest appearance on his television show a few years ago, she was asked by the late Louis Lomax, "What are the physiological differences between Lesbians and other women?" Susan, who more recently, as part of her "liberation," felt the need to tell her mother about her Lesbian life, was equally appalled when her mother grasped her hand and asked very solemnly, "But why don't you have an operation, dear?"

Because there is no such operation. Neither our bodies nor the way they function is different from those of other females. Like other women we come in all sizes and shapes. Some of us are tall and lanky; some of us are short and fat. We are young and old, beautiful and homely, blonde and brunette, short-haired and long-haired, fair-skinned and dark-skinned—whatever the combination or variation. And no matter how you may look at it, we are and must be recognized and dealt with as women. In order to understand the Lesbian, it is therefore necessary that you think of her as a living, feeling, thinking human being: a woman. The Lesbian looks, dresses, acts, and *is* like any other woman. The only thing that distinguishes her as a Lesbian is her choice of another woman as her sex, love or life partner.

Wherever you find two women living together you cannot assume, however, that they are Lesbians, since many heterosexual women share apartments out of economic necessity or for companionship. Nor can you be sure that two women, because they date men, are heterosexual. It may only be a cover to protect their Lesbian relationship from gossip and innuendo. Karen recalls the time when a coworker who was driving her home after an overtime stint at the office declared emphatically, "I can spot a 'queer' every time!" The fact that she was talking to one had completely escaped her.

Another fallacy is the assumption that "it takes one to know one": that there is some telltale sign, Morse Code signal or knowing glance exchanged between Lesbians at a mixed gathering. In all likelihood any Lesbian present at such a gathering would be very much on guard lest she give herself away—even to one of her own kind, whom she still regards as a threat in such social situations.

Appearance can also be misleading in trying to detect a woman's sexual orientation. Nancy, on return from a camping trip at Yosemite National Park, told us she had finally figured out the way you can tell the Lesbians from the straight women. The "stomping butch" types wearing men's jeans and boots usually had a husband and a number of kids trailing along behind them; the Lesbians, however, wore capris or women's slacks so as to appear more "feminine" and not so obvious.

The American public puts much stock in the professional opinion of medical doctors: "They ought to know; they are the authorities." Pardon us if we disagree—and with good reason. Our "authority" is personal experience, not only with leading the life of a Lesbian, but also with reading so much of the literature that indirectly affects that life.

The August, 1957, issues of two national magazines, on the newsstands at the same time, carried articles which purported to describe and enlighten the public about Lesbians. "What Makes a Homosexual?" in a publication called *Actual Medical Cases* written by Hugh Barnes, M.D., stated: "The homosexual female is characterized by deficient fat in the shoulders and at the girdle,

firm muscles, excess hair on the chest, back and legs, a tendency
to over-development of the clitoris. There is also a tendency
toward a shorter trunk, a contracted pelvis, under-development of
the breasts, excess hair on the face and a low-pitched voice."

However, Edward Dengrove, M.D., writing on "Homosexuality
in Women" for *Sexology* magazine, had this to say: "Contrary to
the popular conception of the woman with homosexual tendencies, she is not necessarily, or even usually, the extremely masculine woman, aggressive, strong and muscular, mannish in physical
appearance and dress, lacking all the delicacy and gentleness we
associate with the feminine. . . . For most Lesbians are not women
who are pretending to be men, but rather women who cannot
express their normal sexual drive in relationship to men, but must
direct it towards other females instead. Even in the sexual sphere,
the Lesbian remains essentially feminine, with the natural desires
and reactions of a woman. . . ."

Which one has the Toni? No wonder the public is confused!
And no wonder many Lesbians who have sought therapy have
found themselves explaining the whole phenomenon of homosexuality to their doctors.

Even though more is known about the Lesbian today than ever
before, the stereotypes still persist, reinforced by what little has
been recorded in history and by subsequent literary accounts. The
history of female homosexuality is probably as old as the history
of the human race itself; archaeologists have discovered prehistoric
cave drawings of female figures engaging in homosexual acts
together. But the term *Lesbian* is derived from the island of Lesbos, a triangular area of land in the Aegean Sea off the coast of
what is now Turkey. Sappho, famous Greek lyric poetess of the
early sixth century B.C., was supposed to have established a school for
young girls and/or a cult for female homosexuals on the island.
Historians and translators are at such variance about the details
that Dr. Jeannette H. Foster, former librarian for the (Kinsey)
Institute for Sex Research and author of *Sex Variant Women in
Literature,* was prompted to point out that, by Ovid's day, there
was so much controversy about Sappho's personal life that it almost seemed as if two Sapphos must have flourished on Lesbos,
"one the great poetess and the other the courtesan of undis-
ciplined habits."

Born out of the Sappho controversy the Lesbian has thus been depicted as a childish romantic at best, or at worst a child molester or prostitute. Prior to the twentieth century the chronicles of history and literature were written almost exclusively by men. References to Lesbians, of course, reflected the bias of the authors, who never depicted women as wholly, or even primarily, homosexual; the male ego could never admit that a woman existed who could have sexual satisfaction without a man. Lesbian episodes depicted in literature take the form of the initiation of an innocent girl by an older woman more experienced in giving sexual pleasure to men, a diversion for the prostitute, an experiment by upper class ladies with their handmaids to alleviate boredom, or the desperate activity of nuns or prison inmates who have been isolated from men. The accounts are devoid of personal devotion in any such relations, and sexual play often involved more than two participants.

There are occasional references, however, to pairs of women who formed "strongly emotional friendships," most famous of whom were the "Ladies of Llangollen": Lady Eleanor Butler and Sarah Ponsonby, two seventeenth century Irish women who settled in a cottage in the Vale of Llangollen in north Wales. While they were sometimes called "the Platonists," it is reported that Lady Eleanor wore men's clothes, that her journal spoke of "our bed," and that neither left their cottage for a single night throughout the fifty years they lived together. Even the accounts of the more recent long-term relationship between Gertrude Stein and Alice B. Toklas have a tendency to skirt the issue of their sexuality.

History also indicates that Lesbianism was existent among certain of the royalty and their courtiers, most notable of whom were Queen Christina of Sweden, Elizabeth I of England, and Marie Antoinette. But most of our knowledge of Lesbians in history is based on innuendo, rumor, or conjecture, and cannot be considered reliable.

The first novel on female variance to be written by a woman appeared in 1788: Mary Wollstonecraft's *Mary, A Fiction*. It is said to be based upon the author's consuming attachment to Fanny Blood, which began when Mary was about fifteen and continued until Fanny's death twelve years later.

Radclyffe Hall's novel *The Well of Loneliness,* first published in England in 1928, was exceedingly daring for its time. After lengthy court hearings, the book was condemned as obscene in the British Isles, simply because of its subject matter and the sympathetic manner in which it was handled. Other books published in England at the same time on the Lesbian theme did not meet the same fate, however, apparently because in them the Lesbian association was either condemned, as in Naomi Royde-Smith's *The Tortoiseshell Cat,* or satirized, as in Compton Mackenzie's *Extraordinary Women.*

Republication of *The Well of Loneliness* in Paris was followed by translation into eleven languages, and fourteen years later the book was enjoying a steady annual sale of one hundred thousand copies in the United States alone. It became the "Lesbian bible." Unfortunately, to the uninitiated the book perpetuated the myth of the Lesbian as a pseudo-male, and many young women, like Del, emulated the heroine, Stephen Gordon, only to find that their lovers, like Phyllis, were not looking for a male substitute. For Lesbians are women who are attracted to *women.*

The first nonfiction book covering Lesbianism as a whole and written by a Lesbian was *We Walk Alone,* published in 1955. While pleading with society to be more tolerant and less condemning, more understanding and less prone to pity the Lesbian as some kind of freak, the author, Ann Aldrich, led her readers "through Lesbos' lonely groves," dwelling mostly on bizarre examples and giving only fleeting reference to those women who are well-adjusted, productive citizens in society.

During the 1950s newsstands were deluged with Lesbian paperback novels which were, despite appearances to the contrary, (im)pure fiction written primarily by men. Those that were written more realistically by Lesbian authors, we have since learned, were rejected by the publishers or altered to fit the "party line" which required either a tragic ending or the ultimate realization that heterosexuality was indeed the only avenue to true happiness.

By the 1960s the trend in Lesbian fiction had changed somewhat. Happy endings were allowed in some instances, implying that Lesbian couples might be able to establish fulfilling alliances. But the quality of the literature still left much to be desired. Of some sixteen hundred titles listed in the bibliography *The Lesbian in Literature,* prepared by Gene Damon and Lee Stuart and published by the Daughters of Bilitis in 1967, the vast majority were earmarked as "trash." And these, of course, were chiefly written by men for male readers.

Led perhaps by the onslaught of these sensational sex novels, often describing Lesbians with male sex partners, and by publicity about the existence of a Lesbian organization, many men found their way to the offices of the Daughters of Bilitis in San Francisco. Some were quite outspoken about their sexual needs; others, more shy, cloaked their desires in a shroud of vagueness. But their interest in DOB was based on the false concept that Lesbians were open and available to men who "understood" and hoped to share in mutual sexual delights.

A tall, burly young man, who could easily have been taken for a police detective, made a special trip from Los Angeles in search of a Lesbian. Object: matrimony. Cliff's problem was that his responses were "feminine" in nature and that he felt trapped in a male body. Coming from a Catholic background, the only acceptable sexual outlet for him was heterosexual marriage. He reasoned, therefore, that he needed to find and marry a woman who would act as his masculine counterpart: namely, a Lesbian.

However, as Del carefully pointed out to Cliff, the Lesbian is not necessarily a male in a woman's body. Lesbianism is not a matter of gender-role designation, but contains within it elements of psychological, emotional, and spiritual involvement between two *women.* While Cliff's immediate and pressing problem was not solved, he did find a friend who was understanding and non-judgmental about his own sexual identity and needs. Del has heard from Cliff that he has since married and is the father of two children. How he and his wife have worked out their masculine and feminine roles we do not know. But we do know that what we call "femininity" and "masculinity" is culturally defined and few people, heterosexual and homosexual alike, fit the molds.

Another young man, Roger, came to the DOB office for help. He was not as articulate as Cliff, and it took Del some time to determine that he was looking for a Lesbian partner with whom to perform cunnilingus. Again Del tried to explain that female homosexuality could not be defined simply in terms of the sex act itself, but had to do with emotional involvement between women; that

Lesbians are not seeking male partners; and that, in any event, DOB was not in the business of pimping. Roger, however, was not easily dissuaded and Del, in exasperation and in need of reinforcements, suggested that, since Phyllis would be getting off work soon, perhaps they could continue their discussion over dinner at a nearby gay bar. Toward the end of the meal Del excused herself to go to the restroom. Roger took this as his cue to "come on" with Phyllis "as the date Del had fixed him up with." When Phyllis cleared up his misunderstanding, he left abruptly and indignantly.

These are only two of the many examples we could offer that Lesbians in our society are perceived by men as sexually permissive in choice of partner and sexual act. Many a Lesbian, too, has been surprised to realize that the heterosexual couple whom she has befriended, whom she believed to be sympathetic and understanding, was actually conspiring to lure her into their conjugal bed.

And so it has gone through the years. The descriptive phrases, commonplace in the literature about the Lesbian, have always been ambivalent and tend to create an aura of sexual mysticism: "the exciting, alluring and tantalizing promise of a woman's closeness"; "a strange, tempting, forbidden love"; "perverse, yet compelling attraction"; "sordid and ugly revelation of the unleashed passions of evil and of love"; "the quirk of nature that lures young women into the lonely, isolated and tragic twilight world." Although such language makes for dramatic effect in fiction and attention-getting headlines for newspaper sensation-seekers, it has little to do with the realities of Lesbian life, and has led to the existing state of confusion among the general public as well as among Lesbians themselves.

Little scientific research has been done on the Lesbian, and what has been done is based primarily upon childhood background and sexual practices. Until recently most subjects were drawn from captive samples of women in prison or in psychotherapy. And it has always bothered us that the emphasis of research has been devoted almost exclusively to causation rather than to those facets of the Lesbian life itself which could help to explode some of the myths and foster better understanding.

We have also maintained a strong objection to measuring the Lesbian in terms of happiness or unhappiness. A Lesbian who is struggling with her identity or who may be trying to repress her sexuality will, of course, be unhappy during that period of her life. The woman who has come to terms with her identity and has crossed the bridge of self acceptance may have gained self confidence but not yet a lover, and so feels lonely and unhappy for a time. The Lesbian who has hurdled the identity crisis and established a meaningful and satisfying relationship with another woman may still feel somewhat unhappy on occasion because of society's strictures. Happiness is not stationary: it is fluid; it fluctuates. As Lesbians we have experienced great joy and happiness and love. We have also known despair, conflict and unhappiness. This is the human condition. The same may be said for heterosexuals, for whose miseries Lesbians have often expressed compassion and empathy. Unfortunately the concern is not reciprocal. The fact that the Lesbian is not generally thought of in terms of her humanity, her close relationship to family, her deep involvement with society, her sameness rather than her difference, is responsible for the negative self image she often adopts or must struggle to overcome.

2. Self Image

It doesn't just happen to you. It isn't as if you wake up suddenly one morning and say to yourself, "I am a Lesbian." Or that you make a conscious decision—"that is what I'm going to be from now on"—as if it were an acceptable goal in life.

Though many Lesbians believe they were born that way, we tend to feel that persons are born sexual: not heterosexual or homosexual, just sexual. And the direction a girl's sexuality may take depends upon her individual circumstances and life experiences, and how she reacts to them. It's rather like a slowly emerging awareness of herself as someone who is different, who is responding in ways that are apparently not usual to others, and yet seem very natural to her.

Sometimes this awareness begins very early in life. While a child of five doesn't know anything about the sex act and couldn't care less, she can experience a strange attraction to other little girls, or perhaps just one girl singled out of the group. She may play with boys and feel a certain camaraderie and affection for them, but the emotional attachment she feels for girls may be entirely different.

Del remembers knowing and playing with a number of boys, but she never related to them with any degree of closeness or fondness as she did with her female playmates. She played tag and kick-the-can and hopscotch with all the kids in the neighborhood, but the game that stands out in her memory was playing "house." Boys didn't engage in this "girl stuff," so Del always assumed the role of husband and father. While the other little girls delighted in dressing up in their mother's clothes and playing the *femme fatale* (which in those days was the flapper), Del dragged her stepfather's old clothes out of the closet, struggled into the ill-fitting pants, which she cinched in around the waist, and rolled up the pants legs to where she wouldn't trip over them. Then she preened in front of the full-length closet mirror and strutted around in her child's-eye view of what it meant to be a man. Wearing the pants in the family had a deep significance for Del. It meant being boss, laying down the rules, making the decisions, being catered to—slippers, pipe, dinner ready when she/he came home from work. It meant being important, being master of the house. It meant being worldly and free to do what one chooses. Del had consciously wanted to be a boy from the time she was six, when the *Liberty Magazine* representative who was hiring youngsters to take over the local routes turned her down, not because she was too young, but because she was a girl. (That's really when she joined Women's Liberation, she says now.)

But Del's masculine image was mostly fantasy. She was never what one generally thinks of as a tomboy. She was never particularly athletically inclined, though she did like to play basketball. While a little girl like Del might today act out as an astronaut the hazards of interstellar space, Del's heroes were fearless lawmen (or outlaws) of the Wild West. It was a proud day when she got the cowboy outfit she had longed for. It was complete with hat, boots, spurs, cuffs, holster, chaps and cap pistol—all except the horse. But she was never man enough to master the gun. She was frightened by the bang of shooting off caps and was forever (and no one has ever been able to figure out how she managed this) getting her fingers caught in the trigger and running home crying to mother or grandma to get them extricated. To this day she hates guns—and the Fourth of July!

Apparently Del's experience was unique. At least we haven't met any other Lesbians who will admit to being as poor a shot as Del, whose masculine self image obviously suffered some damage. She retreated into such indoor sports as cards, checkers, and reading, and decided she would have to depend upon her brain, not her brawn, to prove herself.

But these were not really conscious decisions. Children show an avid interest in something today which may be dropped for something else next week; friends drift in and out of their lives; they learn new skills in school; they visit other households, meet new challenges, observe people in the streets and in the parks, always collecting new impressions, new ideas, new dreams of what life is really all about. Del hadn't thought much about wanting to be a boy until one day she noticed an item in the newspaper about a woman who had a successful sex change operation. This glimmering that such a thing was possible (and it was long before the celebrated case of Christine Jorgensen) started the fantasy all over again.

By this time Del was a bit older, aware of her body and feelings of sexual attraction, and the fantasy took on a romantic interest in girls. But, of course, she never let on, never told anyone about her feelings. She didn't figure her parents would understand. Her close girl friends talked only about boys and dragged her along on double dates, where she pretended interest in her escort while she fumed in silent rage and jealousy when "her" girl kissed the other boy. But Del was one up on him. *She* could spend the night with the girl—even if doing so meant, as it usually did, that Del would lie in a paralysis of fear from wanting to reach out and touch but not daring to.

Del married during her third year at college, when she was nineteen. She hadn't felt any strong attachment towards another girl for some time. She met Jack when she was working on the college paper: he was the business manager and she the managing editor. They started dating and found they had a lot of common interests, and by the time Jack got around to asking her to marry him, she was convinced that she was really in love with him, really in love with a man. Shortly after they were married, Del became pregnant (there was no pill then and damned little sex education) and had to drop out of college.

The Second World War was declared shortly thereafter, and housing in the city became tight. So the expanding Martin family was forced to move to the suburbs. Jack took a civilian job with the army, and what with commuting and long hours, was gone a great deal. But it wasn't his absence that broke up the marriage. His being gone was actually a relief at times, because Del was beginning to question her choices. She was feeling a deep sense of loss and of being trapped: loss of her own identity as a person and being caught in a rigid, narrowly defined role of wife and mother.

She'd had some mistaken idea that she and Jack were on equal terms in a one-to-one relationship, but he reminded her of the exact words he'd spoken when he proposed to her: "I've always dreamed of having a home of my own, and I'd like to have you *in it.*"

Besides their young daughter, whom they both adored, Jack and Del had something else left in common: they both wanted a wife. And when Del fell madly in love with the woman next door, she knew that for all parties concerned she must end her marriage. After the divorce Del dated a lot of different men, trying to prove that she was "normal" and trying to get over her consuming attachment for Sandra. During this time she ran across a copy of *The Well of Loneliness,* and for the first time she was able to put a name to what she had been feeling. She was a homosexual—a Lesbian.

She said the words quietly to herself, let them wash over and through her, and experienced a release she had never known before. The mystery that had plagued her all these years had been solved. She pronounced the words aloud, firmly and slowly: "I am a Lesbian." The relief she felt from having made this self discovery—of knowing, of being honest with herself—gave her a new sense of freedom. Then she repeated the words loudly, defiantly—and proudly. She felt for the first time she was on the threshold of profound meaning in her life. She saw a glimmering of who she was, who she could be. Del had known she was different, that she was attracted to women instead of men, but, like so many other isolated Lesbians, she thought she was the only one. Now she knew differently. There were others like herself.

She spent many hours at the library looking up every reference she could find on the subject. There wasn't much: a few books about the male homosexual, with bare mention of the female. But as she skimmed rapidly through the pages, her stomach muscles began to tighten; she gritted her teeth and fought back tears.

She had been feeling that she at last belonged, that there were other human beings in the world she could relate to. But her elation was short-lived. What she had thought of as love, this desire that for her came from the purest of motives, was really despicable and degenerate, at least according to these books. The love she felt for Sandra, though never expressed, was a perversion, a sign of psychopathology, a crime against nature and a sin against God. The people she had wanted to know about, wanted to meet and relate to, were crude and disgusting. The joy of self knowledge, so dearly bought, had turned into a very sick joke. Her new self image was destroyed.

I am a Lesbian.

A simple statement, it would seem, which merely conveys that the woman expressing it has a preference for women, both erotically and emotionally. But behind that statement may be years, sometimes decades, of soul searching, untold agonies of self doubt and guilt, and painful conflict—conflict between recognition of her inner being and acceptance of an assigned societal role, conflict between the desperate need for family support and despair at the prospect of bringing shame on her loved ones, conflict between her religious belief in God's eternal love for all His children and the negative pronouncements of church doctrine, conflict between celibacy and breaking the law, between honesty and deceit, between abject silence and open admission, between maintaining a dual life and loss of a career, between being crippled or whole, between life and death.

Behind that simple statement—"I am a Lesbian"—are implications so vast that the individual who would survive with any measure of sanity must examine all that she has ever been taught, all that she has ever experienced, all that she has ever hoped or dreamed. Some never make it through this long and lonely journey. They can't face rejection, the concept of being "queer" or different. They believe the myths and accept what they see on the surface of gay life. They succumb to fear and assume the guilt. They cannot play it straight, nor can they adjust to their homosexuality. So filled are they with self negation and self hatred, there is nothing left for them but death.

Del contemplated suicide; others have attempted it, and some have succeeded. Because of our own experience we are keenly aware of the identity crisis every Lesbian must face: that period in her life when she is forced to come to terms with the reality that she is at odds with the society in which she lives. We have known that thoughts of suicide often occur to the young woman, like Del, who cannot reconcile her actual feelings with those expected of her by her family, by her religion, or by her peers. But we had no idea how prevalent suicide is until we learned of a recent (1971) discussion involving twenty Lesbians between the ages of twenty-five and thirty-two, where it was revealed that only two had not attempted suicide when they were teenagers. It was shocking to us that eighteen out of twenty young women had been made to feel so degraded by the realization of their Lesbian identity, their self image so debased, that suicide seemed to be their only out. In our own more advanced age bracket we might expect this sort of revelation, but not in so young a group. We assumed that younger women would have had access to information that had been unavailable to us. What we failed to realize was that while there may be more literature available, it is still just as negative, and society's attitude still just as oppressive. The young Lesbian of today, while she may find out much earlier that she is not the "only one," must still work her way through the homosexual sin-crime-mental illness syndrome before she can accept herself as a person.

Self acceptance is a necessary step in the growing up process of any individual. For the Lesbian it means her very physical survival. But the stumbling blocks deliberately and precisely placed in her way by our society provide for her a seemingly never-ending obstacle course. She jumps one hurdle, then another and another, but there are always more hurdles to overcome. These are hazards and pitfalls which the Lesbian must face over and beyond the ordinary trials everyone meets in life. Families, friends, employers, clergymen, doctors, legislators—all unwittingly but sometimes knowingly—continue to put up the blocks, build the fences and set the traps that prevent the Lesbian from taking her place in the human race.

It is no wonder that some fall by the wayside and give up. We cannot know for sure to what depths of despair those Lesbians who have committed suicide were driven. But we do know the stories of some of those whose self destructive bent was thwarted and of those, like Del, who gave this desperate solution some serious thought. They are pressured by puritanical mores, by the law, or by the misconceptions perpetrated by psychiatry.

In a letter to the Council on Religion and the Homosexual, which was postmarked Fargo, North Dakota, Jeri asked, "Does it really say in the Bible that if you are gay, you will go to hell?"

Jeri was a high school dropout. She had led a rather aimless life, had gone from marathon swimming to roller derby to being a nurse's aide, having held "more jobs than I can remember." Religious bans had not intruded upon Jeri's life very intimately until her ten-year-old nephew, Georgie, was killed accidentally. "I loved him so. He was like my own son—the one I could never have. My girl friend says it's all my fault Georgie was killed. She says that God took him because I have sinned. I just can't go on living with that. I would never have harmed Georgie knowingly—he meant too much to me. Every night I pray that God will take me too, so that I can be with Georgie again. As for my girl friend, well, there's nothing left for us. She is gay, will never be straight, but now, like me, she is nothing."

The fact is that there is one reference in the Bible (Romans 1:26) which describes the "vile affection" of women for each other as "against nature." Although those who cling to a literal translation of the Bible no longer would necessarily put the Lesbian to death, they nonetheless regard sexual relations between women as a heinous sin. In our attempts to explain the Lesbian to certain church groups, we have been confronted in some instances with severe condemnation: give up your evil ways, take Jesus Christ into your hearts, turn heterosexual—or be eternally damned. (This is the approach of Teen Challenge, a group which serves as a sort of Homosexuals Anonymous and watches over any member that may falter.)

One Lesbian we know, who belongs to the Assembly of God, confessed her sin during a regular church service. She was immediately dragged to the altar, pushed to her knees and held there. Her fellow Christians gathered around her and prayed over her *en masse*. They railed and chanted and pleaded with God to exorcise the Devil who had taken over her senses. The trauma of that experience was devastating to Joanne. It left an indelible imprint on her psyche. Try as we all have in DOB, we have not been able to get Joanne to reinstate herself as a person. She still has terrible fits of depression. Nothing can change her feelings as a Lesbian; likewise, nothing can change her conviction that she is doomed to God's wrath.

Religion also had an overpowering and stifling influence on Lucille. She'd gone to a Pentecostal Bible college, and had taken some nurse's training which she never completed. She was nervous and restless, and had changed jobs (clerk-typist) frequently. Unable to accept herself as a Lesbian, she even went so far as to become engaged. After she called off the impending marriage, she became actively involved with DOB/NY. Since she was single, sensitive and stunning, she drew a great deal of attention from the unattached members. She paired off with this one for a while, then that one and that one and that one. Her relationships, though intense at the beginning as she pursued or was pursued, never lasted very long. Lucille, who to all appearances had everything going for her, wouldn't let anyone touch her. She could make love to another woman, but she wouldn't allow herself to be made love to in return. When asked why by a bewildered partner, she was unable to say. "It's just the way I am."

She was the way she was because as a little girl she had provoked the self righteous rage of her father. He had caught Lucille masturbating. To him she had committed an unforgivable sin. Despite her mother's objections, he dragged her off to the family doctor, demanding that he operate on her and remove her clitoris—which the doctor did—so that she would not be tempted again, so that she would never again experience the pleasurable physical sensations of sin.

Then, too, there was Daisy, an old friend from Seattle, who came to visit us. With her was Gina, her partner for the last year. Dai, as we remembered her, had always been a lot of fun, was ever cheerful and outgoing. But now she seemed depressed, quiet, mysterious, and extremely nervous. At the first opportunity to talk to her alone, we asked Dai what was wrong. She told us that Gina, a Catholic, had urged her to join the church too, and that finally, about six months before, she had agreed. During the course of Dai's studies of the catechism, the two of them had many consultations with their parish priest. They spoke openly to him about their relationship and questioned him about its religious implications. He told them it was all right for them to love each other: to be homosexual was not a sin. But to have sex was. Dai and Gina were devout, and for the last five months had abstained.

"I can't stand it any longer!" Dai cried out. "Gina wasn't just my friend, she was my lover—and a good one at that. Now I can't let her touch me at all, even to put her arm around me. It's too much—more than I can take."

Ironically, not too long before she'd met Gina, Dai had undergone breast surgery to cut her forty-six-inch bust down to size. She had suffered from an inferiority complex all her life because she didn't qualify as America's sex symbol. She'd remodeled herself to be sexy, and now God had decreed that she lead a sexless life.

Self image? What kind of a self image has the church given the Lesbian? Less than human, sinner, celibate, unnatural, perverse, immoral, graceless, shameful, unstable, unworthy, evil-minded, accursed, wicked, impure. That is what is laid on the Lesbian when she seeks spiritual enlightenment and guidance. Out of a group of twenty-five women attending a DOB discussion on religion, seventeen had been raised in the church, but only two still attended services with any regularity.

Fran said she goes to the Episcopal Church because she needs to, when she "feels guilty." She denied that her homosexuality had anything to do with it, really. "Attending church fills my need for peace and quiet—for retreat. It gets me outside of myself and at the same time forces me to dig inside of myself. And I find a certain fulfillment of my spiritual needs."

Neva, who considered her Methodist-Baptist background an essential part of her life, said that going to church services helped her both spiritually and socially. She needed to be with her "own people," even though she admitted she traveled under false colors. "I'd be rejected if they knew I was a Lesbian. It's not sinful if they don't know."

On the other hand, Vickie, who had been a member of the Presbyterian Church for twenty years and who had actually met her lover there, said she and Roberta had given up the church. "As far as the church was concerned, our relationship was sinful. One or the other had to go. The church went."

A young Chinese woman, Mei, observed, "Sometimes I feel as if the church sanctions sin just so that people will have something to repent. To me, that's negative. I'm looking for something more positive, something that will draw out the best in me, not just dwell on what some may deem the worst."

Certainly the church has nothing positive to say to the Lesbian. In fact, in coming to terms with herself, the first charge she must face is that, because her sexual expression is not procreative, she is "unnatural" and therefore "sinful"—a religiously inspired attitude which permeates our culture.

This notion can be traced to early Jewish history. Barrenness, in the Jewish struggle for survival as a people, was a curse. It was vital to the small Jewish tribes that their people copulate to populate, and it was so written in the Old Testament. Prior to the seventh century B.C., homosexual activities had been associated with Jewish religious rites, just as in other cultures elsewhere in the world. But upon their return from their Babylonian exile the Jews established the Holiness Code, which sought to fence out the alien world and set up rules for the separation of the Chosen People of God. It was then that homosexual acts were condemned as the way of the Canaanite, the way of the pagan. Homosexuality was thus proscribed as an indication of or adjunct to idolatry, *not* as a sexual crime. (A clear case of guilt by association, we might add.)

The saga of Sodom and Gomorrah has perhaps been the most influential of biblical references in justifying our civilization's abhorrence of homosexuals. Scholars have justified this condemnation on the grounds that the men of Sodom who surrounded Lot's house demanded to "know" his two male visitors, who were foreigners. The demand to "know" these men has been interpreted to mean knowing them carnally (homosexually), and it is for this wickedness that biblical scholars have assumed God punished the people of these cities by destroying them.

However, Dr. D. S. Bailey, an Anglo-Catholic theologian in England and author of *Homosexuality and the Western Christian Tradition,* points out that such justification hinges on the single Hebrew word *yadha* (to know). According to Bailey this verb appears in the Old Testament 943 times and is used to refer to coitus fewer than a dozen times. When it is used in the latter context, it always refers to heterosexual intercourse. Bailey therefore concludes that the men of Sodom were not seeking sexual knowledge of Lot's male visitors, as previously supposed, but were merely expressing a desire to *know* these strangers, to find out who they were and what they were about. Bailey also points out that Lot was an alien, a sojourner in Sodom, and that he had flouted custom by not presenting his guests to the established residents of the city before taking them into his home. Thus

Bailey maintains that the destruction of Sodom and Gomorrah apparently had nothing to do with homosexuality, as previously supposed.

Theologians are constantly reinterpreting religious tenets in light of current knowledge and circumstances. They point out that biblical passages cannot be taken literally, but should be viewed in the context of the times in which they were written. Dr. Robert Treese, professor of theology at Boston University, also suggests that homosexuals who reject the Bible and therefore religion are being just as literal as those who condemn them. But it is only in recent times, because the sexual revolution taking place in our society forced them to, that theologians have again directed their attention to homosexuality. In their continuing search for the meaning and ethics of human sexuality, many theologians have discarded old beliefs. Few any longer hold to biblical and legal requirements which limit all sexual intercourse to the "missionary position" within marriage with the sole expectation of bearing children. More liberal attitudes, referred to as situational ethics, are chiefly concerned with relationship, regard and responsibility towards one another.

For instance, Joseph Fletcher, professor of social ethics at the Episcopal Theology School in Cambridge, Massachusetts, and author of *Situation Ethics,* says that there is nothing in the teachings of Jesus about the ethics of sex, except adultery and a condemnation of divorce as a correlative matter. The Christian ethic, Fletcher contends, should have no interest in reluctant virgins and technical chastity. Sex needs to be demythologized and freed from romanticism on the one hand and from puritanism on the other.

People are learning, Fletcher claims, that they can have sex without love and love without sex, that sex can be used for recreation as well as for procreation. He concludes that sex outside of marriage isn't wrong unless the persons involved hurt themselves, their partners, or others. "Whether any form of sex (hetero, homo or auto) is good or evil," Fletcher states, "depends on whether love is fully served."

Most liberal church thinkers don't want to go that far. That would equate homosexual with heterosexual conduct. To accept homosexuals is to condone homosexuality and they can't bring themselves to that posture. There is still Saint Paul, they say.

Others, however, admit that Paul did not single out same-sex relations as being more heinous than other sins. Helmut Thielicke, distinguished German theologian, cautiously questions whether that might mean that Paul was concerned over the *way* of homosexual behavior, which might be analogous to adultery, polygamy, etc. The problem then becomes "sex as a depersonalizing force versus sex as the fulfillment of human relationship," according to H. Kimball Jones, author of *Toward a Christian Understanding of the Homosexual.*

Theologians find that the old arguments against homosexuality don't hold up so well in the context of loving relationships, as they have become increasingly aware that the established criteria for heterosexual marriage (love, commitment, concern and responsibility) can be, and often are, found in homosexual relationships. But then they wriggle out of the problem of acceptance by raising the question of whether or not the homosexual identification is absolute, whether or not it can be changed. If it is not constitutional, if the homosexual was not born that way, if it is learned behavior that can be unlearned, then the religionists can more comfortably accept the homosexual, sinner though she or he may be, with tolerance and forgiveness. This seemingly more liberal stance is the lure of the missionary that will beckon the hapless homosexual sinner back to the Way of God—the way of heterosexual righteousness.

Most of the recent statements from major Protestant denominations struggling with the relevance and ethics of today's sexual revolution demonstrate a common agreement on at least three points with regard to homosexuals: (1) they have been badly treated by the church; (2) they should not be summarily condemned, but accepted into the church community; and (3) sexual acts between consenting adults in private should be taken out of the realm of the law.

The homosexual is apparently no longer to be ostracized and punished. She or he may be accepted as a sinner, alienated from God, but with some presumed chance for reconciliation. Just how this can be accomplished is not specified. There is still a marked resistance to the concept that the homosexual can partake of the good life within the homosexual experience. Church liberals find it easy enough to offer righteous Christian

tolerance to those who are "unfortunately and irreversibly" homosexually oriented. But they are still rooted in the myth of Adam
and Eve, still rooted in the concept of procreative sex (recreative
sex now being accepted, but for heterosexuals only), despite the
evidence that homosexuality has existed since antiquity and was
once accepted practice in religious rites. They are unable to accept
homosexuality as a variance on the continuum scale of human
sexuality as shown in the Kinsey reports of actual behavior of
American men and women. Churchmen are all too willing to praise
the Lord and pass the buck to pseudo-psycho-social "scientists"—
let *them* find the way out of the dilemma. The liberal Christian
attitude, in the meantime, amounts to condescension, a salving of
the heterosexual conscience. There is no Good News yet for the
Lesbian or the homosexual.

Inroads into religious thought and re-evaluation are a slow and
cumbersome process. Lesbians live in the *now*. For the most part
that still means rejection in most church circles. Laurie, for instance, was referred to Del by a desperate Methodist clergyman
who had received a phone call from this twenty-one-year-old offering him thanks and encouragement because he had spoken out
from the pulpit for an understanding of homosexuals. For herself,
though, Laurie indicated that she had reached the end of the line.
The only answer to her own religious conflict was suicide. She
came from a Southern Baptist background and knew that she
could not be a Lesbian and still be part of the church she loved.

Since her suicidal inclinations were prompted by religious teachings and since the clergyman was knowledgeable about homosexuality, Del asked why he was referring Laurie to her. The minister claimed it would be helpful if Laurie could identify with
someone like herself who had "made it" or at least resolved her
own conflicts.

Del tried to talk with Laurie, explaining that the Bible could
not be taken literally, that theologians were beginning to review
religious thought as it is related to the homosexual, that questions
of sin and guilt were not as simplistic as they might appear, that
certainly heterosexuals didn't have a corner on the God that was
Love.

"Stop, stop it!" Laurie screamed and burst into tears. "All you
are doing is confusing me more. There can be only *one Truth!*"

When she quieted down, Del tried a different tack. She asked Laurie about her Lesbian friends whom she had met in the army. "What about them? Do you consider them to be evil?"

"No, no, of course not," she sobbed. "They are beautiful people. They are good in their own way. I could never condemn *them*!"

"And yet you condemn yourself," Del pointed out.

For months Del wondered if somehow she had gotten through to Laurie, worried about what had happened to her. She learned eventually that Laurie had taken her problem to her uncle, a Baptist minister, who had promptly placed her under the care of God—and a psychiatrist. Then, recently, at a service of the Metropolitan Community Church, a fundamentalist church for homosexuals, Del ran into Laurie again. She was still a little shy, though more self assured, and she indicated she had found her acceptance in the church. With it she had found self acceptance, of course. It showed in her carriage and glowed in her face. But the story of how she got there, the years of self chastisement, of trying to change to a heterosexual orientation, followed by years of agonized religious re-evaluation—that story was not told.

Biblical condemnation of homosexuality, though more explicit with reference to the male, nonetheless carries over to the female. Women with a strong church background or some personal or professional commitment to the church have particular difficulty in accepting themselves as Lesbians. An Illinois seminary student, Dolores, gradually came to realize that in deepening her relationships with the women in her consciousness-raising Women's Liberation group, she was emotionally and physically drawn to one woman in particular, to Sarah. It was a shocking revelation to her that she not only loved Sarah but was somehow "in love" with her. As a representative of her church, Dolores had attended workshops on sexuality and had gained a great deal of objective knowledge. She had acquired a certain understanding of and empathy for homosexually-oriented persons. She saw acceptance of all dimensions of sexuality as part of today's process of social change and counted among her friends a number of gay people, both male and female. In recognizing her feelings for Sarah, however, she also recognized that, if they were to enter into a relationship, the term "Lesbian" could be applied to her—Dolores. This made the oppression real. Love, sex, relationship: these were concepts she could accept. But the stigma attached to being a Lesbian and the labeling of herself as Lesbian—this was hard to take.

Many women share Dolores's consternation. They engage in Lesbian relationships, often move in together, but never discuss or admit their homosexuality, even to themselves. For in so doing they must work through the guilt, the fear, the sanctions society and church impose on them. As long as they don't admit it, it doesn't exist and they need not suffer the consequences.

Luckily for us, neither of our families went to church. Although Phyllis's grandfather had been a Southern Methodist preacher, her mother did not require that she or her sister Lorna go to Sunday School. Perhaps because he, too, had been subject to a rigorous religious training in the Presbyterian faith, Phyl's father concurred. So Phyllis managed to escape the wrath of God. On the other hand, while Del's folks only set foot in a church when a friend or relative married or died, they did insist that Del and her sister, Merle, go to some kind of service every Sunday. They didn't care which church they went to, only that they went. So both of them tried out various denominations, their choice being determined more than likely by the faith of their current friends.

Luckily for Del, too, one of her early childhood friends belonged to Unity, an offbeat religion that embraces metaphysical concepts. There she learned that God was Love and that God's love was manifested in all beings everywhere. This knowledge was to hold her in good stead when she later encountered the hellfire-and-brimstone fanatics. Her faith in God's love remained unshakeable, though her faith in people sometimes wavered. This basic faith also helped her during those trying times when she later struggled over her Lesbian identity.

Phyllis didn't undergo the same painful process of self analysis as Del. She always had the sort of philosophy of life which may be likened to that of some medical doctors: despite the weight-watching fads, they refuse to prescribe diets. They reason that a person's body will let him or her know what it needs in the way of nourishment, what is "good for it." The same concept, as far as Phyl is concerned, may be applied to other human needs, emotional, spiritual and sexual.

Prior to meeting each other, we had both rejected organized

religion. We each felt that one could be religious without attending church. Our rejection of and antagonism toward the whole concept of organized religion has been reinforced over the years as we have witnessed the damage the church has done to the Lesbian, to the male homosexual, and to many heterosexuals, especially to women. To us the church is a monolithic monster that preys upon people's fear of death. Rather than raising the consciousness of its constituents, the church forces people into following rigid rules which only oppress consciousness. Rather than being life-affirming, the church is life-denying.

Some homosexuals, while pushing for church reforms, are not just quietly going to hell. Depending upon their personal convictions or early religious training, some have become atheists or agnostics, while others have rationalized the negative aspects of the church and still continue to follow their faith. Still others have sought and found their own gay churches and synagogues. As for ourselves, we are members of the Prosperos, a metaphysical group that offers spiritual enlightenment and a sense of being that has meaning for us. We have also found meaning in the Sunday "celebrations" of San Francisco's Glide Memorial United Methodist Church, whose minister, A. Cecil Williams, has brought together a racially and sexually integrated congregation in which there is a real sense of joy, love and community.

The Lesbian's problem in our society doesn't just rest with the church. Despite avowals of the separation of church and state, the sin became a crime. The language of our legal statutes (right out of the Talmud) retained its religious flavor and fervor: the "infamous" or "abominable" or "detestable" *crime against nature,* as it is referred to in the laws of thirty-seven states. No other offense, not even murder, is prefixed with such judgmental choice of words—words which cannot help but influence "impartial" courts and juries as well as those legislators who are being called upon today to repeal these laws. It is the English common law, having its origins in the Judeo-Christian tradition, which became the basis for the American system of jurisprudence.

We need to note here that at no time in England was Lesbian behavior proscribed by law. This was probably due to the relative unimportance of women in society. There is a popular story that this oversight in the law was once posed to Queen Victoria, who decried the suggestion, dismissing the thought as impossible. "Two *ladies* would never engage in such despicable acts!" There was a subsequent, and unsuccessful, attempt made in Parliament in 1921 to include Lesbian practices under the law. The law against male homosexual acts, enacted during the reign of Henry VIII, was finally repealed, as far as two consenting adults in private are concerned, in 1967.

Our Puritan forefathers added a refinement to the English law by including Lesbian sexual practices, either specifically or by inference. Just as it is not a sin to *be* a homosexual, only to act it out sexually—so it is with the law. Nowhere in the law can the words *homosexual* or *Lesbian* be found. But certain sexual acts, often performed by heterosexuals as well as by homosexuals, by women as well as by men, *are* illegal, though enforcement and prosecution are generally directed almost exclusively against male homosexuals. The language describing these acts is somewhat varied and sometimes vague, allowing for great leeway in interpretation. Researchers who have attempted to determine in which states the female homosexual may be advantaged by omissions of the law are at wide variance. Such information is really of little consequence to the Lesbian, since cases involving overt homosexual activity between women that have actually reached the courts are extremely rare.

Because of her nature as a woman and undoubtedly, too, because of her physical body structure, the Lesbian usually finds it more convenient and comfortable to confine her sexual calisthenics to the privacy of bedroom or home. Laws against private adult activity are virtually unenforceable. Complaints can only be brought by "peeping toms" or revealed in divorce or custody proceedings where an indignant husband or horrified relative may have accidentally walked in at an inopportune moment. A *1984*-style spying on private bedrooms may become a reality, according to some, if the polarization between the forces for and against social change continues. Lesbians may yet feel the pinch. But the point is that the Lesbian, no matter how discreet she may be, no matter how sincere and loving her personal feelings, is labeled a criminal. When by chance she is arrested on some non-sex-related charge, her Lesbian identity, the guilt she has been made to feel, is always a factor.

Many years ago we recall there was a sensational "murder" case in a small rural community in the state of Oregon. Tanya, a young woman of twenty-four, was found dead from a gunshot wound. Jackie, a very masculine-appearing woman with whom she had been living for the past two years, discovered her body when she came home from marketing. The authorities took Jackie in for investigation. Though she vehemently protested her innocence, they held her on suspicion of murder. She insisted that the shot was probably self inflicted, that Tanya had been despondent because of ill health.

During the weeks of the investigation, two communities became aroused over the sheriff's action: families and friends from neighboring farms who had known Jackie for years and had accepted her as a friend despite her seemingly peculiar ways; and the Lesbian community of Portland, the underground subculture which Jackie and Tanya had been a part of on their infrequent visits to the city. The first community was verbal and supportive of Jackie. The second discussed the case among themselves but remained silent. Some Lesbians knew for a fact that Tanya had been ill and in much pain from a kidney ailment, but they didn't dare to come forward and verify even this much of Jackie's story. Their reasons were twofold, and both had to do with self preservation. They couldn't afford to expose themselves in the first place. But if they did brave it, would their presence hinder more than it would help? There had been no mention of a Lesbian relationship in the papers. Why chance bringing that out into the open? Underlying these rationalizations, of course, was the guilt—the tremendous guilt of betrayal, of not standing by a friend in need. A collective Lesbian conscience was salved by the eventual dismissal of charges and release of the suspect. Jackie went back to the farm and to her friends. She has never been seen again in her old haunts, the gay bars of Portland.

Although a Lesbian is seldom subject to prosecution for her sexual activity, she is always aware that it is regarded as criminal. Heterosexuals, on the other hand, performing the same acts, do not give a thought to or are not even aware of their own criminal behavior. The Lesbian cannot get away from the fact that she is branded as sinful and illegal on the basis of that label alone. No matter how creative she may be, no matter how great her personal contribution to society as a whole, no matter how exemplary a life she may lead otherwise, she is always damned. This knowledge cannot help but be damaging to her self image.

Donna recalls the time in her youth when she stormed out of a gay bar after having quarreled with her lover. In a rage she raced down the street. When she turned the corner, she came face to face with a policeman. "Arrest me, officer," she shouted. "I'm a Lesbian! Arrest me, arrest me, officer, I'm a Lesbian!"

The startled policeman looked at her in dismay. "Go home, lady, go home and sleep it off."

Unfortunately for the Lesbian, like Donna, her sexual identity too often becomes her primary identity. Ideally she should consider herself as a person first, a woman second, and a Lesbian only third. But because of the negative connotations and all the constraints that go with it, she is thrust by forces outside herself to protect the Lesbian part of her nature. It then becomes a primary concern. It is only when she can denounce the idiocy of the religious scriptures and legal strictures that bind her and can affirm her Lesbian nature as but a single facet of her whole personality that she can become fully human.

Even Phyllis, who because of her work in the homophile movement is knowledgeable and prepared for most eventualities, can be taken aback. As the victim of a hit-and-run accident, she called the police. While she was sitting in the back of the squad car, the officer taking her report radioed in to headquarters for a routine check. She heard him giving her identification. Then he used the phrase "DOB." How did he know, she wondered, before she realized he was referring to "date of birth," not "Daughters of Bilitis."

It is the knowledge that one's private life is regarded as criminal that tends to make Lesbians feel guilty. Consequently many plead guilty to charges of which they are innocent. In a gay bar raid, for instance, most of the women arrested plead guilty to "disorderly conduct" charges, even though they are guilty merely of being on the premises. They are really pleading guilty to being Lesbians, not to any public misconduct.

It should be obvious by now to the general public that prohibitive laws do not deter homosexuality. They only make homosexuals more miserable and open avenues for misuse of the law or for blackmail. They do not serve society's purpose and should be repealed, as has already been done in most countries around the world. As early as 1955 the American Law Institute approved in final form its "Model Penal Code," which incorporated a recommendation that since "no harm to the secular interests of the community is involved," private sex acts should be considered crimes only when force or fraud is used, or a minor involved. At this writing only five states (Illinois in 1961, Connecticut in 1970, Colorado and Oregon in 1971, and Hawaii in 1972) have complied.

By an ironic turn of events, with the revised criminal code which became effective July 1, 1970, the state of Kansas has reduced sodomy penalties for homosexual adults (of either sex) from felonies to misdemeanors, but has let heterosexuals, married or unmarried, who may perform acts of oral or anal copulation, off scot-free. Delaware and Texas appear to be moving in the same direction. The *very same acts* would thus be legal for heterosexuals, but illegal for homosexuals. Such legislation aptly illustrates a gross miscarriage of "justice" and the inequity of our legal system.

The United States remains the last stronghold of excessively repressive sex laws. According to Kinsey, if all sex laws on the books were enforced, approximately 10 percent of the population would be supporting the other 90 percent in jail. Even churchmen, who are still tentative about sexual freedom, see it as a moral issue only. They, too, fail to see it as a legal issue.

Where private sexual acts have been removed from the purview of the law, either by design or oversight, solicitation laws have generally been retained. In other words, it may be all right to do it, but don't ask anyone! Solicitation laws thus may be invoked by the zealous law enforcement officer who dresses and acts in accordance with the current mode of the gay set and sits around in a gay bar, encouraging or enticing some guileless homosexual into "making a pass" or into suggesting, "Come up to my apartment." The gay man has every reason to believe the newcomer would be a willing partner to private adult sexual activity. Thereupon the officer identifies himself and places the "offending" homosexual under arrest.

While this type of police work is generally limited in its application to apprehending male homosexuals, there have been similar cases reported to us whereby policewomen have been used as decoys in gay bars to ferret out Lesbians. One case in point was the wholesale arrest of more than a hundred homosexual men and women in a bar called Hazel's in Sharp Park, California, during the mid-1950s. Another arrest was made in a bar in Oakland, California, when an unsuspecting Lesbian invited a policewoman to dance.

Most women have been taught how to ward off unwarranted and unwanted advances from men. To us, it is inconceivable that men as well as women cannot learn to say no to an undesired homosexual overture without resorting to the police for protection, or to violence and hysteria. Homosexuals are easily discouraged. Most Lesbians we know would not only take no for an answer, they would not be apt to ask the question in the first place unless they had reason to believe they would receive a favorable response. It took Del more than two years to make the proverbial "pass" at Phyllis. What prompted her bravado was the urgency presented by Phyl's announced plans to leave Seattle and return to San Francisco. It was a "now or never" situation.

While the questions of the validity of the sin and the legality of the crime of homosexuality were being debated, late nineteenth century scientists began to wonder if there wasn't some special cause for what they termed "sexual inversion." Homosexuality up to then had been accepted as a natural "unnatural" phenomenon, so to speak, and was consequently never questioned within that definition. But behaviorists noted that no matter how zealously society tried to prohibit or repress its expression, in generation after generation homosexuality continued to manifest itself in a minority of the population. Scientists thus began to probe into the area of human sexuality and to examine homosexual behavior in particular to determine its cause or causes, presumably to find the means for curing or preventing it.

From the beginning, theoretical treatises on the "disease of inversion" carried the imprint of centuries-old religious superstition. In 1869 Westphal, professor of psychiatry at Berlin, referred to homosexuality as "moral insanity" because of its "contrary sexual feeling." In Italy, in 1875, P. Mantegazza called female homosexuality an "error of nature." Most late nineteenth century sexologists debated the pros and cons of homosexuality as being hereditary and/or pathological. In his study of female homosexual behavior the German author Iwan Bloch observed that women in attendance at Lesbian parties and dances wore men's clothing and called each other by masculine nicknames, leading him to the conclusion that such behavior was obviously a "sickness."

Thus was the "scientific" background laid for the advent of Sigmund Freud who, at the turn of the century, formulated his theories about libido (a person's sexual impulse, drive and/or energy) and its permeating influence on all of our emotions and thoughts. Out of his works grew a cult, based in the moral and legal traditions of the past but with a new mystical language. This pseudo-science of psychoanalysis has had a profound impact on modern attitudes toward homosexuals and is largely responsible for the shift in recent years from the syndrome of labeling homosexuality "sin" and "crime" to that of labeling it "mental illness."

Freud postulated that a homosexual component can be found in the sexual development of every human being. There remain in everyone, homosexual and heterosexual alike, the residual manifestations of bisexuality; but the homosexual, having failed to repress his "natural" homosexuality at puberty like most people who then progress to a heterosexual commitment, represents instead a case of "arrested development." For a girl to make this transition to womanhood the sexual primacy of the clitoris must be abandoned to the vagina.

In his famous "Letter to an American Mother" Freud wrote: "Homosexuality is assuredly no advantage, but it is nothing to be ashamed of, no vice, no degradation, it cannot be classified as an illness; we consider it to be a variation of the sexual function produced by a certain arrest of sexual development. Many highly respectable individuals of ancient and modern times have been homosexuals, several of the greatest men among them (Plato, Michelangelo, Leonardo da Vinci, et al.). It is a great injustice to persecute homosexuality as a crime, and cruelty too."

Freud's followers, however, ignored their idol's affirmation of homosexuality and chose instead to latch onto the "arrested development" phrase. They backed it up with his theories on "fixation" or the "Electra complex" (strong emotional attachment of a daughter for her father) and "penis envy" (attributed to the psychological makeup of all women) as the common denominator, as proof that female homosexuality, like male homosexuality, is an expression of "sexual immaturity" and a symptom of some deep-seated, underlying neurosis.

From case histories of "disturbed" Lesbians the psycho-pathological profession has made assumptions and hypotheses. It has offered theories and rationalizations as possible explanations for Lesbianism. These are as variant as their subject matter. Every-thing—every circumstance, every dream, every thought, every inci-dent, every interaction—in a Lesbian's life makes her a Lesbian, if she already happens to be one. The fact that many of the same things are experienced by women who identify as heterosexual, however, is never recognized nor explained.

Take, for instance, the causation theories that relate to fear. The list includes just about every fear imaginable to woman: fear of the opposite sex, fear of injury or of being emotionally hurt by a man, fear of pregnancy, fear of venereal disease, fear of submission, fear of penetration, fear of rejection, fear of the un-familiar (as contrasted with the familiar), fear of inadequacy, fear of rivalry, fear of growing up and assuming the adult responsi-bilities of motherhood. These fears are accompanied by other feel-ings, according to the malady-mongers, of love and/or hate for mom and/or dad, sibling jealousy and rivalry, loneliness, rejection, neurotic dependency, strong masochistic impulses, orality and sa-dism, lack of self restraint, self pity, narcissism, insecurity, inferi-ority, hurt pride, defiance, lack of self confidence, loss of self esteem, and the excessive wish to survive (to which we might add, "What for?").

There are myriads of causal factors alluded to in the profes-sional literature. Some of the more popularly touted concepts are: heterosexual trauma or disappointment (meaning he was a lousy lover), having been sated with males (presumably referring to pros-titutes), seduction in adolescence by an older female (more often the youth is the aggressor), childhood seduction by a member of the opposite sex (apparently no matter his age), rape (but that's "normal"), masturbation (after marriage boys are true blue, girls are taboo and so are you), first sexual experience with someone of the same sex (finding it pleasurable), tomboy behavior in early childhood (also apparent in pre-heterosexual girlhood), concen-tration on athletics in adolescence (physical fitness for the young female is limited to making herself attractive to the boys), sexual segregation in girls' schools or camps (sometimes has its compensations), inability to make affectional peer relationships (which is a "no-no" either way), absence of sex education (for hetero and homo alike), early sexual tensions (it doesn't happen to "nice" girls), preoccupation with breast development (that's a societal hangup), compulsive preoccupation with sexuality in general (ditto), sexual apathy of husbands (obviously the wife's fault), frigidity (ditto), repulsion for the male body (you've said no too often and too long, just as you were taught), defiance of male superiority (right on, sister), and renunciation of femininity (whatever that is).

If that isn't enough, there are also more recently developing theories relating to the speeding tempo of modern life, the growing independence of women and their lessening need for marriage, increasing masculinity in women, and unhealthy nervous systems of men. And always with us, of course, is the assumed "psychophysiological predisposition to be mentally aberrant."

All this was what Del learned about herself after hours of agonized reading at the library. They were talking about her, a Lesbian. And they were right. Lesbians do suffer from feelings of rejection, loneliness, isolation, fear, insecurity, hurt pride, lack of self confidence, loss of self esteem. Del felt all these things and more. She was indeed sick. She displayed all the symptoms of melancholia: excessive brooding, depression, despondency, dejection and despair. How could it be otherwise? The realization that she is considered sinful, criminal and mentally ill can be overwhelming and devastating to a young mother of twenty-five, particularly when she sees what she experiences as simply a state of being and expression of love.

Del knew she could no longer squelch her Lesbian nature. It was part of her, inseparable, and she had to deal with it. But there was no one she felt free enough with to talk to about it, and as far as she knew, she'd never met any other Lesbians who might be able to shed some light on her seemingly hopeless plight.

She could never talk to her parents about it. Besides the shame and the hurt, which they didn't need, she could only heap blame and guilt on them, which they needed even less. The parents of Lesbians have not been spared the judgments of dementia-disposed diagnosticians: every display of love and affection is questionable; every act or non-act is rejection; every quarrel or dispute is evidence of abnormality; every interaction between them as individuals has a name in psychological jargon; every interaction between them as a couple and their daughter can be classified by sterile pseudoscientific language. Del discovered that the tyranny was all-pervasive, the tyranny of self appointed, self anointed guardians of the nation's mental health (read that "illness").

Dad, it seemed, may be weak and ineffectual; on the other hand, he may be strong and domineering. He may be seductive, or he may reject his daughter. But mom is usually the culprit—strong and domineering, usually critical and unsympathetic, because she often entertains wishes to be a prostitute or has unconscious (or sometimes conscious) anti-heterosexual attitudes. She's probably a latent homosexual. Daughter may feel competitive with the mother for the father's affections. She may resent and rebel against her parents' strictness and puritanical attitudes. The parents may have wanted a boy, or a sibling may have expressed preference for a brother. Perhaps the daughter is responding to a lack of affection and approbation from her parents. There may have been family discord, a separation or divorce. Parents are usually described as sexually maladjusted, alcoholic, neurotic, or sometimes even psychotic. But whatever their faults, the daughter experienced a fixation, a strong positive emotional attachment to one and its counterpart (hatred) for the other—all of which supposedly wound up with the daughter being strongly dependent on her parents while at the same time acting out her defiance of them. No matter how you look at it, the picture painted by psychological theorists was not pretty.

Del could not identify with the parents the books had described. They seemed unreal, like automated skeletons without flesh and blood, without the human equation. Parents need to be viewed in the context of their times and the level of their awareness, as must Lesbians, and all other people for that matter. Del's parents were two lovable human beings who had worked hard to raise a family during the depression years. Certainly they made mistakes, but they did their best with the tools and information they had. There was no Dr. Spock to rely on then. Sure, her stepfather favored her sister, but she was *his* daughter and that made sense. Besides, Merle was pretty and cute, and, sure, this did lead to some "sibling rivalry." But both her stepfather and her mother had always been very supportive of Del. He had instilled in her a thirst for knowledge and had spent many evenings going over her lessons with her; her mother had wanted Del to have the education she herself had never had, and from the start had put hard-to-come-by money away for college. Both contributed to Del's sense of identity, that of a unique human being who could attain whatever goal she worked for, if she stuck with it. Of course, there were family squabbles. That was as inevitable as the generation gap that eventually ensued. Her stepfather sometimes drank too much with "the boys from the office" before coming home to dinner, and sure, his sense of humor sometimes turned to ridicule that really hurt. Probably there could have been more display of affection in the family, but in between the not-so-good times were many happy memories: of trips to the country, early morning nature walks in Golden Gate Park before school, parties and friends, encouragement and proud moments of personal accomplishment shared.

Del's parents didn't raise her in a vacuum. They encouraged her associations with others and her wide reading habits. Karen Horney's *Self Analysis,* for instance, stimulated her to sift through memories, understand the interaction which caused childhood resentments, ferret out incidents in her life that may or may not have contributed to her identity as a Lesbian. Nothing in her self examination, nothing in her reading, convinced Del that her parents were to blame—unless it was her strong sense of self determination which they had encouraged. In that, perhaps, they had failed to prepare her for her role as a woman in our society. Woman's role, Del discovered to her consternation, is culturally prescribed, leaving little room for self determination. Finding she'd been miscast, she made her exit from the scene.

Del wondered what effect her being a Lesbian might ultimately have on her daughter. Her new-found revelation hadn't really changed how Del felt about Janey, but their relationship could certainly be ripped apart and Janey even taken away from her if Del's new identity were divulged. Yet how was she to cope with her feelings if she didn't find some release? How could she plan and build for the future if she could not find someone who would understand—someone she could share her misgivings with, who would help to steer her in the right direction? Del was trapped in herself, in a problem that appeared insoluble.

Finally she worked up enough nerve to reveal her feelings and her dilemma to a couple of her women friends, who were, of course, straight. They were a few years older than Del, and, as it turned out, far more sophisticated. They patted Del on the head and said they doubted she was a Lesbian. But since she needed to find out for herself, they took her in tow and introduced her to the gay bars of San Francisco's North Beach. One of these women became Del's confidante. For hours on end she listened, allowing Del to unload all her frustrations, all her misgivings, all her pent-up emotions. The other woman became Del's first lover.

While Phyllis had no difficulty in dealing with the right or wrong of her newly chosen way of life, she did experience difficulty with other people's attitudes. She remembered all too clearly the mistake she had once made of telling a married friend, Elsa, about Del (that was when we were still just "friends") and having her husband forbid Elsa to have anything more to do with Del—or with Phyllis, if she and Del continued to be friends.

Like most Lesbians who have only recently "come out," Phyllis became very self conscious. She felt somehow that she'd changed, that just by looking at her anyone would automatically "know." She avoided people's eyes and blathered about inconsequential minutiae, interspersed with nervous laughter, and zealously avoided any personal references.

But it isn't in Phyllis's nature to be a vegetable, quiet and passive. She is a vibrant, gregarious, social being—and a lousy liar. She knew she couldn't continue to prattle indefinitely. She also knew she'd never be able to carry it off if she invented a boy friend, as so many other Lesbians do, so she began to talk to her friends— perhaps a little hesitantly at first—about "us." "We" saw this movie last night, "we" bought a car, and "we" moved from a furnished apartment to a house of our own. And when the company Phyl worked for issued limited shares of stock for purchase by employees, even her boss was aware of what he called her "partnership" and fully expected that the stock would be in both names.

Finally one Friday evening, over cocktails after work, Millie, who always played the comic, became very serious. "Phyllis, I'd like to ask you a personal question. It's not that I want to butt into your personal affairs, but it just seems to me it would be a lot easier if we could be honest with each other."

Phyllis was startled, and braced herself for the worst. Millie blurted out, "Are you a Lesbian?"

When Phyl nodded affirmatively, Millie hugged her and laughed, "We guessed a long time ago. Pat and Holly too. But we couldn't figure out how to let you know. We all wanted to tell you that it doesn't make any difference."

The joy of relief, of venturing to speak the dreaded word and finding it's really all right, called for a celebration. They phoned Del and invited her to join them. Besides, they were low on funds and Del had just been paid.

Del established a similar friendship with her coworker Lisa, and, like Phyllis and Millie, talked about the forbidden subject. In this case, however, Del was the one who initiated the discussion by offering her confidence. Lisa responded in much the same way as Millie. And sometime later, when the boss was planning another dreary company party to which spouses were invited, she suggested, "Why not ask Phyllis, Del's roommate?" From then on Phyl was included as a part of the "company family": that benevolent image American businesses try to establish among employees and employers.

"To tell or not to tell": that is a constant question. Because we met with some measure of success does not mean we would recommend that every Lesbian run out and spread the news about herself. There's probably enough of that going on behind her back as it is. Sharing a confidence depends upon how much confidence you have in the others involved. It is also predicated on your own awareness that you have been accepted as a person, that you already have a basic relationship, and that this knowledge you impart simply adds another dimension to your personality, but doesn't change it.

The dilemma is best explained in this excerpt from an anonymous letter appearing in *The Daily Californian* following a 1965 series of articles on homosexuality:

"I am a Lesbian. I am also a senior at Cal, a woman, a liberal, and most important of all: a human being. I do not consider myself sick. I am not mannish, queer or insane. Besides studying for a profession at Cal, I work here. My associates at work and my fellow students are not aware of my sexual preference: they regard me highly. I sometimes wonder to what extent their attitude towards me would change if they knew of my deviance. I have a hunch that I would regret finding out.

"I have homosexual friends here. Curiously enough, I know few Lesbians at Cal and many male homosexuals. There are many people who, I am almost certain, are homosexual but since I cannot be sure, I can't approach them and thereby reveal myself.

"The problem really is not finding someone to talk to—the problem is finding someone to talk to freely. One gets tired of living a life of pretense. Instead of saying to a fellow who asks for a date, 'I can't make it' or 'My boy friend and I have already made arrangements for tonight,' thereby inhibiting a further relationship, I would welcome the freedom to answer honestly, 'I like you as a person, but have no sexual interest in you. If you can share my feelings, I would like a friendship to develop between us.' "

Another woman, Gert, felt altogether differently. She wanted to make a complete break with the past, with the straight world. Recently divorced, she had been living with Chris for about six months. She told us how happy she was, how finding and living the gay life had been for her a radical change for the better. Though she'd lived all her life as a heterosexual among heterosexuals, she protested she now had nothing in common with them, that they no longer spoke the same language. "I just can't *stand* straight people anymore!"

This makes as much sense as do the parents who turn against their daughter when they learn that she is a Lesbian. Have they all changed character? Have they really changed so drastically? Aren't they all the same basic people they were? How can this one word "Lesbian" make so much difference in their lives?

Lily told us that she was sixteen when she became consciously aware that she was different. "I was not in the least smitten by boys, as everyone else seemed to be, but I most certainly was by a few of the girls. I had no trouble admitting this to myself because I had learned as a child that, if I told no one, I could think any and all thoughts that came to mind. Perhaps my atheistic upbringing helped here. There was no God in my universe who could read my thoughts. I assumed they were absolutely safe.

"What I 'knew' at sixteen was that society would consider me far worse than the worst criminal and that my protection lay in telling no one and in a most careful watch over my behavior. This, I now see, was remarkably wise of me. To tell anyone in those days would have been to get myself hopelessly twisted up inside, perhaps never to recover."

By the time she entered into a Lesbian relationship some six or seven years later, Lily had pretty well resolved the emotional conflicts between her inner life as a homosexual and the heterosexual facade required to protect it.

Though there have been some strides in public education about homosexuality, especially in the last five years, Del's predicament of twenty-five years ago is shared today by countless women. After Jess Stearn's book *The Grapevine* was published, the Daughters of Bilitis was deluged with phone calls and letters. One frightened and frantic married woman phoned three thousand miles across the country to break through "eighteen years of silence." Another from Iowa, who did not realize that DOB is a volunteer organization with office hours at night after work, kept the answering service operator, a man, on the line for forty-five minutes, so desperate was she to talk to someone. And "Delaware" (that's the only way we were ever to identify her) wanted to support the organization's work anonymously because her socialite family would "die" if they knew she was a Lesbian.

Letters postmarked Klamath Falls and River City revealed the complete isolation of the Lesbian in a small town, the Lesbian who cannot lose herself in the anonymity of big city life. For her it is a tragedy when the DOB magazine is late coming out. For her a magazine is the only real contact she has with "her people": those who understand, who share her problems, who hold out hope for her dreams.

The ones who finally made their way to the DOB office, to meet and talk with us in person, told heart-rending stories of how difficult it was to make what, for them, was a first public appearance as a Lesbian. Mary said she'd been there every day for a week, even sat on the stairs for hours at a time, then had gone home only to come back again for another try before she could steel herself for that final step which would take her through the door and into the office of a known, publicly declared Lesbian organization. Even though she knew there were others like herself behind that door who were ready and willing to welcome her, eager to offer her reinforcement as a person, she still had to identify herself: not by name or address or place of employment, but as a Lesbian, and an anonymous Lesbian at that. The stigma attached to that label is still so great that many, though help is offered from many other quarters today, are still unable to accept it.

A lot of people, who fear us because we are different and hate us because they fear us, have built up an elaborate labyrinth of words, centuries in breadth and length, to hoodwink us and themselves into believing we are morally depraved, legally reprehensible and emotionally defective. When we try to respond, try to explain the fallacies and the invalid premises upon which their arguments are based, we meet still another barrage of rhetoric. We then become defensive, apologists or injustice collectors.

How do we break this vicious circle? How do we beat this rap? How do we establish some semblance of stability and sanity in our lives when we are constantly bombarded by these destructive influences? If you are like Phyllis, who is an inveterate optimist and independent thinker, you have an inner, unshakeable faith in yourself and never let what other people think determine what's best for you. It's your life, which no one else can live for you, and it is you who reap the benefits or the consequences of your decisions.

At any rate, Phyllis didn't undergo the same painful process as Del. As we indicated before, she'd not really thought about homosexuality prior to meeting Del. She was twenty-four then. Her self image and her life experience had always been heterosexual, though she had been interested in women and sought them as friends. She admired women, had an appreciative eye for a pretty face and a trim figure, and occasionally fantasized about what it might be like to feel and touch them. But this she accepted casually and never associated with any sort of sexual connotations.

"Delaware," on the other hand, never resolved her conflict. One evening we made a date for dinner when she was stopping over in San Francisco en route to Hong Kong on business. We had been intrigued by her furtive phone calls and felt concern over her inability to accept her sexual identity. She came from a wealthy family that traveled in high society at a national level, and fear of exposure to her was paramount. Something had happened, and she simply had to talk it over with someone.

We were not prepared for what we saw: an attractive woman in her mid-thirties, stylishly and expensively dressed and coifed but with a hangdog turn of the head, like a child who has just been admonished. She was unable to look us in the eye as she poured out her story of having made a drunken pass at an old family friend. Nothing had been said of the incident since, but it was preying on her mind to the exclusion of all else. What did the woman think? Would she tell her family? Had she told anyone else? Should she say something to her? What should she do?

The incident, as it turned out, was not as recent as we had thought. We convinced her to forget it. Since nothing had happened in the interim, the whole thing was best ignored. We turned the conversation to her work and her trip to Hong Kong. A totally different person emerged right there in front of us: an animated, vibrant, confident woman, with head held high, who knew what she was about. She could tell a good story, had a marvelous sense of humor and kept us entranced over coffee and after-dinner brandy. But at the mere mention of the word *homosexual* she became Cinderella at midnight, reverting to the frightened child with the hangdog expression.

Our hearts went out to her. We knew how she felt, the anxiety she was experiencing. And we were angry—angry that this intelligent, delightful woman with so much creative potential could be reduced to such a state because of the shame that had been foisted upon her as a Lesbian.

We wished that she shared our anger, for we had learned that the expression of hostility, of righteous indignation, was a stepping stone from martyrdom and self pity to self acceptance. We wished that she could see herself as we had seen her: a person of wealth, not in money, but in the human qualities of warmth, humor, ability and strength. We wished she could understand that awareness of herself as a Lesbian need not change those positive attributes which she indeed possessed, that she was no less a person because she was sexually different. We wished she had reached that point in life where she could say: "I don't care what other people think. *I* know who I am, and that's all that matters." For it is then and only then that the Lesbian can achieve self acceptance, that ingredient so necessary to her well being. Without it she must hide, lead only a half life; without it she will be unable to rid herself of the emotional cancer deep inside her, forever festering and poisoning her mind and her body. With it she can withstand rejection and scorn, take the calculated risks in life, and find her niche in society.

But self acceptance in our society is not easily achieved. We preach individuality while we demand conformity. We recognize the diversity of subcultures and religions in America while we pledge allegiance to rigid puritanical precepts. We insist that the rights of minorities are protected by the United States Constitution while we abridge them daily through segregation and discrimination, bigotry and hypocrisy.

Fortunately there is a dawning awareness in the so-called helping professions that homosexuality is merely a variation in the total spectrum of human sexuality. A few in the psychiatric profession, like Drs. Thomas S. Szasz and Ronald D. Laing, are reminding their colleagues that theirs is a theoretical field, not an absolute science. They deplore the celerity and capriciousness with which the profession labels various human conditions as mental illnesses simply because they differ from the majority.

In his book *The Myth of Mental Illness*, Szasz refers to psychiatry as a *theoretical* science based on the study of personal conduct, which in the beginning was closely allied to the tradition of philosophy and ethics. Gradually, however, psychologists came to consider themselves "empirical scientists" whose experimental methods, observations and theories are allegedly no different from those of the natural sciences of physics and biology. Szasz contends that as long as they are addressing themselves to the questions of how man lives and how he ought to live, this cannot be true; ethical problems cannot be solved by medical methods. He labels psychoanalytic theory based upon the cause and effect model of classical physics as "historicism" that does not take into consideration valuation, choice and responsibility in human affairs. Szasz also expresses concern about the reclassification— based on no matter what the norm—of behavior like homosexuality as mental illness.

In "Legal and Moral Aspects of Homosexuality," appearing in the anthology *Sexual Inversion*, Szasz claims that the goal of converting the homosexual to heterosexuality is incompatible with the purely "analytic" enterprise of the therapist, whose role ideally is to help the patient learn about himself, others, and the world about him. To accept heterosexuality as a social value because of its biological value is a delusion, and he likens such psychotherapeutic efforts to value promotion, not value analysis.

Drs. Laing and Aaron Esterson, Scottish psychiatrists, in the preface of their book *Sanity, Madness and the Family,* point out that the diagnosis of a particular mental illness could differ between two psychiatrists from the same medical school, between different schools and between countries. But when these diagnostic disputes occur, there is no court of appeal. "There are at present no objective, reliable, quantifiable criteria—behavioral or neurophysiological or biochemical—to appeal to when psychiatrists differ," they say.

This is why we have often stated that theories about the etiology and treatment of homosexuality are much like verses in the Bible: it is possible to pick and choose those quotations which most nearly approximate your own thesis. What we are talking about, in either case, is value judgments. It is this point we must make clear. We speak subjectively from our own experience, which we have openly admitted in our introduction. But it must also be understood that psychological theories are based upon people's subjective evaluation (no matter how objective they may try to be) of their observations of a number of their fellow human beings, who have communicated to them their subjective experience.

Dr. Laing, in *The Politics of Experience,* says that natural science is concerned only with the observer's experience of things, but there is a vital relationship between the behavior observed and the *experience* of the person whose behavior is being observed and that there is no traditional logic to express it. "The relation between the experience and behavior," Laing asserts, "is the stone that the builders will reject at their peril. Without it the whole structure of our theory and practice must collapse."

What we call "normal" in today's society, according to Laing, is the product of repression, denial, projection and other forms of destructive conditioning. The "normally" alienated person then, by virtue of the fact he acts more or less like everyone else, is taken for the sane. Other persons, who are out of step with the prevailing state of alienation, are then labeled by the "normal" majority as bad or mad.

Like the religious and legal disputes, debate continues among psychologists, psychiatrists, sociologists and anthropologists as to how to classify homosexuality. While a few proclaim they have managed to reverse the identity of a very small percentage of their patients, the great "silent majority" of analysts puts its energy into helping its clients adjust to their homosexuality. They help them to accept themselves as Lesbians or as homosexuals, but still with tongue in cheek. For they could, but do not, take a public stand against repressive sex laws or against oppressive societal attitudes. So, after months or years of analysis, the Lesbian may have her inner conflicts resolved, but outwardly she must still cope with a hostile heterosexual society. Not to reveal the errors in translation and interpretation of the Bible regarding homosexuality; not to include homosexual along with heterosexual relations within the new code of sexual ethics; not to repeal laws proscribing private sex behavior; not to expose the myth of mental illness, which labels deviance, from no matter what the norm, as a disease—*these* are the real sins and crimes and sicknesses.

The facts the public has been led to believe are based upon mythology, fantasy, rationalization, theory, conjecture, personal bias and hysterical hyperbole. Because of this, the Lesbian must go it alone. She must find her own destiny out of her own guts. How she manages her difference, how she feels about herself on learning of her homosexuality, how she confronts those societal attitudes that proclaim her less than human because of a state of being: these are part of every Lesbian's story. Some Lesbians succumb to society's disregard for people and wind up in purgatory or jail or the asylum. But hopefully most learn, after years of bitter inner warfare, that they are people—people of worth and dignity—and that what is important really is not how others view them, but how they view themselves.

3. Sexuality & Sex Roles

What do Lesbians do sexually? The question has been asked by men and women, homosexual and heterosexual. Sometimes they get an answer, but not always.

During World War II, a woman passing as a man and "married" to a woman was unmasked at the army's physical examination. Phyllis read about the case and ran to ask the "older, wiser" woman in her college dorm, "What can two women do together?" The answer she received was, "Use your own imagination." The trouble with that is you can never be sure if your imagination is playing tricks on you or not.

A young friend, whose mother asked her what Lesbians do, ducked the question. "I don't know. I never asked one"—which, as she wrote us, was true. "I've never asked a Lesbian what she did with another woman. I just read a few choice books and let the rest come naturally."

Mothers do seem to be curious about the subject. When Paula told her mother she was a Lesbian, she followed up by saying, "You can ask me almost any question you want about the subject." But when mother asked how Lebsians made love, Paula told her that was one of the questions she wouldn't answer. Several weeks later the mother told Paula that she had found out what Lesbians do. "How?" asked Paula. "I went to bed with one," replied her mother. "It was a very pleasant experience." Poor Paula, bound by the ground rules she herself had set, could not ask her mother for the details.

Paula's reticence about her sex life is not unusual. Most Lesbians, as most women, consider sex a very private matter and will not discuss it. In the early 1960s a researcher, working with DOB's research director, sent out a questionnaire to find out what Lesbians do sexually. This caused much consternation. Even though the answers were to be totally anonymous many women refused to fill out the questionnaire, all of which makes us wonder if the pseudoscientific book *Lesbianism Around the World,* by R. Leighton Hasselrodt, M.A., isn't really science fiction. The book, citing a study never fully identified, had little to say about Lesbians or their life styles. Its only concern was Lesbian*ism* (how they do it), and it even purported to establish which way is the most popular in various parts of the world: a clear-cut example of pandering to the heterosexual male's prurient interest, and curiosity, about Lesbians.

Phyllis, along with several male homosexuals, was speaking to a group of seminary students one evening in 1968. The class varied in age from eighteen to forty and included both men and women, many of the latter wives of the seminarians. At the break the professor called Phyllis aside. "When we reconvene would you tell them how homosexuals have sex?" he asked. "Surely they know," Phyllis retorted. "Oh, no," said the professor. "And if you don't tell them, they'll be bugging me all week about it."

In 1967, Ms. N filed suit in Sacramento to regain custody of her daughter, custody which had been granted to the father at the time of a divorce. During the sensational hearing Ms. N admitted engaging in "homosexual activity" with three different women in her own home, but not in the presence of her children (she also had a son by a previous marriage); they had been left at the babysitter's for the night.

"Just what does that entail? What do you do?" asked the Honorable Joseph G. Babich of the Superior Court.

Ms. N refused to answer, invoking the Fifth Amendment. But the judge persisted. "There is no such definition in the Penal Code of a homosexual, is there? . . . This is what I'm talking about. Everybody bandies this word about, and yet we don't have a definition. Now, I would like to know what she does with the other women that constitutes the act. Maybe she just shakes hands with them. I don't know." The transcript of the case indicates that the judge never did find out.

There is nothing mysterious or magical about Lesbian lovemaking (except, perhaps, for the two people involved). As Dr. William Masters and Virginia Johnson have found in their sex research, the body goes through certain physiological changes during the sexual cycle whether the initiator of the cycle is you, a partner, or an inanimate object. The mystery and the magic come from the person with whom you are making love. Everything that one woman does to another can be done also by a man, but for a Lesbian that would change everything. It isn't the actions or the act: it is the woman involved who makes it more than just "physiological changes."

What do Lesbians do sexually? Very much the same thing a man and a woman (or a man and a man) can do, with the exception that there is no penis present. There are a number of ways that two women can seek and find sexual gratification together, ways limited only by the imagination of the persons involved.

The three most common techniques used in Lesbian lovemaking are mutual masturbation, cunnilingus and tribadism. Mutual masturbation consists of manipulation of the clitoris, caressing the labia, and/or penetration of the vagina by the fingers until sexual excitation or orgasm occurs. This can be done simultaneously by the partners or in turn. Cunnilingus is the stimulation of the clitoris, the labia, and sometimes penetration of the vagina by the tongue of the partner. Again, this can be done by one to the other or, in the "69" position, by both at the same time. Tribadism, on the other hand, involves one woman lying atop the other, followed by up and down rhythmic movements to stimulate the clitoris of each. It is a technique which may fulfill "butch-femme" fantasies, but which takes time to master. There may be variations of position, but satisfaction comes from stimulation of the clitoris by the friction of movement against the body of the partner.

There are two other methods by which two women may achieve sexual gratification, but they seem to be relatively rare in practice. One of these is the use of penis substitutes or dildos, made usually of some rubber product and shaped and colored to look like a penis. This idea tickles the fancy of most men who cannot feature women enjoying or being satisfied sexually without a penis. However, the dildo's most prevalent use is by heterosexual women in masturbation. The truth is that the great majority of Lesbians and/or heterosexual women have never seen a dildo. Women who feel the need for inserting a penis substitute in the vagina to fulfill their heterosexual fantasies are more apt to use homemade improvisations, such as a candle, banana or cucumber. But sometimes, like the glutton who heaps his dinner plate too full, they may overestimate their capacity.

It is important to emphasize that a penis (or penis substitute) is not necessary for a woman's sexual gratification. As pointed out in the epic book *Sexual Behavior in the Human Female,* published in 1953 by the Institute for Sex Research, most heterosexuals, both men and women, do not realize that sex between two women may be "as effective as or even more effective than" techniques used in heterosexual coitus. As Masters and Johnson discovered in their research and reported in their book *Human Sexual Response,* and what the Kinsey people also pointed out, is that the first third of a woman's vagina, the lips of the vagina and the clitoris contain virtually all of the nerve endings which serve for sexual stimulation. The inner two-thirds of the vagina has very little sensation, although some women receive a heightened sense of satisfaction from the feel of something deep in the vagina or hitting the cervix.

In all studies (and there haven't been all that many) about Lesbian sexual practices one unanimous finding has been that the use of penis substitutes is relatively rare. We are sure that most Lesbians have tried something at one time or another, but for continuing satisfaction in sex there is nothing like a living, breathing, responding person. As one Lesbian declared during a discussion one evening, "If I wanted a penis for sex I'd go find a live one, not a fake."

The remaining technique is anilingus, use of the tongue in and around the anus. The finger of one partner may also be used to stimulate the anal region, which is an erogenous zone.

As in the case of any sexual communication between two people, full knowledge and prowess come only by practice. Further, there are a number of possible variations on these basic techniques. We should mention here that Lesbians (dare we say "women"?) don't just hop to it, as some men do. Foreplay (embracing, kissing on the mouth and other parts of the body, breast fondling and sucking, nibbling at the ear, and touching and stroking various erogenous zones of the body) is important to women in lovemaking—and men, too, if they will only admit it.

What bothers us, however, is the bald statement by psycho-analysts that these practices, like breast stimulation, gratify the Lesbian's thwarted maternal instinct. The breast is an erogenous zone of both the male and the female. Does that mean that the man who derives pleasure from having his partner stimulate his nipples is gratifying his maternal instinct? Does that mean that all American males are really frustrated babies because they were weaned away from their mothers' breasts at a tender age? Does that account for their "breast fetish"? Psychoanalysis (which is nothing more than a "secular religion," according to Dr. Szasz), by its emphasis on the "immaturity" of various sex acts and foreplay, is simply a carry-over from the early religionists who forbade sex unless it was for the purpose of procreation. On the other hand, more knowledgeable sexologists and marriage counselors point out the various erogenous zones of the human body and encourage variation in sexual technique to buck up a tired heterosexual relationship.

These, then, are the techniques, open to much variation by individual women. They have been listed in books before, primarily in those of a scientific or pseudoscientific nature. This has been helpful to many a young Lesbian—at least she can read up on the subject. Not so long ago about the only way you could educate yourself was to go to a gay bar and pick up (or be picked up by) someone more experienced than yourself. We may have made progress in taking sex out of the realm of the hidden and unknown, but baby, we've still got a long way to go!

Although books may be helpful to a Lesbian in figuring out what to do sexually, the same books will undoubtedly have a lot of other rubbish about homosexuality in them. And, because the seeker probably knows little about the Lesbian except that she is one, she is liable to accept the statements in the book as true.

As the years have passed we have been alternately enraged, amused and discouraged about books and articles written about female homosexuals. The worst yet is the book by David Reuben, M.D., called *Everything You Always Wanted to Know About Sex but Were Afraid to Ask*. This book, a runaway best seller when first published, has been reprinted in fifteen languages. Unfortunately for the homosexual, male and female, this means millions of people have and will read Dr. Reuben's statements about homosexuals, all of which are distorted half-truths which stereotype the homosexual much as bigots used to stereotype Blacks as "happy chillun."

Because of a complaint lodged by the Dutch Society of Homosexuals (COC), and despite a court ruling based on freedom of the press, the Dutch publishing company of A. W. Bruna & Son agreed to refrain from further distribution of Reuben's book in Holland. Justice W. H. Overbeek, while dismissing the complaint, called the book "shallow, insignificant and bigoted" and allowed that these "American assertions" about homosexuality would not stand the test of criticism in the Netherlands. The management of the publishing company, in withdrawing publication, admitted they had decided too hastily and therefore too carelessly to translate the American "sexseller."

Dr. Reuben, true chauvinist that he is, does not spend as much time in his book on the Lesbian as he does on the male homosexual, but in the little space he does devote to the subject (in his chapter on prostitution!) he manages to cover a lot of erroneous zones. As with his answers about male homosexuals, his opinions about Lesbians make one wonder if he has ever met any, let alone read any of the literature about them.

In response to the question "What do female homosexuals do?" he quips, "One vagina plus another vagina equals zero." Lesbians, he indicates, are forever looking for love where there is none, for an unavailable lasting sexual satisfaction. Contrast this attitude with the remarks of the Kinsey staff or of Dr. Earle M. Marsh, assistant clinical professor of obstetrics and gynecology at the University of California Medical Center. At a 1968 series of lectures on sex, Dr. Marsh was quoted as saying: "It's too bad that every male cannot have instruction from a female homosexual prior to marriage. Only a female homosexual really knows how to make love to a woman. We, as men, are kind of duds along those lines."

Dr. Reuben does manage to cover all the sexual techniques; what he ignores in his explanation is the reality of any kind of emotional involvement or relationship. He says Lesbians do seem to "make out" a lot, kissing, stroking, etc., but that this is merely to build an illusion of romance. Apparently in his world Lesbians are just like a lot of men: they go right to work with no preliminaries. He also brings up two of the semi-myths about Lesbians:

the use of the dildo, and the Lesbian who has an unusually long clitoris which can be inserted in the vagina and who, therefore, is in great demand. We disposed of the dildo myth earlier. As to the other, there are variations in clitoris size among women just as there are in penis size among men. We have read that spider monkeys have been observed with a clitoris almost as long as the male's penis, but we haven't run into Lesbians with such unusual attributes, nor have we heard from others about any.

Although Dr. Reuben devotes an entire chapter to misinformation about the male homosexual, he kisses off the Lesbian with four "answers." This short shrift treatment of the Lesbian is indicative of Dr. Reuben's treatment of women in general. His section on menopause is unbelievably medieval in its concepts, as evidenced by his statement, "Having outlived their ovaries, they may have outlived their usefulness as human beings." Considering this demeaning attitude, how any woman can bother to read further is beyond belief.

Reuben makes the flat statement that the majority of prostitutes are female homosexuals. Now that's a myth we surely thought had been laid to rest. Most of the few books written on Lesbians have included a section on prostitution and, conversely, most of the books on prostitution have included a section on Lesbians. But more realistic and less moralistic looks at the world's oldest profession have shown that prostitutes enter their line of work for two primary reasons: money and sex, in that order. The concept that most prostitutes are Lesbians simply doesn't hold water, although there are some who are and who, we assume, entered the field simply for the money.

Such a one is Betty, an attractive blonde in her late twenties. Because of certain physical handicaps, her guilt about being a Lesbian, and a drinking problem of some years' standing, Betty had had a hard time of it. She had tried college and failed, tried business school and failed, tried living with a woman and failed. She finally ended up in Chicago on welfare and in analysis. The latter worked. Her self esteem rose, her drinking ceased, and she started her own business. She became a prostitute—and a good one. No pimp for her; this was strictly a one woman show. Betty is off welfare now and earning more money than she had ever dreamed of. She works hard at her profession, learning new techniques and gimmicks to please her clients. She's still a Lesbian—women are for loving, men are for business. Or, as one Lesbian poet has written, "Man can only fuck what I can love."

But, more often, the prostitute becomes a Lesbian, or engages in Lesbian relations for her own emotional gratification, *after* her "business" experiences with men have left her with feelings of disgust and revulsion. Ellen Strong, in her article "The Hooker" which appeared in the anthology *Sisterhood Is Powerful,* describes her own reaction. She became a homosexual for a few years because she found she could still respond sexually to women, though she no longer could to men. Her experience with women was what sustained her emotionally during this period of her life. It filled her need for love and involvement at the time, but it did not change her into a Lesbian.

In a one-man show of inconsistency, Dr. Reuben touts fellatio and cunnilingus (male and female oral copulation practiced by homosexuals) as desirable and pleasurable and perfectly all right to practice—for heterosexuals. Though he admits that the most undersexed man or woman could be brought to "an explosive orgasm" by using this technique, he nonetheless pooh-poohs it when it comes to homosexuals. The act is the same, whether between members of the same sex or the opposite sex. Yet, while admitting that female orgasms begin and end with the clitoris, Reuben still insists that oral sex is good *only* when it is followed by heterosexual penis-vagina intercourse. Since he is not a woman, since he cannot experience the "clitoral" orgasm, since he wants and needs the vaginal penetration for his own penis satisfactions, this may be very true for him. It does not necessarily apply to all women, most especially not to the Lesbian. And the "maturity" of the vaginal orgasm as opposed to the "immaturity" of the clitoral orgasm is just so much double talk to confound the Lesbian into thinking she is missing something. Most Lesbians agree that "you shouldn't knock it if you haven't tried it." They have tried it. They know what they are missing, and they are glad of it. Instead they have found something else which is far more satisfying. Can't we let it go at that? Must we continue to measure the intensity and quality of orgasms? It's a child's game, like saying, "Mine is bigger and better than yours!" It proves nothing except that certain people derive sexual satisfaction in different ways, the measure of which can only be known to the individual experiencing it.

Although she is most often seen solely as a sexual person by straight society, the Lesbian has as many sexual problems as do her heterosexual sisters. For she is caught in the same morass of sexual suppression as are all women in this country. By and large, she is raised to prepare herself to become wife and mother and helpmeet to her male mate. She is still taught that woman must save herself sexually for her husband—the nice girl doesn't play around. She is taught that woman is not aggressive—at least not obviously—but rather uses devious (feminine) means to achieve her ends. She is taught to conform, insofar as possible, to the outward appearance of the "ideal woman" which has been given her by television, the motion pictures and magazines. She is taught, more often than we would like to think, that sex is something evil or dirty and not, heaven forbid, something which is pleasurable and joyous.

It is not at all strange, then, that the Lesbian often grows to adulthood denying her sexuality, afraid of her sexual feelings and, in many instances, unaware and unknowledgeable of what they mean and how to cope with them. You can imagine the chaotic state of mind a young Lesbian may suffer: not only is she, like every woman, basically ignorant about the real meaning of sexuality, but as well, she is faced with the horrifying fact that the sexual feelings that are surfacing in her are directed toward another woman. It is little wonder, then, that a percentage of Lesbians find themselves frigid (or nearly so), that many Lesbians are completely passive and cannot bring themselves to reciprocate and make love to their partners, and that a number of Lesbians never have any sex at all.

To understand the Lesbian as a sexual being one must understand woman as a sexual being. Historically, in America woman was considered nonsexual, by men and by herself, until the end of World War I. It seems incredible now, but prior to that time it was considered totally "unladylike" for a woman to enjoy sex. So heavy was this pressure that some women had operations for clitoris removal so they would not act in such an unseemly manner. From this background women started the long and still not completed fight to regain control of their own bodies, the long fight to be considered full natural sexual beings and not merely vessels for a man's pleasure.

What is woman fighting against? The double standard, not just in the area of sex, but in all areas of life. She is fighting against the myths, still perpetuated, that she is destined for one man, and only one man, and must be pure and chaste until she finds him, if ever. She is fighting against the concept that sex is purely for procreation, not for recreation. She is fighting against the rules made for her by all-male religionists and against the ridiculous concept that she is not "all woman" or "mature" until she experiences the male mythology of the vaginal orgasm. She is fighting for lovers who will consider her needs, not just their own pleasure, lovers who will recognize her as an orgasm-seeking human being and who will be (hu)man enough to work with her for mutual pleasure.

Woman today, although more free than ever before in this country, is still bound by the invisible shackles of the past. She needs the help of her sisters and brothers to break out of the prison of the past and into the freedom of mutual respect and opportunity.

What, then, is the effect of our sexually repressive society on the Lesbian? It is far-reaching and varied and very much in parallel with the sexual schisms of those women making a heterosexual commitment. Imagine a young woman of eighteen years who has finally sorted out her feelings, her emotions, her sexual responses to find that they all point toward the fact that she is a Lesbian. At the same time she will find that she is considered illegal, immoral and sick; a man-hater, a woman-seducer, masculine and hard—all this by the heterosexual society.

Further, considering that most young women of eighteen in this country are very naive about sex, either theirs or anyone else's, it follows that our young woman probably hasn't the foggiest notion of how to go about making love to another woman. In fact, she probably hasn't any idea of how to go about meeting another woman of like persuasion. Depending on her background, she either feels that sex is a good thing, a bad thing, or just a thing. These values will be with her as a Lesbian, just as they would have been with her had she been heterosexually oriented. Fate will have something to do with the outcome. Her first sexual contact may be with an experienced Lesbian, in which case at least she will have some idea of what goes on; it may be with someone as inexperienced as she. If this is the case, much will depend on the attitudes of both women toward sex.

A third possibility for our eighteen-year-old is that she may have had her first introduction to sex with a man. According to a study on "Sexual Behavior of the Female Homosexual" done by Drs. Marcel T. Saghir and Eli Robins, of the Department of Psychiatry at Washington University School of Medicine in St. Louis, more than three-fourths of the Lesbians studied had had heterosexual intercourse. For the majority this occurred between the ages of twenty and twenty-nine and was primarily done in a spirit of testing and experimentation rather than because of strong sexual arousal.

We mentioned earlier that many Lesbians are frigid, a concept that blows the minds of most straight persons who have always thought of Lesbians only as sexual beings. It also blows the mind of the Lesbian suffering from this problem! It shows, too, that heterosexual women do not have a corner on the frigidity market created by society's oppression of women.

Pat, a professional woman in her forties, sought help from us recently because she couldn't achieve orgasm with another woman, and even through masturbation it took a very long time. It was also apparent that she did not feel good about being a Lesbian and was deathly afraid to let anyone straight know her sexual orientation. With the help of a vibrator and much, much endorsement that it was all right to be sexual, she was able to retrain herself, not only to orgasm but to multiple orgasms. In the process, she began to feel much better about herself as a person, even though she still isn't shouting to the rooftops about being a Lesbian.

Although the great majority of Lesbians make love to one another, there are some who either refuse to make love to their partner or who refuse to be made love to. The former is usually a woman with one (or all) of three problems. She has been brainwashed into thinking that women are passive in sex; she is new at the game and afraid she won't perform correctly; or she really feels sex is dirty and can't bring herself to action. Given half a chance, with the right partner, she can overcome all three of her blocks.

But the woman who won't let anyone make love to her, who can only be the aggressor, has a much deeper problem. Mac, very much the sophisticated businesswoman during the day, metamorphosed into very much the "male" and "husband" when she was at home. Her "wife," who didn't work, literally brought Mac her slippers and pipe. "I can't let Jan touch me sexually," she explained. "It would destroy the illusion. Besides, the man should be the aggressive one." It was unfortunate she hadn't ever discussed the matter with Jan, for Jan didn't have any illusions that Mac was a man. She loved *her* and would much have preferred a woman-to-woman relationship. Jan had tried discussing the matter with Mac early in their relationship, but had run into a mammoth wall of stubbornness and had given up.

The gay terminology for a couple like Jan and Mac is "butch and femme." As mentioned earlier, we were very much caught up in this "tradition" when we started living together. But so was everyone else! Especially our heterosexual friends, Sue and Sam. When we went to gay bars, the same roles were being acted out all over the place.

Our butch-femme relationship was perhaps less overt than some, since Phyllis drove and Del didn't (obviously, driving a car is a masculine thing); Phyllis could at least drive a nail relatively straight, while Del had problems with anything like that. Both of us could (and did) cook, and neither of us liked to wash dishes, clean house or iron (so we seldom did).

What confused us were the concepts of what was masculine and what feminine. Phyllis tended toward more tailored clothes—boy-type shirts and suits—was that masculine? Del was sensitive, emotional, romantic—was that feminine? Or weren't these words, *masculine* and *feminine,* culturally defined and socially scripted? Did they really have anything to do with the way people really were? We decided *no* and started acting as people, as ourselves, as women rather than as caricatures in a heterosexual marriage. But it took us a while.

Why did the butch-femme idea arise, and why has it lasted? For one thing, it isn't difficult for women, no matter what their age, to look around and see that it is an advantage to be a man. It seems fairly logical, also, that if you are sexually attracted to a woman, you should play the "masculine" role. Especially if what you have in mind is getting yourself a wife! Two women setting up house-keeping have only the model of the heterosexual marriage: the division of labor along strictly sex role lines. Again, when you look at heterosexual marriages, it certainly comes out clearly that the male has the better deal.

The stereotype of the dyke is an extreme of the butch. A young woman who has decided she is a Lesbian may only know of this stereotype: a masculine looking woman a la Stephen Gordon in *The Well of Loneliness*. So she dresses and acts the part she thinks she must as she makes her first tentative forays into homosexual society. In some Lesbian circles, she is likely to find herself pressured into declaring herself either butch or femme, and that she is expected to conform in matters of dress, speech and action to the prevailing mode of the group she hopes to join.

There are also Lesbians who truly believe they are more "masculine" than "feminine" and that they were born so. One assumes that they equate masculine with aggression, power, superiority, etc., while they feel that feminine means passivity, inferiority, softness, etc. A friend of ours in her fifties who has always played the butch role put it this way:

"Now I know that many middle class Lesbians insist that there is no such thing [as butch-femme]. But *I* know there are masculine and feminine Lesbians. There is me . . . and I now know that I cannot be unique. . . . I met and fell in love with a decidedly feminine Lesbian, not the least bit hung up over her femininity. In her I found my deep inner nature reflected, the polarity opposed to hers.

"The butchy appearing Lesbians (the 'baby butches') often as not turn out to be quite feminine. I think these are the ones that lead some Lesbians to deny the existence of any sexual polarity. I'm not sure what the reasons are for this kind of self misidentification, but I suspect one reason to be the equating of feminine with inferior the world over.

"*I* know that sexual differentiation is here to stay. It does not follow a simple one-to-one correspondence with biological sex. I cannot be attracted by another masculine Lesbian. As I put it, I'm psychologically heterosexual."

Although we don't agree with Nella we do know a number of Lesbians who would: because that's the way they feel, or at least the way they have rationalized their feelings against the inferior status of being a woman. Strangely, it is those women who feel that they are "born butch" who tend to ape all the least desirable characteristics of men. In this case one may well say to these butches, "Up against the wall, male chauvinist pig!" For to consider oneself a heterosexual, to stress that male and female are opposites which presumably attract, is to accept the entire male-imposed doctrine that woman's place is indeed in the home serving the male. Much of the polarity between men and women has centered around procreation. But the sex act itself is neither male nor female: it is a human reaching-out for the ultimate in communication with another human. The roles men and women (or butch and femme) play in our country are only acting, not honest and equal relationships between two human beings.

We can't stress too strongly that the great majority of Lesbians think of themselves as women and are looking for (or have found) another woman with whom to share their lives. Many go through the "butch" stage for reasons already mentioned, to which might be added the identification factor. If you look like any other woman on the street, how in the world are you going to find other Lesbians, or, more to the point, how are they going to find you? So stereotyping yourself may serve a plus function at the beginning of one's gay career. Thankfully, the vast majority of those now proudly flaunting their "butchhood" in gay bars and meeting places around the country will shift to their true identity as woman as they become older, wiser, and more sure of their identity as a person.

One who has gone through all the stages is a very old and dear friend of ours, Toni. Del first met her in Seattle when she was a slim, dark-haired and attractive femme, playing the role to the hilt in slinky dresses, much makeup and the works. After Del moved to San Francisco, we lost track of Toni until one night, in a rather raunchy gay bar in North Beach, Del said, "My God, isn't that Toni?" And indeed it was, but hardly the same Toni she had known so well in Seattle. This Toni was a bit heavier, hair short and slicked back, no makeup and dressed completely in men's clothes.

Toni joined Daughters of Bilitis, at our insistence, and as a result of the group's example, its unspoken pressure, she toned down her dress. She was still very butch, but she wore women's slacks and blouses. It seems old fashioned now, in this day of rampant individuality in clothing, but one of DOB's goals was to teach the Lesbian a "mode of behavior and dress acceptable to society." What DOB meant by such a suggestion was that all persons should be free enough to dress, and feel at ease, in the appropriate attire for any situation, from evening gowns to bathing suits. We knew too many Lesbians whose activities were restricted because they wouldn't wear skirts. But Toni did not agree.

"You'll never get me in a dress," she growled, banging her fist on the table. But she became fast friends with a gay man, and over the months he helped her to feel comfortable with herself as a woman.

We met Toni for dinner before the theatre one night. There she was in all her glory, neatly turned out in dress, hat, gloves and high heels, the very epitome of a middle class matron. The only different note was the lack of lipstick. "My mother never wore it, so why should I?"

Today Toni, like many women, often wears pants to work. But she is not wearing them now to reinforce some vague concept that she is "male." She is wearing them for the same reasons other women do: they give you much more freedom of movement than skirts, and they are warmer. She's still not wearing lipstick, but neither are a lot of younger women. Perhaps Toni was merely ahead of her time in her mode of dress and behavior, since individuality in dress is much more acceptable to society now.

We were most amused by the letter DOB received many years ago from Alyce of New York. "I guess you could call my roommate and me mild transvestites—that is, we wear slacks almost always on our off-work hours. We are comfortable in them and we have no problem adjusting to the stares of the passersby. We consider dresses, high heels and stocking holders the most uncomfortable contraptions men have invented to restrict the movements of women so they cannot walk very far, lift many things, or sit with their legs apart in warm weather." You can bet that the Lesbian is glad that her preferences in clothing have at long last caught on.

When Phyllis was shopping in Macy's one day, she stepped into the elevator along with some young "hip" types. An older woman, in a knit suit, with her hair carefully groomed, looked them all over and blurted out, "I'm the only 'straight' person in this elevator!" Realizing what she'd done, in an effort to apologize, she said, "I have to work." Phyllis, who has become relaxed about dress both at work and on the street, had to do a double take before she realized that "straight" to the woman had referred to clothing—the woman's skirt and heels as opposed to the slacks and jeans the others were wearing.

"Polite" society still judges people by the clothes they wear. "I was once a part of the mixed up kids who look like men and aren't—who look for trouble and get it," Jayne told us. "Do you know what Chicago does to people like that? Every door they walk through is in danger of being locked forever. Luckily I met someone who stripped me of my precious clothing and replaced it with eight years of schooling. My first lesson was: I am a woman and that's something to be proud of." So the debate continues: whether to dress for comfort or for what society or the dress designers consider "feminine."

We have found some interesting anomalies in the butch-femme pattern over the years. One which crops up rather consistently is women—usually divorced and, we suspect, not Lesbian at all—who pair up with butch Lesbians. In these partnerships the entire male-female dichotomy is acted out to the nth degree. The femmes insist that their butches wear only male clothing and that they appear and act as nearly like the stereotyped male as possible. Marty, who succeeded more in looking like a young boy than a man, although she was in her thirties, told us: "I wouldn't mind wearing women's clothes. It would make life much simpler. But Ruth won't hear of it. She threw all my dresses and things out."

Most of these femmes have been divorced more than once. It appears that they have been so badly treated by men that they can't bear the thought of remarrying. Yet their only knowledge of a relationship is that of man to woman, so they fashion their own "man" out of the woman they can relate to. It does not make for a happy situation for either party, and usually the twosome doesn't last very long.

In the early sixties we ran into what must have been the very epitome of a butch-femme couple. Leslie and Carol had contacted DOB in San Francisco to announce that they were moving from

Washington, D.C. They told us what train they were arriving on and asked us to meet it—and to get them a room in a hotel that wouldn't object to their dog and cat. We did. You couldn't miss them when they got off the train: Leslie in pants and trenchcoat, Carol in skirt and much jewelry, and the very large dog, the furry cat. We took them to their hotel, had a drink with them, and then split. It was a bit much for us. Besides, we hadn't been too much help. Since we both went to hairdressers, we were unable to recommend a barber for Leslie, and it was obvious that Leslie didn't think much of Del as a butch. Phyllis, who was in slacks, didn't really qualify as the zenith of femininity either.

Leslie and Carol attended several DOB parties, but didn't really fit in. Carol would be the only one there in a skirt and, as Leslie grumbled, you really couldn't tell who present was butch or femme. At that time everybody was wearing capris and blouses. Almost everybody had short hair, and almost everybody wore lipstick. Obviously it wasn't a proper group of Lesbians.

Leslie and Carol took a house in Marin County and one weekend asked us to dinner. They were intelligent women, and the evening was pleasant, if a little too alcoholic. But the topper came after dinner, when Leslie indicated Del was to remain with her in the dining room for brandy and cigars, while Carol and Phyllis were banished to the parlor for woman talk. We went along with the gag, but it was certainly a new trip for us. The subject under discussion in both groups, it turned out, was Leslie: how brilliant she was, how many degrees she had, but how she wanted to become a veterinarian's assistant so she could always wear pants. It seemed an awful waste of talent and potential.

The minority of Lesbians who still cling to the traditional male-female or husband-wife pattern in their partnerships are more than likely old-timers, gay bar habituées or working-class women. The old order changeth, however, and as the women's liberation movement gains strength against this pattern in heterosexual marriages, the number of Lesbians involved in butch-femme roles diminishes. There can, however, be some strange situations, even in a world where women's consciousness is being raised. We recently heard of a leader in the women's movement in Los Angeles who speaks out strongly against male domination and chauvinism. Yet in her relations with another woman, she plays the traditional male chauvinist butch role—not because she wants it that way, but because her friend insists.

Lynda, speaking as the new "woman-identified" woman of Gay Women's Liberation at the 1971 Council on Religion and the Homosexual symposium, was challenged by someone in the audience because of her apparently masculine attire. But Lynda explained, "This short haircut, because it is mine, is a woman's hair style. These so-called men's boots, because I am wearing them, are women's boots. This pipe, because I am smoking it, is a woman's pipe. Whatever women wear is women's wear. It is a matter of individual choice—and comfort."

Individual choice, too, is granted (if sometimes grudgingly) by Lesbian feminists to their sisters who still cling to their butch-femme roles. When a number of "enlightened" Lesbians, during the 1971 Gay Women's West Coast Conference in Los Angeles, loudly and openly ridiculed a traditional-style wedding taking place between two women at the Metropolitan Community Church, other truly enlightened sisters were enraged. To add their opprobrium to that which these women were already experiencing from society was, to them, unwarranted and unconscionable. Coming from them it was even more oppressive than the societal oppression they had gathered together to protest. Differences though there be in philosophy, politics or life style, the right of individual choice and of human dignity is basic to the sisterhood. What is rejected, however, is the transference of male chauvinism in adopting traditional sex roles. Most Lesbians, whatever their life style, are striving today for more egalitarian relationships.

We have watched the decline of the butch-femme concept of relationship for sixteen years. It has been a gradual decline, and, as we mentioned, the stereotype has not yet vanished. As a life style it has many disadvantages, as does the same concept—person as property—when applied to the heterosexual union. One of these disadvantages is the jealousy which invariably creeps in. Jealousy of one's partner, especially obsessive jealousy, indicates an uncertainty of the relationship and bears witness to the fact that the two partners feel somehow possessed, like chattel, by one another. Observation would indicate that more jealousy is engendered in a butch-femme relationship than in a woman-to-woman partnership, probably because of this underlying possessiveness. If you are sure of your partner's love, if your partner is a person and not a thing, then jealousy either doesn't exist or is extremely minimal. The high incidence of jealousy imputed to the Lesbian by many of the so-called experts on the subject simply doesn't exist.

Certainly we had a problem with jealousy early in our togetherness. While Del was babysitting with her daughter, Phyllis was still dating Jim. Now Jim was a holdover from Phyllis's "straight" days and had been the only person she had known, of her own age, when she had returned to San Francisco from Seattle prior to her commitment to Del. She had never been remotely romantically interested in Jim, though he was in her, but she hated to "hurt his feelings" by making the break. And at that time she surely didn't have the nerve to tell him she was a Lesbian.

For obvious reasons this whole situation didn't sit well with Del. It just didn't seem right, and she wasn't convinced there was "nothing" between them. Phyllis did break the friendship off, but not before some dramatic scenes between us. But Phyllis laid down the law. One of the reasons she had broken up with the man she had been engaged to had been his unreasonable jealousy. She wasn't going to go through that again. So she flatly told Del she would not tolerate any jealousy. And it worked. By and large, we have not been troubled with jealousy over the years. We know where we stand with each other.

While there is a certain amount of jealousy among Lesbian couples, as between heterosexual couples, the Saghir-Robins study indicates that jealousy comes in last as a reason for relationships breaking up. Further, many women who break up their relationship as lovers remain fast friends. This wouldn't be possible if the split had come over jealousy rather than a change in, or loss of, emotional attachment, the reason given for most "divorces."

Illustrative of the changing attitudes among Lesbians are Helen and Ann, young, socially aware, hip and long haired. Helen, twenty-five, has been married and Ann, twenty-one, holds deep religious commitments. Both are active in DOB and the women's movement. They have lived together for a year now, sharing love and work. Coming down the street holding hands, dressed in jeans and old army shirts, their long blonde hair hanging free, they certainly don't fit any of the stereotyped images of the Lesbian. There is no butch or femme in their world. But there once was.

"When I first got involved in gay life," Ann says, "I decided it was best to be butch. So I found a girl and we settled down. She did all the womanly things and really fussed around the house, making curtains and ruffly things. She looked to me to make all the decisions—she acted as if she didn't have a mind at all. It was a drag. So, I did what any self respecting male would do: I went out and found another girl."

It didn't take Ann long, however, to find out that equality in a relationship was important. And, says she, "There's certainly no problem being bored with Helen—she's got a mind of her own for sure."

Much change has taken place in the way all women (straight or gay) in this country think about sex roles and personal relationships. There appear to be three strong influences: (1) a questioning of religious dogma, exposing myths and re-examining the taboos, thereby developing a new code of sexual and social ethics; (2) research on human sexuality, opening up avenues to more widespread sex education, and discovery of "the pill"; and (3) the various liberation movements which all decry the use of labels to separate people and which raise the question of what it really means to be human.

Masters and Johnson, in their classic *Human Sexual Inadequacy,* found that religious orthodoxy was the single biggest contributor to sexual dysfunction, a fact those of us who have worked with homosexuals have known for years. The guilt heaped on those women, straight or gay, who have been brought up in Roman Catholic or fundamentalist religions particularly, can be unbearable. It is the cause not just of sexual inadequacy, but of alcoholism, drug addiction, misery and suicide. While Protestant denominations in this country are beginning to rethink traditional attitudes, their statements are still too cautious and tentative—and too late for many.

Though many churchmen have come a long way in understanding the humanity of homosexuals, many are still caught up in medieval concepts. Just recently a young woman called Phyllis to ask about scriptural references which didn't damn the homosexual. She indicated that she had gone to a Methodist church in San Francisco seeking understanding and help in solving her dilemma. "I'm married," she said, "but I believe it is a great mistake for me. I asked the minister why it was wrong for me to live with the woman I love in a union that seems so very natural. I asked why it would be right to stay with my husband in a union that is unnatural for me and to which I could never give my all. The minister's reply was that only if I stayed with my husband would I be 'welcome' at his church."

The homophile thrust for freedom and equality has forced some clergymen at least to recognize that love and sex between two persons of the same sex can be, and are, equal to and as valid as that between two persons of the opposite sex. Such a realization leads inevitably to a re-evaluation of the sacred institution of marriage. If the church recognizes love between two homosexuals, it cannot very well continue to condemn love between two heterosexuals who have not bothered to "sanctify" their love through wedding vows. Theologians are presently wrestling with these problems.

Change is also coming about in terms of women's sexual awareness and activity. Because of better birth control methods, especially the pill, women are for the first time relatively free of the fear of pregnancy. They are less tyrannized by their biology and thus begin to question their traditional roles. The women's liberation movement serves as a catalyst, challenging all women to question both their sexual and social roles. As a result, many more young women are experimenting sexually than ever before. In fact, if there is truly a sexual revolution in progress, it is among women, not men. A recent survey of the sexual activity of college men and women made by the Institute for Sex Research indicates that, when compared to earlier figures (approximately twenty years ago), the number of men engaging in premarital sexual intercourse has remained static, but the number of women so engaging has doubled. This, then, does at least establish basis for the hope that woman, whatever her sexual orientation, is moving toward more acceptance of herself as a sexual being.

The advent of the "flower children" in 1967 brought with it a marvelous idea: to take each person for what she or he is as a person, not for skin color, sexual orientation, status or any other artificial quality. Out of this idea of love came a great deal of sexual experimentation among people of the same and opposite sexes. If you grooved on someone, a logical extension of that feeling was sex—and it didn't matter what the sex of the grooved-upon was. Thus the idea of bisexuality, always with us, became much better known.

This concept of bisexuality was extended into the women's movement. As women in their small consciousness-raising groups began to come to terms with themselves and sought an equal partnership with men, they found that their husbands and/or lovers were not so willing to give up their roles of supposed supremacy. Their men, not having gone through the same consciousness-raising process and not understanding how they, too, are oppressed by their own stultifying "male" roles, were still clinging to the status quo, still steeped in male chauvinism. As a consequence, and because these women could not and would not turn back to the old ways, many of them vowed not to have anything more to do with men until such time as they could come together as equals. Having become more sexually aware and having made this decision, these women were then faced with finding alternatives to heterosexual coitus for their sexual satisfaction. Their options were: celibacy, masturbation, or Lesbianism. A good many, preferring and needing a close personal relationship, have deliberately chosen the latter. The experience of both the hippies and woman-identified women would indicate that the "nature" of mankind, which has heretofore been obscured by biological and biblical scripting, may indeed be bisexual.

Those naturalists who have condemned homosexuals not only point to Adam and Eve, but to lower animals as proof that our true nature is to be heterosexual. However, biologists have observed homosexual contacts in widely varied species of mammals, and anthropologists have found homosexual practices in almost all cultures. Biologists have observed homosexual activity in rats, mice, hamsters, guinea pigs, rabbits, porcupines, marten, cattle, antelope, dogs, cats, goats, horses, lions, sheep, monkeys, chimpanzees and pigs.

Drs. Clelland S. Ford, anthropologist, and Frank Beach, psychologist, in their book *Patterns of Sexual Behavior,* claim that human homosexuality is the product of our fundamental mammalian heritage of general sexual responsiveness. Cross-cultural and cross-species comparisons suggest to them that a biological tendency for inversion of sexual behavior is inherent in most, if not all, mammals, including the human species. They, of course, added that homosexuality, while prevalent, is not the predominant sexual activity observed in these societies and animals.

Freud, we pointed out earlier, postulated that a homosexual component can be found in the sexual development of every human being and that there remains in everyone the residual manifestation of bisexuality. Wilhelm Stekel, a coworker with Freud, stated flatly in his book *Bisexual Love*, "All persons originally are bisexual in their predisposition. There are no exceptions." It was his contention that the struggle between the two components of a person created neuroses and anxieties. At the age of puberty, however, the heterosexual represses his homosexuality, sublimating it in the more acceptable proprieties of friendship, nationalism, social endeavors and gatherings. The homosexual, on the other hand, somehow pushes the "wrong" button and represses his or her heterosexuality instead. But in either case, since no one manages to overcome his tendencies toward the other type of sexual behavior completely, both homosexuals and heterosexuals carry within themselves a predisposition to a neurosis. But here is where the heterosexual bias steps in. Somehow it turns out, according to Stekel, that homosexuals *are* neurotic because of their unexpressed heterosexual potential; heterosexuals, however, merely have the potential for neuroses because of their unexpressed homosexual component.

In more recent times Dr. Albert Ellis, sexologist and executive director of the Institute for Rational Living in New York City, has stated that those persons who are either exclusively heterosexual or exclusively homosexual are neurotic. The Kinsey studies verify that American men and women are not necessarily as exclusive in their private sexual behavior as they may pretend publicly.

It has seemed to us, as we have met and talked about homosexuality and human sexuality with thousands of persons, that indeed we all have the potential to respond erotically to both sexes. That we do not use this potential is due to the church-imposed morality under which we all suffer. A child is born a sexual being, neither hetero nor homo. As Dr. C. A. Tripp, psychologist, pointed out in 1965 during a symposium at the University of California School of Medicine, most human sexual behavior is *learned*. It is only in the lower animals that it is totally instinc-

tive. The higher on the evolutionary scale you are, the less instinctive are your sexual reactions. So our life experiences "teach" us
our sexuality, which may turn out to be hetero, homo or bi. The
Kinsey staff, in *Sexual Behavior in the Human Female,* pondered
the fact that given the physiology of human sexual response plus
our mammalian background of behavior, "it is not so difficult to
explain why a human animal does a particular thing sexually. It is
more difficult to explain why each and every individual is not
involved in every type of sexual activity."

The evidence indicates we may be purely sexual at birth, but
that our society channels us primarily into accepted modes of
behavior or, sometimes, those not so acceptable. We may have the
capacity for bisexual response, but social mores from both sides of
the fence tell us *no*.

At least three-fourths of the Lesbians we have known have had
heterosexual intercourse more than once, either in a marriage situation, while dating, as an experiment out of curiosity, or as a test
of sexual identity. For the majority of these women the experience was good, erotically: that is, orgasm was achieved and there
was a pleasurable feeling. But there was not the emotional involvement which was present in a Lesbian sexual relationship. And that
is what makes the difference. As Masters and Johnson so well
argued, an orgasm is an orgasm, no matter how it is achieved. The
body goes through the same physiological pattern, whether orgasm
comes through a loved one or the edge of a vibrating washing
machine. The "quality" of the orgasm differs—not within the body,
but within the head. There is, after all, a great deal of difference
psychologically between your lover and your washing machine.

What has happened with the advent of a more permissive part-
ner-changing and sex-switching sexuality is that a number of Lesbians have gotten pregnant, accidentally. A heterosexual woman
on the prowl will usually take the pill, or use some other method.
A Lesbian caught up in the concept of loving persons as persons is
very likely to be totally unprepared for a roll in the hay with a
sperm-spouting male. This happened to a friend of ours who,
having nothing special going with a woman, ended up in bed with
a young man she had met and enjoyed. It was a classic tale—one
shot and she was pregnant. In this case all has turned out well. The
young woman is mature and intelligent. She has subsequently set

up housekeeping with an equally intelligent and mature woman. She decided to keep the baby and the two of them appear to be doing a better job of child-rearing than many heterosexual parents. This, however, was a unique situation. It could have happened to someone not so mature who didn't want children (or wasn't ready to take on such responsibility) and who would have faced the trauma of all unwed mothers: do I keep the baby, have it adopted, get an abortion—or kill myself?

Over the years we have known a number of persons who considered themselves bisexual. Their complaint, almost universally, was that no one understood the bisexual, that she or he was much more discriminated against than a homosexual, since the straight community usually considered the bisexual to be homosexual while the gay community figured the bisexual to be simply a homosexual who, for one reason or another, hadn't yet been able to admit this fact. The bisexual, then, who has not repressed her or his ability to respond erotically to either sex and who might very well be expressing the true "nature" of the human species, is spurned in both the heterosexual and homosexual communities. Perhaps if these two warring camps declared a truce and discontinued the practice of repressing one or the other of their same-sex and opposite-sex response components, we might have a chance of finding out what the nature of sex is all about.

With the givens of Freud and Stekel—that we all have both heterosexual and homosexual inclinations, either of which, if repressed, leaves us with a predisposition to a neurosis—then insistence on a heterosexual identity as the only acceptable one obviously is detrimental to every one of us psychologically. Because we have bowed to the Judeo-Christian tradition, we have been bound to the unhealthy antisexual (not just antihomosexual) attitude that pervades our culture. We have never allowed people to respond to one another openly and reciprocally without rigid role definition. If we were allowed "to do what comes naturally," we might possibly come to understand the ambisexual nature of the human animal. If the idea of sex could be cleansed and the guilt we have felt about it could be purged from our minds, we would be rid of our sexual frustrations and hangups. We could expand our consciousness beyond our present preoccupation with the who-what-why-where-and-how of the mechanics of genital contact and fascination with the measurements of physical attributes (breasts, penises and orgasms). Allowed the freedom to be human, we might find that a new sexuality would emerge, encompassing not only the sensual, but also the trans-physical qualities of love, empathy and concern for one another's personhood, regardless of gender.

4. Life Styles

As is undoubtedly the case with many other Lesbians, our way of life has undergone many changes during the nineteen years we have been together. The first year was pretty stormy. While we had been close friends for more than three years, living together was something else again. In addition to the usual adjustments a heterosexual couple would be expected to make, we also had to cope with the problems entailed in leading a dual life.

As we mentioned, Del's daughter spent a good deal of our "honeymoon" with us, and Phyllis still had a boy friend in tow. Further, Phyllis's going out on a date while Del stayed home with Janey didn't do too much for Del's butch image. Also, there were other demands from our respective families which meant going our separate ways, and this was especially trying during holidays like Thanksgiving and Christmas. Each of our families related to us as daughter and friend. They were totally unaware of the implicit in-law relationship of that friend. Although we wished to spend the holidays together, we were consequently duty-bound to our respective families and were forced to deny our own family unit. Del's family usually opened Christmas packages on Christmas Eve, and Phyl's on Christmas morning. These were command performances, hidebound family traditions not easily broken, so that we had difficulty working "us" into the schedule. Eventually we took our respective sisters into our confidence, neither of whom had any difficulty whatever in accepting our relationship. That was reassuring to us personally, but not very helpful with the rest of our family problems since both sisters warned us not to tell our parents.

Early in our relationship, Del trotted Phyl down to the neighborhood bank to open up a joint checking account; some months
later we opened a joint savings account. We really hadn't discussed
financial arrangements, but Del was determined that ours was a
"marriage," and that included mutual ownership of all assets—
which in those days consisted of a bookcase made of boards and
bricks, countless books and records, a radio-phonograph, and a
motley collection of dishes, utensils and linens—hardly anything
worth writing a will about.

We have since learned that many Lesbians do not pool their
resources, as we did. Rather they each put up half of the rent and
food money and maintain separate bank accounts. When it comes
to furniture, some even go so far as to purchase "my" chair and
"her" chesterfield, apparently so there will be no hassle about property should they break up housekeeping. To us, this sort of
arrangement implies a built-in failure of the relationship, a sort of
self fulfilling prophecy. We weren't taking any chances.

One friend, who came into our lives at a much later date, explained that she felt "no relationship can last anyway." Like Ann
Aldrich, who wrote *We Two Won't Last*, Claire figured each affair
to be an interlude, and that inevitably the partners would grow
apart and split. Her pattern, we noted, was one of choosing a
younger woman as a partner, living with her for three or four years
and then breaking off. Instead of "growing apart," we concluded
that Claire's partners simply "grew up" and left the nest, that she
was repeatedly taking on the role of "mother" instead of establishing a one-to-one relationship.

As we said before, Sue and Sam were our only close friends in
the beginning. Everything was fine between the four of us, but
when other guests entered the picture, then we became their unmarried women friends. It wasn't always easy to make this sudden
switch in roles—most especially since we were newly together in a
butch-femme relationship. For Del it meant a complete about-face
from masculine to feminine, from married to single, from lover to
friend. It meant opening herself up to the old man-woman social
games in which she was expected to follow rather than take the
lead, in which she was supposed to be coquettish and coy. The
role, which had always galled Del anyway, was even more devastating under these circumstances—it was emasculating. It stripped

Del of her masculine illusions about herself and destroyed her self confidence as a lover. It enraged her, too, to watch Phyllis take it all in stride. Phyllis had always been an inveterate flirt. She enjoyed attention, even from men. As Del reluctantly played the role, she couldn't help wondering if it was really only an act to Phyllis. As an undeclared couple we had no rights. That our relationship was clandestine was not our choice. But we were nonetheless vulnerable, subject to many doubts and fits of jealousy.

Although we loved Sue and Sam dearly and had some hilarious times together on their houseboat in Sausalito, we still felt a keen desire to know and become part of the gay community. All of our friends were straight, and we missed not having any gay friends. Our only tie with the gay world was our own private sense of "belonging" to each other. While for the most part, we could relax and be ourselves with Sue and Sam, still there was something missing. We needed, too, to relate to gay people who would understand the subtle differences between heterosexual and homosexual relationships. We needed to know more about the gay life itself and how others managed it in a straight society. Above all, we needed a sense of "community" with others like ourselves—the feeling of security and respect that a homogeneous group affords its members.

We looked up a couple of Lesbian friends Del had known before we met, but they had split up and were very much preoccupied with their own problems. One had found a new lover who was possessive and antisocial, who certainly couldn't be bothered with two naive bumpkins. We knew there were lots of other Lesbians in San Francisco. We'd been to the gay bars and we'd looked at them, just like all the other tourists on the Broadway bar circuit. But we were shy, and we didn't know how to go about meeting them. They were mostly in-groups, where everybody already knew each other, and they seemed to be wary of strangers. Not knowing gay bar "etiquette," we felt totally inadequate and fearful of intruding ourselves where we might not have been welcome. So we just looked and watched, longing to share in their camaraderie, longing to be a part of this nebulous in-group, but not knowing how to break through.

Phyllis took a temporary typing job and came home one evening all excited because she had spotted a young woman she was just sure was "one of us." She wore her hair short, her clothes were tailored, she had a deep voice, and her mannerisms seemed to be indicative. "I just know she's gay," Phyllis reiterated. "But I just can't go up to her and say 'I'm gay. Are you?' What do I do?"

Short of coming right out with, "Are you gay?" Phyllis dropped every hint she could to her coworker, since there was nothing about her own appearance that would give any indication that she herself was a Lesbian. "She couldn't help but know—if indeed she is a Lesbian," Phyllis told Del the next night at dinner. "When we had our coffee break today, every other word I said was 'gay'—the weather, the time we had last night, etc. But she didn't let on, if she understood."

Most Lesbians, we have learned since, make it a practice to keep their private lives completely separate from their work, even though they may be aware of the presence of others in the plant or in the office. Someone else might overhear a conversation and put two and two together, or the other Lesbian could unwittingly make some remark that would be a dead giveaway. Then, too, personal involvements could lead to petty jealousies and sticky office politics. Consequently most Lesbians observe an unspoken moral code of not exposing one another, a sort of mutually protective loyalty pact. Any of these reasons could have been why Phyllis's coworker refused to bite at her "gay" bait. Since she has finally passed the stage of believing that every woman who wears a Pendleton jacket is gay, Phyl now says, "Besides, she may not have been a Lesbian at all. Just because she fit the stereotype. . . ."

One night, when we were once again making the gay bar scene, we stopped in the 299 Club and struck up a conversation with the bartender, who turned out to be a neighbor just around the corner from us. But more important, he was gay. We soon became fast friends with Mack and his lover, Ronnie, an unemployed female impersonator.

Fortunately this was shortly before Halloween, a world-renowned holiday for homosexuals—a sort of gay Mardi Gras festival with colorful and spectacular costumes, when the men dress up as women and the women dress up as men if they so choose. It is a night when by tradition police relax their tight surveillance of gay bars, much as they do parking meters on other holidays. It is a festive occasion, for which many "drag queens" may spend hundreds of hours and dollars on a lavish, elegant gown that will be worn only on this one night of nights. We made a date with Mack and Ronnie to go to the Beige Room.

Phyllis and Ronnie decided to dress alike and for a lark enter the "drag" contest together. They found some black satin material which they fashioned into mini-skirts with a sexy slit up the side and wore matching multicolored striped tops, black berets, black fishnet stockings and very high heels. This qualified them as stunning French apache dancers, if not prize winners. Most DOBs have seen Del more often than not at their Halloween parties only as an electioneer pushing her favorite candidate for the coming Tuesday election or as a picket carrying a sign reading "Down With Costume Parties." But that night Del herself went in costume, as a gay priest. She borrowed Ronnie's jacket to wear with her slacks, took the collar off a white blouse and turned it around, pinning it to her black shirt, bought some bright orange iridescent socks and plunked a man's hat on top of her head.

As we were waiting for Mack and Ronnie to pick us up, the doorbell rang. The children down the street had come for "trick or treat." Del, forgetting completely about her get-up, went to the door and loaded their bags with candy. She was taken aback when one little boy looked up solemnly and said, "Thank you, Father."

Another incident the same night occurred on our way home. We were hungry, and, considering our costumes, decided to stop at Ott's drive-in, where we could eat in the car. But before our orders came, Ronnie announced he had to go to the bathroom.

"Well, you can't go to the men's room!" Mack snapped.

"But you can to the women's room," Phyllis added. "Come on."

So the two apache dancers started off, with Del trailing along behind them. Ronnie and Phyllis entered the women's room with no trouble at all and were happily ensconced in their individual cubicles when they heard a woman scream, "There's a man in here!"

Del, who had just come through the door, was as startled as the woman when she realized that she, Del, was the intruder and not Ronnie.

"It's—er—Halloween, you know," she muttered, as the woman left.

On a Friday night shortly thereafter we brought Ronnie with us to the 299 Club where Mack was on duty. During a lull late in the evening, Mack beckoned to us, "Come here. I want to show you something." We followed him through a door at the end of the bar and into a huge, well-equipped restaurant kitchen, then through another door to a darkened dining room that was equally well furnished, with booths along the sides and tables in the middle, allowing for a seating capacity of about fifty.

"The boss says that we can have this rent-free if we would serve dinners. He figures it would draw some bar business. That's all he's after," Mack said.

Before we had time to say anything, Mack continued, "I thought that since Ronnie and Phyllis aren't working they could take it on. Ronnie could do the cooking, and Phyllis could wait on the tables."

"But how much money would be involved in setting it up?" practical Del, the bookkeeper, asked.

"If we stick to a simple one-item specialty menu, it wouldn't take much," Mack replied. "How about steak, baked potato, green salad with roquefort dressing, and coffee? It's simple to prepare and fast-order. If it catches on, we've got it made!"

So with *our* fifty dollars (Mack had found the place, and besides he and Ronnie were broke) we were in business. And the only thing it made was life more complicated. When Del was off work evenings and weekends, Phyllis had to work—a life style well calculated to cause some marital friction. It became increasingly difficult to explain to Phyllis's parents why she was busy most nights and weekends. She didn't feel somehow that she ought to tell them about her business enterprise. To top it all, Tad's Steaks took our brilliant idea and made it a going thing on Powell Street, eventually opening a chain of restaurants in several major cities.

We gave up on the restaurant business and began to think of alternatives. Phyllis had been unsuccessful in finding employment in journalism, as she refused to work on the women's page. (She'd been a police reporter in Chico before moving to Seattle.) She was reluctant to take a job in an office. Both of us were becoming increasingly irritated with our parents and the time they demanded of us separately. We wanted our couplehood, and we felt agitated because we couldn't tell them so. Phyl's father displayed his wariness of Del, and when on those rare occasions she was invited to the Lyon home for dinner, she felt extremely self conscious and uncomfortable. She squirmed her way through the evening—a costly personal price to pay for the "togetherness" we didn't really feel there.

One night, when we were unloading our gripes on Lorna, Phyllis's sister, she warned, "One of these days you're going to blow it. Why don't you two get out of town?"

That sounded like an excellent idea. But where should we go? Lorna suggested Santa Barbara, where she just happened to know a gay fellow. But we had always wanted to go to New York and we suspected that there would be lots more than *one* gay person there. So we made our decision to leave for the east coast. Phyllis went back to work in an office; we purchased a used station wagon on a six months' contract and started saving our money in earnest for the trip. We figured that within the year we would be on our way across country.

Our trip was delayed, however. As soon as we made the last payment on the station wagon, it broke down. So we bought a brand new one, this time not taking any chances. But it would take another eighteen months to pay it off.

Once we had decided to leave and had picked a specific date of departure, we became more relaxed with our families. We could afford to put ourselves out a little. It wouldn't be too much longer anyway. And much to our surprise, the family "problem" solved itself. As we relaxed, so did they. With tension gone and some time having elapsed, our parents became more accepting of us as a pair. Now when we went to visit singly, we were asked why we hadn't brought the other one.

We did not feel the same urgency to leave. The trip to New York, though still planned but not announced, was a year off anyway. We decided to find another place to live in the interim. Our new neighbors upstairs, we figured, were having nightly wrestling matches with the best two falls out of three. We could live with the fact that the pictures on our wall were always askew, but when the glass on our coffee table started to jump, that was too much.

Since we were going to all the trouble of moving, we felt we should find a better place, preferably with a view. We skipped Nob

Hill and Telegraph Hill—they were out of our class—and started to comb the slopes south of Market. That's when we ran into the "for sale" sign in front of a split-level, four-room "dream" house on Red Rock Hill. We took it, dubbed it "Habromania Haven" (habromania: a type of insanity characterized by delusions of a pleasing nature) and have been happily deluded ever since. The fact that the place was fifty years old, needed repairs, and didn't even have a closet escaped us entirely. It had a gorgeous view.

We had a nightly ritual of having coffee in front of the big picture window and staring raptly at the lights of the Bay Bridge and downtown San Francisco. Before the novelty wore off, we were interrupted one night by a phone call from Nancy, whom we had met at the 299. She, her girl friend Priscilla, and some of their friends were thinking about starting a social club, a club for Lesbians.

We were finally to meet our Lesbian sisters. We eagerly jumped at the chance. That marked the beginning of a long and time-consuming, but very rewarding, involvement which was to put us in touch with countless Lesbians around the world, bring us practical knowledge of ourselves and the society in which we live, and afford us the opportunity to help bridge the communication gaps.

The fifteen years which followed were to be rich ones, years in which we were to find a broad range of Lesbians. Among them could be found those who exemplify the very best and the very worst of the human condition. But the vast majority of them lead quiet lives much akin to the lives of most other Americans. Unfortunately for the Lesbian, she is stereotyped as primarily a sexual being. This stereotype often turns a quiet life into one of quiet desperation and brings about a turning away from sex and/or involvement with other Lesbians simply because such noninvolvement seems the only "safe" way to survive in a hostile society. It is ironic (but consistent with America's confused view of sex) that a large number of people whom society would castigate for sexual variation, i.e., Lesbians, actually don't engage in sex at all, or do so very rarely. We have known a number of women who fit in this category: women who have identified themselves as Lesbian, who suffer through all the fears that they may be found out, that they may lose their job, that they may face rejection from friends and family, and yet have never found either the woman or the nerve to change their status from one of being to one of doing.

Ann, a schoolteacher in her early thirties, was a shy and quiet but willing worker in the early days of DOB. Although she made some friends, she also built a shield around herself which seemed to say, "Don't get too close." And no one did. To this day she lives a self sufficient but lonely life, untouched by human hands. True, she has never suffered the pangs of unrequited love, nor the hurt of rejection by a woman, nor the agonizing decision to break off a love affair. But then neither has she known the warmth and soul satisfaction of love and companionship with another person.

On the other hand, Elsie, a highly-placed social worker in Chicago, led a hectic, romantic, emotional and highly sexual life in her younger days. The list of her affairs was almost endless; none emerged as a lasting one. Her commitment to sex and her enjoyment of it were open and free. As she got older, however, and moved up in her profession, she began to fear the exposure which might come from those she wooed and won. After a close shave, brought about by the indiscretion of a young woman she had stopped seeing, Elsie phased out her sexual life. From that time forth she concentrated on her profession and on a nonsexual involvement with a circle of friends.

There are, we discovered, two types of "loners." One is excruciatingly shy and may spend years of her life waiting for the right moment, hoping that the time will present itself when she can openly declare herself to the woman she adores. The other fancies herself a Don Juan, and for her the chase is the thing.

Charlotte had fawned after Gert, a divorcee, for six long years, waiting until her sons were grown and away from home, hoping that then they could move in together and something "would happen." Of course, she never told her friend how she felt, or of her dream. And when the boys went into the army, Gert cleared out too and moved to Seattle.

"Now what a problem when she comes back to visit!" Charlotte said. "I don't care much to see her. I was crushed when she left and have only recently gotten hold of myself. I can't bear any more torture. She doesn't understand why, and I can't explain."

Charlotte had withdrawn into herself. She felt a growing resent-

ment toward her friends because she was unable to be truthful and
straightforward. She began to avoid them. Fortunately, she enjoyed her own company and was the type of person who never ran
out of things to do. By chance she picked up a book that mentioned DOB in New York, and because of her correspondence and
affiliation with that group, her horizons are widening once again.

Another Lesbian, Kate, doesn't entertain the fear that paralyzed
Charlotte. If anything, she's much too bold and flirts with danger
constantly. She works in the office of a major oil company in Los
Angeles. The office is quite large and contains row upon row of
desks at which very attractive young women sit and type, sort
mail, do billing, etc. Kate loves her job—and most of the women in
the office. She's "scored" with at least nine of them in two and a
half years, which is almost as good a record as some of her male
superiors. But the last time she made a pass at one of her coworkers, she picked the wrong one. She was reported to their
supervisor. Kate didn't lose her job, but she's been told in no
uncertain terms that company employees are off limits for her
"cruising."

We don't know how you'd classify Beulah. She'd certainly led a
full life. She'd worked at all sorts of odd jobs, but was at heart an
artist, a student of life who always found something to laugh at,
even in times of distress. It shocked us when in her late fifties she
went into a convent. It was out of character—her language had
always been so well punctuated with swear words and her stories,
though fascinating and well told, were far too racy for the monas-
tic life of a nun. It wasn't necessarily her devotion to religious
pursuits or her love of God that "called" Beulah, though. As it
turned out, she had just broken up with a woman after ten years,
during which time she hadn't worked. She discovered that re-entry
into the business world at her advanced age wasn't too easy,
especially when you don't have any references and are a woman.
Rather than go on welfare she sought refuge and security within
the church.

There are also "loners" that come in twosomes. Some couples
do not choose to mix with or identify with the homophile community in any way. The fear of exposure is of course the major
reason for isolation. But there is another reason why such a couple
prefers to travel exclusively in heterosexual society. One or the

other, or both, may be fearful of the competition that other gay women may present. If a partner doesn't know other people and has no contact with them, she is less apt to wander. Such a couple will isolate itself from the gay world either in mutual agreement or at the demand of one partner or the other.

After twenty years of such lone togetherness Zelda and Marney came to the DOB office. Marney had seen a copy of *The Ladder,* and her secret longings for the companionship and social outlet of a group could no longer be suppressed. But she was obviously too eager, too enthused over her new acquaintances, and too involved in DOB activities to suit Zelda. They didn't stick around, though they did invite us over to their home for dinner a time or two. Then we heard they'd moved—left the Bay Area completely.

Some such couples extend themselves only to heterosexual couples. Others more commonly find their friends among gay men. Wanda told us that the only close gay friends she and Sally had were men because they were more available, more supportive, and you could relax with them more easily. "With them there are no sexual connotations. But if you were a previous friend to some one partner of a Lesbian couple, there is always a barrier—you are forever a threat to their relationship."

But some couples are loners not so much by choice as by circumstance. Merle and Jean are farmers. Because of the novelty or eccentricity (depending on your point of view) of two women tending chores without a man around, it's taken them a while to become accepted in the small rural community where they are located. Their "gay" life is limited to their own relationship, reading material, sporadic correspondence and infrequent visits from friends they had known before they "retired." Occasionally they run into pairs of women in town whom they may wonder about, but if they become acquainted at all (which is seldom, because of the demands and constant attention to their crops and farm animals), nothing is said. It takes too long to build up to such "confessions." There isn't enough time.

By and large, most Lesbians opt for a one-to-one, long-term relationship as an ideal. The most common question put to a couple is, "How long have you two been together?" Whether or not these pairings last, as in heterosexual marriage, depends upon the degree of their maturity, their level of sexual adjustment, how well their personalities mesh, how much they have in common and how well they manage their outside commitments.

Society's refusal to recognize their "marriages" has been a source of friction and anguish for many Lesbians—and for many reasons. Because she becomes aware of her homosexuality and acts upon this self knowledge does not mean, as people often suppose, that the Lesbian automatically rejects all of the values she has been taught. For every Lesbian has been born of a heterosexual union, has been brought up and conditioned in a heterosexual family and environment, and is steeped in a predominantly—almost exclusively—heterosexual culture. And the Lesbian, being a woman, has been steered throughout her early life toward an expectation of falling in love and getting married—though her mentors did not have in mind her doing so with another woman.

Despite society's prohibitions, as with so many of our laws that would regulate what we may drink or smoke, many Lesbians have devised various ways to circumvent laws and traditional public policy. Marriages, for instance, have been performed between two women. This necessitates the rather hazardous practice of one partner adopting a male identity, posing and passing as a man and husband.

One such case in France was reported in *Aufbau,* a New York German newspaper, in 1961. Ginette and Bernadette exchanged marriage vows in front of the mayor of St. Cloud and again before the parish priest in that same city. Bernadette's parents found their son-in-law "Philippe" (Ginette) a little strange. He was a tiny and dainty fellow with a mustache and huge, dark glasses, but he could prove he earned a good salary, and Bernadette had insisted on him for her husband.

When their masquerade was discovered, Ginette and Bernadette were placed on trial in Paris—not for the marriage, which was declared legal by the judge because it had not been annulled—but for committing eleven offenses in order to obtain the documents necessary for the marriage, including a marital capability certificate. The judge smilingly declared that Philippe was "entitled to all other rights due as a husband," but this did not prevent him from meting out one-year sentences to both women, despite their plea that they had harmed no one. The judgment did not carry with it a stipulation that their prison terms be served in different jails, however. "Even the judge did not want to be that cruel," the article concluded.

Of course, there have been mock marriages performed in the gay community, with a friend performing the ceremony, followed by a reception at a gay bar for the newly wedded couple. But there have also been genuine religious services held in a church. These aren't weddings as heterosexuals know them, but convenant services, a recognition in the sight of God and the church of the bond between the two persons involved.

We had occasion to witness such a "Celebration of Commitment" at an Episcopal church when a friend, Joyce, invited us to a service for her and Madeline, which was to be performed by her pastor and with her parents in attendance. Joyce was jubilant when she broke the news to us. This tall, pensive, sensitive young brunette had been through years of struggle with her parents, her church and her psychiatrist. Finally she had received the blessings of all three to be herself.

Dressed in a simple pale blue suit, her eyes brimming with joyful tears, she solemnly made her vow to Madeline, "I give you this ring as a token of our covenant, vowing to live in close friendship, to strive for fuller knowledge of your being, and to care for you above all others. I pledge myself to realize your needs, encourage your full potential, and to love you even as I love myself. May God be between me and thee forever."

Knowledge of this service, like the many others that have been performed, was limited to those involved, their families and/or friends. But in March of 1971 a reporter from the *San Francisco Chronicle* got wind of a covenant service for two male homosexuals at which the Reverend Lloyd Wake, of Glide Memorial United Methodist Church, officiated. The story appeared in the paper, complete with pictures. For weeks Mr. Wake was beseiged with hate letters, and demands were made upon Bishop Charles Golden that Wake be defrocked. Righteous heterosexual Christians still think they have a corner on love—and God. To their minds, anyone who might think otherwise should be thrown to the lions.

The first religious marriage in the nation designed to bind two persons of the same sex together legally was performed in Los Angeles June 12, 1970, according to a report in *The Advocate*, a homophile newspaper published in that city. Neva Joy Heckman

and Judith Ann Belew were married in a simple double-ring ceremony performed in their home by the Reverend Troy D. Perry,
pastor of Metropolitan Community Church. What makes this particular ceremony different from the covenant services previously
described is that the rites were conducted under a provision of
California law that allows a common-law liaison to be formalized
by a religious ceremony, and a church certificate of marriage to be
issued. Under these circumstances the law does not require that
the couple obtain a marriage license, the church certificate being
sufficient to prove the legality of the marriage. The Reverend
Perry altered the traditional heterosexual vow, having Neva and
Judith respectively "serve in the office of" husband and wife. Unfortunately, however, in looking up the specific statute involved,
our attorney found that it clearly states "*man* and wife."

Two other courageous women, this time in Louisville, Kentucky, sought a writ of *mandamus* and declaratory judgment from
the circuit court when they were denied a marriage license by the
Jefferson County clerk. While the 1798 Kentucky marriage statute
does not specify that a marriage contract must be between two
persons of the opposite sex, County Attorney J. Bruce Miller indicated he had reviewed public policy in Kentucky since the law was
written and was of the firm belief that neither then nor now has
the state legislature ever intended two practicing homosexuals to
be blessed with the sanctity of a marriage contract. "To the contrary, it has outlawed their sexual activities as being against public
policy and contrary to nature. . . ."

The fact that one of the applicants, Marjorie Ruth Jones, was
thirty-nine and the mother of three children, provoked Miller to
add that nowhere in the union of these two women could he find
"the requisites of a happy home, the love and affection desired by
society, or the proper concern for the children involved." He went
on to say that "the pure pursuit of hedonistic and sexual pleasure
. . . is obviously no statutory implied reason for marriage" and that
the officials of Juvenile Court and the Metropolitan Social Services
Department should investigate whether the mother "by her
actions and behavior, both publicly and privately, had been guilty
of contributing to the delinquency of a minor" in the case of her
fourteen-year-old son. Ms. Jones's other children are an eighteen-
year-old daughter and a son in the armed forces.

Tracy Knight, twenty-five, "the other half" in this action, who is a dancer in a Louisville night club and also runs a massage parlor, said she wants homosexuality "legalized instead of being pushed into a corner . . . like it was a freak thing." She deplored the public's weird ideas about orgies and dirtiness, as evidenced by Miller's statements. David Kaplan, one of the two attorneys representing the women, said they would fight the case through to the United States Supreme Court, if necessary.

This story, and that of Jack Baker and Michael McConnell in Minneapolis, were carried by the national news services. A debate on the merits and validity of homosexual marriage ensued in a number of local newspapers across the country. The *San Francisco Chronicle* ran a series of comments on this controversial issue by clergymen and municipal officials as well as by the local and vocal homophile community. An editorial of July 16, 1970, concluded:

"Members of the heterosexual majority derive great security, pride and social acceptance from this 'rendering public' of an honest, social commitment in the eyes of 'God and Man.' It would seem only in keeping with the times that consideration be given to allowing the homosexual minority the same rights to this sense of fulfillment."

The Minnesota Supreme Court ruled unanimously on October 15, 1971, that Baker and McConnell were properly refused a marriage license despite their claim that to deny gay couples the same benefits as straight lovers is unconstitutional discrimination. Justice C. Donald Peterson stated in the opinion, "It is unrealistic to think that the original draftsmen of our marriage statutes, which date from territorial days, would have used the term [marriage] in any different sense from an opposite-sex one."

Two Black women, twenty-one-year-old Manonia Evans and twenty-five-year-old Donna Burkett, were refused a marriage license in Milwaukee on the same grounds. However, there is an assembly bill pending in the Wisconsin legislature's judiciary committee which would amend the state marriage law to permit marriage between members of the same sex.

Aside from the Metropolitan Community Church, the only other religious body to recognize the sanctity of homosexual marriage is the San Francisco Meeting of Friends (Quakers). On November 14, 1971, the Meeting adopted the position "that the same standards of judgment in matters of morality and acceptable behavior which we apply to heterosexual persons should also be applied to homosexual persons" and that this principle should be extended "to all levels of social and economic life"— including marriage. The Meeting stipulated that "if a request for a homosexual marriage is before the Meeting, the Clearness Committee should have on it at least one person who is an acknowledged homosexual, and who is also a member or at least a frequent attender of the Meeting."

While marriage for homosexuals is still being tested in this country, newspapers have recently reported legitimate Lesbian marriages in England and Bangkok. In some areas, at least, people are beginning to respond to the needs of homosexual couples.

It is a mistake, of course, to assume that Lesbians, any more than heterosexuals, "walk off into the sunset and live happily ever after," a conclusion that movies are fond of prescribing for heterosexual couples. Lesbians have their marital problems too, but unfortunately until most recently (and it is still all too uncommon) there has been no marriage counseling available for their taboo relationships. Society tries to pull them apart rather than help to keep them together. Dr. G. DiBella, who is affiliated with Metropolitan Hospital in New York City, has been doing research with gay couples who have been together at least ten years in order to develop a marital counseling program for homosexual couples. Occasionally we have also run across marriage counselors in San Francisco who have worked with gay people. This is an area, or occupation, where there is a definite need.

While it is true that the two of us started out in 1953 on a "till death do us part" and "faithful forever" basis, formalizing our relationship has never appealed to us. We consider love and sex our own private affair and much prefer "living in sin." We have no hangup with God. Our troubles stem from Man, for whom we have no need in our togetherness and from whom we do not require magic words or mystic ritual to solemnize our love or make it binding.

Besides, we have witnessed all too often what happens when a common-law husband and wife have been pressured into marriage. Somehow the love and concern they once felt for each other give way to possessiveness and the demand for certain rights institutionally bestowed upon them, and the couple winds up in the divorce court. What keeps us together is not a piece of paper or words. What keeps us together is *feelings*—of love, commitment and mutual respect.

We certainly champion those women who, because they feel a genuine, deep, personal need for public and religious recognition of their union, are willing to fight for their equal rights. And we must admit that if their efforts to legalize homosexual marriage should materialize in our lifetime, we just might give the idea some serious consideration. The economic exploitation of homosexuals who are always considered to be "single" persons, no matter what their true marital status may be, and who are taxed on this basis at the highest possible rate, has always been particularly galling to us. As a minority people we have always had to pay a disproportionate share of the tax burden, but without the benefits accorded to heterosexuals.

For some, marriage means a religious sacrament and commitment. For others it may also take on a legal significance in terms of community property, the filing of joint income tax returns and inheritance rights. Recognition of a Lesbian union might also serve to validate the couple who wished to take on the legal responsibility of adopting homeless, unwanted children. It would also simplify insurance problems, making the couple eligible for family policies, for family rates on airlines travel and for that matter, for "couple" entry to entertainment functions, too.

Financial and legal protection of mutual assets is always a problem to a Lesbian couple. When we bought our new station wagon and made arrangements for a loan at the bank, the branch manager asked if we didn't want to take out a nominal insurance policy which would automatically pay up the balance in the event something happened to one of us. Then he corrected himself. Coverage for us would require that we take out *two* policies, not one, as in the case of a married couple. Later we got into the same thing when we signed up for a home owners policy with All State. The main office canceled us out on the grounds that their home owners policy was designed for one family, and as far as they were concerned we represented "two" families. We would therefore have to get separate policies for fire, personal property, liability, etc. We eventually found an insurance broker who obtained adequate coverage for us in one package, but we have heard of cases where insurance was canceled altogether on homes owned by two males. That there is an unwritten law in the insurance industry that homosexuals are a bad risk—they throw wild parties—has been verified by insurance brokers "off the record."

Naming the beneficiary on a life insurance policy can be troublesome too. The forms require that you also stipulate your relationship to the beneficiary. Insurance salesmen and employers (in the case of group policies covering workers in a business firm) are apt to ask embarrassing questions if you put down "friend." What about next of kin? Don't you have any living relatives? Some Lesbians have settled for "partner," but that misnomer is suspect too. We solved the problem by leaving insurance proceeds to our estate and then drawing up wills. Needless to say, we have left all our worldly possessions to each other. However, our attorney pointed out that in the event we were both killed in an automobile accident, the law would determine which one of us died first and our estate would then go to the other's heirs. We therefore named Janey, Del's daughter, and Lorna, Phyl's sister, secondary heirs in both wills. They both know each other and happen to be very fond of each other, so there is no likelihood of any contest.

But for those Lesbians whose families may be intolerant or hostile to their Lesbian liaison, there is small protection. Wills have been broken by greedy relatives, and the Lesbian partner, no matter how long the relationship existed, is still regarded as a non-relative and usurper. One vivid example is the treatment of Alice B. Toklas by Gertrude Stein's family—Ms. Toklas did not share in the author's estate and died a pauper.

It is not uncommon to find Lesbian couples who have been together for twenty years or more—a partnership well established, but unrecognized legally or socially. During such a long-term relationship it is safe to assume that as a pair they have acquired a certain amount of community property. Protecting the rights of the survivor to this mutually owned property and protecting her from financial loss pose untold problems for the Lesbian couple— rights and protection which heterosexual couples take for granted and which society, too, accepts and reinforces.

Only recently we met Laura, who was grieving over the death of

Thelma, her partner of thirty-five years. At the same time she was faced with the stark reality of California's inequitable laws. She and Thelma were technically "unrelated," but Laura was the "widowed" survivor in joint tenancy; thus the law could exact three times as much inheritance tax from her as from a heterosexual widow. She was unable to prove (since they kept joint accounts) that she had actually made half of the payments on their house or that she had made 50 percent of the deposits to their checking and savings accounts. She was assessed 10 percent of the total value of their mutual holdings—including even her half held in joint tenancy, along with bank accounts, home furnishings and auto. The savings account, of course, was meager after Thelma's long protracted illness. Consequently Laura had to sell their home, which they had bought to "protect them in their old age," to raise the cash to meet the taxes. Leaning on her cane as she slowly descended the steps for the last time, her eyes as gray and misty as the fog that settled around the house, Laura screwed up her lined face into a half smile and said wryly, "Those stairs were getting pretty hard to climb anyway."

But there are many other problems a Lesbian couple must face because their union is not recognized. There are problems relating to children, custody questions arising out of divorce proceedings and adoption, which we will go into when we discuss the Lesbian mother. There are other problems in that Lesbians are children themselves, i.e., daughters. Because, to all intents and purposes, the Lesbian is the "unmarried daughter," it falls to her in our society to take on the responsibility of caring for an aging or ailing mother or father.

Monty, a thirty-five-year-old Black X-ray technician, whose mother was diabetic and going blind, was forced into this position by her married brother and sisters. She complained bitterly that they wouldn't even come over and offer her relief time, though they lived in the vicinity. She and Darlene, her Lesbian partner, from whom she had separated in order to move back into the family home, hardly had any time alone together. If Monty wanted an evening out or had to go shopping, it was Darlene who came in and stayed with mother. By the time the poor woman died, the damage had already been done. Darlene had found someone else who had no family ties.

When Marilyn, who had been living with Jenny in Portland for
five years, went back to Massachusetts for her father's funeral, her
mother took it for granted she would come back home to stay.
Mother had a spacious and regal house in Boston, which she didn't
want to give up, but she couldn't live there alone. She needed her
daughter's companionship now. Marilyn obviously had no ties—no
husband—so why not? Why live in some miserable apartment with
some lonely woman (who could find another roommate easily
enough) when she could have everything she wanted here and live
in the lap of luxury? Her mother really needed her now and was
not easily dissuaded.

Marilyn was wrestling with that one the last time we talked to
her and Jenny. The suggestion was made that with mother's
wealth she could hire a companion, but Marilyn said her mother
wouldn't hear of such a thing. Also, she didn't have any close
friends left. All she had really in the way of any personal relationship was Marilyn. What about her brother? Couldn't he help? Well,
he was married and lived in Texas. It was impossible for him to
take on the responsibility.

"It's up to you, Marilyn," Jenny shrugged, "if you intend to let
your mother run your life for you."

But the pull was still there—and the guilt, always the guilt, if
something should happen and you weren't there. Or if by your
refusal, by acceding to your own needs, by living your own life,
you might be frowned upon as selfish and hedonistic, as shirking
your filial duty. And then, too, you just might be cut out of the
will.

"You whites have it comparatively easy," Kathy, a young
Chinese woman, declared to a group that had crowded into a
booth at a nearby restaurant after a DOB meeting. "The Chinese
family is so close knit, so clannish. It was a real struggle for me as
an unmarried daughter, to get out from under the family roof and
into my own apartment. It's bad enough that my roommate is a
Caucasian, but if they knew she was also a Lesbian—wow!"

"Maybe it's easier for us to get out on our own, but the rest of
the trip is pretty such the same," Jackie observed. "Tell me, do
they ever stop bugging you about 'when are you going to get
married?'"

"When you get old enough, dear, they do," Phyllis winked.

Roberta and Sharon didn't separate when Roberta's father, a retired widower, needed help. He had fallen and broken his leg. When he was released from the hospital, they moved him into their apartment where they could care for him together. Certainly this addition of a third party into their household cramped their style. They don't feel that they can tell the old man, since previous conversational references to homosexuality indicated an unwillingness on his part to deal with the subject. Consequently they have been afraid to have company in and don't get out very often. But Roberta and Sharon are older; their "salad days" are over, and they decided they could make the adjustment far better than father probably could.

We resent society's bald assumption (which goes for siblings as well as for parents) that an "unmarried" woman does not have and is not entitled to a personal life. We also resent those women who allow themselves to be pushed into such a position. We have known many Lesbians who were trapped at home until a widowed parent died. Only then, when it was too late, were they free to seek a life of their own. Feeling very strongly about our own twosome as a family unit, we vowed this would never happen to us. When we bought our house, we were not unaware that it was too small to take anyone else in—we have one bedroom and one double bed. Certainly we would be concerned with the health and welfare of our parents and would contribute, if need be, to their support. But neither of us would return home; nor would we invite a parent to live with us. It's because we care—about them as well as ourselves. We have different life styles and commitments, which none of them would understand or be able to adapt to in a live-in situation.

There are some parents who do come to understand. When Carrie's father died, her mother asked her to stay for a while. The sudden loss of her husband had completely unnerved her. Sandy, Carrie's lover, phoned almost every evening. They'd not been separated before during the six years they'd been together. Sandy worked in an insurance office and had her daughter to care for too, so it was about a week before she was able to get over for a visit. But when she finally arrived, the look in her eyes and Carrie's automatic loving embrace told the whole story.

Carrie's mother smiled, "Forgive me, my dears. I didn't understand. You don't belong here, Carrie. Go *home*—with Sandy."

Vera, who was in her forties, suddenly found herself surrounded by Lesbians. Her two daughters, one in her early and the other in her mid-twenties, had each recently "confessed" to having women love partners. Between the two of them they gave mother a liberal education about homosexuality. Vera tried to understand and opened her home to their friends. She generally sat around and listened—sometimes in amusement, other times in utter amazement.

One night, Corky, the younger one, came rushing into her mother's bedroom to tell her, "Guess what? That woman who moved in next door a few weeks ago—you know who she is. We've seen her working in the garden. Well, tonight I saw her in the Cask. How about that? That means she's gotta be gay!"

"That's nice, dear," Vera murmured sleepily. She'd only half heard or understood what Corky had been saying.

But her two daughters, Corky and Stella, started plotting. Wouldn't it be great if mom met some "nice woman" and settled down? The one next door (they'd found out her name was Lenore) was the right age, and she was personable—a little quiet, but maybe she was just shy. So Corky and Stella became terribly interested in gardening all of a sudden. They watered the lawn until Vera thought it looked more like a swamp. And they kept pestering poor Lenore asking her nonstop questions about plants, their names, what kind of fertilizer they required, etc. Eventually they invited their new "friend" over to dinner, and gradually she became a regular visitor. Whenever she was over, Corky and Stella greeted her profusely, but managed to give her space and time alone with Vera. They hugged each other with delight when their mother announced one evening, "I hope you don't mind, but Lenore asked me out to dinner and a movie tonight. There's supper in the oven for you."

Lenore and Vera became close friends. Lenore fell in love with Vera in time, but the whole idea of having a woman as her lover was completely foreign to Vera. If that were her daughters' choice, that was fine for them. But for her? No. But she became very fond of Lenore, and somewhat dependent on her companionship. She didn't want Lenore to get serious, but she didn't want to lose her either. She kept Lenore dangling for years. Finally, when the girls left home, Lenore and Vera did try living together. It lasted only a short while. They found they were both older and pretty set in their ways—their ways didn't jibe. But they still see each other and are still close friends.

Living arrangements of Lesbian couples are also influenced by professional careers. As a woman, to whom education and job opportunities have heretofore been very limited, the Lesbian has had to "pull herself up by the bootstraps," a refrain her Black brothers have heard for years. Once she has attained any measure of success in the business and professional world she is not likely to give up what she has gained. She will cling stubbornly to the niche she has cut out for herself. She feels she must hang on to a good job when she can find it. As a result, many professional women who may be classified as Lesbian couples are in jobs that keep them apart and prevent them from living together.

Harriet, for instance, is a principal with tenure in the Philadelphia secondary school system. Her Lesbian lover works for the government in Baltimore, has worked her way up to a supervisory position, really likes her job and doesn't want to leave. A transfer for either of them would mean taking a position of lesser status and pay. Though Harriet and Joycelyn are a couple of four years' standing, they have never lived together, except for weekends and vacations. They are looking forward to the day when they can retire and build their long-deferred home on the land they have purchased in New Hampshire.

Esther is a successful businesswoman. She runs her own contracting firm, very much a "male" business. She works with men all the time—employs them, plans and deals with them at every level of the construction industry. She is very conscious of being a woman in a man's domain. She is sharp and shrewd, and she can match wits with the best of them. But she must be careful to maintain her "feminine" image, since the success of her enterprise depends on her being able to command the respect of the men in the business. Es has a swank home in the Berkeley Hills where she lives "alone," according to her success story which was written up in the women's pages of the *Oakland Tribune*. Her lover is totally invisible to the outside world.

According to Edie and Elaine, who lived in Honolulu for eight years before moving to the mainland, "Gay life there is lousy for residents and fine for tourists."

"You see, the island of Oahu is so small it takes only two and a half hours to drive all the way around it. And there's the military and security clearances to worry about," Edie explained.

"I'll bet there are only fifty Lesbians—sixty at the most—on the island. There are four gay bars in the 'Cocktail Center,' but only one caters to women. They're mostly mixed," Elaine put in.

"Yeah, and being in the service, we didn't dare go to the places often. When we did go in, it would be just for the cocktail hour and dinner. We used to park the car several blocks away," Edie said. "And we didn't dare stay any later for fear we'd run into the shore patrol."

Bobbie and Dale, as two civil servants in the federal system, are so frightened by the thought of exposure that they maintain separate households, even though they live in the same city. Other women, pretending to be just "roommates," take apartments with two bedrooms, the second of which usually becomes a den that is easily converted when family or straight friends come to visit.

Then there are those Lesbians who marry homosexual men to take the pressure off, an arrangement that sometimes leads to strife when they choose to live together, even when it is understood that they may each have their own separate love life. Lorrie found that Dave expected her to play the role of subservient housewife and elegant hostess when he lavishly entertained his friends at dinner parties. He resented it when she brought her friends home, however. She was supposed to do her "catting around" outside.

Tom, Harry, Jane and Mary tried another variation that worked out quite satisfactorily for them. They got married—Tom to Mary and Jane to Harry, bought a pair of flats, with the women moving into one and the men into the other. When the occasion called for it, they switched from their gay to their straight roles simply by walking up or down a flight of stairs with a few clothes and a toothbrush.

There are many close-knit, inbred Lesbian cliques to be found in suburbia. These groups of women, who keep their activities a very closely guarded secret, usually have professional status or social position to protect. Because of this, if a couple breaks up, they usually find their next partners from within the group. In one such circle of eight friends, we noted that Connie had lived for a time with each of the others, and that several others had traded partners a time or two. We concluded that they had some sort of "musical chairs" arrangement. Occasionally, though, the field is broadened by a member of the clan finding a new partner on the outside and bringing her into the group.

Many teachers, while forced into the closet during the school year, lead a relatively free life during the long summer vacation. Some pile their gear into a camper and become vagabonds for three months, stopping here and there to do some fishing, hitting all the tourist spots along the way, and seeking out the gay bars they may not dare to visit in their own locale. Others buy or rent a cabin in the country as a hideaway for weekends and vacations. But many don't feel really safe until they get out of the United States. They head for Canada or Europe and in some cases become entangled in complicated, long-distance romantic involvements.

Louise met Valerie in London one summer. They hit it off immediately and became so attached to each other that parting was extremely difficult when Louise had to return to Dayton for the beginning of the new school year. As so often happens, "absence makes the heart grow fonder," but correspondence had to suffice until the next summer when Louise could hurry back to London. During the second trip she and Valerie seriously considered the possibility of a more permanent arrangement in closer proximity. Louise had tenure in the school system, and had arrived at "that age" when she felt she could not give up her job and lose her pension. Valerie, on the other hand, had a small business in which she was doing moderately well. She was willing to sell out and join Louise in Dayton. However, there was still another problem to be reckoned with. Valerie had a chronic kidney ailment which required constant medical attention amply provided for by the British socialized medical care system. If she were to come to the States, cost of her medical care would be prohibitive. Practically speaking they were at a stalemate. "If only we'd met ten years ago . . . ," Louise concluded.

Ruth has been carrying on a long-distance romance with Marjorie between Victoria, British Columbia, and Palo Alto,

California. While allowing for more frequent visits during Christmas and Easter holidays as well as summer vacations, these trips and interim phone calls can be costly in time as well as money to a young graduate student who is working for her Ph.D. in sociology. Ruth hopes she and Marjorie can settle their citizenship problems soon so that they can be together permanently.

Aside from the external obstacles to a Lesbian's choice of life style, there are always the eternal psychological ones. Perhaps the most prominent internal pressure is the hangup with the Christian concept of monogamy and fidelity. Jeanine, for instance, ended her friendship with Tomi abruptly when she came to the realization that Tomi had "seduced, or at least tried to seduce, every girl friend I ever had. We'd been friends for almost twenty years! And somehow it just never penetrated. After the episode with Relta last week, though, I began to think back. Sue just laughed at Tomi. Gerry told her to go to hell. Although Flora was intrigued and flattered, Tomi didn't really make it with her either. She did with Lorrie, though," Jeanine recounted. "What kind of a friendship would you call that? Sick—that's what it is!"

Most Lesbians lead quiet unassuming lives and expect fidelity from their partners. There are some, like the heterosexual swingers, who may opt for extracurricular activities. And sometimes one partner will stray, with or without the knowledge or consent of the other.

Interestingly enough, as some Lesbians are striving for recognized marriage, others, particularly the younger ones, are seeking less traditional modes of relationship. As the years rolled by and we had piled up a respectable "together" record, we found that some of our friends were looking to us as an ideal or model couple. "If you two ever break up, I'll jump off the bridge" or "I'll give up gay life" were some of the comments. However, the scene is changing today. They're not saying that anymore.

Now some of our younger Lesbian friends are willing to allow us this one-to-one relationship if that is our bag, but they don't want to be restricted to this old hat kind of life. As with youth elsewhere they are protesting the validity of the nuclear family. We therefore find younger Lesbians (and some not so young) who feel perfectly free in playing the field, in entering into an affair with another woman without the thought that it will, or must, last forever. Communes are forming among Lesbians; non-monogamous relationships are being experimented with: sexual freedom indeed seems possible in certain circumstances. In all these experiments, the desire is for the freedom to choose alternate life styles.

Carl Wittman, in *Refugees from Amerika: A Gay Manifesto*, published by the Council on Religion and the Homosexual, explains it this way: "We have to define for ourselves a new pluralistic, rolefree social structure. It must contain both the freedom and the physical space for people to live alone, live together for a while, live together for a long time, either as couples or in large numbers; and the ability to flow easily from one of these states to another as our needs change."

Along with the concept of communal living another arrangement has developed: a contract between the two women involved, a one- or two-year lease, so to speak, which can be renewed or dropped at expiration date depending upon the success of the mutual venture. This alternate life style, which developed out of the encounter group and liberation movements, requires that the parties involved in the partnership be honest with each other, state clearly what they want out of the relationship and what they are willing to give, and evaluate their successes and failures, much as a profit and loss statement, at regular intervals. These Lesbians don't want to stay together out of misplaced loyalty or because of historical longevity; they want to be sure that the challenges continue, that they don't grow stale, that they continue to grow and develop personally and together.

Politics is becoming an increasingly important factor in Lesbian relationships. We have often said that if one of us had been a Democrat and the other a Republican, as in the case of Phyl's folks, we would never have made it together. We take our politics and our "cause" too seriously. Presently we are highly dissatisfied Democrats who are becoming more and more radicalized. A society that has developed technologically from the horse and buggy to the space age in the short span of this century must learn to respond as readily and as rapidly to revolutionary social change as to evolutionary scientific progress. The fact that government has not responded, has not been as visionary with respect to human needs as it has been to scientific data, has led to implications far more serious than mere political dissent. The liberation movements, as we see them, are religious crusades that are heralding a new age for human kind. The labor pains that precede any new birth are now being felt by all people. The Lesbian, too, is affected by these forces of change.

The urgency of the Black movement and its turn toward a more militant stance posed a dilemma that became too much for Linda, when she became a community organizer for the poverty program at Hunter's Point in San Francisco. She lived in nearby Daly City with a white woman. They'd been together for about four years, and while Linda loved Rhonda deeply, she became more and more restless and morose. By day she worked for and with "her people" in the ghetto. By night she lived a middle class existence in suburbia. The two didn't jibe, and she finally split. Afterwards, she came to see us, to explain, and to ask us to look out for Rhonda.

Many Black women who had been involved earlier in the homophile movement found themselves forced to make a choice between the two "causes" that touched their lives so intimately. One of them wrote a play that was a hit on Broadway.

A short blonde with a turned-up nose and determined chin, Pru, a professor of history at a small Lutheran college in the Midwest, took her sabbatical and went off to New York City. She had wanted to do some historical research on women, to find "herstory" in order to introduce a new and relevant course much needed on the campus of this church institution. While in New York, she joined Women's Liberation and became "liberated" enough to move on to the Radicalesbians. She had been a closet case, needless to say, at the college.

It was a new and exhilarating experience for Pru when she found herself marching with her gay sisters and brothers—twenty thousand strong—carrying a sign, "I'm Gay and I'm Proud" in the parade down Sixth Avenue on June 28, 1970. The demonstration climaxed "Gay Pride Week" and was held in commemoration of the Christopher Street riots the year before when homosexuals stood up to the police to demand their rights as citizens.

"I can't really describe it—the feeling that experience generated in me. Earlier I had championed the DOB teamwork silently from the farthest seat in the stadium. But that day, I was on the field myself. Now I feel free—to be myself," Pru told us later.

After that she decided she couldn't go back to the stultifying atmosphere of the college and wrote a letter of resignation to the administration. She received a reply from the president asking, "What about your financial commitment?" The terms on which her sabbatical had been granted stipulated that she must return and teach for at least two more years or repay the sabbatical wages. Pru told them they could not expect reimbursement from her for three very good reasons: first, it was at least three years from the time she first requested the sabbatical until it was actually granted, which should take care of the time element of her obligation; second, as a woman she had never been paid a salary commensurate to that received by male professors of lesser qualification and, if she and other women on the staff were paid at proper and equal scale, the college would actually owe her and all of its female employees hundreds of thousands of dollars; and third, she didn't have any money now and had no prospects for employment in the immediate future.

"P.S. I'm a Lesbian!" exclaimed Dora, a member of her small group in Radicalesbians, when Pru read her the letter before mailing it.

"And a second P.S.," Pru added: "You should be glad I'm not coming back. If I did, I'd turn that place inside out."

The Women's Liberation, Gay Liberation and Third World Liberation movements have had the same effect on Lesbians as on others in the general community. Some women have reacted in fear and become more conservative; others have accepted the challenge and have moved to a more radical stance. Interracial couples, like Linda and Rhonda, have undergone tremendous upheavals in their lives, which were tentative at best anyway because of racial prejudice from bigoted landlords, family pressures, and the job discrimination they faced as women and as Lesbians. Other couples have had heated arguments over the pros and cons about coming out into the open, of the wisdom of being "up front," knowing that societal attitudes about homosexuality cannot change until they do. Some have dropped out of society completely, like May, a Third World woman, who left New York and went to Detroit to be a community organizer for the revolution.

In her paper "Double Indemnity: The Negro Lesbian in the Straight White World," Eleanor Hunter, a sociology student at the University of California at Davis, points out that the primary fears of the Black Lesbian relate to bringing shame on her family and being ostracized from the Black community, on which she is dependent not only for social interaction, but for her very survival.

The Black Lesbian, as with all Blacks, is necessarily instilled with a consciousness of her color and given a set of psychological tools so that she can function safely in a hostile, dangerous and potentially lethal white world. The Black community, aside from the built-in social institutions of the ghetto, is a psychological community where a feeling of unity is engendered out of common activities, interests and grievances. The Black Lesbian is very dependent upon and committed to this community, and this commitment precedes and exceeds her Lesbian commitment, which is even more severely castigated in Black circles than in white when it becomes known. There exists no such sense of community for her white Lesbian sister, who has developed her "consciousness of kind" as a Lesbian, but never as a white—unless perhaps she lives in the South.

While Lesbians of both Black and white races have not shown any eagerness to divulge their sexual identity, this added dimension causes the Black to burrow even deeper underground. Those Ms. Hunter interviewed emphasized the large number of latent Lesbians among Blacks, women whose very strong attractions to others of their sex were neither defined nor acted upon, but which were sublimated in strong friendships. Those who acted out their ·Lesbianism, who lived together, for the most part had few, if any, gay friends and dated men to keep up a front.

"Indeed, it would appear that whereas in the white community deviance is imputed on the basis of the observed commission of homosexual acts, in the Negro community deviance is imputed on the basis of the observed omission of heterosexual ones," Ms. Hunter stated. Thus Black couples go to great lengths to keep their Lesbian identity secret, and those on the loose find it next to impossible to find a partner. There are some Black Lesbian cliques, hard to find though they be. They are mostly groups of ex-servicewomen who found each other in the armed forces. But the Black Lesbian, on the whole, is more often led into alliances with a white woman—rhetorically, at least, the "enemy"—or she is forced to sublimate her sexual preference entirely.

The minority of Blacks who surface and become part of the

more visible gay life are to some degree alienated from the Black community and generally establish their permanent relationships with white women. By so doing, they thus suppress their Black identity and travel almost exclusively in the white world. Ernestine, a former vice president of New York DOB and a Black, said she'd never gone with a Black woman. Despite white people's impression that there is more sexual freedom among Blacks, she pointed out that there may be more freedom to participate in sex—but not a variety of sex. Blacks are "still very caught up with other people's definitions of how to live, so they can't explore yet."

That didn't mean that Ernestine preferred white lovers necessarily. They were the most available. "I would like to be able to really communicate with a Negro Lesbian. This would be a perfect situation as far as I am concerned. I only wish more Black women felt free enough to join DOB."

Interracial "marriage" for the Lesbian makes life even more complicated and requires further complicity. As one Black noted bitterly, referring to her previous white partner of many years who had recently taken a new lover, "Well, this will be the first time in twelve years that Karen's been able to take her girl friend home."

But while Blacks find it difficult to take the long step into the gay community, which is still relatively underground despite a growing minority of vocal liberationists, more and more whites are taking the giant step of what Evelyn calls the "truth trip." She is torn between being honest with herself and those she associates with on the one hand and hanging onto her chosen profession as a social worker on the other. The more she wrestles with her dilemma the more she realizes she can't have it both ways. The fact that she is working in a profession which should but does not affirm the Lesbian's sexual orientation makes it virtually impossible for Evelyn to be truthful. Besides, she hopes someday to be able to adopt a child under the new "single parents" adoption program. The importance of the reasons for her silence do not make her hypocritical stance any easier for Evelyn. She is in continual struggle with her two selves: the one that cries out to be freed and the other that is silenced by expediency and compromise.

With the advent of the Gay Liberation Front have come two

senses of the term "coming out." It used to mean the physical experience that "made" a woman into a Lesbian, her "debut." In today's jargon of the streets, to "come out" means public revelation, openly identifying oneself as a Lesbian or homosexual by "coming out of the closet."

The visible, verbal and "organized" homophile community can be likened to the tip of an iceberg. The vast majority of Lesbians are far from liberated in the sense of being open with their associates. There are still far many more in the closet than out. Professional women who have been able to declare themselves openly, like Phyllis, have unique jobs with foundations or institutions outside of the system, where emphasis is on people and their contributions, not on labels. But these opportunities are, of course, very rare. Some offices are more sophisticated and ready to accept gay people openly. And we've heard of a few Lesbians who have been able to survive being the butt of jokes in industrial plants. But such openness, at least at this stage of the game, is still somewhat hazardous.

Take Ellie, for instance. She's in her fifties and lives alone in a rented house in a lower middle class residential district of Alameda. When the woman next door proved to be friendly and started stopping by several times a week, Ellie enjoyed and was grateful for her companionship.

One day, however, Ellie blurted out that she was gay. Her friend was surprised and asked a few probing questions. She came by a few more times after that, but not so often, and finally her visits ceased altogether, leaving a void in Ellie's lonely life.

"Why did you tell her?" Phyllis asked.

"I don't know—I just did! I never did such a thing before in my life!" Ellie exclaimed. "I just don't know what came over me. I didn't have any ideas—no designs on her," she added. "I just wanted to be friends. But telling her about me—being honest—that sure did it!"

Gay Liberation's challenge to all in the closet to "come out," to be honest, is having just as profound an effect upon older Lesbians as it is on the younger generation. For some, like Ellie, the effect is on the unconscious, which may surface in many strange and compelling ways. For others, like the gray-haired Vassar alumna and social worker who found her gay pride in the New York parade, it is a new consciousness to be dealt with. She wrote a letter to the editor of the alumnae magazine, in which she spoke of what Vassar meant to her as a Lesbian undergraduate and president of the student association: the loneliness, the inability to express to anyone her own needs, the system that assumes everyone is heterosexual. However, our Vassar alumna did not feel free enough to sign her name. Her lover of fifteen years is also in an uptight profession and warned, "Don't you dare!" The letter, sent anonymously, was never published.

Then there was Mabel. She came out with a bang a few years ago. She was a thirty-five-year-old nurse who suddenly found herself in love with another nurse (female) who was already "taken." She plunged into DOB affairs, became the social chairman and arranged the various picnics, dances, brunches and spaghetti feeds. She wanted to meet "girls, girls and more girls" and what better way?

In between the monthly DOB socials, if you wanted to find Mabel any evening, all you had to do was go out to Fin Alley, a bar that catered to Lesbians. There you'd find Mabel going ga-ga over the go-go dancer or tablehopping during intermission. It wasn't that Mabel drank much—she didn't. She was merely engaged in her favorite sport: girl watching. Night after night she went through the same routine, as if she were jet-propelled. She couldn't bear to be alone, just had to be with Lesbians, yet she was ever aware she was courting danger—danger she'd be found out and lose her career.

After a year (we never could figure how she lasted that long) she retreated back into her closet to stay. Now she travels in a professional women's social circle, playing golf and bridge "with the girls." We wonder what would have happened to Mabel if she had ventured forth during today's climate of "liberation." Would it have made a difference?

We have been referring to the married Lesbian primarily in terms of a woman-to-woman relationship, but there are also many Lesbians who are heterosexually married. Like so many others they may have known attractions to members of their same sex, but dismissed them as "schoolgirl crushes." Or they may have been revolted by the seamier side of the Mafia-run gay bar scene of New York: too much drinking, the unreal quality of the butches and femmes, the instability of constantly changing partners, the loneliness, the hardness of the habituées. Failing to realize that heterosexuals could also be disillusioned by the sleazy straight bars if they thought that was all there was to heterosexuality, they look for some man to take them away "from all that," hoping to find security and stability in marriage. Others were simply unaware of homosexuality, let alone their own tendencies, until later—sometimes much, much later, after ten or twenty years of marriage.

Ellen, one of those who turned her back on gay life, did not find until she was going through menopause that the homosexual side of her nature could no longer be repressed. The tug of war that was going on inside her had made her physically ill, to the point that her husband insisted she see their family doctor. The physician knew there was something wrong with her mental state and chalked it up to the fears and emotional trauma many women are supposed to experience during the "change." She knew what her problem was, but couldn't tell him, lest he say something to her husband. Besides, she loved her husband and their children. She didn't want anything to happen to disturb their family relationship.

Luckily, when she found Los Angeles DOB, Sandy and Sten were there. These two sensitive and helpful women were near her own age and took her in tow. Ellen, who was now forced to face her past and her gay sisters whom she had rejected, needed the warmth and affection Sandy and Sten radiate. They listened, and they understood. That was all that was needed. Ellen was able to return home somehow reassured and better able to cope with her feelings.

In expressing her thanks for their kindness, Ellen wrote: "About half or more of my purpose was accomplished by the time I left you that first day. The pressure of years—just to talk—not to be alone—but even more, to be accepted for what I am in all ways without pretense, no lies, no deceit. I began to feel clean again—I don't know how else to say it—that's not quite right, but as close as I can come. I was completely exhausted when I left, but the next morning there was a sense of peace I haven't known for at least three years. By the time I said goodbye the following

Wednesday, when I saw you again, I felt a peace I had not known since childhood. All this because I'm once more in control—not being driven by thoughts and actions that were contrary to 'me' and completely out of character. I believe I can handle my personal problem now, but, of course, only time will tell. This I do know: I'm now calm, my fears are no longer exaggerated all out of proportion, and I'm looking forward instead of remembering the past and longing for an end to the present."

Another wife, Becky, had a brief fling with Susie. But then Susie became too serious and demanded that she make a choice, a choice Becky was not prepared to make. It wasn't that she was after a cheap or frivolous affair—she was very much attached to Susie. Yet she couldn't make the break with her husband, whom she also loved in another way. And there were the children to be considered. When forced to a decision some, like Becky, retreat to the heterosexual side of the proverbial fence. Others make a complete break with the past and cross over to the life of the Lesbian.

A regally attractive Black woman sought us out because she had recently become aware of her feelings toward women. She had been honest with her husband, had talked it over with him, and he had agreed she probably ought to find out more about the subject. But it was one thing to talk about it and quite another to act upon it. The seeds of jealousy and uncertainty overcame his intellectual understanding. He stormed up to our house, where a DOB party was going on, stomped in, grabbed Marcie by the arm, and steered her down the stairs and into their car. Not a word was spoken, and many present didn't even realize the incident had happened. We never saw Marcie again.

Jory of Illinois canceled her subscription to *The Ladder* because she was getting married. "After seven years of gay life I believe that I have at last made a successful break from what I consider the worst possible existence for myself. I've found that the security of marriage means far more to me than the heights of emotion and certainly more than the depths of despair. I can't tell you how thrilling it is to be accepted by my family and by his family at face value. I've almost forgotten to be afraid of what people are saying or possibly thinking of me—no more of that awful feeling of 'everyone knows,' " her letter explained.

Perhaps Jory made the right choice for her. But then perhaps she traded one set of problems for another. Marsha reflects on her same decision of twenty years ago:

"Basically I guess what I have come to see and understand in myself is my complete shut-out of expression from all except those very few I have loved, in whatever form or kind of love that may have been. With those few I have never been quite adequate; I could only strive to be as they wished, and not as I was or am. Give nothing to the hundreds of people you meet, let no one see your feelings or read your thoughts (a friend of about five years told me once that I was as 'cold' a person as she had ever known), let no woman touch you even casually (I've even abhorred shaking hands), but be demonstrative with the male because that is acceptable and to be cultivated. And then when I loved—whether child, friend, parent, husband or lover—I could only give all I was, and it was never enough."

Miriam Gardner and Jody Shotwell both wrote articles for *The Ladder* describing the plight of a woman who dwelled in that borderland where there were two laws of gravity pulling her in opposite directions: one toward the emotional fulfillment of a Lesbian relationship and the other toward the responsibility long ago assumed for husband and children. These women do not act out of boredom. To them a Lesbian liaison is not a "lark." It is a necessity that springs from the deep roots of their inner being.

But a relationship with a married woman is unsatisfactory, indeed unbearable, to the Lesbian who seeks a monogamous and lasting union. For her the times of separation are extremely lonely, and she has too much time to think. She begins to feel that she is being used, becomes jealous of her male counterpart, drinks too much, and becomes morose and argumentative as she wallows in self pity.

"What are you? A Lesbian who strode down the matrimonial aisle out of ignorance or error? A heterosexual looking for fun and games on the side? Or a bisexual who wants it both ways at the same time?" she asks.

The situation between the two becomes ugly. The beauty of what had been becomes a nightmare of bitter accusation, jealous rage, tearful pleading—and rare bliss when there is time left to make up. Del knows the scene all too well. That first affair of hers, which we mentioned in passing, was with a married friend.

Whenever DOB has received some publicity in the media, the biggest response has come from heterosexually married women. Some complain about their sex life and wonder if a Lesbian relationship might bring them satisfaction. Some only recently discovered, after marriage, that they had a strong Lesbian component in their makeup. Others, who had deliberately given up the gay life for the security of heterosexual marriage, find they cannot ignore their Lesbian nature. They aren't necessarily looking for sexual or romantic contacts, but for understanding, for a chance to express the feelings which they have tried so long and so hard to contain. Others are torn between a Lesbian affair they need and want, and their prior commitment to their husbands and children. But all have one thing in common: there is no one, no public service agency, no priest or therapist they feel they can turn to without being held in jeopardy.

The need for adequate and nonjudgmental counseling is paramount. Recognition of the latent homosexuality in heterosexuals and conversely, the latent heterosexuality in each homosexual is essential, if we as a people are ever to resolve our sexual hangups. The need for realistic sex education, not just the biblical or reproductive variety, is vital. The National Sex Forum in San Francisco has recently developed an educational program for those in the helping professions (medical doctors, psychiatrists, psychologists, social workers, teachers, clergy, et al.) so that they may provide such counseling in the future. The Forum, which takes an aesthetic view of human sexuality, emphasizing both the value of sexuality and of proficiency rather than constraint, makes the following assumptions: (1) the most significant factor in sex education is that sex can be talked about casually and nonjudgmentally; (2) individuals should be allowed meaningful exposure to a realistic objectification of the range of behavior into which their own experience and those of other humans fall; and (3) the person who teaches, counsels, or gives advice (regardless of professional qualifications) should have a low burden of sexual guilt feelings so as to be of service to others rather than serving his or her own needs. Unfortunately, the assumptions of the National Sex Forum are not yet widely accepted, and in the meantime, the Lesbian suffers.

What we have been describing are various life-style adaptations which take place after the Lesbian has met others like herself. How did she get to that point? As we have already indicated, Lesbians are difficult to distinguish from other women. So how do they meet?

The most obvious place is the gay bar which can be found in quantity in most large cities; even small cities usually have at least one. Most such bars cater to male homosexuals for very economic reasons: as men, male homosexuals have better paying jobs and therefore more money than most Lesbians. Other bars play to a mixed crowd; a very few are devoted to an exclusive Lesbian clientele. Some of the latter exclude men entirely unless accompanied by a woman, the converse of the discrimination against unescorted women in some exclusive hotel and cocktail lounges. Lists of these bars can be obtained in U.S. and foreign editions of *The Address Book* or *Gay Guide,* available at most gay bookstores and newsstands or through various homophile organizations. A newcomer to a large city can generally find out where the action is by asking a cab driver.

Finding a gay bar doesn't spell instant success, however. Most serve a repeat clientele, people who already know each other and who tend to come in couples or in groups. They might eye a stranger suspiciously, wondering if she really knows what kind of a place she has happened into. And if she is shy, it may take a visiting Lesbian a few visits to become acquainted. Sometimes she doesn't meet anyone that interests her romantically or sexually, but she strikes up an acquaintance who introduces her to others, and then she meets their friends. Then her circle gradually widens outside of the bars.

We don't recommend the "mail order bride." Some Lesbian couples have gotten together through correspondence—but not always on order or by invitation. Suddenly, instead of a letter in the mailbox, you open your door one morning and find the object of your infatuation there on your doorstep prepared to move in. Occasionally a Railway Express package with some of her belongings may precede her as a forewarning of what is yet to come. These gifts from outer space generally come with mixed blessings, and we have yet to hear of a case that lasted.

Other Lesbians meet through the homophile organizations. If there is no Lesbian group in their locale, the male organizations are still a source of contact. A few other women do show up. And then, too, most male homosexuals have at least a few Lesbian acquaintances or friends they can introduce a woman to.

But one word of warning to the seeker: one or two tries aren't enough. All too often in the Daughters of Bilitis we have noted that newcomers (whether they be older or younger, white or Third World, single or "married") come to one gathering, don't find the person or persons they are looking for and never return. At the next meeting, however, there is often an entirely different gathering, a group, or a person, who might have interested them had they been there. For instance, as we are writing this, DOB/SF is a very young (under twenty-five) group for the most part, but by the time you read this the group could have changed drastically. And whatever the group that may be visible, there are always the many invisible contacts DOB has to tap.

In small towns where there are no gay bars or organizations, there is usually a gay clique comprised of both men and women. They frequently hold house parties and include both sexes as a cover from nosy neighbors, since there is less chance for the anonymity afforded in large cities.

Because a gay subculture exists in most large cities throughout the world and is easily accessible to the knowledgeable, the Lesbian traveler has little trouble learning the ropes in a foreign country. Armed with addresses and phone numbers of friends of friends and with lists of homophile organizations and gay bars, she is able to make immediate contact with others of her own persuasion. And if you are a Lesbian lucky enough to work for a travel agency you can sometimes make the "grand (gay) tour" at cut rates.

Lesbians in other countries are now emerging, like their sisters in the United States, into a more visible existence. Canadian women, for instance, have had a good deal more reticence than their Yankee sisters. Some of them, on visits to San Francisco's freer atmosphere, have said that they had old friends, sometimes of twenty years' standing, whom they assumed to be gay, but the subject had never been broached. But the Canadian scene has

changed somewhat since the repeal of laws against homosexuality
and because of the influence of the Gay Liberation Movement.

Val Vanderwood reported in *The Ladder* of April/May, 1970,
that although there have never been any laws against Lesbianism in
England, it should not be presumed there are no social pressures or
public censures. They most certainly do exist. English women are
still not likely to tell their parents, friends or employers that they
are Lesbians. However, they do have one advantage over their
American counterparts. As girls they are not pushed to date as
early as American youth are, nor are they pushed so hard to be
"popular" and to get married. This at least takes a bit of the
pressure off.

In describing "Gay Life in Holland" in the December, 1961,
issue of the same magazine, Karin Storm said, "To understand the
position of the Lesbian woman in Holland you have to know a
little about the Dutch character. The Dutch have very little imagination—their matter-of-factness is known all over the world. As
long as you don't bother people here they won't mind your business. But one thing: don't be obvious. Dutch people don't like
anything which is out of normal. 'Being like everybody' is their
slogan." Karin also indicated that people there "can't understand
(and 'not understanding' means to the Dutch often 'not believing')
that a woman—being of the inferior sex—can prefer the love of
another woman to that of a superior man. . . . The Lesbians in
Holland are not divided so clearly in 'butch' and 'femmes' like in
the States," Karin observed. "Most of us look rather feminine . . .
it's rather natural, I suppose. We are 'gay' because we love women.
If we prefer make-believe men, it's hard to understand."

In the Netherlands, even though a boss might discover an employee is a Lesbian, he would not be apt to fire her. The reason:
everybody is understaffed. There are about ten gay bars in at least
three of Holland's cities—Amsterdam, Rotterdam and The Hague
—but the clientele is mostly men. Dutch Lesbians, like those
in America, prefer small friendly gatherings at home. But enter-
taining in Holland is more difficult, since few can afford a house or
a flat and must rent rooms from landladies who would not accept
gay tenants.

"Altogether you could say that our gay life is rather quiet. If
the American novels about gay life tell the truth (which I can

hardly believe) it will seem rather dull to you. But, believe me, it isn't!"

Recent American visitors, like Cynthia, concur. She was struck by the relaxed atmosphere and the friendliness of her Dutch gay friends. On a visit to Amsterdam's COC, the oldest and largest homophile organization in the world, Cynthia was impressed by the "complete lack of paranoia, regret and heartache regarding the homosexual's identity. First of all, he or she is devoted to working and living a purposeful life, regarding themselves, first of all, as human beings. Homosexuality is secondary, it having been a matter of choice, not the 'I couldn't help it' attitude most Americans have. There simply are not the mental hangups. I can't help but believe it is because of a solid identity structure, and secondly, because homosexuality is regarded as choice, personal choice, and is not influenced by the questions of Victorian morality."

Lesbians in Scandinavia, according to Michael Holm, editor of *Uni,* a European international magazine published in Sweden, are a particular breed of women. "They are free of prejudices, independent, do progressive things in other fields too. Many of them come from other countries, have left family and country behind them and started a new career of some kind here. They have strength, will power, and intelligence—though I am sure there are homosexual women of all kinds, just as there are homosexual men."

Technically, Lesbianism "does not exist" in Catholic Southern Europe (though Holm says he has many subscribers from these countries). Little is known about the Lesbian in Asia, but we do know that there are at least three Lesbians in Indonesia. Ger found her way to *The Ladder* through some friends in Holland with whom she had been corresponding. Her story, which was revealed in her letters published in the June and November 1964 issues, is typical in that she, too, was convinced that she was "the only one."

"In Djakarta, this city of millions, surely there are hundreds of my own sort—women who are waiting, wondering, yearning, as I do. Then why can't I find them, why are they so invisible, so concealed?"

In her youth Ger had experienced some intimacies with other Indonesian girls, who "are very caressive of their own accord, and no one will think anything of it if they embrace you in public. It is a common habit. They love to hang on your arms, even on your neck, pressing their cheek against yours, overwhelming you with compliments about your good looks, the scent in your hair. . . . But don't make the mistake to get any wrong ideas—they would run from you as if from mortal danger. . . . But, of course, they *have* to marry, that's a strict custom, and the family will see to that. Only a few are independent enough to risk a family row and maintain their freedom. And they are looked upon as pariahs. There is nothing more humiliating than to be called an 'old maid' in this country—and but few have the courage to face it of their own free will."

Ger expressed her shame because she, too, found that she couldn't resist the coercion to marry. "But it lasted only three months before I revolted against my captivity and broke free. I didn't love my husband, of course. It was just plain cowardice that made me surrender. I couldn't stand being different and being talked of. If I had just one friend, one person like myself, I would have resisted any pressure. But there was no one—I didn't even know there could be—I was still convinced I was the only one in the whole wide world. And I couldn't stand it—it was too much to bear by my lonesome self."

Ironically enough, it was Ger's husband who enlightened her. He had some American novels, which she read, and she was eagerly seeking more. "Even books and other reading matter are hard to get and because our money has no value abroad we can't order anything ourselves. We are dependent on what the bookstores are allowed to import. And that is not much—mostly textbooks and very rarely a few pockets."

With her divorce, Ger's family disowned her. She had disgraced them. She didn't gain anything but her solitary freedom, for, as she said, "there was no one waiting for me at the end of the line." But at least she had learned that there were others like herself in other parts of the world.

The second installment took on a much happier note. It began with a secretary Ger met, whom she describes as "fun-loving Rora." They became friends and confessed to each other that they were Lesbians. Rora, too, had thought she was "the only one." They moved in together as friends ("just friends"), and Rora introduced Ger to a group of male homosexuals she had known. From them she learned more about gay life and acquired more books.

Then she met Hetty at a party. Hetty "had a very interesting face: narrow, with sharp features and sparkling cat-green eyes." Rora and Ger invited her to visit them. "She came—and didn't leave again!"

But, of course, the story wasn't that simple. Hetty, it seems, as with all good Indonesian women, was married, and she had a seven-year-old son. She had no trouble sorting out her feelings of love for Ger and indifference to her husband, with whom she had been staying for appearance's sake and because of the child. But her son—what about him? Ger let her fight her struggle alone, watching powerlessly from a distance, yet sharing her pain and despair. Hetty finally came to her own decision to obtain a divorce and to give up her son—a hard and painful choice to make.

It is interesting to note that Ger, in her aloneness and search for those who shared her inclinations, was aware at the time of so-called women's clubs in Indonesia, mostly high society, where they literally "commit" Lesbianism just for the fun of it. Out of boredom they take up the unique hobby of "maintaining young girls, preferably art students, as their so-called protegées. . . . I know, they tried it with me, too." But Ger, like other Lesbians around the world, was not just looking for sex. She wanted love—and found it.

Though customs and language may differ from country to country, Lesbians are pretty much the same around the world. Even in nations where laws proscribing homosexual activity have long since been repealed, the stigma attached to being a Lesbian still remains. The Lesbian thus leads her life at many levels, with varying degrees of openness. She meets her partners more easily in gay bars, at homophile organizations, by correspondence and world travel. She also meets others by chance acquaintance on the job (as we did), in the waiting room of the doctor's office, in the classroom, at the veterinarian's, at the laundromat, at the supermarket or in the women's movement. Such chance acquaintances may require playing a "cat and mouse" game for a while to determine that what one suspects about the other is really true. What happens after that, what life style the Lesbian adopts, is determined by how much she is inhibited by cultural conditioning, religious persuasion, family ties, and economic dependence on the status quo. All of these factors have a direct bearing upon the Lesbian's personal relationships. The life style she adopts is generally not so much a matter of choice as the means she employs for her own self protection. But as more and more Lesbians become self determined rather than society driven, new and more open life styles for Lesbians will necessarily emerge.

5. Lesbians Are Mothers Too

We met in 1949 in Seattle where we were both working for an outfit that published a series of trade journals. Del was editor of the daily sheet and Phyllis the assistant editor of the weekly and monthly magazines. It was the type of firm that hands out grand titles to women in lieu of pay. Del had been billed by the boss as "a gay divorcee" (he didn't know how gay) when he apprised the staff of the fact that he'd hired her in San Francisco and that she was en route, making some business stops on the way.

Phyllis decided to give a party to welcome the new addition to the staff, and most everybody came. But the guest of honor, who didn't feel too comfortable in such social situations at the time, kept disappearing. Every time Phyllis searched her out she found Del in the kitchen, at the makeshift bar, holding court with some of the men. She even smoked cigars. Later in the evening Phyllis came upon an even more interesting scene. All the men had their ties off and were showing Del how to knot them. It was a great party, Phyllis reflected afterwards, even if her new coworker did seem a little odd. She's a strange sort to be a mother.

Mothers in our society may be odd or strange, but never "queer"—or so most people believe. Lesbians obviously can't have children. Theirs is a "sterile" relationship that is nonprocreative. "Poor things, they will go through life without ever being fulfilled as women—never knowing the joys and heartaches of mother-hood," or so the story goes.

Well, the news is that many Lesbians are mothers, and they are raising their children well, or raising them poorly or raising them indifferently, just as their heterosexual counterparts do. Mostly these are women who were unaware of their Lesbian tendencies until after they had married and had children. Or they are women who suppressed their Lesbian feelings, convinced, as most heterosexuals are, that these feelings merely represented a natural phase in their lives and would disappear after they experienced marriage and motherhood. There are some women, too, who consciously rejected the gay life in favor of the more societally accepted and respected heterosexual relationship.

Later, when their Lesbian nature surfaces and demands recognition, they are faced with decisions that affect not only their own health and happiness, but that of many other persons close to them—their husbands, their children and their Lesbian partners. Some of these mothers choose to remain in their heterosexual marriages "for the sake of the children." Others, feeling that tensions which would necessarily arise would be destructive to all parties concerned, obtain divorces. By keeping silent about their Lesbian feelings, they manage to retain custody of their children. But then they are faced with still another dilemma: whether to remain single or to establish a Lesbian relationship.

There is no provision in this hetero-sexist society for the Lesbian mother. But her existence cannot be denied—nor can her relationship to her children. In the past she has been treated like a leper, a threat to her own children. Court rulings have disregarded any possibility of her being named legal guardian in custody cases; the disregard has been on the false assumption that as a Lesbian, she cannot adequately serve her offspring's many and varied needs. Husbands, by their sole claim to heterosexuality, have been awarded custody regardless of their suitability as parents. The onus is on the mother, and the label "Lesbian" is enough to deny her her children.

As a result many women have been held captive in unsatisfactory marriages. Others, who have managed to obtain divorces and custody of their children, live under the constant threat of exposure, of being declared unfit mothers solely because they are Lesbians. They are forever vulnerable. Ex-husbands or male in-laws, because they suspect the relationship between the mother and a "roommate" or because neither of the women will submit to their unwanted advances, have thus been able to threaten what otherwise are peaceful and loving households offering a wholesome environment for the children. Unwitting and trusting female relatives, unaware or unbelieving of the predatory actions of their spouses, are misled into being accomplices in having the Lesbian mother declared "unfit" and her children taken away from her.

We know of such a case in Moscow, Idaho. The divorced father, a drunk and a gambler, long ago split for Nevada and has never been heard from since. The mother, her three children and her Lesbian partner of almost four years have in the meantime established a close-knit family unit. Vickie, the mother, in her mid-twenties, is a warm and outgoing person. She is admired and respected in the community—if someone is sick or in need, she is right there offering her help. But what her neighbors don't know is that she is a Lesbian. What they don't know is that her brother-in-law, Jake, has been trying to seduce her for the past year, even going so far as to expose himself in front of Vickie and her children. What they don't know, too, is that her roommate, Lola, has also been subjected to the same assaults and threats. "You're just a couple of queers!" Jake jeered. "If you won't submit I'll have the kids taken away from you."

Despite the unsavory situation with which they have been forced to cope, these two women felt comparatively safe, since Jake had no actual proof that they were indeed Lesbians—not until Vickie made the mistake of confiding in her sister, Sally, one day. As sisters they had always been fairly close, and when Sally asked Vickie about her relationship with Lola, it only seemed natural to Vickie to be honest with her. She felt that, given the chance to talk it out, Sally would understand. The affirmation was all that Sally was after. She did not want to hear any more. Jake had put Sally up to asking Vickie, and she ran to him with the proof he needed. Sally and Jake, childless heterosexuals, are now threatening Vickie that they will expose her as an unfit mother, a Lesbian, and will themselves seek custody of her children.

What recourse does Vickie have? We know of only one case where custody of children was awarded to a declared Lesbian mother, and that was an uncontested divorce where the mother was older, was well established in the community and had the support of clergy, doctors and the attorneys as well as of relatives and friends. Vickie feels she is in good standing in the community, that many of her friends would rally behind her, even if it became known she was a Lesbian. But her own sister is against her, and there is no known case on record where a judge, given the choice between a homosexual and a heterosexual household in which to place the care of children, ever ruled in favor of the homosexual one. The best Vickie could do in a court hearing would be to divulge Jake's untoward behavior and possibly prevent his and Sally's claim to the children. But the children would probably be declared wards of the court, be separated and placed in foster homes. Vickie wants to fight the case. She's been a good mother and doesn't see how the court could rule against her. Lola wants to flee, pick up bag and baggage and move across the border, "get lost" in another state and re-establish themselves in a new setting. Vickie must make the choice: to stay and fight for her "rights," which are nonexistent to date, or to flee from "justice."

Vickie and Lola are individuals trying to live full productive lives in a society blind to some of the deepest human needs. Their situation is representative of what many Lesbian relationships are subjected to because of the public's total lack of understanding and compassion. In a divorce or custody case always, and perhaps rightly, the primary consideration is for the children. But the mother, even if she is a Lesbian, obviously needs to be considered too, as does the father, or other "blood" relatives who may be involved, as in this case. What is "best for the children" and for the others is not always so clear-cut as our heterosexually prejudiced family welfare and court systems pretend.

"What of the children of Lesbian parents? What happens to them?" A psychiatrist who was counseling a young father in the throes of divorce phoned Phyllis and posed these questions. Though his wife had admitted to being a Lesbian, the client still respected her as a person and as a mother. He didn't want to cause any trouble or take the young daughter away from her, if only he knew there were similar cases that had proved all right. The psychiatrist thus wanted to know if there were any books, any papers, any data on the subject which might help his client come to his decision about the custody of his child.

There is no such body of information available. If it is difficult or impossible to obtain a census of Lesbians in general, it is doubly so in the case of mothers who wish to maintain custody of their children. Of the mothers we happen to know, most have small children; there are some teenagers, but only a few have as yet reached adulthood.

During the early days of DOB we found that a number of our members were faced with the problem of rearing children in what society would call a "deviant relationship." They had problems with ex-husbands and fathers who exercised their visitation rights and at the same time made disparaging remarks about the "room-mates." These women were ever on guard about their Lesbian relationships and often given to doubts as to whether they were "doing the right thing." To answer their questions and allay their fears, we arranged a series of discussions with some women whom we felt might help: Rhoda Kellogg, one of the original Suffragettes and director of the Golden Gate Nursery School; Eleanor van Leeuwen, specialist in parent education for the San Francisco school system; and Faith Rossiter, psychotherapist.

While the DOB mothers discussed such things as physical and emotional growth of the child, how to detect and deal with defects of speech or learning habits, the burning question was, of course, their own deviance from the societal norm and what effect this might have on their offspring. It became clear that any straying from one's sincere feelings or true values could be said to be deviant, so that there could be deviant heterosexuals as well as deviant homophiles. Love and security in the home overshadow almost all other factors in determining the emotional stability of the child. The guest resource people emphasized that if a youngster knows love, gives love and receives love, and knows he or she is wanted, chances are the child will turn out to be normal and well adjusted. The emotional stability, the maturity of the parents—male-female or female-female—necessarily determine the background of the child. Therefore, they warned, "the basic thing is to accept and understand yourself, and then the rest of the world as it is."

The three women in this discussion series had suggested that mothers looking for general information on child development should use the library of San Francisco's Family Service Agency. That was in 1957. But while Lesbian mothers may have traipsed to the FSA and used the facilities of its library, they did not dare to discuss the problems they were facing with the counselors also available there. It was not until 1971, when the agency was chal-

LESBIAN/WOMAN

lenged by the homophile community to deal with homosexuality
openly as a family problem, that these women could feel free to
express their doubts and problems without fear of reprisal from
what they assumed to be an uptight guardian of the heterosexual
family.

A beginning step toward more realistic help for the homosexual
was taken when the Family Service Agency directors responded to
an ad hoc homophile committee's request by naming two declared
homosexuals, a man and a woman, to their board. Del, Sally
Gearhart of Gay Women's Liberation, and Rick Stokes, president
of the Council on Religion and the Homosexual, had appeared
before an agency committee and then the board itself with a request for two board members, two counselors and two community
organizers. These positions were to be equally divided between
men and women—all declared homosexuals.

Their presentation pointed out that all homosexuals come from
families and stressed the need for proper counseling not only of
homosexual youth, but of their parents. Though two gay people
were named to the board, the hiring of gay counselors and community organizers would have to wait until funding was obtained.
Unfortunately the action by the agency was taken at a time when
it was facing financial difficulties. Plans were laid, however, for
working with the present counselors and other members of the
staff to establish a more realistic approach to homosexual problems which can exist within the family.

Dr. Harvey Kaye participated in a recent DOB discussion in
New York at which a panel of Lesbian mothers talked of their
experiences. One had a three-year-old daughter who never had a
father in her home; another had had no homosexual relations until
after her divorce when her child was fourteen, but when this girl
met her mother's lover she was hostile; a third woman had been
divorced when her daughter was fifteen and her son eight and had
then lived happily with a woman for five years, though without
overt affection in front of the children. In no case had these
mothers told their offspring that they themselves were homosexuals.

The audience asked: How can you change society's attitude
toward the Lesbian if you won't tell your own kid? At what age
should children be told about homosexuality? Will a girl brought

up in a gay household become a Lesbian? Dr. Kaye advised mothers not to tell the three- to eight-year-olds of one's homosexuality, since at that age the child is working out his or her own sexual identity. He suggested it would be helpful to have male friends around the home as father substitutes. He also claimed that a Lesbian parent will rarely have a homosexual child.

"It's too bad about the mother—she made her choice to lead a Lesbian life. But she should think of the child's welfare. She should give up her children so that they might have a better chance in life," declare self-righteous heterosexual parents, who are themselves responsible for the inequality of those chances in life. They fail to realize, too, that most homosexuals had that "better chance" in their own heterosexual homes.

Some women, who haven't yet worked through all the negative expletives thrown their way and who accept society's evaluation of them, have succumbed to such pressures and given up their families. Others—like Ms. N, who didn't agree, who loved and wanted her children—have fought for their custody through the courts.

While Judge Babich never satisfied his curiosity about what Ms. N did in bed, he did hear Dr. George Gross, psychiatrist, testify that she "had many of the fine qualities that we think of in terms of a stable person, a reasonable, sensible, sensitive, aware person, a person who is interested in her children, in the things children need, is aware of some of their basic emotional needs in the process of growing up." Dr. Gross also stated in regard to Ms. N's management of her sexual activity, "I can't see that it—activity in and of itself—would have any adverse effect upon the children."

But then comes the clincher. He qualified his previous statement by adding, "I do not believe that a homosexual adjustment is the best type of sexual adjustment, if we're thinking about the ideal for an individual."

"Can you give us an idea, an estimation of how many people have made an 'ideal' sexual adjustment in society? Is this a common thing that a psychiatrist finds?" Blackmon, Ms. N's attorney, countered.

"I think it's impossible for him to answer that. He hasn't tested us all yet," the judge interceded. (Nor had he "tested *us* all yet," we would add.)

However, the good doctor did say that in his "professional opinion" all people have various degrees of sexual difficulties in the process of growing up that can come forward and have some effect on the child. He said he always shied away from the question of "parental love" because it had so many ramifications. But he agreed with her attorney that Ms. N had affection for her children and a warm relationship with them, and "this affection and this warmth and strength of their relationship would lead her to be a good parent in the sense that she cares properly for their needs, both physical and emotional."

Under cross examination, however, Dr. Gross also agreed with Mr. N's attorney that she would have more difficulty than a heterosexual person in encouraging the children to seek a heterosexual relationship and that her homosexuality would impair her ability to impart the "traditional concept of morality to her children."

Asked if Ms. N would have difficulty in overcoming her homosexual tendencies—overcoming them to a heterosexual adjustment—the doctor said yes. Pressed further on his views of psychiatric claims of so-called "cure," he said that there were people who hold to the view that homosexuality can be "cured." "But I do not, and I don't think many psychiatrists do."

"Can you tell us whether or not homosexuals exhibit a greater attraction to young people than heterosexuals, as a group?"

"I'm not familiar with them as a group."

On redirect examination Blackmon tried to establish that Ms. N, aware of her problems as a homosexual mother, could indeed cope with them in rearing her children. Dr. Gross foresaw difficulties in role identification at many levels with a growing child, but admitted a heterosexual parent could have the same or even more difficulty in terms of relationship with children.

"Is it likely that her children will be homosexuals?" Blackmon asked.

After saying there were no studies available and that you can't really predict this sort of thing, Dr. Gross nonetheless ventured the "guess" that Ms. N's children would have sexual difficulties, but he refused to guess whether they would be of a homosexual nature or not. Mr. Winter, on his redirect examination of the witness, established that the first six years were formative years in regard to sexual problems and sexual outlook toward life. Ms. N's children were four and seven years of age.

The judge asked if the children would be better off with a heterosexual father, to which the expert witness admitted not knowing the father well enough to make such an estimate. But then he added the inevitable observation, "Given everything else equal, of course, I think the heterosexual analogy represents a better type of overall judgment."

Blackmon asked Dr. Gross if the four-year-old girl was having difficulty at this stage of her development. But the judge ruled that since the doctor had not examined the children, but only the mother, he was in no position to have an opinion on the matter.

"I'm having difficulty with 'all other things being equal' that we have tossed around," Blackmon protested, to which Judge Babich responded, "Well, the doctor's had trouble with the 'good' and 'bad,' so. . . ."

When Mr. N took the stand he recounted the events of the couple's separation, his wife's moving from Oakland to Sacramento with the children, and his subsequent visitations. He had suspected his wife of having homosexual relations, which were confirmed by Ms. N's mother because she'd walked in on her and Sandra. Mr. N then took both children away from his wife—the seven-year-old son, who was not his but Ms. N's by a previous marriage, as well as his own daughter "because I just gave her an ultimatum like she couldn't possibly have him in an atmosphere like that—I wouldn't allow it."

The judge, exercising his judicial "discretion," found that the "best interests" of the four-year-old required that she be with her natural father with visitation rights to the mother in his presence. The fate of the son would have to be settled in a separate litigation. When Blackmon questioned visitation rights only in the presence of Mr. N, the judge conceded this might create ill feeling, but still required the presence of an adult third party agreeable to both, hopefully, "a relative who has no problems."

"I want this child protected, and if the lady takes therapeutics and the psychiatrist can assure me, then I will look for unrestrained visitation." So stated Babich in his august judgment.

We knew another woman whose case was similar to Ms. N's.

Prior to the divorce, however, she had allowed her husband to commit her to a state hospital for the mentally insane. If she had Lesbian tendencies, obviously she was crazy. However, the shock treatments and all other treatment that she was subjected to in the hospital didn't alter her sexual preferences. She, too, admitted her homosexuality in open court, but the judge in her case, while expressing sympathy, could find no "precedent" whereby a homosexual parent had ever been awarded custody of children. He accordingly gave custody to the father, who really didn't want the child and only wanted to get back at his wife because she had failed him, had wounded his heterosexual male ego. Some time later he gladly turned over the responsibility for the care of his daughter to her Lesbian mother, without so advising the court.

In the meantime, the damage had been done. The mother, who was a brilliant and sensitive woman, was never able to reconcile the trauma of her hospital experience, the trauma of the contested divorce, the trauma of having her child wrenched from her. Nor was she later, when she once again had her daughter with her, able to escape the societal-imposed guilt and the fear that any slip, ever so slight, might again mean intervention by the authorities. She became an alcoholic, though she would never admit it. She managed to hold down a desk job in a large insurance office and provided for her daughter's needs. But she could never accept herself, and she never resolved the inner conflict that was hers to bear.

In the January, 1965, issue of *The Ladder,* under the heading of "Living Propaganda," Ms. B writes of a success story: "I reached a personal crossroad in 1964. After eighteen years of marriage and four children, after a long, desperate attempt to keep a marriage together that was stifling to both partners, I sued for divorce and openly declared my love for a woman and our intention to make a future life together. With the custody of the children at stake, I gambled, because I believe deeply that there is justice for the homosexual.

"I was frank and honest with both my own and my husband's families, both our lawyers, and with the physicians and clergy who were involved—including three pastors from three different denominations. Because I had worn the mask with fair success, some were shocked and unbelieving. Some had always felt I was 'different,' but could never quite put their fingers on how I was different.

"All but a few of the relatives stood by me in the divorce. The remarkable thing is that the most narrow-minded and prejudiced of them agreed that I'm certainly not 'sick.' The most prevalent response was, "But she is so good, a good mother, a good house-keeper, a good person! My husband's attorney could not uncover anything derogatory about me, an acknowledged Lesbian. And I have won uncontested and complete custody of the children.

"My friend and I are discreet and have used good judgment when admitting our homosexuality. I do not advocate random admissions, as that can be unwise. However, in my case it was possible to be honest not only with attorneys, physicians and clergy, but also with carefully chosen neighbors and friends. There has been much less prejudice than one would expect."

Of course, Ms. B speaks from the vantage point of maturity and experience. Her children were past the ages of two or six or eight, depending upon which "authority" you listen to, and their own sexual identity was already established. She also had reinforce-ment, people who would stand by her. And the divorce and cus-tody proceedings were not contested.

Del went through a contested divorce herself. Her husband had intercepted a couple of mushy notes she had written (but never sent) to the object of her affection next door, an affection that had not been and never was to be overtly expressed. Del knew how she felt, but she figured that didn't constitute a transgression which could be held against her. She persisted in the divorce action, though Jack tried to threaten her with the notes in order to persuade her to drop it. She never mentioned the damaging evidence to her attorney, even during the confrontation between both attorneys and clients in a room adjoining the courtroom—the one final attempt on the part of the lawyers to effect a reconcilia-tion, if possible.

When Del wouldn't budge from her decision to proceed with the divorce suit, Jack's attorney held up an envelope and waved it above his head. "You know what we have, don't you? Do you want us to use them against you? We will, you know."

"Yes," Del stared him directly in the eye, "I know. Do with them what you will," she said wearily. "I still want a divorce!"

Jack's attorney made good his threat and, during the court

proceedings, introduced the notes in evidence. Del's attorney
looked at her quizzically, as she leaned forward watching the judge,
who glanced briefly at the notes and denied the motion to include,
saying they were irrelevant to the case.

The relief Del experienced cannot possibly be described. For
the "co-respondent" in the case, who actually had no idea what
was going on, was in the courtroom. Del was spared the embarrassment of having her infatuation for her revealed publicly.

Del was granted her divorce and awarded custody of Janey.
Jack was to continue making the payments on the house (would
you believe they were only $35.00 a month then?) and make a
like monthly contribution toward Janey's support. But the legal
wrangling was not to end there. Ms. C (for "co-respondent") had
asked Del if she could move in with her temporarily, since she
herself was obtaining a divorce; and, of course, Del couldn't say
no. But Jack was damned if he was going to make the house
payments as long as "that woman" was living there. So Del had to
brave another court appearance. This time the judge told Jack in
no uncertain terms that Del's choice of a housemate was none of
his business and that withholding the payments he had ordered
was an act constituting contempt of court.

The period of adjustment following the divorce, the inevitable
arguments with Jack when he came back after taking Janey for a
weekend outing, the frustration of living with a woman she was
attracted to but dared not approach, the torture of trying to figure
out who she really was and at the same time maintain a somewhat
stable household and home life for Janey—all this was indeed trying for Del.

When Janey was three, Del learned that a neighbor was placing
her son in a private school in Belmont. Janey and Matt had been
fast friends from the time Janey had first toddled outside to play,
and Janey begged Del to let her go to school too. Del decided
perhaps this might be a better arrangement than the babysitter she
had then. She sold the house out from under them, placed Janey
in the school, bid Ms. C goodbye along with all the frustrations she
represented, moved to an apartment in the city where her job was,
and had Janey home with her on weekends.

By the time Janey was six Jack had remarried. He and his bride
of several months were convinced they could not have children

and asked Del to let them take Janey. They could provide her with the security of a real home with *both* a mother and a father. After much soul searching Del relented. As an "army brat" Janey was subject to orders but exposed to world travel. She even spent a couple of years in Europe. But when in the vicinity she visited Del on weekends and during school vacations. That's how she happened to be with us during our "honeymoon."

Lest young Lesbian mothers, on the heels of Ms. B's success story, decide to bare their souls and throw themselves on the mercy of our unmerciful courts, we would remind them that Ms. N's case is much more typical. We would remind them of their age and experience; we would question them as to whether they themselves were that together personally and within the community in which they live.

Unfortunately for children, heterosexual and homosexual parents alike usually have their babies when they are very young, while they are still finding out who they are and what the world is all about. They generally "grow up" along with their children.

When we showed the transcript of Ms. N's case to an attorney friend, he said he hoped we would warn all Lesbian mothers. "Be as candid as you can without giving evidence which can be held against you. Honesty and sincerity won't get you any place with the prevailing attitudes of today's society."

He added that Ms. N's attorney should have at least stood up and made a statement after the judge rendered his decision—a statement to the effect that he hoped "there would come the time when society and the courts would base a custody case on the character and ability of the mother and not on whether she was a Lesbian."

There are attorneys and attorneys just as there are psychiatrists and psychiatrists. It was particularly ironic that the attorney who involved DOB in Ms. N's case had previously fought DOB. He was then working for the Legal Aid Society, but had previously represented the state against the Council on Religion and the Homosexual, DOB and other California homophile organizations in their bid for a booth in the educational pavilion at the state fair. When faced with a case on the other side of the fence, the attorney did not hesitate to seek help and knowledge from those he had previously moved against. He needed funds for a psychiatric examination of his client, which DOB provided, and the name of a Sacramento psychiatrist who would be experienced in this area of expertise. Unfortunately we were not acquainted with professional persons in the Sacramento area, but did send some suggestions gleaned from knowledgeable Bay Area psychiatrists.

Dr. Gross was not one of them. Dr. Gross, if you recall, admitted he knew nothing of homosexuals as a group. The judge gave weight to his testimony that a heterosexual adjustment for the parent was "generally" preferable to a homosexual one, though he admitted that Ms. N exhibited all the positive qualifications expected of a good mother, and that not all heterosexual parents were free of problems that might affect their children. Nowhere in the transcript was there a similar psychiatric evaluation as to the attributes of Mr. N as a father other than his identification as a heterosexual—a fact that, to us, is not impressive. It tells nothing of the man's character or his ability to raise a young daughter. We hear so much about how little boys need a father figure. What about little girls? Don't they need a mother? And is Ms. N less a woman or less a mother just because she happens also to be a Lesbian?

Although the courts were not involved, another woman, Rose, fought an entire self image to recover her daughter. She was a Mexican-American who had come west after her release from Cook County jail. She'd been in some sort of scrape and had served a short sentence, at which time her small daughter had been placed in an orphanage. She was determined to make good, get herself a steady job, create a wholesome home environment and then demand that Dorinda be returned to her. She made good her resolves and in the process acquired herself a "wife." Rose had been extremely "butchy" and rough. With Nan's influence and help, she learned how to dress and act more in keeping with the image she wanted to project—that of a stable, responsible, well-mannered, feminine-appearing epitome of motherhood.

All projects were go. She'd made the transformation economically, physically and psychologically. She was the pillar of middle class matronage and was now ready to tackle the Establishment to get her daughter back, and that she did with a vengeance! With determination, perseverance, persistence, nagging, cajoling—whatever the situation called for—she gathered letters of character reference, letters affirming her unblemished employment record, letters confirming her newly acquired standard of living, letters attesting to her home environment, letters from clergymen, attorneys, social workers, teachers, and psychologists. All those who had known Rose before were truly impressed with her transformation. If getting her daughter back meant all that much to her, certainly she should have her. She'd proved her sincerity, and she gave every indication of being able to make good.

The plan worked. It was a happy day when Rose returned from Chicago with Dorinda and took her home to Nan. All went well for about a year, but then Rose began to slip back into her old ways. She began to act more like dad than mom, and she and Nan began to fight about it. Then Nan left Rose—left her to cope all by herself. That didn't work out at all. So she packed up Dorinda and took her to Arizona, where she had relatives. Not that she didn't love Dorinda—she did. But being a "mother" just wasn't her bag.

Lesbian mothers who find living in a heterosexual family facade unbearable and decide to go their own way, face some very real problems—quite apart from the edicts of the courts and the vindictiveness of ex-husband/fathers and other assorted relatives. With divorces behind them and young children in their care, Lesbian mothers have many more decisions to make. Is it possible to provide my children with a wholesome environment and still maintain my love life? Should I bring my lover into the home?

Some, like Belle, decide that it's too risky. She ventured out once long ago to participate in some of the DOB discussions, but not for long. Unable to cope with any possibility of exposure, she opted for the spinster life—but with children. She has devoted herself solely to "mothering," to what she believes to be the welfare of her children. We still hear from her every once in a while. She phones us when she "can't stand it any longer," when she needs "to hear an adult voice and be able to talk and discuss things above the childhood level."

Others, who choose to remain single like Belle, nevertheless find it impossible to deny their own sex drives. They manage a furtive affair once in a while, but refrain from becoming too "involved." These guilt- and fear-ridden affairs, which can never be allowed to get too close to home, certainly cannot be very satisfying, but they are "safer."

But many Lesbian mothers try to establish ongoing relationships and introduce their partners into the family unit. If the mother has thus chosen the Lesbian life, then two questions emerge. Do I tell my children, and if so, when and how? And what should my conduct toward my partner be in the children's presence?

These two big questions lead to other questions. What if the kids in their innocence say something about "us" to the other kids and it becomes part of the neighborhood gossip? What effect would that have on the children? Should we tell them in order to protect them from such an eventuality? But would they understand? Wouldn't such knowledge only confuse them? When should you tell them anyway? At what age? Dr. Kaye said not before eight, but if they ask you before then, what do you say? What if you tell them and they reject you?

The answers, of course, come down to how comfortable the mother is with her homosexuality, how mature she is in her response to the many pulls and demands on her from her children, her lover and her society. Some mothers manage to keep their secret all their lives, but most realize that there will come the day of reckoning when the secret will come out and they will have to deal with it.

Andrea, the alcoholic mother we mentioned earlier, became obsessed with a burning compulsion to level with her high-school daughter, Jennifer. So great was her burden of guilt that she simply had to unload it or go mad. At every gay gathering she sought out the other mothers and questioned them incessantly as to how they had handled it when and if they had told their children. Some had managed the situation quite well, but they cautioned Andrea that you can't simply spring it on a young girl, that you must prepare her for such a revelation. Otherwise it could have disastrous effects.

We can only conjecture as to how, in her shame and guilt, and perhaps under the influence of alcohol, Andrea explained the "facts of life" to her daughter. It was not surprising to learn later that Jennifer had gone to the school counselor and that the home environment of this young student was under investigation.

We had been out of touch for a number of years. Unfortunately when Andrea died and Jennifer phoned to advise us, we were out of town. She wrote us a note thanking us for being friends to her troubled mother, indicating that it had taken her a while to understand, but that in time she and Andrea had been able to come to terms. Jennifer's husband had been most helpful in bringing this about.

Del always felt that there was a calculated risk that when the time came that her daughter learned the truth she might be rejected. But she felt, too, that if she built a good relationship with Janey, the stigma of having a Lesbian for a mother might be overcome. Besides, Del never did feel comfortable in the role of mother anyway. She detested "momism." She had always rebelled at society's labels of motherhood and womanhood which, to her, restricted personhood. Her view of mom was more as a guide, counselor, teacher—and above all, friend.

The inevitable day came. One evening at dinner Janey, by then a teenager and college student, wanted to know, "What is that club you and Phyllis belong to, mom, that takes up so much of your time?"

A heterosexual friend, who was a guest at dinner and who knew what the score was, immediately began to chatter about something else. But Janey was not to be put off. "I still want to know the answer to my question." Del thought that called for a private mother-daughter session and told Janey the next time they were alone together she would tell her all about it.

The next evening, as it turned out, Phyllis went over to see her parents, and Del and Janey were indeed alone together. Del waited for Janey to ask her question again. When she didn't, she broached the subject herself, since keeping one's promises had always been a cardinal rule between them. Del got out some copies of *The Ladder* and told Janey all about the Daughters of Bilitis.

"That's all very interesting," Janey said, "but how come you and Phyllis are so involved?"

We had thought that she must have had some inkling of our circumstances, even if she wasn't sure. Janey had moved back to San Francisco with us to go to college; many of our homosexual friends, both male and female, had been in and out of the house, and we had even taken Janey to several gay social gatherings. She had remarked about the masculine nicknames of many of our women friends, and had echoed her church youth group's hilarity

when its collection totaled $69.00. But the news that Del was a
Lesbian and that the two of us were living in a Lesbian relationship came as a complete shock.

"I just thought you were friends. I certainly never thought of
you as having sex together! As a matter of fact, I always thought
that if I didn't meet the 'right guy,' I'd like to establish such a
warm and close relationship with another woman, like you and
Phyllis have."

Del cautioned Janey about talking too openly about it. She
referred her to some books if she wanted to learn more, and
suggested the names of some psychologist friends in case Janey
might like to discuss the subject with a third party.

"Is it all right if I tell Kevin?" Janey had a steady boy friend.

"Sure," Del replied. "What I meant though was that a lot of
people don't understand, and they can give you a bad time."

Kevin was none too pleased with Janey's news. But together
they went to the college library and read up on the subject of
homosexuality. At one point they had qualms about its being
hereditary: they'd come upon the Kallman study of identical twins
where both turned out to be homosexual, strongly suggesting that
genetic factors are involved in the etiology of homosexuality. But
as we have already indicated, although some still cling to the belief
that there is an inherent predisposition, the preponderance of
psychoanalytic theory suggests homosexuality is either a learned
pattern of behavior or an expression of one facet of the ambisexual nature of human beings. Eventually, as they pursued their
study, Janey and Kevin dissolved their fears regarding their future
offspring. They decided we were okay and that our homosexuality
was okay too.

When they announced their engagement, and we had offered
our blessings, Kevin grinned shyly, "I guess I'm really a lucky guy.
I'll have two mothers-in-law instead of just one!"

Most people think that one mother-in-law is enough. Having
two mothers-in-law did pose some problems for Kevin. As mother
of the bride, Del invited the prospective bridegroom's parents over
for dinner. Apparently Kevin's step-father sized up the situation
immediately. He took Kevin aside later and told him what he
suspected, that Janey's mother was involved in a Lesbian relationship—a fact Kevin felt compelled to deny.

Johnny found himself in a similar predicament when he brought some of his high school buddies home one afternoon after school. They checked out the place and started asking Johnny some pretty pointed questions. Who was this Meg, this woman who was staying there with him and his mother? How long had she been living with them?

Johnny said she was a friend and that she'd been there about five years.

"Is she a queer?" one young man demanded.

"Of course not!" Johnny was adamant in his denial.

"Well, they sleep in the same bed together, don't they?"

"What's the matter with that? We have only two bedrooms, and one of them is mine," Johnny replied. "You've got rocks in your head!"

"Does your mother ever date? Does she go out with men?" his friend pursued the subject.

"Yes, of course, she does. They both do. There have been lots of men over to the house." Johnny insisted there was nothing wrong or peculiar about either Meg or his mother.

The incident, though, puzzled him somewhat. Why would Dick say such things? His mother had never remarried in all these years, and Meg didn't ever mention the possibility of marriage for her either. On reflection that seemed rather odd, since most women were setting their traps to catch themselves a husband. So Johnny took the whole question to Blanche, his mother. She told him that what his friends had suspected was true and explained her relationship to Meg and to the men friends they had—that they were homosexuals too. "You've got to be kidding! They don't look or act like fairies. Why, Gary is every bit as much a 'man' as the coach of our basketball team. He can't possibly be gay!" cried Johnny in disbelief.

That bit of news really bothered him more than the fact that his mother and Meg were Lesbians. He loved them both, they'd been great to him and he guessed they were entitled to find happiness in their own way. Johnny's early childhood had been filled with violence. He remembered all too well his father coming home drunk and picking an argument, oftentimes venting his temper by beating up his mother. When Johnny had come to her defense, he had gotten it too. Life had been a lot different since the divorce, since Meg had come to live with them.

Johnny kept his newfound knowledge to himself. He continued to play dumb as far as his nosy, accusing friends were concerned. It was none of their business. They wouldn't understand.

Sometimes the parental "confession" takes a different turn. "I didn't have to tell my daughter—she told me!" Gretchen announced to us. "I'd been divorced about a year. During this time I'd plunged myself into all sorts of activities, particularly the civil rights movement. In CORE I met this Black woman. She was different from all the women I'd ever known. She wasn't pretty— she was handsome. I admired her looks, but there was also an intensity about her that fascinated me. I invited her to the house for dinner a number of times in hopes that our friendship would deepen. I wanted so much to get to know her better. But as I did, my fascination began to change into something else. I began having these strange feelings, this strong attraction I had only felt for men before."

Gretchen went on to say that, as she puzzled over her feelings, she became withdrawn. After dinner, while her daughter Helen was doing the dishes or studying, she would build a fire in the fireplace and just sit and stare and think.

Finally one evening Helen came and joined her. She curled up on the footstool and gazed up at her mother. Then she reached over and put her hand on Gretchen's knee. "What's the matter, mom? You've been so quiet and moody lately. Something is bothering you."

"It's nothing I can talk about." Gretchen grabbed for the Kleenex and dabbed at her eyes.

Helen was silent for a moment. Then she rose and put her arms around her mother. "Is it Beth? Are you in love with her?"

"Yes, Helen, I think so," Gretchen admitted after a momentary pause. "But I don't understand it. I've never felt this way about another woman before."

"So? You never ate soul food before you met Beth either," Helen replied, as she began to assume the role of counselor. She told her mother if she really loved Beth it was all right, that she needn't feel guilty about it or try to hide it and that the situation, however troublesome it might be in the neighborhood, could be worked out.

There is always the problem of how the mother and her Lesbian lover are to conduct themselves in front of their children. Most older women have made it a practice of withholding any form of physical expression, even ordinary displays of affection. But younger women of today say this isn't natural, it's unhealthy. Kids should grow up in a more relaxed atmosphere, where love and affection are openly expressed. "What's wrong with holding hands or putting your arms around one another or kissing in front of the children?" they ask. "Other women do it. It's accepted among heterosexual women. Why are we Lesbians so uptight?"

Of course, not all Lesbians cotton to the idea of tying themselves to a partner who has children. At first Phyllis was not too happy with the prospect of having Janey with us. That was only until she got to know her. Now Phyllis is as much a mother, mother-in-law and grandmother as Del.

But Molly remained adamant. She told Luella right from the beginning, "I'm not having any kid living with me!" Luella's son had been in a foster home, but during his adolescent years had become unmanageable. She knew she was going to have to do something about him, knew she should have him with her. But Molly wouldn't hear of it. Luella had been with Molly for five years. She didn't want to lose her, but she also loved her son and felt responsible for him. She felt guilty too because of the years that had already come between them. Luella tried and tried to get Molly to at least give it a try. But Molly stood her ground. "It wouldn't work. I just know it!"

There were weeks, even months of indecision—and constant arguments. Finally they hit on a solution. They bought a duplex. Luella and her son live in one unit and Molly in the other. This arrangement seems to have solved their impasse. Luella is able to meet the needs of both her son and her lover and receive the love and satisfaction which each provides her. We suspect, however, that she is also saddled with the housework of both her domiciles.

In some cases, roles are played out, as with Lou and Brenda. It was Brenda who sought us out. She and Lou had recently found each other and wanted to get a place together, but Brenda had two children, a boy and a girl, whom she had to consider. Could such an arrangement possibly work out? This was Brenda's first experience with gay life. Lou was pretty "butchy," which both attracted and repelled Brenda. If two women were to bring up children, that's what they'd have to be—two women. It's the only way it could work. At least that's what Brenda was telling us when she left.

Shortly thereafter she invited us over for dinner. She wanted us to see their new place and meet the rest of her family. When we walked in, Lou was on the floor tussling with Teddy, the three-year-old boy. Then she started tossing him up into the air and catching him—one, two, four times—until Teddy yelled, "That's enough." But Lou tossed him up in the air once more, and he screamed, "I said that's enough, daddy!"

We can only assume that Brenda and Lou decided that every little boy needs a male figure in his life, a father, and that's the role Lou was to play. But we wondered how this role playing would turn out when Teddy started bringing the neighbor kids in to play and they told him in disgust, "Your daddy is a *girl*!" We never did find out. Brenda and family moved away soon after that, and we lost touch.

For the most part, a Lesbian mother can meet the questions of relationships with a child in the same way that a good heterosexual mother can. The child is a person and deserves to be treated as such.

Adele, when she brought Sadie home to live, sat her fourteen-year-old daughter down right then and explained the situation to her. She figured Janice was old enough to know, and she didn't want to take any chances that she find out from anyone else. A short time later they all went together to a softball game. Janice surveyed the crowd and became aware that they seemed a lot more masculine in dress and behavior than most other groups of women she was used to seeing. She pointed to a hulking butch-type, cigarette dangling out of the corner of her mouth, who had been foul-mouthing the umpire. "I don't want to be like that," Janice said disdainfully. Her mother assured her she didn't have to be. In the ten years since then there has been no mention of homosexuality from Janice. Adele and Sadie have always been discreet and have been rather cagey about what friends they invite into their home. Other than the expected family quarrels, which erupt in heterosexual families too, there has been no friction with Janice. She is obviously fond of Sadie and respects her relationship with Adele. Janice is now in college, dates young men, and is obviously heterosexual in her own adjustment.

Del, as a mother, felt strongly about Janey's learning to analyze a situation and come to her own decisions, to think of her American heritage in terms of its original ideals of individualism, which have somehow turned into a tradition of coercion to conform. She recalls with a special fondness the time she and four-year-old Janey were on their way to visit grandma. Del suggested they skip down the hill.

"But mommies don't do that!" Janey exclaimed. But this mommy did, and from that time on, every time they came to that hill, mother and daughter skipped down it together.

Then there was the summer when Janey came to stay with us. She was fifteen. We asked her about college, but while she seemed genuinely interested, she was also very indecisive about the prospect. Janey was an excellent student and was going into her senior year at high school. We persisted.

"But dad says there's no use my going—it costs too much money—unless I know what I want to do, what I want to take up." Then Janey's voice broke. "And I don't know!"

While we both, in our college days, knew exactly what major we wanted to take, despite admonitions from our elders that it wasn't a field for women unless we wanted to teach—journalism, that is—we also remembered the many students groping their way along, changing their majors as their interests shifted or as they found the right focus for them. We pointed out to Janey that there was no urgency to decide fully on a major until her junior year, that the first two years provided a general background anyway.

"But dad says it's a waste of money to send a girl to college unless she's going to do something with her education," Janey added.

We thought differently. Here we were, two journalism majors, Phyllis working as a traffic manager for an import-export firm and Del keeping books for a trucking outfit. But neither of us would have traded the life experience, the broadening of our perspective, which could only come from our college education. We told Janey so.

"You'll have to make up your own mind," we told Janey, "but

know this: If you really want to go to college, we'll see that you get through."

A few days later we noted there were many things Janey was unable to make up her mind about. As with so many young people, apparently her heterosexual mother and father figures were also quite authoritarian in their approach to child rearing, making all the decisions. Phyllis, as another mother to Janey, expressed her concern to Del. We both felt the parents' role to be one of laying the groundwork, of molding and guiding the young person so that she would be prepared for life when she was on her own, when she would be forced to make decisions at every turn. So together we launched a campaign. We started forcing Janey to make decisions—what to have for dinner, where we should go on the weekend, or what movie to see. This didn't mean that she was in command for the summer and we her lowly subjects. It meant that she had a voice in group decisions, it meant she could express her preferences, it meant she was an integral part of our family unit with all the privileges—and all the responsibilities.

We had to admit that by the end of the summer Janey, in contrast to the mousy young thing she was when she first arrived, might be a bit much on her return to Jack. Del asked what form of punishment she generally received for her transgressions when she was at home.

"I usually get sent to my room," Janey replied.

"Well, here are some books." Del pulled a few volumes out of the bookcase. "You'd better stock up. I think it's going to be a long and sometimes lonely winter for you."

Children can even think mother is "groovy" or "cool." Phyllis groaned inwardly when another young student from State wandered into her office looking for source material for her term paper on homosexuality. "Oh, not another one!" she muttered impatiently to herself. "I just don't have time for it. She's probably going to tell me the paper was due yesterday and will want me to do the research she's been too lazy to do herself."

But this case was quite different. Phyllis didn't mind helping when her visitor offered the information, "You see, my mother's gay, and I think it's groovy. I'd like for other people to understand that. I think I'm heterosexual though. I really dig boys!"

When a partner has been introduced into the home, the Lesbian relationship itself does not always work out, of course. While the children may become very attached to the partner, the mother may become unattached. As in heterosexual divorces, such a separation can be very upsetting to the children. A child may find it extremely difficult to part with the partner who is not the true parent. When this happens, it is most helpful if the mother and her "ex" can remain friends.

Mary couldn't have been more devoted to Willie if he'd been her own son. She missed him terribly—as he did her—when she and Barb split up. But Barb harbored no ill feelings and was sensitive to the bond between Mary and Willie. So, like Barb's divorced husband, Mary, too, is allowed "visitation rights." She often takes Willie to the zoo or to the circus when it's in town.

Another fear the Lesbian mother must face is what will happen to her children if she should die. This was a very real and imminent problem for Jenny, who had a chronic heart ailment. She knew her days were numbered—one more attack, and that could be it. She brooded over what would happen to Kenneth, her ten-year-old son. She didn't want him taken over by his father's family or hers; neither of them was a prize. And she wanted Kenneth to have the best possible chance in life, as any mother would. She fretted over all the possibilities and decided that if Ericka, her lover of three years, was willing to take on the responsibility, that would be best all the way around.

Ericka was very attached to Kenneth. She regarded him as she would her own son, but she had many misgivings. There could be all sorts of trouble from both families, and she would be regarded as an outsider. What claim could she have really to Kenneth in the eyes of a judge who would ultimately make such a decision? It's relatives that count, not "friends." They consulted an attorney who drew up Jenny's will naming Ericka executrix and stipulating her as Kenneth's legal guardian.

What Jenny had prepared Kenneth and Ericka for came to pass—she died one night in her sleep. But her legacy, her fondest desire that Kenneth and Ericka continue on together in her absence, did not. A fierce court battle ensued involving both families. Ericka, distraught over Jenny's loss, was unable to bear up under the strain of heated accusations, self doubts, the nagging question of whether she could really manage Kenneth's education all by herself, and the continual harangue by those sitting in judgment that "every boy needs a man in the picture." She did manage to block the two immediate families, as Jenny had wished, however. Kenneth was turned over to a male cousin and his family, in whom Ericka had some measure of faith. This helped somewhat in the anguish she felt because she had been unable to accomplish Jenny's dying wish. But Jenny had asked too much.

There are other Lesbians who are not mothers, but who would like to be. Their desire for children does not override their Lesbian commitment, however. Some have experimented with artificial insemination. Others, like Delia, have deliberately picked out a likely father and allowed him to seduce her hoping she would become pregnant right off so that repeat performances would not be required. It is only recently that some Lesbians have been able to adopt children legally through privately arranged adoptions or under the "single parents" adoption program, although the adoption agencies are not aware that the women are Lesbians.

One couple, who had a definite butch-femme relationship in their youth, had wanted a child so badly that they made various attempts at artificial insemination without success. Many years later, when they were in their forties, they eagerly greeted us with the news that they had a baby. They had adopted the baby of an unwed mother in Lillian's family. By that time Bo, the butch, was less obvious as a Lesbian and more obvious as a successful businesswoman. The couple had a spacious home with a swimming pool outside the city. There would certainly be love and security in that home. We only hoped that their fondest dream did not come true too late in life, for Lesbians can be just as prone to spoiling children as heterosexual parents.

Judy, who had passed muster in her thirties and obtained a license to operate a foster home, legally adopted another Lesbian's son. So as not to encounter future difficulty with the natural mother, she and her Lesbian partner moved out of town. The adopted mother has a natural gift with children. She was a playground director and had always worked with youngsters. She has all the qualities of a good mother: humor, warmth and infinite patience.

Another Lesbian, a medical secretary, adopted a baby through the regular channels. She had no difficulty since she was Black, was adopting a minority child, and has an aunt living with her to care for the boy while she is at work.

A friend of ours, Craig, came back from a trip to San Diego. He'd spent a week with Claire and Marlene, who had taken over Claire's niece when her mother had died six months before. Craig couldn't get over it—the terrific change he'd witnessed in these two women. "To see them together you'd believe they'd always been a family. It's great for little Candy too!"

But what of those mothers who did not brave the divorce court, who chose rather to remain with their husbands "for the sake of the children?" A trim, matronly PTA-type told us, "I was brought up in a middle class family where there was no discussion at all about sex (let alone about homosexuality!). I thought I was the only one. I managed to suppress my homosexual tendencies, convinced myself I was 'in love' and married. But it wasn't 'me.' It wasn't my kind of life. Except that it *is*—I'm trapped in it. I have three lovely children. They're what makes it bearable. If I want to keep them, which I do, there is no other option open to me."

"As a Lesbian who 'passes' in the straight world," another mother told us, "I have had strong feelings both pro and con about the two-faced kind of existence that I have felt it necessary to live to date. And I wonder—if either of my daughters should find herself with my inclinations, have I left any guideposts? Have I left on the road a spark of hope, a ray of light to make the burden a little lighter or her adjustment less painful? Or will she be doomed to silence, as I have been?"

In another instance, after seventeen years as wife and mother, an Oregon woman indicated the only thing that had made possible her living so long with mask intact was her deep personal relationship with God. She was then praying to Him to give her the courage to make the break she should have made long ago.

Rita lived in Baltimore with her husband and four children. Charlotte lived in Washington, D.C. with her husband and three youngsters. Yet Rita and Charlotte were lovers. They managed to get away for a weekend together about two or three times a year. Somehow that had to sustain them. Neither one of them had any training or work skills, no way to support their families even if they had wanted to venture out on their own.

Then there was Mona. Her kids had grown up. She was free. And some twenty years later she looked up her "true love" hoping to take up where they had left off. She was too late. What "had been" had been.

"I found out only the innocent can be brave. At least I found myself backtracking, and it didn't make me very proud of myself," Ginger told us one day. Her story gave us insight, another slant on what it means to a woman and her children when she must remain silent, must repress all that is homosexual in herself, shying away from all reference to the dread subject which might give her away.

Ginger's daughter, Gwen, came downstairs one morning ready for school, and Ginger noticed she wasn't wearing her new blouse. She asked her why.

"I forgot today is Thursday," Gwen replied.

Ginger asked her what that had to do with it—already knowing the answer.

"Today is Fairy Day, so I can't wear green."

"Do you know what a fairy is?"

"Yes, that's a homo."

"Will wearing green make you a Lesbian?"

Gwen got the connection immediately. "No, but the kids would think so." She started to laugh. "The whole thing is pretty stupid, isn't it?"

About half an hour later, as she was getting ready to leave for the bus, Gwen stopped her mother again. "Isn't this what you've been teaching me not to do all these years—doing something just to be one of the crowd?"

Ginger answered, "Yes, it is."

"Then I think I'll go change."

"Do you—do you have time?" Ginger faltered.

Gwen glanced at the clock. "No, I guess not." She hurried off to catch the bus.

Later Ginger asked herself, "Was I right or wrong? Was I simply trying to protect my daughter from being hurt? Or was I protecting myself? I honestly don't know. But I do know this: had it been anything other than homosexuality I might have taken a different action, as I have often done in the past. I have tried to

teach Gwen to do her own thinking and come to her own decisions. But this time the seeking of an 'out' was immediate and
almost instinctive on my part."

Ginger frowned as she reached for the words. She was obviously
troubled by the incident, and she was searching for its meaning. "I
have tried to teach Gwen not to parrot anyone, but to think and
then decide for herself—until she hit this blind spot in her mother.
In all else I can be the champion, can't I? But not this."

"I don't have a black face," she went on, "so I believe, teach and
preach civil rights. I am not a Jew, so again I champion their cause.
I am not a commie, an alcoholic, a dope addict, an Indian, or
member of a minority group—except one. I live and believe and
work and try to pass on to my daughter a respect for all—all
except one, that is. That one has been one big blank in her life
because it has simply been non-existent in my life since the day I
married."

But Ginger smiled as she recalled Gwen's resolve to change, to
go ahead and wear her new green blouse on Sweet Thursday. "It
seems the teaching has carried over—transferred, so to speak. I
know I was proud of Gwen at the same time I myself felt shame
and guilt. She was the one willing to show courage, not I. But I
took that chance away from her because in her innocence she
didn't know her action might have a backlash and that her mother
was among those 'guilty.' I'll never know whether I was right or
wrong, will I? How simple (and uninteresting) it would be if everything was either black or white without the infinite number of
shades between."

Another wife and mother of fifteen years wrote us, "Daily I
watch and guide my two daughters as they are growing into
womanhood. Fear tears at my heart that some innocent situation
may imply that either one may have homosexual tendencies." We
would add that she is probably choking her daughters, repressing
their natural affection for their female peers and generally inhibiting their relationships with half the population.

Such mothers have swallowed, hook, line and sinker, society's
male-imposed dictum that the role of woman is to serve man as his
wife and mother of his children. They have been brainwashed into
believing heterosexuality is the only viable way of life, have never
accepted themselves, live in constant threat of exposure, and care-

fully steer their children into stereotyped sex roles. Obviously heterosexuality was not "easier" for them. Have they, as Lesbians, been happy in their self imposed traditional roles? With all their lies, with all the pretense and deceit, with all their fears and the guilt they heaped upon themselves, did they really lead constructive, fulfilling and satisfying lives? Or did they, in their eagerness to conform, end up full of bitterness, self pity and martyrdom? How sweet is their reward when the children grow up and leave home? The satisfaction that they did their best, gave what they could to maintain the status quo which bound and gagged them, which chained them to ill-fitting definitions of femininity and maternity, which stifled their individuality and which finally left them alone and bereft? For what? So they may watch their daughters and sons repeat their dismal stereotyped performances with their grandchildren? To keep the wheel turning which grinds women ever so slowly, but oh so definitely, into desert dust?

We cry for these women who pay homage to the great god They. We pity them for their slavery to the Jones family. We have shared their agonies, their anguish and their despair. We have been there too.

But many of us have ventured where they feared to step. Tentatively at first, yes. It was never easy, but neither was it easy for those women who remained trapped in their marriages. We knew that the subtle (and not so subtle) nuances that go on between ill-mated fathers and mothers do not escape children. Divorce—even at the risk of losing our children—in most instances was a far better alternative than staying together in a sham relationship. We had a lot to learn: about ourselves, about children and about other people. We had a lot to learn about honesty, how to withhold information and yet be as candid and open as possible. But one thing which we always knew and which sustained us was this: nothing can be as soul rewarding as being true to yourself, accepting yourself for what you are—a Lesbian—and leading your life, no matter what the obstacles or what other people may think, with the self confidence and conviction that you are a worthy human being in your own right.

Knowing this, how could we, as Lesbian mothers, possibly say that our children should be either heterosexual or homosexual? They must simply be themselves, whatever that is. Only they can know that. We can give them the tools that can provide them the courage to explore the journey of selfhood, as well as the stamina and support they may need to nurture and protect that self once it is identified. But only self acceptance opens the door to a new, enriching and fulfilling life.

Out of such concerns, expressed in a workshop at the Gay Women's West Coast Conference, evolved the Lesbian Mothers Union. A group of Lesbian mothers have joined together to eliminate the threat of losing their children and to alleviate the pain of their isolation. They offer each other help and support during those crisis periods when they must make decisions as to whether or not to remain in the "safety" of a heterosexual marriage or to strike out on their own, whether to give up their children or to fight for them, whether to hide their identity or to be open and honest. In their rap sessions Lesbian mothers question traditional concepts of raising children. Many reject the need for a father figure or male substitutes as role models for their young sons. They don't want their sons to grow up to be like their fathers or like most men in our society today. They want to raise a new breed of men who know that their manhood does not depend upon the subjugation of women.

Presently the Lesbian Mothers Union is working cooperatively with San Francisco's Family Service Agency to develop a program which would include a redefinition of what constitutes a family, confrontations between Lesbian mothers and the agency's counseling staff to assess the agency's clinical approaches to families headed by Lesbians, a research study to evaluate the quality of care and home life of the children of Lesbians, legal aid in obtaining expert witnesses for contested custody hearings involving Lesbian mothers, and a mass media campaign to educate the public about the realities of the Lesbian life style. The Lesbian Mothers Union also sought and received a promise of legal support from the National Organization for Women for a test case involving custody of children where the mother is a known Lesbian.

There is, at least and at last, some glimmer of hope, however slight, that society is ready to begin to deal with the problems Lesbian mothers face. But, as with any effort towards social change, it will require pioneering, some risk taking, a great deal of courage and dogged determination.

"Gay is Good" is more than a slogan. It signifies a way of life that need not and cannot be measured in heterosexual terms. Continued comparison is useless and serves no one. If our granddaughter should turn out to be a Lesbian or our grandson a homosexual, we would hope that Janey and Kevin would accept them as they are. There is every indication that they would.

When they were living in the Village, a married student housing complex near the university, Janey wrote an article for their monthly mimeographed magazine entitled "Thoughts on Homosexuality." Here is what she said:

"It all began during my first year at college, when someone in my family informed me that she was a Lesbian. How would you react to something like that? My reaction was shock and wonder. But as time went on I realized how unimportant to our relationship that fact was. She didn't suddenly become something twisted and evil. She is still the same wonderful person, and I love her.

"Since then I've learned a lot about homosexuals from this person and from people I've met through her. . . . The first, most obvious, thing I learned was that homosexuals do not fit society's stereotype. . . .

"Secondly, I've learned that some homosexuals, like some heterosexuals, have affair after affair after affair, while others find lasting love relationships that are no less than marriages. . . . If such true love is possible between two friends of the same sex as well as between those of opposite sexes, certainly it must be possible between lovers of the same sex. True love is a special relationship between human beings, and we are talking about human beings. . . .

"While I think there are some psychologically and emotionally healthy homosexuals, I wouldn't be surprised if there were a larger percentage of homosexuals who were neurotic or disturbed people than the percentage of heterosexuals who are neurotic or disturbed. Just think of the pressures these people are subjected to. Parents renounce their homosexual children, children renounce their homosexual parents, ministers and priests deny them any hope of salvation. . . .

"It must be awful to live your life in secret, fearful of exposure that might mean ostracism and loss of job. Homosexuality may not mean slavery in society, but it certainly does not mean freedom. But then, I'm a part of society, and I know that we're all human beings. What do you think?"

What *do* you think? Shouldn't society take into consideration that the Lesbian mother is a person—a person who may be deeply concerned and committed to the welfare of her children? Shouldn't court decisions as to the custody of her children be based upon her merits as a person rather than on her sexual preference? If, as it seems to be, society's interference in her relationship to her children is based solely on the expectation of whether or not her offspring will make a heterosexual adjustment, it must be remembered that Dr. Kaye and others from the helping professions have indicated it is extremely rare that a Lesbian mother will have homosexual children. It's the other way around: most homosexuals are spawned from heterosexual marriages.

It cannot be automatically assumed either that just because a father is a heterosexual he will be a good father any more than it can be assumed that all women will make good mothers. The ability to reproduce has nothing whatever to do with child-rearing. What is involved is the love, concern, responsibility and maturity of the parents, not whether that parent is heterosexual or homosexual. What is involved is that the children grow up to be whole persons—self reliant and self assured—not whether they are heterosexual or homosexual.

6. Growing Up Gay

"Please, don't just throw this away and forget me! I'm so thankful that it is real! DOB, I mean. A few hours ago I was almost afraid to look your address up in the phone book for fear that, since DOB is something I want to exist so very much, it would all be another lost hope. But, thank God, I found it to be true. You don't allow membership to anyone under twenty-one. *Why*? People like me who are floundering around trying to start a career and stay out of trouble are the ones who really need you. We're alone and it's all so very new and sometimes frightening. I'm sick and tired of loneliness. I want desperately to belong, not to some leather jacket group, but to DOB. How else can I retain my self respect and peace of mind simultaneously? If it is impossible to allow membership and participation to someone my age (nineteen), can you possibly let me subscribe to your publications? Please. . . ."

The above letter, from Tish, arrived at the DOB San Francisco office in 1965. It was only one of many received over the years from teenage Lesbians seeking some kind of stable group which would help them get their heads together. Unfortunately, Tish was right, DOB didn't accept members under twenty-one—in fact, at that time DOB as an organization was afraid to even speak to anyone under age. The twenty-one-year-old age limit, now dropped to eighteen by most homophile organizations, has to do with the fear of being charged with "contributing to the delinquency of a minor." As far as we can see, the "contributing" is mostly done by a callous society which fails to realize that sex is a reality for

most young people very early in their lives. Feelings, sexual orientation, fear and confusion start far before the magic age of
twenty-one. DOB/SF changed its policy and began to allow
women eighteen years and over to attend functions other than
those where liquor was served—but the women still can't become
members until they are twenty-one. Even eighteen isn't young
enough. Many need friendly counseling and a chance to identify
with a group much earlier.

Another nineteen-year-old wrote from Indianapolis: "Please
send me some literature about religion and Lesbianism. I'm not
sure what stand the Catholic Church takes. I know it condemns us
because we practice birth control. I want to be a good Catholic,
but I'm a Lesbian. Please help me." She had been lucky, for she
had spoken to a priest who had told her that God did not condemn her. But she knew, too, that he was only one priest and that
he didn't speak for all the others. She might have encountered a
priest who would have told her she was damned to hell: others we
have talked to have run into that kind.

"I really understand the point you were trying to make when
you said Lesbians are brought up as women, and they aren't
trained to be aggressive in the pursuit of a partner, in the way
young men are," wrote Hazel, also nineteen, from Phoenix,
Arizona, in response to the April, 1971 *Playboy* symposium on
homosexuality in which Phyllis was a panelist. "I know what you
meant. I am hung up on someone who is twenty-four. Maybe that
sounds far fetched, and you'll say she's too old for me. I really
care for her though. But I don't know how to let her know. You
just can't go up to a chick and say, 'Hey, are you gay?' So how
would one go about this?"

Hazel went on to say that she couldn't talk to her parents, and
that she had made an attempt to discuss her Lesbian feelings with
her physical education teacher. "I figured she was gay, too. But
when I followed her home after school one day, she gave me the
cold treatment after that. There's just no one to talk to. I hope I
didn't make a mistake by writing to you, too. It took a lot of
nerve out of me to write this letter."

Our concern about gay youth, although extending to the male,
has been primarily focused on the young Lesbian. We can identify

much more readily with a young woman's problems than with those of a young man, but in addition, the young Lesbian is truly more disadvantaged than the male. As a female and a homosexual she has two strikes against her from the start. Add youth for a third strike. If she happens to be of a racial or ethnic minority she has a fourth strike. The picture can look pretty dismal.

The young women themselves have pointed out the problems as they see them:

"I don't know where to meet Lesbians. I know there are bars, but I'm too young. Besides, I don't think I would want to go to a bar."

"I'd like to have more friends—there are some groovy girls at school—but they keep talking about boys and dates. I feel awkward. I don't fit in."

"Lee and I are fortunate, we have each other. But we can't be open about it, we can't go to the school dances as a couple."

"When I read *The Well of Loneliness* in high school I knew I was a Lesbian," said Pam. "I didn't dig the idea of acting and dressing like a man, though, and I didn't want a girl who did. But I thought that was where it was at. It would have been a fantastic help to have known some Lesbian couples not caught up in the butch-femme thing. I went through four years of shit before I got things straight in my head, thanks to Gay Women's Liberation."

Pam, who was now in college, had indeed had a hard time of it. She had dated, and had sex with boys in high school, but had been more strongly attracted to girls. Her parents, caught up in their own concerns, paid scant attention to her and gave her little sense of love and affection. In her search for love she placed an ad in an underground paper—and received an astonishing number of answers. "All of the women who replied were heterosexually married and they were only interested in sex relations," Pam said. "I asked them, don't you want anything more? The answer was always no."

Then Pam discovered some other Lesbians, a group much involved in the heterosexual role playing. She was seeking a monogamous relationship and love: "If I had to be a butch or a femme to fit in, I decided, I'll do it!" She "fell in love" with a slightly older, much more experienced and very butch woman. As she played the role, Pam pointed out, "I became extremely passive and masochistic. I idolized her. She could do anything she wanted with me." When that affair ended, Pam drifted into another, with a woman of similar traits, and continued almost as if nothing had changed. Then the two began going to Gay Liberation dances where they met other Lesbians. From there it was only a short skip into Gay Women's Liberation and the beginning of a painful process of self re-evaluation.

"People kept asking me, 'Why are you playing roles?' and I didn't have a very good answer." In the process of finding an answer Pam broke up with the woman she was living with and has since kept herself relatively unentangled. "I think I want to settle down with one woman some time," she says, "but there is no hurry. In the meantime, I want to meet as many people as possible and really get myself together. When I do meet the right person, I want it to be for keeps."

Claudia and Lisa had been lovers and constant companions throughout their high school career. When their parents bugged them about dating, they found two male homosexual lovers and the four double-dated—to the delight of the parents. The arrangement worked out well, and between the two young women there was very little role playing. "We didn't feel guilty about us," Lisa said, "but we did about our parents. We were afraid of hurting them. And we had to play games constantly so they wouldn't find out."

Claudia graduated from high school a year ahead of Lisa and went off to college. She and Lisa saw each other on weekends and holidays and all was going smoothly until Lisa's mother found a cache of letters that Claudia had written. The confrontation was fierce, although the "culprits" denied all implications of Lesbianism. They hoped by so doing that they would still be able to see each other. But the parents scotched that—they were forbidden to meet and had to do so on the sly.

They managed, always with great effort, to get together occasionally, but the added pressure on a relationship already overburdened with secrecy was too much. Lisa vowed she would come to Claudia when she turned eighteen. However, she still lives at home with her parents, although she is now almost nineteen. "When I talk to my parents, you can just see them turn off," she says despairingly, "but if I leave home, I won't be able to afford college. And it would hurt them so. . . ." The parental power, coupled with society's disapproval, imprisons young Lesbians as efficiently as would iron bars.

Tish, tall and attractive, came to see us after writing DOB. She was delighted to meet some "settled" Lesbians and impressed with the length of time we had been living together. We all enjoyed her visits, but it was clear that we were of another generation. She was looking for someone to go to the beach with, to dance with, to do zany things with. We didn't quite make the grade as exciting companions to someone nineteen.

Because of her need to be a part of a group and to be with people of her own age she gravitated to San Francisco's Tenderloin, an area north of Market Street inhabited by social outcasts and rejects of many kinds: the old, the poor, the prostitute, the pimp, the hustler and the homosexual. The latter are usually young and, in most cases, profoundly mixed up. It certainly isn't the best place for a young woman to be prowling around. But Tish met friends there, young people like herself. She also discovered pot and pills and a whole seamy side of life she hadn't known about. The newness was exciting and so was the danger, the lawbreaking. All the rules she had known went by the board. Why sleep when you could always take "speed" to stay awake?

Tish had enrolled in San Francisco City College, but her long, late hours and increasing use of drugs soon made her a virtual dropout. Before we lost track of her completely we had invited her to a meeting of the Board of Directors of the Council on Religion and the Homosexual. For a long time we had been concerned about the underage Lesbian and homosexual, and it seemed that the newly-founded CRH was the ideal vehicle to start something: the clergymen involved could lend an aura of respectability and any upset parents could be referred to them.

Tish made an impassioned plea to the board, spelling out all the compelling reasons for some kind of youth program. The Board, all male except for us, listened agitatedly. After she finished and we had made a motion to start a gay rap group for teenagers, the discussion began. For the most part the clergy sat silently while the male homosexuals castigated us for bringing someone underage to the meeting and went through all the tired old reasons why CRH couldn't dare deal with anyone under twenty-one. Needless to say, our motion was defeated—and so were we. It has been of no help to Tish that some three years later CRH did away entirely with any age restriction on membership and in 1970 began a rap group for teenage Lesbians under the tutelage of Dianne, a twenty-seven-year-old gay teacher with a powerful commitment to individual freedom, especially for women.

In the meantime, we had gotten acquainted with Nancy, also nineteen, through DOB. She had been devoted to her mother and had been absolutely shattered when she died. A shy person of average intelligence, she was fearful of people, unsure of her own ability, afraid to speak up lest she make some sort of mistake, positive that anything she did would be wrong.

At a CRH meeting one evening we introduced Nancy to Nadine, another nineteen-year-old. Nadine, it appeared, was Nancy's opposite. Poised, well-spoken and seemingly sure of herself, she had a fresh innocence about her that was most appealing. When the two young women left together after the meeting, we grinned fatuously at each other—we had done a good thing! And so it appeared. The two girls were inseparable and Nadine had helped the person within Nancy to come out. Nancy left her sister's home in Oakland and moved into the house where Nadine lived with an assorted group of young people.

However, the assortment was a bit too much for Nancy, as all the young people in the house were heavily into the drug scene. Nancy enjoyed pot, but the use of other drugs frightened her. She eventually moved out, back into her sister's home, and back into the shell from which she was beginning to emerge. When she reached twenty-one, she joined DOB and slowly has been working her way into an awareness and acceptance of herself and her potential as a person.

We recall the anguish on the faces of the sixteen-year-old Catholic girl and her friend as they related how they had been thrown out of their parochial high school in Los Angeles.

"I guess," Mary said, "someone had ratted on us. Tess and I were in the cloakroom alone. . . ."

"We thought," Tess chimed in.

"Yeah—all I did was kiss Tess on the cheek," she continued. "Then the sister was there and she dragged us both into the principal's office—she slapped us and called us dirty perverts. . . ." Mary's voice broke.

The nuns held a trial (more like an inquisition) with both girls, their parents, the school hierarchy and the six-member student council present. The entire proceedings were taped. Both girls "confessed." They were expelled from the school and advised that should they apply to any other school a copy of the tape would be sent with their transcripts.

What was their recourse? Did they receive "due process"? Of course not—they received what most minors receive in this country, a kangaroo court based on the premise that you are guilty and there isn't a chance that you can prove otherwise. Both youngsters came from working class homes which were strictly Catholic. Their parents were dumbfounded by the events; they were embarrassed and chagrined; they did not stand up for their daughters; they believed their church could do no wrong.

When Mary and Tess, after recovering somewhat from the shock, did try to enroll in another high school, one designed for those who have dropped out and want to return, they found that the nuns were as good as their word. "We can't have anyone like you in this school," the registrar said primly. What happens now to two sixteen-year-olds whom society has forced to leave school?

On all sides the relationship of adults to teenagers is deplorable. Sex education, whether at home, in the school or in the church is a farce. Sex is not just biology and reproduction: it is emotions, sensations, pleasure and pain. When these feelings are at variance with the unimpassioned rules of the majority, it is almost a certainty that the young person involved can use someone to talk to, someone to help her sort out her anxieties and confusions and, most specifically, someone to reassure her that no matter which way she swings sexually she can live a happy and fulfilled life.

The teenage Lesbian should be able to find a group made up of young women in her own age range. She needs people with whom she can socialize, can discuss mutual problems and experiences, can have sex with if the occasion and desire occur. A sixteen-year-old Black, an extremely attractive, intelligent and sensitive person, wrote Phyllis: "I fear I must contact you when I'm in the city because I am depressed far too often . . . sorrows must be shared."

The attitude of Americans toward "children" (which includes everyone until they are twenty-one) is still totally unrealistic, although there have been some positive improvements in recent years as a result of the demands of youth. But the improvements have not been in the area of sex education, nor has it been in parents' understanding of or ability to communicate with their offspring.

In many cities, community-minded citizens have set up twenty-four-hour telephone answering services to receive calls from bewildered youths who feel they cannot communicate their problems to the adult world. Most of these SOS lines were motivated by concern about the drug scene in the youth culture. According to volunteers who answer the phones of Sacramento's "Youth Crisis Line," however, the preponderance of calls are cries for help in dealing with teenage pregnancy and homosexuality.

A typical call was that from a sixteen-year-old who said she was aware of her Lesbian feelings which she simply couldn't and wouldn't convey to her parents. "I tried to talk to my minister, but he said that was an 'unclean' word. He told me I shouldn't ever say it again—or even think it." There was a long pause. Her voice quivered as she continued, "But that's the way I feel, the way I am. I need to know more about it. I so desperately need to talk to someone who will understand and who will help me to understand." Her voice became more shrill, as she begged, "Please, please tell me. What can I do? Where can I go?"

Every one of us needs someone to talk to openly and honestly, to share ideas, dreams and hurts. The teenager who is not gay has her problems, too, but can usually share most of them with someone close to her. Not so the budding Lesbian, unless she is fortunate enough to find a friend like herself. But even then, there are two naive youngsters sharing their ignorance.

Most of our counseling with youth has been on a friendship basis—primarily listening, but also asking pertinent questions and answering their questions when we could. We know, either from our own experience or from that of others, what the youngster is going through. (We learned early that, even with the best intentions, young women rarely took our advice. Most young people still "learn by experience.") Not just teenagers, but older women, too, have sought us out and found it helpful to be able to talk to a Lesbian, to someone like themselves, who is able to be open and honest. As Alicia said several years after she had written Phyllis: "When I got Phyl's letter saying 'as a Lesbian I know what you are going through' it blew my mind. I knew then there was some hope that I could live honestly too."

One of the questions put to us over and over again as we have spoken to straight groups about homosexuality is, "If you had a young person right on the border line between homosexuality and heterosexuality, wouldn't you push her toward the latter?" Our answer has been and is, a resounding *NO*. We wouldn't push anyone in either direction. There has been far too much of pushing people into slots that they either didn't fit or weren't ready for. The decision has to come from the individual's own self knowledge.

For instance, whether Tess and Mary, the two young women thrown out of high school for supposed Lesbian activity, are truly Lesbians, has yet to be determined. But regardless, they will probably be Lesbians because they were pushed, marked, and stereotyped as Lesbians by those adults who most feared such a result. When speaking to groups, especially high school students, we try to emphasize that it is quite common to have schoolgirl crushes and that even having a Lesbian affair doesn't necessarily mean that you are a Lesbian. But we also point out that if you identify as a Lesbian (and a few probably will), it is important to realize you are still the person you were and should keep the same sense of values you had prior to your new-found discovery about yourself.

To many young women the family is a symbol of cultural oppression and of self destruction. Any real or fancied misdemeanor makes them vulnerable to parental indignation and to the withdrawal of their love and affection. "We live in a microscopic world bounded by two people, our parents," they point out. "As children we have no chance to argue, no chance to find options or alternative life styles to the nuclear family that our parents proclaim is so wonderful."

Madge spoke strongly about the way her family had prejudiced her against homosexuality, had made her aware of the stigma attached and had, in fact, indicated that sex was evil, even while giving lip service to the modern idea that sex is a good thing—in marriage. "It never entered my head that I was doing anything wrong," she said of her affair with Ellen, "until my parents laid on me a sense of guilt and shame and a sense of alienation—from them, from Ellen and from all of society."

In her search for some semblance of sanity, Madge went to a

social worker who recommended that she seek psychiatric help at the county hospital. But Madge found she couldn't get such help without her parents' permission, and she felt, "I'd rather die than have them know I'm queer."

Del remembers all too well what it means to be a teenager, and, later, the crisis years of her twenties after she left home. She scoffs at those people who say, "I'd give anything to be young again." Of course, they always add, "and know what I know now." But you can never "know" what everyone must learn through pleasure-pain experience. Though we learned that all too often mom and dad were right about a lot of things, we also know they were wrong about a lot of other things.

At ten Del declared ever so emphatically, "I'm never going to get married." She was reminded of this statement by the mother of one of her childhood girl friends, when, at eighteen she announced her engagement to Jack. While it is true Del's parents didn't pressure her towards marriage (as a matter of fact, her mother tried to dissuade her on the grounds she was too young and the fear she would not finish college—which she didn't), all her girl friends were either engaged or already married. Pressure from one's peers, especially when you are young, is difficult to withstand. Most of the young women Del associated with, however, were older than she, since she had skipped a couple of grades during grammar school.

The young people of today probably never heard of games like "post office" or "spin the bottle." They're much too sophisticated these days for that. But these adolescent games, designed for experimental kissing between opposite sexes, could be extremely embarrassing for a reluctant Lesbian. And at the George Washington High School dances, Del would have much preferred to join the line of boys who wanted to dance with Lana Turner (she was called by her given name, Judy, then).

In those days there were no options for the teenage Lesbian. Even now they are extremely limited—and not very good. As Madge learned, unless you are twenty-one, or can prove you are an emancipated woman, i.e., living alone and supporting yourself, you cannot get any kind of therapy, counseling or medical attention without your parents' permission. One youngster, from a middle class Chinese family, was referred to Phyllis by Suicide

Prevention. She had been to literally every psychiatric clinic in San Francisco but, like Madge, was adamant that she wouldn't seek her parents' permission for fear they would find out what she feared: that she was gay. As a result she never did get any professional help and, as she got older, left home and drifted into the hippie scene, seeking her self through the psychedelic subculture.

Attempts to talk to parents, to reason with them, to make them understand are fraught with many dangers. Whether to tell one's family or not has always been a problem for the Lesbian. Today, with so many in the gay liberation movement advocating total openness, it is even more difficult to make the decision. If you are a teenager and you keep hearing older (and presumably wiser) homosexuals shouting, "Tell your parents, tell your boss, tell the world—don't be ashamed!" the pressure can be fierce. Unfortunately there is no general rule about telling; each case is different. So many variables exist: the relationship between the parents and between them and their daughter; the family's religious background; the parents' attitudes toward sex—the list could go on and on. Discussion with older Lesbians and with her peers can be vital to a young woman as she tries to get herself together and resolve this difficult dilemma.

Many families openly fight Lesbian relationships. At sixteen, Maureen was whisked off to a psychiatrist when her wealthy parents discovered her high school "romance" with Sam. They had been worried about her because she talked of Sam constantly, but she had never brought him home to meet them. When they accidently learned that Sam was short for Samantha, they knew why. They were hysterical. Such a state of affairs in *their* family was intolerable. It was impossible that Sam could have such a hold on Maureen, for all her blubbering that they were " in love."

Maureen was confined to quarters. She was not allowed to go out; nor could she receive phone calls or mail. She was sent off to another school out of state just as soon as it could be arranged. But Maureen kept running away, kept returning to Greenwich Village in New York seeking word of Sam. The gay grapevine always worked. But whenever they found each other, so did the private detectives Maureen's family had hired. And they would be separated again. Finally, in desperation, Maureen's parents placed her in a sanitarium where she was to receive intensive and extensive care.

By the time she was eighteen Maureen made good her escape, never to return. She found Sam and they left New York, hitchhiking three thousand miles to California. During their stopovers in various cities they sought out the gay community which provided temporary shelter and food. They worked at odd jobs to carry them over the lean times in between. But they always seemed haunted and pressured to move on, to get as far away as they could from Maureen's imperious parents.

When Maureen and Sam finally found DOB, they were broke and hungry. We brought them home with us, and they stayed for a month—long enough to draw their first pay checks so they could finally have a "home" of their own. Sam found a job in a factory and Maureen a position in an office. But when they were just barely beginning to feel settled, off they fled again. Someone had been asking pointed questions, and they somehow knew Maureen's folks had picked up their trail again.

For a number of years after that we would hear occasionally from Maureen and Sam. But it was always the same story. They'd made several trips across this vast country of ours. They had little else than "each other" and an overpowering fear of discovery. They were everlasting vagabonds.

"It's something that's in your blood. It's your life. You can't get away from it," Ted Lewis, old time vaudeville entertainer, said of show business in a recent CBS interview. Lewis recalled how he kept running away time and again until his parents finally gave in to his burning desire to become a part of the theater. Parents of declared Lesbians might take heed.

The helping professions do not always "help." We've seen too many disastrous results from the prevailing parental pattern of shipping their daughters off to the psychiatrist when they discover they have Lesbian tendencies. Most psychiatrists know little about homosexuality and even less about Lesbians. Too often their advice is that this is only a phase, a case of mistaken identity, that the girl will get over it and live normally—as a wife and mother.

To most adult counselors, even the most enlightened ones, when teenagers come to them with problems relating to homo-

sexuality, it means an "identity crisis." They have accepted
Freud's thesis that most youngsters experience homosexual feelings until after puberty when these feelings shift to heterosexual
ones and that young Lesbians, in seeking their help, are still trying
to make this transition. Over how long a period of time do they
think this "after puberty" transition stretches? For most teenagers
we have encountered the identity crisis they face is not whether or
not they are Lesbians—they know that—but what to do about it.
The problems they face in a society geared solely for heterosexuals
relate primarily to how to meet other Lesbians and how to socialize.

Several years ago a sympathetic and understanding high school
counselor in one of San Francisco's ghetto high schools tele-
phoned Phyllis at work. "I've got a fifteen-year-old girl who is
having identity problems," she said. "Could you see her?"

"Sure," Phyllis replied. "Have her call me about the time. Can
you give me more information about her?"

"She is in my office now," the counselor said, "I'll put her on
the line."

The voice that came over the phone sounded young, scared,
sullen, and Black, but not confused about her identity. "If I come
down to see you, will I meet some people like me?"

Although the number of various counselors referring people to
homophile organizations is increasing, there is still a vast and unfortunate lack in understanding and knowledge by many. Lily's
experience was typical. She had come under the custody of Juvenile Court as a runaway and was being placed in a group home
situation. She only had a few more months to go before she was
eighteen and was being very careful that no one found out she was
a Lesbian. At the intake discussion the director, a rather austere
Black woman, explained the way the all-girl home operated. "We
don't have any homosexuals here," she said with a look of distaste,
"so you don't have to worry about that." Her few months in the
home, really a progressive place for juvenile "delinquents," were
sheer hell for Lily, as she struggled to get through individual and
group therapy without disclosing her homosexuality, always remembering the director's tone of voice as she mentioned "homosexuals."

Most institutions charged with dealing with juvenile girls are
totally lacking in any concept of caring about those of their flock

who are Lesbian. When discovered, such girls are isolated, placed in solitary as it were, and forbidden any contact with other girls. They are usually thrown into some kind of "mental health" treatment where all the emphasis 'is on "curing" their homosexuality rather than on the examination of other problems which are troubling them. Such conduct is extremely damaging to youngsters, whether they are gay or only think they are.

A really mixed up situation involving juvenile court in Sacramento had one of our gay friends, a social worker, almost climbing the walls. The cast of characters included:

Doris, a runaway from a totally repressive home situation.

Joyce, who was carrying on an affair with Doris.

Meredith, Joyce's partner of ten years.

Sally, our friend, a social worker, but not connected with the juvenile division.

Doris's problem was that she had to find a foster home for the next six months until she was eighteen, or else face being sent to the California Youth Authority as an incorrigible runaway until she was twenty. She had been in a group home, but had run away from it (for one day's time) after a derogatory discussion of "queers" had taken place. Her probation officer was unaware that she was a Lesbian, and that fact did not enter into the decision of what to do with Doris.

Joyce, very aware of the problems involved, and concerned about Doris, called Sally, whom she knew slightly, and asked her help. Sally, who had gained a well-deserved reputation among Sacramento's younger Lesbian community as a sympathetic and skillful counselor, agreed to do what she could. Doris came to see her, and in the interview expressed her doubts about her relationship with Joyce, especially since Meredith was acting more and more depressed and upset over the whole situation.

Sally checked all her sources, but was unable to come up immediately with a foster home. She continued her counseling with Doris who was becoming most agitated over not only the situation about the foster home, but also over her connection with Joyce. Joyce had told her that their affair was known to Meredith, but that it didn't matter to her. Doris was not so sure—her observations indicated otherwise. She wanted out, but yet she didn't. Sally's conversations with Joyce were most unsatisfactory; Joyce denied any problem with Meredith and said she couldn't bear the thought of breaking off with Doris.

Sally was beginning to lose patience with Joyce, and when Meredith attempted suicide with an overdose of pills, she really blew up.

"If you two don't get some professional help," she told Joyce, "I'm going to get out of this whole mess. You're old enough to know better. And this intrigue certainly isn't helping Doris any." Joyce agreed, but although she and Meredith did make some effort toward finding a counselor, it wasn't a very serious one.

Doris's probation officer found her a temporary foster home and things settled down for a bit. But Doris was still seeing Joyce constantly, even though she kept telling Sally she wanted to slow the affair down.

"If I could only level with Doris's probation officer," Sally said to us one night. "I really think it would be best all around if Doris was sent away from Sacramento. But my hands are tied—I can't level with the probation officer because I don't know what her reaction would be to knowing Doris is gay. She might be one of those who would ship her off to the Youth Authority. And that sure wouldn't help Doris."

It would indeed have been easier for all if Sally could have explained to Doris's probation officer why she thought Doris should have been placed out of town. It ended with Doris being placed in a permanent home and finally telling Joyce she didn't want to see her any more. Joyce flipped and created a scene, almost getting Doris thrown out of the foster home. Then Joyce attempted suicide and was committed involuntarily. She was later released on the condition that she get additional psychiatric help. Meredith finally joined in the counseling sessions.

Almost all of the trauma could have been avoided if the people involved could have been honest about their Lesbianism at the beginning. Young Lesbians—and older ones, too, for that matter—often need help because of their emotional entanglements, just as heterosexuals do. That they do not often seek or obtain counseling is due only partly to their fear of exposure. There is also the underlying apprehension that their actions and emotions will be prejudged when labeled Lesbian. They feel that their problems are not unlike those other people face and should be treated in the same manner. Consequently, homosexuals, when they do seek help, usually try to find gay counselors with whom they can identify.

In the "helping" professions—doctors, psychiatrists, psychologists, social workers, clergy, etc.—there are many homosexuals. But they are not generally free to say to a client "I'm gay, too." Though it would be of immeasurable help to the client, it might just bounce the therapist out of a job. Most such professions are licensed by the state and the license can be taken away on the grounds of moral turpitude if homosexuality is indicated. This creates a waste of talent, for homosexuals trained in therapeutic practices could not only be of much more assistance to their gay clients if they could be open about their own life style, but would be fine consultants for heterosexual therapists who usually know little about the problems confronting gay people. In addition, homophile counselors have usually struggled with heterosexual problems (since they were brought up in that system), while straight counselors may have never wrestled with homosexual problems. Yet a Lesbian psychologist told us she would lose her straight clientele if it were known she was gay because people would automatically assume she couldn't understand her heterosexual patients.

Heterosexuals often have difficulty in understanding our claim that homosexual counselors can deal successfully with heterosexual clients, but that the reverse isn't necessarily true. There are several reasons: homosexuals are exposed all their lives to the heterosexual life style and its concomitant problems; most of their professional training is in these areas; and homosexual counselors are not biased against heterosexuality and would not be disposed to prejudge their clients. While more enlightened heterosexual therapists do not feel it imperative that homosexuals change their sexual orientation and do encourage their clients to adjust to their homosexuality, their approach is still, more often than not, judgmental or patronizing. The implication is that homosexuality is an unfortunate substitute for heterosexuality and that the homosexual must make the best of his "affliction."

In all our years of working with Lesbians we have found that those women who were unwillingly placed in therapy by hysterical parents have been the most hostile and the most mixed up. It has taken them literally years to sort out the confusion that incompetent and unknowledgeable counselors have created. Many have run away from home to escape the pressures built up by the therapy sessions and the attitudes of their well-meaning parents. Others, in order to put an end to therapy, have learned to play the game—they lie and pretend change, telling parents and therapists "what they want to hear." Mothers and fathers who are contemplating such a move would profit by taking the time to explore what it would mean to them to try to change their own heterosexual orientation.

Most authorities in the field of child behavior are agreed that the sexual pattern of a person is set somewhere between the ages of two and eight. Once set, the probabilty of total change is practically nil. It seems to us that one of the most harmful things parents can do to their daughter is to drag her through an endless series of encounters with psychiatrists, doctors or clergymen, most of whom know nothing about homosexuality, little about how young persons think and feel, and in addition hold the traditional male chauvinist views about the role of women.

As we have reread Ann Aldrich's books of the fifties we have been struck anew by her sense of defeatism, her use of the words "abnormal," "perverse," "neurotic." When they were first published, these books brought a ray of light into many a Lesbian's life, but they also reinforced the idea that, although you could manage to struggle through life as a Lesbian, it was an inferior and much less desirable way of life than heterosexuality, than husbands and children. The majority of young people we are in contact with today do not buy this concept. They feel that it is not possible to segregate persons by their sexual activities, that the worth of a person comes through doing, not being. To which we can only say, Right on!

Much of the "literature" about the Lesbian presents her as sort of a super lovemaker, one whom no woman can resist. She is shown in a series of seductions, usually of much younger women. More usually the "seductions" are similar to the one described below by Naomi, now married and a mother:

"All memories of Sarah and the sporadic contacts by mail have always been tinged by guilt on my part even though she married and now has three children. I knew her when I was eighteen and nineteen and already at the university. She was still in high school, and she came to the summer camp where I was a counselor. She was (and is) quiet, shy, deep, intelligent and had a crush on me, her counselor. I found her attractive and took advantage of the crush. Only lack of knowledge on my part prevented me from doing things that I would have felt even guiltier about later. The next school year I learned the term for what I almost 'did' to Sarah; the book called it 'bringing out.' "

But attitudes are slowly changing. Today's young women have much more going for them than their sisters in other generations had. They are more sophisticated and knowledgeable about sex in general, and the subject of Lesbianism and homosexuality has been much in the news. Although the various gay liberation groups around the country differ in method, politics, secondary goals and strategy, they have one thing in common: unlike many of their older sisters and brothers they are not ashamed of their homosexuality. Gay is good, gay is proud. This attitude certainly has beneficial results for young men and women today as they seek to establish their personal and sexual identity.

Not all young women have problems when they realize their sexuality is aimed at girls. Many slide smoothly through life, backed up by understanding parents, or by an optimistic view of life or by good fortune in the other Lesbians they come into contact with. Annette recalls how the awareness of her sexuality literally burst upon her and her family some years ago when she was seventeen.

"I had been fascinated for two years with an 'older' woman, Marge, who was a year ahead of me in high school," she said. "I had played all kinds of games to get her to notice me—and finally all my efforts worked. She asked me on Tuesday to go to the movies with her on Friday night. And, of course, I said yes! I was so excited I couldn't wait to get home after school. As soon as I hit the house I told my mother about my 'date.'

" 'That's nice, dear,' mother said, looking puzzled. I don't think she quite knew what to make of it. I was so overwhelmed I really didn't notice her reaction. Then I told Tom, my older brother.

" 'But she's a girl.'

" 'So what?' I bounced away, leaving him open-mouthed.

"I told dad the minute he arrived home from work and left him totally perplexed too. Aunt Rose was there for dinner and, as I bubbled throughout the meal about Marge—how smart she was, how pretty, how good in debating and athletics—I found my aunt watching me quizzically. I later found out about the conversation she and mom and dad had had after I'd gone upstairs to study.

" 'What in the world has come over Annette?' dad had asked. 'Why should she get so excited over going to a movie with a girl friend?'

" 'It is just a case of school girl worship,' mom thought. 'Marge is older than she.'

"But Aunt Rose was not so sure. 'Haven't you doting parents ever noticed Ann's lack of interest in boys and her evident interest in girls?'

"It seems they had," Annette added, "but they really hadn't thought about what these things might mean. As a matter of fact, neither had I. But Aunt Rose proceeded to enlighten mom and dad and then later, me. It worked out well—a total understanding between all of us and never any feelings that I was doing anything wrong or bad. I sure have a lot to thank Aunt Rose for. Also Marge, for it seems my instincts were correct. We became lovers for a while until she went off to college. We're still in touch with each other, though only on a friendly basis."

As we indicated earlier, the "experts" are in sharp disagreement about the causes of homosexuality. Peter and Barbara Wyden, in their book *Growing Up Straight,* have also noted this and have taken the position (as we have) that resolution of these opposing views is impossible at present, and, at any rate, unnecessary to their purposes. Their concern, however, is with the prevention of homosexuality, which necessarily implies a cause-and-effect relationship. Our concern is with those young women whose identity as a Lesbian is already clearly established—with what happens to them and how they manage their lives. Implicit in this concern, of course, is our belief that Lesbianism is, and must be accepted as, one facet on the continuum scale of human sexual expression and that a Lesbian relationship is, and must be accepted as, a viable life style.

The Wydens, despite their protestations to the contrary, have had to accept certain psychological theories as a premise for the preventive measures they advocate. In their message to apprehensive parents they say that Lesbianism is almost impossible to detect in pre-adolescence. "Tomboyish" characteristics, unlike "sissy" behavior in boys, cannot be considered grounds for suspicion.. Since all girls tend to enter into deep friendships with other girls, especially in adolescence, even this cannot be considered a conclusive factor. Evidence that a girl is not accepting her "femininity" is the only real signpost that a daughter may be moving towards a Lesbian identification, the Wydens conclude. They cite these clues to the wary parent: a girl wanting to be a boy, her mother's refusal to dress her in attractively girlish clothes, her refusal to play with dolls, her fear of normal contacts with boys and her revulsion to physical contacts with boys at the dating age. The budding Lesbian would also tend to be a loner and would have intense crushes on another girl, a teacher or some other older woman.

The Wydens stress that parents must and do act as models of behavior for their children. They say that the mother's acceptance of her role as a truly feminine woman will communicate itself to a daughter. On the other hand, if parents are unsure what constitutes appropriate male or female behavior or are competitive, their children are bound to be confused. How parents behave together, displays of affection between them and sharing of activities, also affect their offspring. But one word of caution: togetherness does not mean sameness. In sexually normal homes the definition of *"la grande difference"* is taught naturally and early. Girls get dolls and help mother in the kitchen. Boys don't cry and help daddy mow the lawn.

This sort of drivel is precisely what women are protesting today: rigid role definition and the fact that femininity is defined by a woman's place in the kitchen or bedroom. While the Wydens applaud equality for women, they are disturbed by the increasing competitiveness of the female, who, they claim, weakens the masculinity of her husband and sons. They give credit to Dr. Marvin H. Hurwitz of the Downstate Medical Center, State University of New York, for this additional observation: "In adolescence a girl must make her peace with her fears of passive and masochistic wishes whose fulfillment are vital elements of femininity." In *Growing Up Straight* a woman's femininity would appear to be reduced to her ability to complement the male by dressing so as to be sexually attractive to him, by catering to all his needs while passively and masochistically subjugating her own, and by training her daughters to accept this same preconceived, culturally-and-biologically-destined female sex role. If there is any correlation between the model behavior parents are told to emulate and the incidence of homosexuality, it has to be the oversell of stultifying, self sacrificing female sex roles that might cause a girl child to rebel and seek her personhood in a Lesbian relationship. The heterosexual relationships she sees in her family and in those of friends are not as complementary nor as complimentary as her elders would have her believe—even in the most "ideal" cases advocated by psychoanalysts.

Perhaps this is best explained by the Radicalesbians, a collective in New York City, in their treatise *The Woman-Identified Woman*: "A Lesbian is the rage of all women condensed to the point of explosion. She is the woman who, after beginning at an extremely early age, acts in accordance with her inner compulsion to be a more complete and freer human being than her society—perhaps then, but certainly later—cares to allow her. These needs and actions, over a period of years, bring her into painful conflict with people, situations, the accepted way of thinking, feeling and behaving, until she is in a state of continual war with everything around her, and usually with herself. . . . To the extent that she cannot expel the heavy socialization that goes with being a female, she can never truly find peace with herself. . . . It is very difficult to realize and accept that being 'feminine' and being a whole person are irreconcilable. Only women can give to each other a new sense of self . . . a new consciousness of and with each other which is at the heart of women's liberation, and the basis for the cultural revolution."

This does not mean that Lesbians reject their femininity or are unhappy with being women, as the Wydens suggest. It means that they reject male definitions of what it means to be a woman and are unhappy with their "assigned roles." It means they rebel against a dehumanizing society which denies them any opportunity for self realization. Most Lesbians neither hate men nor fear them in the sense that psychologists theorize. What they abhor is the game playing, the lack of sensitivity by men towards women, and the feeling of being trapped in a make-believe world. They recognize that men, too, are victims of the false values of the

system. For the heterosexual models, He-Man (aggressor and pro-
tector) and She-Woman (passive and protected), which the
Wydens wish to perpetuate, are the stereotypes from the Stone
Age. They are ill-fitting roles for the twentieth century. Lesbians
as little girls sense this. They know there has to be something more
in life for them than the housewife-mother routine. Some see the
man as "top dog" in a lopsided male-female relationship, and in
their confusion they try to mimic the male for a while. Others
know instinctively that it is only through relationships with
women that they can come to understand what it means to be a
woman. In the process they do not reject their femininity—they
affirm it.

Because of his wide experience in sex research and his broad
acquaintance with the homophile community, we expected a more
positive and less traditional statement from Dr. Wardell Pomeroy
in his highly touted manual *Girls & Sex*. While he is careful not to
moralize or condemn exclusively female relationships, he strongly
suggests that women choose this direction for the wrong reason,
because of a rejection of males rather than an acceptance of
females. He also warns that "by taking this sexual path, a girl is
sentencing herself to live in the shadow of society's disapproval
and is closing the door to marriage and children." While Pomeroy
acknowledges that Lesbian relationships "can be as pleasurable, as
deep and as worthwhile as relationships with males," he concludes
that girls need to think long and hard before going against society,
which has such strong taboos against homosexuality. His book,
like all the others, is geared for the predominant heterosexual
society. Still caught in society's prohibition against the possibility
of nudging any of our young, even ever so slightly, towards a
homosexual orientation, Pomeroy's book on sex for young girls
offers little message or comfort for the teenage Lesbian or her
parents. Additionally, the book is sexist. Pomeroy still expects a
women to be "ladylike" in all outward appearances, but a "broad"
in bed. "It is important for girls to understand this dual nature of
their lives as soon as possible."

From our experience we can say positively that parents of Lesbians should *not*: throw their daughter out of the house or disown
her; scold, nag, weep, wail and recriminate; withdraw their affection; pretend her Lesbianism doesn't exist; force her to cut off her

relationship with another woman; or pressure her into marriage with the hope "it" will disappear. Withholding information and reading material about homosexuality from a teenager will not thwart her identification as a Lesbian if it is there. It can only be a delaying tactic. She'll find other ways of obtaining Lesbian literature, and it would be far better if she could share her search for knowledge in this area with her parents instead of having to be secretive about it. Two instances come to mind where DOB's magazine *The Ladder* got into the hands of persons under twenty-one. A father called the DOB office one day asking that we cease sending the magazine to his daughter in college. He was kind enough to say she had probably falsified her age, but he was adamant that she should not receive this kind of literature.

In the second case we received a letter from an obviously irate mother in Wisconsin threatening to kill Del (who was the editor at that time) if we didn't take her daughter, Mary, off the mailing list. The only trouble with that letter was that she didn't give us a name or address. We did look to see if we had anyone named Mary in Wisconsin, but were never successful in finding anything. We did not hear from the woman again.

What can parents *do*?

If the parents of daughters with a homosexual orientation want them to be happy, creative and contributing members of society, they will have to think carefully about their attitudes toward homosexuality and toward their daughters. They will also have to work actively on whatever level they can to change the laws and attitudes of society which make of the Lesbian a second-class citizen.

Young people who are new parents or who will be parents in the future need to work toward bringing their children up in an atmosphere of mutual trust, respect and love. They can raise their children without stereotyping them in sex roles, so that those children know they are individuals who can strive for any goal. They can be open about sex in all its variations, letting their daughters know there are many life styles for her to choose from and that all are equally valid. Knowledge is the great destroyer of fear. They must establish a rapport with their daughter from the very beginning so that, if she discovers she is a Lesbian, the entire family can work together to help her find a way to fulfill her destiny with the least possible trauma.

If it is too late for you to follow the steps outlined above, if there is no closeness nor understanding between you, and you find out a daughter is a Lesbian, *DON'T PANIC*. Just *listen*. In our society today so few people ever take time out to listen, to hear, to tune in on what the other person is saying or feeling. Listen carefully and non-judgmentally. Give your daughter a big hug, and tell her you understand, even if you don't completely. She is still your daughter, and if you loved her before you found out, you love her still. Tell her that.

Once you've gotten over the shock—the realization that it is your daughter and not someone else's who has identified as a Lesbian—then it is time to go more deeply into the subject. If you didn't react negatively to her confession and if you listened, chances are that you can still talk to her, you can yet establish communication, a mutual respect and rapport. She will need and want that more than ever before. Remember that whatever values you instilled in your daughter when she was a child are still hers. If you and she can remember that, there is no reason why she can't lead a fulfilling and responsible life as a Lesbian in spite of contrary prevailing public opinion.

As one father told us, "What I am just beginning to learn is that the most important thing I can do for my offspring is to let them 'spring off' in their own way, in their own time. I am also learning to be honest with myself. I am continually asking myself if these hands of mine, or these words of mine, that I place on them are really for purposes of nurture—or are they for control?"

Encourage and support your daughter, don't try to control her. Encourage her, too, especially if she is in high school, to socialize with a wide variety of persons of both sexes. Sometimes young women have a tendency to withdraw and become too introspective. Yet part of everyone's growing up is influenced by involvement with other people and in outside activities. Even though she may choose another young woman as her partner, she is still a part of the larger society. Her future depends upon her ability to get along with other people and to function in society. But that doesn't mean she must allow others to define her identity or the behavior that is appropriate for her. That must come from within her own being.

If she and you can't work it out together, if you need additional support, then try to find a competent, understanding counselor. Here we are in agreement with the authors of *Growing Up Straight.* Help from a counselor should be sought only *"after making certain that the counselor is, in fact, experienced with homosexual problems and has a sympathetic attitude toward homosexual patients."* (The words and italics are theirs, not ours.)

If you don't know of an experienced counselor, see if there is a homophile organization in your area and ask for a referral. Or ask at the medical school or psychology department of your local college or university. But be sure you make your requirements plain—that you want a counselor who can help you *understand* homosexuality, not one who is hung up on changing or curing homosexuals.

Above all, remember that the discovery of her sexual orientation has not changed your daughter. It has just added a new dimension to her life, and to yours.

7. Lesbian Paranoia —
Real & Imagined Fears

Fear, at some time or another, plays a big part in the life of every Lesbian. For the most part her fears are real; only rarely do they slip over into the realm of the imagined fear, of paranoia. These fears stem from the knowledge that for a woman to love another woman is at variance with society's expectations. Thus there is fear of public opinion and resulting ostracism. Fear of identification as a Lesbian leads to fear of ridicule, fear of rejection, fear of group association, fear of the homophile community, fear of police, fear of family, fear of forming friendships, fear of loneliness, fear of losing one's job or career, fear of loss of respect, fear of displaying affection, and, perhaps the greatest and most disastrous fear of all, fear of self acceptance. For self acceptance is the only weapon against fear, and even that is not enough. Most of these fears are well founded for, as members of an out-group, Lesbians are subject to reprisals from all quarters of society: friends, family, employers, police, government.

The idea that the Lesbian, as a woman, has fewer problems to face than the male homosexual is simply not true. She may not be as readily identifiable as the gay man—but she knows who or "what" she is, and until she is ready to accept herself as a human being, as a woman and as a Lesbian, she will always identify herself in society's terms: as something apart from the norm, perhaps even sick. Thus those women you see greeting each other with

kisses and hugs in public places are much more likely to be heterosexual than homosexual. Molly told us that, in accompanying
some women friends to a restaurant, one of them who was lame
took her arm. "She needed support, and it was a natural move for
her. But it was not natural for me. I learned when I was about
fourteen that one does not do this. I don't believe I have ever so
much as touched a woman in public since that age. So when Jane
took my arm I instinctively tightened up to withdraw, then looked
at her and slowly relaxed. But I was still self conscious."

She went on to say, "I've never learned either to give or receive,
either by verbal or physical contact, demonstrations of affection.
It has been all or nothing—either I gave completely to the three
women in my life or I gave nothing at all by way of verbal or
physical demonstrativeness."

Phyllis, who has always been a demonstratively affectionate person with a habit of touching people, confesses to a slightly different problem. "Occasionally," says she, "I feel self conscious
when I touch some of the women in the office. It isn't that I'm
afraid they'll think I'm a Lesbian—they know that. It is rather that
I'm afraid they will misunderstand, that they will think I am, like
a man, making a pass at them. But I try to suppress the hesitation—I wish more people could be physically as well as verbally
communicative. A pat on the hand or head can convey a lot when
words aren't adequate."

Molly's case is a fairly typical one where the struggle to lead a
dual life, to present a conforming heterosexual facade to the
public, stifles even the most innocent and natural movements of
friendship toward others. Putting on an act and constantly hiding
one's feelings often inhibits honest emotion, even with a loving
and understanding partner.

Many younger Lesbians today are refusing to accept the dual
life style. Like the woman in the Gay Pride Day parade in New
York who carried a sign reading "I'm a Lesbian and I'm Beautiful,"
they are beautiful in their uninhibited and natural approach to
life. "Why can't I walk hand in hand with my lover?" they ask.
"Why must we follow stricter rules than the straights do? Love is
love—if there were more of it the world wouldn't be such a mess."

Most Lesbians, however, have found their survival in leading a dual life. By day they are heterosexual, complete with imaginary boy friends; during evenings and weekends with homosexual friends, they "let their hair down," though they are still often apprehensive. It is true that it is accepted in our society that two women may live together as roommates. Since a woman is still paid so much less than a man, everyone recognizes that singly she could not afford to maintain as nice a household as she could by pooling her meager earnings with another woman's. Also, the thinking goes, the poor thing hasn't been able to catch a man and, since population figures show the demand is greater than the supply, she may never get a husband. Let her find another lonely woman and the two of them can make the best of their rejection. Somehow it is thought that the disparity between men and women in our society should really be a good cover for the Lesbian. It's a neat theory, but it doesn't work that way, because always the Lesbian knows her own true identity. She is self conscious and ever on the alert lest some word or gesture give her away. Sometimes she tries too hard.

One possible situation that most Lesbians dread, and why so many disdain those who "look the part," is the one chance encounter. You are walking down the street with your parents or some coworkers and you run into one of your Lesbian acquaintances. There you are, suddenly face to face with a friend you think is "obvious," and you can't afford to be exposed in present company. What do you do then? Do you look the other way and pretend you didn't see her?

We've made it a rule not to say or do anything by way of recognition of the Lesbian who is with people we don't know unless she gives us the cue—or unless, of course, we are in our "straight" street clothes. But even in these instances, when no one else could possibly know the difference, we note the discomfort displayed. The Lesbian in hiding is always self conscious, trapped in her own guilty knowledge and unable to interact with Lesbians naturally in a social situation.

When Elena came to DOB she was twenty-six, intelligent, attractive and had a pleasing, albeit nervous, personality. A former teacher who had dropped out, she had been working a series of secretarial jobs for which she was well qualified. There was

nothing about her appearance or behavior which fit the stereotyped image of the Lesbian. Yet she had been fired from job after
job because she was gay.

"I just can't understand it," she told us. "I am so careful. I
don't make friends with the other women—I'm friendly but not
too much—and I keep my private life to myself. Yet at one place a
woman accused me of making a pass at her! I hadn't done more
than say good morning. I'm beginning to feel paranoid," she
laughed, "as if someone is really out to get me. But I can't imagine·
who."

We couldn't imagine who either, and the best the three of us
could determine was that Elena had been so good at covering up
her private life that she had projected an impression of "difference," of "oddness" or "queerness" that had eventually led to the
conclusion that there was indeed something "wrong" with her and
since no other name for it was available it must be that she was
homosexual. This may have been it; at any rate, on her next job
she loosened up a bit and had no more trouble.

We are still haunted by remembrance of Kerry, a beautiful
young blonde who came to one of the early public meetings of the
Daughters of Bilitis. Despite all efforts to publicize the meetings
the attendance was primarily from the homophile community.
Kerry, shy and questioning, gave all the appearance of being a
misplaced heterosexual, to the point where a member remarked to
us, "Do you suppose she knows what sort of a group this is?"

It turned out she did. She was newly aware of her Lesbian
tendencies and was seeking more knowledge and an opportunity
to meet others like herself. It was the age-old story of the hunt for
"the one and only"—except she had conjured up some very precise
specifications: an older woman, a motherly type. And it appeared
that Del fitted the bill, if only as a counselor.

There were many long sessions with Kerry, who never seemed
to be able to hold down a job because her employers were always
suspecting her of being a Lesbian. Since there was nothing in her
appearance that would cause this, we reasoned with her that there
must be something she was saying or doing that provoked people
to suspect her, that she must be projecting this feeling by her
interrelations with the office personnel.

The problem persisted and she underwent psychotherapy, but

when her paranoia reached such proportions that she cried hysterically that *every* Yellow Cab driver in the city honked at her because they "knew" about her and people threw rocks against her
apartment window because she was a Lesbian, the psychiatrist
recommended that she commit herself. There followed a series of
sojourns in and out of Napa State Hospital. The last time we saw
Kerry it was hard to realize that she had ever been the sweet
young thing we'd first met. The shock treatments had taken their
toll. She didn't speak of her fears anymore. She was hardened. She
was now even more intensely and openly seeking another woman.
All she wanted from us was our help in finding that "older
woman, the motherly type" who would give her the love she
sought so desperately.

The fact is that Lesbians must work, and guarding their jobs is
what accounts for the bulk of their paranoid feelings. Yet, if it
could be made known to employers, they might just find that
Lesbians can be counted among their most reliable and responsible
employees. An article by Jo Harper in the April/May, 1969, issue
of *The Ladder* points up some of the reasons Lesbians may, and
often do, make better employees than their heterosexual counterparts. They have a single-minded attitude toward their careers because they know they must work—there is no husband in the
background on whom they can depend. Often, as the "single"
woman in an office, they are available for overtime or weekend
work where those with families can't spare the time. They can be
more flexible with relation to vacation schedules since they don't
have to go while the children are out of school. Lesbians usually
don't spend long periods on the telephone talking to their lovers,
nor do they spend time flirting with the girls in the office. A social
worker felt that her own (Lesbian) minority status helped her to
understand and relate to the minority persons she worked with,
and a teacher believed she was better able to handle cases of
adolescent same-sex crushes than were heterosexual teachers. And
finally, the article pointed out that most Lesbians, rather than
waiting for a man to come around to do the heavy work, would
move their typewriters or files themselves.

Most Lesbians are happily and productively working. In some
cases there is no intense fear of disclosure; in others the fear is
there as a nagging possibility. Some women realize that discovery

might well happen some time, and they lay plans for coping with the situation, should it occur. But others, who have not been able to surmount the big fear of self acceptance, have a deeper problem. If you have said to yourself "I am a Lesbian. I know and accept this as a part of me. Now I can go about the business of living," you obviously have a firm base from which to operate. But if you haven't been able to take the step—if you are playing games with yourself, if you fear the consequences of non-conformity in society, you are building a life on a foundation of quicksand.

Those most zealously guarding their reputations (though sometimes not too judiciously) are women who have attained some measure of professional status. Very few such women have offered their much needed services to homophile organizations. (Florence Conrad, DOB's research director for many years, is one of the rare exceptions.) Some root for us from the sidelines and make infrequent donations of time or money. Others damn us for bringing Lesbianism into the open, fearing that as the public becomes more aware people might take a second look at them. And, unfortunately, there are many whose attitude is "I've got it made. What can DOB offer me?"

Some of the more injudicious ones are rather funny. Phyllis recalls talking to a teacher one evening in one of San Francisco's wilder Lesbian bars (since closed). "I would love to join DOB," said the teacher, "but I simply couldn't. I'd be afraid of losing my career." How she could say this with a straight face while standing in this swinging bar (which we were sure was going to be raided at any moment) dressed in jeans and plaid shirt, defies understanding.

Recently Phyllis received a telephone call from a therapist who had finally come to the conclusion that she really ought to be doing something for her own people. "It occurred to me," said the voice over the phone, "that many gay women would like a Lesbian therapist. So I'm calling to volunteer." Phyllis was delighted. She had had two such requests for a Lesbian counselor in the past week which she had been unable to fill. She suggested the woman come over to the office the next day and talk with her about it.

That did it. Well, no, she wasn't prepared to meet with Phyllis. She thought she could just leave her telephone number for referrals. And, no, she wasn't about to reveal her name.

"But—" Phyllis sputtered, "how can we possibly make referrals to a therapist we don't even know? Even more important, how can I refer a scared Lesbian to a scared Lesbian therapist? Besides, as in any other profession there are good and bad therapists. Why, just today we had a similar offer from some marriage counselors, a husband and wife team, but, after talking with them and finding out what their attitudes really are toward homosexuals, I couldn't possibly recommend anyone to them."

"I see your point," said the anonymous therapist. She made an appointment to see Phyllis the next day, but did not show up.

Ever on the alert for anything which might put their livelihood in jeopardy, many Lesbians are fearful of identifying with the homophile community. While they may envy those who congregate in freedom and camaraderie, they shun homosexual groups lest they run into someone from work or connected with work. They still shy away, even when it is pointed out that, should they run into a fellow employee or professional colleague, the other person more than likely would only be there for the same reason that she is.

We have witnessed a number of occasions when someone, in the middle of a sentence, goes "Oops!" and starts running for cover. And then the laughter. "What are *you* doing here? I had no idea you were gay!" Such an encounter often relieves the tension at the office or marks the beginning of a new friendship. We have yet to hear of a case of disaster.

There are those Lesbians, however, who feel extremely threatened by other homosexuals who are employed by the same firm. A Lesbian may go out of her way to deny that she shares the others' propensity lest they unwittingly give her away. A Lesbian who has fought her way up to a management position despite discrimination against women may guard her post zealously. As a cover she may be extremely hard on those who work under her whom she suspects might be homosexual. She may even go to the extreme of spreading rumors about another employee in order to direct attention away from herself.

Sandy laughs when she recalls the time she was reported to her boss in Portland by a fellow employee as "nothing but a damned Lesbian."

"I knew that when I hired her," her boss replied. "She's a

damned good worker. I can depend on her. I don't have to worry about her getting married or pregnant. And, furthermore," he said to the accuser, "*you* are fired!"

Few Lesbians are self employed; most work *for* someone else. In one way or another then, they must learn to protect themselves from laws and social attitudes which could cause them to lose their jobs.

The fact still remains that, regardless of all the sanctions against them, Lesbians do seek jobs and are employed in all of the (to them) *verboten* fields of endeavor. They are employed in federal, state and city civil service. They are in professions requiring state licenses. They *are* playground directors, teachers, social workers, nurses, psychologists, librarians, doctors, attorneys, psychiatrists, probation officers, architects, accountants, engineers, diplomatic corpsmen.

Aileen, now working for her master's degree in social work at an eastern college, wrote us: "Before I started thinking of myself as a Lesbian, even though I was one, I never worried about being found out. As I look back on it, I've done all the things it is illegal for me to do! I've been a social worker, a teacher, and a worker in the Peace Corps—all three of which won't take Lesbians. Hah! It is indeed a strange world."

In the face of all the pressures brought to bear to discourage them, why do Lesbians persist in these vocational fields? Wouldn't they be better off in private industry? Or at least in some other line of endeavor?

For one reason, there's the money. These vocational fields are the best paid for women. Not all women are satisfied with mediocre jobs at mediocre pay. The two of us were satisfied, however, with such mediocre pay. It allowed us to carry on a voluntary, extra-curricular vocation. And, Phyllis's long years of learning in DOB have paid off in her present position as associate director of the National Sex Forum.

Most Lesbians who pursue careers in fields where they are not welcome are dedicated to their professions and make important and needed contributions to society. Many of them somehow still believe in our American society and the institutions which oppress them. They foresee social changes and want to be where the action is, and they still share the American dream, the ideals *you* instilled in them when they were youngsters.

Lesbians who are employed in civil service (whether federal, state or municipal) and who are professional persons who must be licensed by the state suffer a more acute fear of job loss than do Lesbians in private enterprise.

Nora, a psychiatric social worker, had been employed for six years in a Veterans Hospital in Colorado. One day she was told to report to the office. When she walked in, a tape recorder was going and the man behind the desk told her that anything she said might be used against her.

Nora was shocked. She couldn't understand what was happening to her, or why. No explanation was given, although later she discovered that someone had written a letter to a Congressman stating that Nora was a Lesbian. The investigator had been flown to Colorado from Washington, D.C., to check her out. She found that extensive snooping had already taken place, as the investigator queried her about her history. They already had a rundown of all the places she had lived for the past twenty years, who her woman friends were, who her roommates had been, statements from previous neighbors, landlords, etc.

Her interrogator mentioned that Nora's six-year work record was exemplary. "The only way you could possibly be dismissed," said he, "is if we can prove you are a Lesbian."

Nora, who managed a remarkable job of keeping her wits about her, denied the charge. When asked if she was a member of the Daughters of Bilitis she admitted knowing about DOB, but indicated she was not a member. She breathed a sigh of relief as she remembered that her subscription to *The Ladder* had lapsed some time ago and she had not yet renewed it.

As soon after the inquisition as she could manage she phoned us long distance to advise us of her predicament and ask that her name be removed from all mailing lists. She said that her fellow employees had rallied 'round and had sought help for her from the American Civil Liberties Union in the event the government decided to move against her. We reminded her, as we have done with other Lesbians in the professions, that information contained in *The Ladder* is quite relevant to a psychiatric social worker and need not be incriminating. (Many doctors, attorneys, nurses, teachers, psychologists, etc., who are not homosexual do subscribe to the magazine. DOB receives countless calls from clergy, psychiatrists and attorneys for information which will help them better serve the needs of their clients.) Nora survived the investigation, but she has since changed jobs and is no longer in civil service.

Others have not fared so well. Faced with the enormity of a federal investigation they melt in their tracks and make admissions that can be used against them. Some recognize they have neither the stamina nor the stomach for such a full scale onslaught and simply take the easy way out by resigning.

The federal government has been the greatest offender of all in discriminating against the homosexual in employment. While the general public is under the impression that exclusion of homosexuals from federal employment applies mainly to positions which require a security clearance, it has been the position of the U.S. Civil Service Commission that homosexuals are not suitable for appointment or retention in *any* federal post. The commission concedes that by itself, evidence showing a person has homosexual tendencies is insufficient to support a rating of unsuitability on the grounds of immoral conduct. Nevertheless, as one Civil Service Commission appeals examiner put it, "to require employees to work with persons who have committed acts that are repugnant to the established and accepted standards of decency and morality can only have a disrupting effect upon the morale and efficiency of any organization."

Where there is suspicion, as in Nora's case, the Commission launches thorough investigations—at a cost to the American taxpayer of some twelve million dollars per year—that might lead to proof that the individual has engaged in or solicited homosexual acts, whether or not these acts were conducted in private by consenting adults. The investigations have not stopped at examination of arrest records, records of conviction, medical evidence or admissions records: suspected homosexual employees have been trailed, their neighbors and fellow employees have been interrogated, and their mail intercepted. Never once have these investigations been related to their competence on the job, but only to their sexual preference.

Homosexuals are no longer willing to accept such employment

prejudice hands down. They are citizens, they pay their taxes like everyone else and feel that, like heterosexuals, they are entitled to work in the federal system to the limit of their capabilities. There are a number of cases pending against the U.S. Civil Service Commission, some of which have been going through the courts for years.

In what could be a far-reaching decision that could change traditional government practices toward homosexuals, U.S. District Judge John H. Pratt, in October, 1971, ordered the Defense Department to restore security clearances to two declared homosexuals. He ruled that the Bill of Rights prohibited the government from subjecting homosexuals to "probing personal questions" about their sex lives as an invasion of privacy or from withholding security clearances for refusal to answer such questions. He further ruled that even if the government managed to obtain information from other sources concerning the type of detail they had tried to elicit from the homosexual plaintiffs, it cannot be used to deny security clearances. Such details, he said, lack the necessary connection to determine whether or not the individual is a security risk.

The myth that homosexuals are security risks because of their vulnerability to blackmail persists. But why are they vulnerable? Because of society's attitudes—and society's attitudes can't be changed because, in the eyes of society, homosexuals perform those "perverted acts." We cannot stress often enough that those "perverted acts" are regularly performed by heterosexual and homosexual alike, but for the most part are only attributed to the homosexual.

Further, there is absolutely no evidence that the homosexual per se will be more disloyal to his or her country if faced with a blackmail threat than will a heterosexual. Heterosexuals *do* commit acts which make them vulnerable to blackmail. Out of hundreds of cases of treason, breach of security or disloyalty in recent history, only *two* homosexuals (British, not American) have been blackmailed into giving secret information to an enemy nation. Additionally, only five alleged homosexuals have defected to the Communists. Even granting the "possibles," that is a mightly low percentage for the homosexual population, and yet our legislators and the press persist in spreading the lie that homosexuals are security risks. Please note there was not one Lesbian among the above-mentioned seven, though there have been a number of heterosexual women who have been blackmailed into giving up secret data to a foreign power.

So, since it is a matter of record that there are no known Lesbians who have been found guilty of turning over secret information to any enemy power, and since it has been proven that hundreds of heterosexual men and women, and at least two male homosexuals, have been found guilty of the charge, we suggest that *only* Lesbians should be allowed "top security" positions in our government.

It is not because there are no Lesbians in security positions that this remarkable record has been attained. We know many Lesbians who, despite all the precautionary and Machiavellian machinations of the federal government, do hold or have held security clearances. We also know many who have served, or are serving, overseas in responsible government positions. Furthermore, we have already indicated that the Lesbian is a chameleon sort of creature who, besides not being easily ferreted out, very definitely has learned how to keep a secret.

Another area of federal employment conducive to paranoid fears of discovery may well be the women's branches of the U.S. armed forces. Many young Lesbians are attracted to the services because of the travel opportunities, the chance to learn a trade, the promise of security, the persuasion of family tradition. They often find themselves caught up in what the homophile community has called "periodic, Gestapo-like purges."

We won't easily forget the strong emotions which were generated by a discussion of Lesbians in the armed forces sponsored by the Daughters of Bilitis. Neither of us had ever been in the service and, although we were aware of the injustices, stupidity and waste of personnel due to the military's attitude toward homosexuals we, like most other people, felt the disadvantage was primarily with the male who suffers lifelong economic loss because of a less than honorable discharge.

Not so. The stories we were told by those who had lived them had all the melodramatic elements of a Class B movie. Although the outward disadvantage is not as great, since women are not required to divulge their draft status or show their discharge except for certain positions, the trauma and psychic scars are still there. The treatment these women have received from the United States military has had an indelible effect upon their lives. Its impact is as great as that of the Nazi concentration camps on surviving Jews.

For those who are not familiar with the mechanics of a "purge," it goes something like this. The armed forces are aware that despite careful screening, a certain percentage of all the women entering the service will have "homosexual tendencies." The purges are conducted by the male investigative agencies "with a little help" from the women. Although the claim is that investigations are only made when there is a complaint, experience indicates that, like police, each base commander has a quota to meet. It usually begins by apprehending some youngster, new to the service and unaware of her rights, and scaring her into cooperation by threats and other third degree tactics. Interrogators usually inform her they will let her off if she will just give them names of other Lesbians. This constitutes the "complaint" necessary to launch a full scale witch hunt which drives through a base relentlessly until the quota is filled. And the informer, who has been duped into thinking she has gained amnesty, finds herself, along with the others, bounced out of the service with an undesirable discharge. If she's lucky, she may be let off with a general discharge.

"For reasons of homosexuality" does not necessarily mean overt homosexual activity, but includes suspicion of tendencies or guilt by association. Many totally innocent individuals have been victims of these vicious investigations, which include confiscating all mail and photographs and rummaging through all personal possessions. A common technique is to lie to the young woman, tell her that her "friend," or friends, have already confessed, implicating her, so she might as well admit it.

The Department of Defense reports that there are very few instances of courts martial; most women are separated by their own signed confessions. But these so-called confessions are meaningless pieces of paper wrung from a group of young people who are lied to, coerced, tricked, frightened and browbeaten into signing. There are even some cases where women have been confined in solitary until they signed, and many instances where they were questioned by male personnel without another woman present, as military law stipulates there must be.

We have run into other cases (and heard of still others) where young women from the ages of eighteen to twenty-two have been interrogated, harrassed, humiliated and ultimately railroaded and discharged for reasons of homosexuality when they didn't even know the meaning of the word. They were not faking when they claimed they didn't understand the terms their inquisitors were putting to them.

We recall two young women, Joyce and Marty, who walked into the DOB national office looking for information about Lesbianism. They indicated they had been ousted from the army on this basis and, if indeed that was what they were—Lesbians—they needed to know more about it.

There is, however, at least one case—Maggie—who claims she is grateful to the navy for informing her of who and what she was. Although a very tall, lanky, and masculine-appearing woman—one who might be "obvious" to others—Maggie was totally unaware of her sexual proclivities. "The guy who questioned me kept referring to me as a 'butch,' " she recalled. "I couldn't figure out what he was talking about—and he didn't believe me, so he wouldn't tell me." She grinned. "After I got out I found out, though."

We have observed that in some cases the armed forces, by their unrealistic and dogmatic approach to homosexuality, are actually *creating* Lesbians instead of eliminating them. Those women undesirably discharged from the services who have come to our attention over the years all became homosexuals. We believe, however, that a number of them probably would not have done so except for the attitudes and treatment they received at the hands of military authorities. For, once the label is branded on the individual, there is some psychological tendency to perpetrate the "crime" for which one has already been found guilty and punished.

Let us offer a particularly vivid example of what we mean. This is a case which we related to Jess Stearn and which he included in his book *The Grapevine.* Tillie, a marine, in all her youthful self righteousness reported Georgie, a WAVE, for having made a pass at her. The authorities went into action. The navy officer was, with all the pomp and circumstance—and humiliation—of a company parade, stripped of her stripes and discharged as undesirable. But during the process of the interrogation and the treatment dealt the WAVE, Tillie became quite distraught and filled with remorse for the suffering she had caused. She tried to befriend Georgie and attempted to make up for what had happened. Then Tillie was given the word. She would be (and eventually was) discharged for "association," if she didn't stop seeing Georgie.

Following her discharge Tillie went back home, but her "discharge" was embarrassing to her family (her father was in political life) and she became a "remittance woman"—"We'll send money. Just stay away from home!" Tillie, just barely twenty, migrated to the city in which Georgie lived. She had no one else to turn to. And this strange chain of events became the bond of a Lesbian liaison which after a couple of years eventually and inevitably broke up.

After the breakup Tillie flipped out, became sexually promiscuous with both sexes, hell bent on self destruction. By twenty-five she had a history of periodic alcoholic busts, was on probation as a result of a manslaughter conviction arising out of an auto accident, and had abandoned her child, the result of a brief and unhappy marriage. She finally got some psychiatric help, and has managed for the past number of years to remain relatively out of trouble and in a Lesbian relationship with an extremely dominant woman, where Tillie is the very passive partner—a relationship which has very heavy masochistic overtones.

So, through the good offices of the military, a young woman who was undoubtedly heterosexual in her orientation found herself thrust into a life style which she didn't fit and with which she was unable to cope. Why? All because a Lesbian made a pass. How many women have been subjected over the years to unwanted and unasked for passes from men? How many Lesbians have been approached by men in the armed services? Does this call for a "purge" of heterosexual men for suggesting what, to them, might be "lewd and lascivious" conduct? Are these young girls tainted for life because someone indicated affectionate or sexual interest in them? Let's be realistic. A Lesbian can be discouraged by a firm and polite, "Thanks, but no thanks," faster than *any* heterosexual male! With proper counseling and handling the marine could have been given a little sex education and taught how to say, "No." And the WAVE could have been admonished and yet gone on in the "career" service job which she loved.

We have known a number of "career" women who have resigned after eight- or twelve-year hitches because it just wasn't worth it. There was always the fear of getting caught up in a "purge," even though they had been very discreet in their conduct. One of these women, Jackie, during her second hitch in the army, had been interrogated during a sweep of the base where she was stationed in Washington. She was absolved shortly after a friend of hers, a reporter on the Seattle *Post-Intelligencer,* threatened the base commander with publicity if he persisted in subjecting the women in his command to such inhumane treatment.

Jackie was given a written notice (carbon copy) that charges against her had been dropped and her record cleared. She was later transferred to another base in the South where she was assigned to the personnel office. She took the opportunity to look up her own permanent file and found that there was no original of the carbon copy notice she had in her possession, but rather a completely different report. She learned she was still under surveillance. That was enough for her. She married a gay boy friend and got out of the service with an honorable discharge.

We remember, too, receiving a letter from a distraught chaplain stationed in Texas. It was his first experience with a military sweep and its effect upon the women who were subject to it. He felt helpless, and deplored the fact there was no DOB branch nearby to help him pick up these pieces of feminine humanity.

As do many other homosexual women, we feel that the Lesbian, by her very nature, is extremely adaptable to military life. Many would be likely to seek careers in the service if it were not for the prejudice against them. As long as these women are qualified, perform their duties ably and conduct their private lives with discretion, they should be allowed to serve. The fact that problems resultant from marriage or pregnancy would not cause homosexual women to drop out of the service should enhance rather than detract from their usefulness to the government.

And if humanitarian arguments are not persuasive, consider the waste of taxpayers' money involved. Estimates have been made that the cost to the government to train each man or woman in the military is from ten to fifteen thousand dollars. That plus the cost of investigations is the amount that is thrown away each time a man or woman is discharged merely for their sexual preference. According to the best knowledge of some ex-servicewomen, out of sixteen platoons in boot camp (comprising forty to seventy-five in each platoon), there are two or three discharges from *each* platoon about every three weeks for reasons of homosexuality. That adds up to a fair amount of our money being flushed down the drain every three weeks at *each* encampment.

Most of the Lesbians who *were* in the service loved the life, their jobs, their country. They view the situation with very mixed emotions. They deplore the treatment they received and are very resentful of their "undesirable" status. Some are obsessed with the idea of getting their discharges changed, though the likelihood is slim. The stigma, the rejection, the loss of dignity, the humiliation—merely for being—is difficult to bear. The charges are seldom based upon actual or flagrant misconduct, but only on suspicion and association. And the scars are vivid and deep and forever sensitive.

We have tried to discourage Lesbians from joining the armed forces. But some young women have difficulty in adjusting to society and feel lost. They view the services as a source of security, as a place where they can "belong." They are determined to make it. In such cases we have tried to inform them about the calculated risks, how to keep their cool in the face of a purge, and we have warned them to be discreet in their personal relationships.

We thought we were being helpful with our warnings, but recently we've been made aware this may not have been so. When Kathy, a nineteen-year-old, first entered the army she was excited about traveling, about the new experiences and people she was encountering. She loved boot camp, even when she was given the duty of cleaning up the latrines from floor to ceiling three times in one long, weary day. Her letters were filled with anecdotes, descriptions of the women in her division and the countryside. She sounded happier than we had ever known her to be. There was order and purpose in her life, and there was at last pride in belonging.

After a few months, however, Kathy's letters took on another tone. She was homesick, true. But there was something more. Because of her constant fear lest she be discovered as a Lesbian she had kept to herself, been afraid to make friends. She was dreadfully lonely and confused. When she was able to get a leave, she headed for the nearest DOB chapter. She needed to talk to people of her own kind, people she could trust, people who would understand her. But the trip offered her only momentary relief. The previous flood of correspondence from her dwindled because she had "nothing to say." Because of her fears she had boxed herself in.

After she had been in the army a little over a year, Kathy witnessed a purge. She was safe, that was for sure; she'd seen to that. But watching from the sidelines was equally devastating. She broke down, was placed under psychiatric care and given a medical discharge.

You've heard the phrase "sick with fear." That's what it meant to one Lesbian in the armed forces. That is the sickness to which the Lesbian may be driven by unreasonably harsh military practices.

Today, with more widespread knowledge of their rights and the more militant stance being assumed by homosexuals in general, Lesbians are beginning to fight back. Sandy and Toni, twenty and twenty-three years of age respectively, who were AWOL from boot camp in Alabama, came out of hiding to address the Western Regional Homophile Conference held in Los Angeles in February, 1970. They sought support from the delegates of twenty-two groups represented. The Lesbian couple said they had not met before September, 1969, when they first became WACs. Nineteen days before their basic training was completed they realized they were seriously in love and so felt they must leave the military.

"The army had not influenced us," Sandy explained. "It was just a matter of two people meeting and falling in love. Under their system, however, there was no place for us." They were being harassed, but it was when they were ordered to discontinue seeing one another that they decided to take an "extended" leave.

"We want other gay people to come out of their closets and stand up for their rights," Sandy declared. "We are going back to demand an honorable discharge."

"But," Toni added, "we are going to force the military to come and get us."

Apparently with the help of Morris Kight, Gay Liberation leader, who had alerted attorneys in Washington, D.C., and Birmingham as well as the American Civil Liberties Union, the two women had offered to surrender to military authorities on Lincoln's birthday in the Los Angeles Unitarian Church. Since the media had been alerted also, the brass didn't show up.

Kight proclaimed, "If the military will not pick up these beautiful, heroic women, then we hereby declare them freed from the military under honorable conditions." His proclamation was approved by acclamation of the conference. Reports since are that Sandy and Toni were indeed granted an honorable discharge after their return to the army base. Some Lesbian stories do have happy endings.

Dr. Franklin E. Kameny, of the Mattachine Society of Washington, D.C., and candidate for Congress in 1971 in the District's first such election, has spent years championing the cause of the homosexual against such conservative and hostile federal institutions as the Congress, the Civil Service Commission and the armed services. In the autumn of 1968 he learned that the army was conducting a purge of WACs in regard to homosexuality, at Fort Myer, Virginia, and at Fort Ritchie, Maryland.

Frank went into action, sending letters of objection to the commanding officers of the WAC companies concerned. These letters pointed out that, if need be, news releases would be sent out making the crackdown a public record and citing the high percentage of Lesbians in the WACs, "a fact which we are sure that the army would not be particularly pleased to have bruited about." (Over the years it has been most obvious that none of the women's services wants publicity. Faced with public exposure they stop their inhuman tactics.)

Two mass meetings of WACs were arranged to instruct them on how best to conduct themselves during such an investigation. They were given careful coaching on the handling of interrogations: "Say nothing; sign nothing; get counsel; fight back." They were told that army investigators have the right to go through their personal possessions and that letters, photographs and address books should be put in safekeeping with civilian friends.

Washington Mattachine supplied them with copies of their leaflet "How to Handle a Federal Interrogation." One of the WACs suggested that possession of the leaflet might, in itself, be compromising. So it was decided to "compromise" everybody. Late that night the WACs literally plastered the barracks with the leaflets. The next morning there were leaflets on bulletin boards, on tables in lounges, on each officer's desk. Everyone had an excuse for having a leaflet in her possession, and this vital information received maximum exposure. Needless to say, post officers were upset and searched frantically for the source of supply.

Frank became involved with the particular cases of Lieutenant X, stationed at Fort Myer, and Sergeant Y, stationed at Fort Ritchie. Both were close friends and had security clearances. Their clearances had been suspended, though without written notice, and they were under investigation. Knowing that regulations permit such suspensions to remain in effect for only ninety days, after which action must be taken either to reinstate or revoke the clearance, Frank demanded that dated written notice of the suspensions be submitted to the two women.

Separate interrogations were scheduled for the two WACs. Lieutenant X's ordeal was called off, however, after a phone conversation between Frank and the interrogator, when Frank pointed out that no irrelevant questions would be answered, that nothing whatever having to do with homosexuality was relevant to the proper implementation of any proper army purposes, and that army regulations pertaining thereto were themselves highly irrelevant to proper military purpose. He added that, if the clearance was to be revoked, Lieutenant X would expect full due process, including confrontation of witnesses, cross examination, presentation of evidence, etc.

Sergeant Y, however, drew the full treatment. According to Frank, her interrogation "was preceded by one of the longest, most elaborate, most complete and meticulously careful statements of her Constitutional and other rights which it has ever been my privilege to hear. It took the interrogator a full five minutes to deliver it." Sergeant Y was asked a series of questions, answers to *all* of which were refused on grounds of irrelevancy. Inevitably, one of the questions was whether she was a member of, or associated with, the Mattachine Society of Washington.

Shortly before the expiration of the ninety-day deadline in each case, the army restored the security clearances of both Lieutenant X and Sergeant Y, and both were returned to full regular duty. However, Sergeant Y was transferred to duty at some considerable distance from Maryland. Other WACs who were caught up in the same crackdown did receive undesirable discharges because they did not choose to resist and fight their cases.

At the state, city and county level there are usually "moral turpitude" clauses in civil service regulations. These would apply if a Lesbian were arrested in a gay bar raid, for instance, or involved in some public notoriety, or if someone reported her to her superior.

Dorothy von Beroldingen, member of the San Francisco Board of Supervisors and former member of the city's Civil Service Commission, told those gathered at the DOB Convention banquet in 1966 that the city did not discriminate against homosexuals, except for certain cases: "jobs where a person is necessarily exposed to the ill, the child or those again helpless to form their own opinions"—meaning, of course, jobs in the schools, the hospitals, juvenile hall, probation departments or the like. She pointed out also that though a homosexual might not be eligible for one job, she or he could be eligible for another position. Discovery of a homosexual in a "sensitive" job would not mean dismissal, but would require a transfer to a different "less sensitive" branch of city government.

In 1967 the City of New York began hiring homosexuals as long as they met all the regular qualifications for employment. Prior to that gay people had been considered unemployable by the city. Subsequently the city's human rights commission asked for power to fight cases of discrimination against homosexuals in jobs, housing, and public accomodations. But Intro 475, which would have enacted this request into law, was killed by a seven to five vote of the City Council's General Welfare Committee on January 27, 1972.

San Francisco, considered avant garde in its treatment of homosexuals, passed the first American civil rights legislation for homosexuals in April, 1972. By a vote of ten to one the Board of Supervisors expanded its job discrimination ordinance to include prohibitions against discrimination on the basis of "sex or sexual orientation" by companies doing business with the city.

Hardest hit by the strictures against homosexuals are the teachers. The Reverend Robert W. Cromey once stated: "If you removed all the homosexuals from the schools in the Bay Area, the schools would have to shut down." As we indicated in the first chapter, a California Supreme Court ruling in 1969 may be of some aid to teachers. The court ruled that a teacher may not have his teaching credential taken away simply because he has engaged in homosexual activity. The state must show that the activity "adversely affected" the teacher's "future classroom performance and overall impact on his students." Furthermore, the American Federation of Teachers has passed a resolution denouncing discrimination against teachers solely on the basis of their homosexuality.

Similar action was taken by the Catholic Teachers Federation (KOV) and the League of School Boards for Catholic Infant and Primary Education in the Netherlands in 1970 after two homosexuals had been fired from their positions in Roman Catholic schools. Even though the court in Arnham had ruled that the school board was not acting unreasonably when it decided to dismiss a teacher for her or his homosexuality, KOV declared that the homosexual way of life should be seen as a valued and acceptable way of life and that the homosexual must be accorded the right to lead his private life in his own manner. One's homosexuality, according to KOV, need not stand in the way of an appointment or the continuation of one's position as a teacher.

There are other pressures besides employment protection pulling at the Lesbian and provoking more fears: the family, religion and the law. The strongest is probably the family. Next, probably, is religion. As we mentioned, Lesbians bring with them into their new sexual awareness all the values and hangups of their upbringing. If they have been raised in a religious family, that religion, even if they have quit its practice, will always be with them and will play a vital part in their lives. In a sense the problems of family and religion are intertwined, since the religion is probably a part of the family life style.

Both conflicts surface in strange ways, sometimes, as with Ann and Terry. We hadn't seen them for a couple of years. Ann had been very active in DOB until she became involved with Terry, a recently divorced social worker. Terry just wasn't comfortable around other Lesbians—she had difficulty relating to them. Aside from a few selected friends, for her they represented another world—a world she didn't want to be a part of—and she certainly had no brief for homosexual rights! So she swept Ann up and off to the country.

A severe flood in the area where they lived prompted us to

phone to see if they were all right. They seemed delighted to hear from us, assured us they were okay and insisted we come to visit them the very next weekend if the roads were open.

We went. Ann was eager to hear the news about DOB, the latest developments on the homophile front, the gossip about this or that friend. All seemed to be going well, when suddenly Ann jumped up from the table and ran for the bathroom. We could hear her vomiting.

When she returned, she was visibly shaken. She told us that, because we were old friends of ten years' standing and we knew she loved us dearly, she wanted to level with us about what had been happening to her during our visit. Since she and Terry had dropped out of "gay life" whenever she came in contact with known Lesbians she became sick to her stomach. "And, dammit— even with you two now it seems!"

Ann had always had a conflict between her religion (Catholic) and her Lesbianism, but she thought she had escaped all that. Since she and Terry had moved away from the city and the homophile scene, she had blocked it out as not relating to her any more. Somehow by living in isolation with Terry, she felt she had shucked off the gay world, which was the object of derision and contempt by the church, her family and society. Although she was still living with Terry in a Lesbian relationship, she had managed, in her mind, to separate the two of them out from "those people" she had previously identified with. And we had brought it all back "home"—where it belonged.

The Lesbians we have known have, by and large, solved their family relationship hassles, although not always totally satisfactorily. In our own case we have always tried to be as honest as possible. We didn't wear a sign, and we didn't go around saying, "I'm a Lesbian" to everyone we met. All of our heterosexual friends knew, and our employers were at least aware of our long-standing partnership. But we never told our parents, though we discussed the possibility many times. Selfishly, at the beginning of our relationship their knowing would have made life a lot simpler for us. But then Del would remember the time there had been a conversational reference to homosexuality and her mother's saying, "It's all the parents' fault." Phyllis, too, would recall her father's remark to her mother, "I think Del is a queer!" made shortly after we'd moved in together. We decided, rightly or wrongly, that it would be easier for us to cope with their not knowing than it would be for them to cope with knowing.

Things changed over the years, however. For one thing, the longer we lived together, the more "things" we acquired together, the stranger it seemed to us that our parents did not know or, at least, suspect. After Phyllis's mother died and her father was staying with us for a while, she decided to "test" him. She had just recently gone to work for the Glide Foundation, and the Council on Religion and the Homosexual had come into being. She figured that was a good entering wedge. But, after enthusiastically telling her father about her "wonderful job, where they even deal with the church's treatment of homosexuals," the best she could get out of him was a noncommittal "Oh?" We decided he probably was aware and didn't wish to talk about it, which was his right, so the subject was never discussed. After he died we did find that he knew, for in the bedroom was an old *Newsweek* magazine containing a quote by Phyllis and identifying her as a founder of DOB.

Others have solved their parent problem in a number of ways. Some have simply disavowed their families and no longer are in contact. Some have been disowned by their parents. Some move far away so there can be little contact. Others, who live nearer, visit rarely either with or without their partners. Some tell their parents, with varying results, ranging from total disbelief to fairly ready acceptance. Another "solution" has been for the unmarried daughter to live with her parent or parents until their death, at which time she is "free."

Nona, a short, stocky, plain-faced woman, had left her home in the Midwest at twenty-five, no longer able to cope with her mother's nagging about her looks, her friends and why she wasn't married. She wandered slowly toward California, savoring her freedom. Her occasional guilt twinges over the scene at home when she left prompted her to mail postcards homeward now and then—but never with a forwarding address. She eventually arrived in California, settled in San Francisco, found a fairly satisfactory job and met Jennifer. After the two women had moved in together and life was moving smoothly, Nona wrote her parents to tell them about her new life and how happy she was.

Unfortunately the parents' response was nonunderstanding and negative. The mother continued to send her daughter clippings about high school friends who had gotten, or were getting, married. Her letters were nagging and plaintive, and always full of intimations that Jennifer was "bad" for Nona. Finally, because the letters from home were always a source of emotional upset to her, Nona discontinued writing and the two moved to another apartment with an unlisted telephone number. She effectively cut herself off from her parents.

Never underestimate the power of parental concern, however. Not hearing from Nona, and not being able to get in touch with her, the parents took their problem to their family minister who, having heard that Glide had something to do with homosexuals in San Francisco, finally made contact with Phyllis. It turned out we had met Nona and Jennifer through some friends, so it was fairly easy to get hold of Nona and say, "Your mother is concerned. Please write her." Reluctantly Nona said she would. She didn't do it right away though, because the parents called Phyllis again. She tried to explain why Nona had withdrawn from them. It was obvious they were kidding themselves that it was Jennifer's fault that Nona wasn't in touch with them. But they did love their daughter and they were concerned for her. Whether it has been possible for them to come together in love *and* understanding since, we do not know.

Despite the fact that Lesbians are seldom arrested, almost never convicted, and are not subject to police harassment to the extent that the male homosexual is, most still have a dread of the uniformed officer and instinctively pull up sharp at the sight of one. (This is, of course, a phenomenon also prevalent in other minority groups these days.)

Del recalls her first encounter with a police officer which occurred in 1949. She had left the Chi Chi Club, at that time a gay bar in the North Beach area of San Francisco, at the 2:00 a.m. closing time and, living in the downtown area, decided to walk home. She stopped at the corner of Broadway and Grant Avenue to look back because a couple of women had gotten into an argument outside the bar. When she turned and started down Grant, she heard footsteps behind her. She quickened her pace, but a hand touched her shoulder. When she turned around, she was face to face with a big burly cop.

He wanted to know her name and address, where she was employed, what she was doing there at this time of night. The only question she would answer was that she was walking home and that she didn't know of any law against that.

The officer countered angrily that, if she didn't answer his questions, he would "run her in" and she would "be lost for seventy-two hours."

Unaware of her rights as a citizen, and knowing nothing about vagrancy laws and police practices, Del still felt she hadn't done anything wrong, refused to identify herself or her place of employment, and insisted on knowing on what charges she might be arrested. All the while in the back of her mind she was wondering if the policeman had seen her come out of the gay bar and if this was the reason he was accosting her.

The cop yanked her across the street, but about this time another officer came along and seemed to have a calming effect on the one who had Del in tow. He then explained he had seen her pause at the corner and that, for all he knew, she could have been a lookout for someone who intended to rob one of the Chinatown stores.

Del repeatedly asked, "Is there a law against a woman walking alone on the streets at night?"

"Just get off my beat, lady, just get off my beat," was all the answer she could get out of the officer. "Don't you have money for a cab?"

Del did, but she "just wanted to walk home."

About the time the officer had decided that instead of arresting her he would rather date her, a cab did come along and Del grabbed it.

This anecdote points out the sad fact that many Lesbians, when they encounter a policeman, immediately suspect he is after them because they are Lesbians. Also, it should be noted that California law now requires that anyone who is stopped by the police must identify himself by name and address, but *not* by place of employment. A common complaint of homosexuals is that police generally make it a practice of phoning employers and apprising them when it is suspected that an arrested employee may be a homosexual, no matter the charges or if the case is dismissed.

Although it is a fairly uncommon practice, policewomen were being used as decoys in gay bars in California during the fifties. This is what the male homosexual refers to as "entrapment" or "enticement," where the officer dresses in conformity with what is the mode at the time for gays, strikes up a conversation with an unsuspecting homosexual, invites and encourages a proposition and then makes an arrest for "solicitation."

At the same time the police and Alcoholic Beverage Control Board of California (ABC) were making raids on gay bars, a practice which even in today's more enlightened climate still takes place in some areas of the country. Charges were generally seemingly innocuous, like "visiting a house of ill repute," "disorderly conduct," or "conduct contrary to the public welfare or morals." Unfortunately many frightened Lesbians have been badgered into pleading guilty to these outrageous charges. They plead guilty not because they have committed the crime they have been charged with, nor because the public has been offended (the only public involved being homosexuals), but because they are made to feel guilty about being a homosexual.

In the case of Kelly's, a bar in San Francisco that catered to Lesbians, police pulled a raid late one night in 1956 and bagged some thirty-six persons (mostly women), arresting them on charges of "visiting a disorderly house." The "culprits" trooped into court on Monday morning for arraignment, whereupon the judge called out the first name and asked how the accused pleaded. "Guilty." The sentence was then meted out: "Ten dollars and ten days in county jail—suspended." The others quickly sized up the situation and decided one simple word, "guilty," and the whole thing would soon be over—no need for the expense of an attorney, no need for further court appearances, no need to lose more time from work or school, no need to be embarrassed any further in public. Like sheep they one by one filed up to the bench to be shorn of their civil rights, not noticing at the time, in their relief, that they had also picked up an enduring arrest and conviction record.

Four young women, however, pleaded not guilty: first of all because they couldn't figure out what they could possibly be guilty of, and second because they questioned the validity of police actions against persons who had not done anything except enter a bar, order a drink and socialize with some of the other patrons. Nothing went on in the bar that was any different from any other (heterosexual) bar. Why was this bar singled out? In each instance (separate trials were held) charges were dismissed. Outside of their acknowledged presence on the premises of Kelly's, the police officers were hard put to describe any disorderly conduct on the part of any of these women or of other persons who had been there. It was not enough merely to call the place a "hangout for homosexuals."

The homosexual is almost always constrained to observe a higher set of standards than is the heterosexual. For instance, the ABC does not prohibit handholding or even kissing between men and women in bars—yet such actions between persons of the same sex, if in a gay bar, can mean that the owner's liquor license can be revoked. We entered a crowded gay bar one night with Alice, a blind friend. Del placed her hand on Alice's shoulder, steering her through the crowd.

"Take your hands off her," the cocktail waitress admonished.

"But she's blind," Del replied. "I'm only trying to guide her."

"Well, the ABC isn't blind!" retorted the waitress, as she pushed by.

A somewhat lighter, but similar, situation happened during DOB's annual St. Patrick's Day Brunch, that year being held in a local gay bar. Three straight women, members of the Prosperos who had, through us, become involved with the homophile community, arrived together. In an ebullient display of love and affection they greeted those present with hugs and kisses, men and women alike, causing the bartender-owner to almost freak out. "They can't kiss women in here, " he muttered distractedly, "the ABC won't like it." The three women, oblivious to the pain they were causing the owner, continued their happy way to an empty table. When we told them how they had broken the rules they were aghast. Not being homosexual they had never before run up against regulations restricting the open display of friendship and affection.

Why gay bars, whether for Lesbians or male homosexuals, should be the concern of any government agency as long as nothing violent or actually illegal is happening is beyond us. Gay bars for the Lesbian, although there are not as many as for the male, serve a needed function for a small percentage of the female homosexual population. They are there if one wants a drink and dinner without playing a heterosexual role. They are there to help you meet others, if you are new in town. They are there for dancing and socializing, as a "club" where a lonely woman can go and feel a part of things rather than only apart. In short, they serve much the same needs as do heterosexual bars.

It is true that for some the "bar scene" becomes a way of life. But for some Lesbians there aren't many options allowed by our hostile society. The Center for Studies of Suicide Prevention recently pointed out that a major cause of suicide is an "extended emotional depression, often coupled with a feeling of unbearable social isolation." People cannot exist in a vacuum. They must have some human warmth and companionship, no matter where they find it.

The myth that Lesbians are all hard drinkers, if not alcoholics, is probably an outgrowth of the fact that the gay bar is a chief point of contact. We know some do drink more than they need to—we have our share of alcoholics—but we've seen more Lesbians who have developed a fantastic technique for nursing one beer for hours on end. This technique—born of necessity because Lesbians as women do not earn as much as males and consequently do not have as much money to spend—accounts for the relatively few gay bars which cater to a female clientele. DOB parties have always had to have soft drinks for the many teetotalers who have attended. Now, of course, as the younger generation forswears alcohol for marijuana, the number of liquor abstainers is on the rise. It is sometimes a sure indication of the generation gap.

Society, then, has placed the Lesbian in a position where she must watch her every move and weigh her every word. Little wonder she sometimes displays symptoms of paranoia. The only resource the Lesbian has had to help her dispel her fears relating to job, family, religion, and the law has been herself, her own self acceptance. A slow change is coming about, however. The Lesbian is fighting back more and more, declaring herself more often. Sparked by the gay liberation movement and bolstered by the feminist movement the younger Lesbian is questioning the dual role, weighing the possible dangers of being open about her sexuality against the very real danger to her personhood of suppressing part of herself—of living a lie.

Each woman must make her own decision; there is no blanket rule covering the art of being honest about yourself. Many women are experiencing great pull from the two options open to them. Nan, open with most of those with whom she comes in contact, still frets about the possibility that she will receive the degree in social work on which she is now working and find all doors to employment closed to her. What then?

We hope the time will come when the Lesbian is free to use all of her ability and creativity in the business of living, not the business of hiding. For many, unfortunately, it will come too late.

8. Lesbians United

Daughters of Bilitis began with eight women: four Lesbian couples, four blue-collar and four white-collar workers, among whom were one Filipina and one Chicana.

The idea originated with Marie, a short brown-skinned woman who had come from the Philippine Islands. In contrast to the United States, the Philippines have no public sanctions or discrimination against homosexuals and Marie envisioned a club for Lesbians here in the States that would give them an opportunity to meet and socialize outside of the gay bars. She also felt that women needed privacy—privacy not only from the watchful eye of the police, but from gaping tourists in the bars and from inquisitive parents and families.

So in our eagerness to meet other Lesbians, we found ourselves on the evening of September 21, 1955, laying plans for a secret Lesbian club. For four consecutive weeks we met to draw up a constitution and bylaws. At the fourth meeting there still remained the question of a name for the fledgling organization.

"How about Daughters of Bilitis?" Nancy suggested.

The rest of us looked at her blankly.

"I ran across this book by Pierre Louys that has in it this long poem called 'Songs of Bilitis.'" Nancy held up the volume she'd been holding on her lap. "It's really quite beautiful love poetry, but what's even more interesting, Bilitis is supposed to have lived on Lesbos at the time of Sappho."

"We thought that 'Daughters of Bilitis' would sound like any other women's lodge—you know, like the Daughters of the Nile or the DAR," Priscilla added. "'Bilitis' would mean something to us, but not to any outsider. If anyone asked us, we could always say we belong to a poetry club."

And so Daughters of Bilitis (or DOB as it is popularly known) came into being. Officers were elected, and Del became the first president. In her acceptance speech she noted that it was time to launch a membership campaign and asked everyone to bring prospective members to the next meeting.

The first official meeting of the Daughters of Bilitis was held October 19, 1955, in a small apartment off Fillmore Street in San Francisco's Western Addition, where Nancy and Priscilla lived. At the appointed time, four very masculine-appearing types arrived to look us over. They strode in, muttered their names, plunked themselves down in chairs, and just stared at us. They were wary and diffident. But they were also defiantly and intimidatingly expectant, as if lying in wait for us to tell them about our dumb idea so they could clobber it.

Since Nancy had invited them (she'd met one in the factory where she worked and two in a bar), we had expected her to break the ice so that we might be on a better social footing before starting the meeting. But she and Priscilla had vanished, gone off to the kitchen to make coffee. One by one the other four DOB members also disappeared. (We never knew we had such a large coffee committee!) And there we sat, the two of us, green and inexperienced in the gay life, left to cope on our own with four hostile strangers.

We made a few stabs at friendly conversation that brought a few grunts and one-word responses. Finally the one wearing a man's suit, who seemed to be the spokesman for our visitors, asked impatiently, "When are you going to start the meeting? We don't have all night!"

So Del took a deep breath and plunged in, explaining that DOB was to be a Lesbian social club with parties and discussion groups to be held in private homes for the time being. Phyllis added that everything would be done to protect the anonymity of the members so that they would have nothing to fear.

"Daughters of Bilitis—how did you ever happen to pick that name?"

Del's explanation was followed by a hoot. "I wouldn't want to carry a DOB membership card in my wallet! What if someone saw it? It's too obvious."

This remark completely astounded us. The speaker, dressed as she was in men's clothes right down to the shoes on her feet, was to us a walking advertisement. She couldn't have been more obvious if she was wearing a sign on her back.

In the beginning we held three functions a month: a business meeting, a social, and a discussion session. Since we were all heavy coffee drinkers, these came to be known as Gab 'n Javas. During these meetings we discussed all the problems we faced as Lesbians, how we had managed them in our personal lives, and how we could deal with the public both individually and as a group.

At one such gathering held in our home, we made the mistake of inviting one of our straight friends. Rae, we thought, had gotten along well with the group. But Marie called us on it later: "DOB is a club for Lesbians. That means *no straight people* allowed."

"At the last meeting we'd been discussing the problem of being accepted by heterosexuals," Phyllis argued, "and one way is to meet them and talk to them."

"The last party was over at your sister's, and she isn't gay," Del added. The others nodded. But to Marie that was quite different.

"Besides, I thought you liked Rae," Phyllis said.

"I do. I think she's really a very nice person. And I'm sorry—but she doesn't belong around DOB!" Marie held stubbornly. "DOB is just for Lesbians and no one else."

That marked the beginning of a long series of arguments about rules and regulations, about the degree of secrecy we had to maintain, about mode of dress and behavior, about dealing with straights as well as gay men, about the possibility of publishing pamphlets explaining our cause. The arguments eventually led to an ultimate rift.

Marie and her friend pulled out first, and later Nancy and Priscilla left too. The group had grown to twelve by then, but a couple of new additions dropped out too. If DOB was only going to be a series of hassles, they didn't want to be any part of it. That left six of us. We sat down and talked over the state of DOB's affairs. We decided it was a good idea, one worth pursuing, even if the odds were against us. So we started out all over again with barely enough members to fill all the slots of the elected officers. By that time our acquaintances in the Lesbian world of San Francisco had broadened, and we were certain we could find more who could see the value of DOB.

Only recently have we realized that the DOB split was along worker/middle class lines. The blue-collar workers who left DOB wanted a supersecret, exclusively Lesbian social club. The white-collar workers, however, had broadened their vision of the scope of the organization. They had discovered the Mattachine Society and were interacting with the men who had already launched what was to become known as the homophile movement. Through Mattachine we heard of ONE, Inc. in Los Angeles and had attended their 1956 Mid-Winter Institute. There we were welcomed warmly by Ann Carll Reid, then editor of *ONE* magazine. "We're so glad to see women organizing! We need you, and we'll do anything we can to help. We'll advertise DOB in the magazine. Also, you can write up a blurb on DOB for inclusion in the book we're publishing, *Homosexuals Today.*"

We felt DOB could meet both needs. Those members who were interested only in the social affairs were free to limit their participation. Parties, picnics and chili feeds could serve as fund raisers for the work to be done by those interested in publishing a newsletter and setting up public forums. But these latter proposals scared off our friends. They didn't want their names on a mailing list, and they most certainly didn't want to mix with "outsiders" (which included gay men as well as both heterosexual men and women).

Nancy went on to found two more secret Lesbian social clubs. The first was Quatrefoil, a group comprised largely of working class mothers and their partners, with a sprinkling of singles. Nancy ruled the group with an iron hand enforcing all the rules that we in DOB had balked at. When Barb successfully challenged her leadership, she went on to establish Hale Aikane, which had all the pomp, circumstance and ritual of a secret sorority. Both groups (now defunct) lasted for some time. Quatrefoil ventured out a few times to meet with representatives of other San Francisco homophile organizations, and Hale Aikane surfaced when they found an old store building which they had converted to club rooms. They sought DOB's financial help, and the two shared the facility for a short while until Hale Aikane went out of business altogether.

So desperate were we for members in the early days of DOB that we coddled, nursed and practically hand-fed every woman who expressed the least interest. We had them over for dinner, offered them rides to and from the meetings—some even moved in on us for days and weeks at a time. Very often our taxi service meant rushing home from work and bolting down a quick dinner so as to leave an hour or so in advance to pick up all our passengers. If there were the slightest evidence that a member or prospect was disgruntled about anything at all (even the weather) there we were, ready to explain, mediate and smooth over hurt feelings and clear up misunderstandings. But this pampering was taking up far too much of our time. Besides, we decided, the organization would have to stand on its own merits or it wasn't worth worrying about.

By the end of its first year DOB had fifteen members, only three of the original eight remaining. We decided to make an all-out push. We started publishing *The Ladder* with Phyllis as editor, and we set up monthly public discussion meetings in a downtown hall. The Mattachine Society was renting several offices on Mission Street, and they sublet half of one tiny room to DOB. A member donated a desk. We bought a used typewriter and filing cabinet. Several San Francisco businesses "donated" small items like paper clips, staples and typing paper. We were in business.

Volume One, Number One of *The Ladder*, a twelve-page mimeographed newsletter in magazine format, made its debut during October of 1956. We were aiming for about 250 copies, but Mattachine's tired old mimeograph only coughed out about 170 that were halfway legible. The cover design, drawn by staff artist B.O.B., showed a line of women approaching a very tall ladder which protruded from the shore of the bay and reached up into lofty, cloudy skies. It carried the legend, "from the city of many moods—San Francisco, California." In the right hand corner was the DOB emblem, a triangle with a *d* and a *b*. Underneath was inscribed the DOB motto, "Qui vive."

The purpose of the Daughters of Bilitis, a women's organization to aid the Lesbian in discovering her potential and her place in society, was spelled out. The organization was to encourage and support the Lesbian in her search for her personal, interpersonal, social, economic and vocational identity. The DOB social functions would enable the Lesbian to find and communicate with others like herself, thereby expanding her social world outside the bars. She could find in the discussion groups opportunity for the interchange of ideas, a chance to talk openly about the problems she faced as a Lesbian in her everyday life. Also available to her would be DOB's library on themes of homosexuality and of women in general. In educating the public to accept the Lesbian as an individual and eliminate the prejudice which places oppressive limitations on her life style, the group proposed an outreach program: to sponsor public forums, to provide speakers for other interested civic groups, and to publish and disseminate educational and rational literature on the Lesbian. DOB also announced its willingness to participate in responsible research projects and its interest in promoting changes in the legal system to insure the rights of all homosexuals.

For today's "liberationists" the original wording of DOB's lofty aims contained many loaded words and concepts, which were to come under fire time and again over the years. Terms like "integration into" and "adjustment to" society, for instance, are no longer viable. Homosexuals today are not seeking tolerance; they are demanding total acceptance. But one must consider the times in which DOB came into being. Just the month prior to the first publication police had raided the Alamo Club, popularly known as Kelly's, loading thirty-six patrons into their paddy wagons. DOB was also born on the heels of the United States State Department scandals of the early fifties when hundreds of homosexual men and women had been summarily fired from their jobs with the federal government when their identity had been disclosed or even hinted at. Most Lesbians were completely downtrodden, having been brainwashed by a powerful heterosexual church and by the much touted precepts of psychoanalysis. There was not the sense of community or solidarity that exists today. Lesbians were isolated and separated—and scared.

The first issue of *The Ladder* contained a "President's Message" from Del challenging the women who received it (everybody we knew or had heard of, friends of friends of friends) to join us in the effort to bring understanding to and about the homosexual minority by adding the feminine voice and viewpoint to a mutual problem already being dealt with by the men of Mattachine and ONE.

"If lethargy is supplanted by an energized constructive program, if cowardice gives way to the solidarity of a cooperative front, if the 'let Georgia do it' attitude is replaced by the realization of individual responsibility in thwarting the evils of ignorance, super-stition, prejudice and bigotry," then Del argued, the lot of the Lesbian could indeed be changed.

We learned later that DOB's was not really the first Lesbian publication in the United States. *Vice Versa,* "America's Gayest Magazine," which was "dedicated in all seriousness to those of us who will never quite be able to adapt ourselves to the iron-bound rules of convention," was published and distributed privately in Los Angeles from June, 1947, through February, 1948. The work of editing, production (typewritten—but with columns justified!) and distribution was all done by one woman, Lisa Ben, who had previously achieved some note in the science-fiction field under her real name. Each copy carried short stories, poetry, news com-mentary, bibliography, letters and reviews of pertinent plays, films or books. Further, *ONE* had put out a special "Feminine View-point" issue (February, 1954) which was written, compiled and edited entirely by women. It was one of the few issues of *ONE* that had completely sold out, and there was still demand for re-prints.

The response to the first issue of *The Ladder* was equally en-thusiastic. We had acquired a post office box, but we were in no way prepared for the volume of mail we received. As volunteers working for DOB after our regular jobs, and small in membership, we were hard put to read it all—let alone answer it!

However, the "President's Message" in the second issue, this time by Del's successor D. Griffin, noted with dismay how many of the letters had expressed fear of being on "the mailing list of an organization *like this.*" An editorial entitled "Your Name Is Safe!" cited the 1953 decision of the United State Supreme Court (U.S. vs. Rumely) upholding the right of the publisher to refuse to reveal the names of purchasers of reading material to a con-gressional investigating committee.

Plagued with fear of identification and fear of being on mailing or membership lists, DOB has been consistently hampered in its growth as an organization and in its outreach into the public sphere. When the organization was founded in 1955, allegiance to such a homophile group was indeed a scary propositon. In the beginning members took pseudonyms or were known to their fellow members simply by their first names.

When Phyllis assumed the editorship of *The Ladder* she also assumed the alias of "Ann Ferguson." About the same time we started the public lecture series, at which meetings, we, of course, publicized the magazine. When someone requested an introduction to the editor, members found themselves calling, "Ann . . . Ann! . . . *Ann!* . . . *ANN!*" But it finally took "Phyllis!" to get her attention. From that point on we cautioned those who intended to use aliases to at least keep their first names or nicknames.

By the fourth issue *The Ladder* carried an obituary—complete with heavy black border. Ann Ferguson had died. "I confess. I killed Ann Ferguson—with premeditation and malice afore-thought. Ann Ferguson wrote that article, 'Your Name Is Safe!' Her words were true, her conclusions logical and documented—yet she was not practicing what she preached. . . . At the December public discussion meeting of the Daughters of Bilitis we got up— Ann Ferguson and I—and did away with Ann. Now there is only Phyllis Lyon."

Before we could get out the third edition of the magazine, which was to inform our Lesbian readers what to do in case of arrest, the Mattachine mimeograph petered out entirely. Macy's sign shop came to the rescue. There were several gay women work-ing there on the offset press. We typed *The Ladder* on paper (printing) plates, and they ran them off. Suddenly towards the end of the month there was a flurry of activity in this Macy's department.

On one particular day, when *The Ladder* was on the press, the boss came into the shop. One worker rushed towards him with a very loud enthusiastic "Good morning, *Mr. Holt!*" detaining him at the door. Another stepped in front of the stack of pages which had already been run off, blocking them from his view. The fore-man, who had been feeding the press, looked frantically for a replacement. She didn't dare ask either of her helpers to move, so she shouted above the whirr of the press, "I'll be through with this job in just a few minutes." Holt waved. "That's all right. You're busy. I'll come back later."

This call was too close for comfort. By that time we had become somewhat more solvent. We had received some publicity in *The Independent,* a monthly newspaper in New York. Our notoriety had spread. Letters, memberships and donations were beginning to pour in. Pan-Graphic Press, a Mattachine-connected printshop, offered to do the work for a nominal fee. But we still had to type the stencils and had the same tedious work of collating, folding, and stapling by hand to do when the pages dried.

Meanwhile the public discussion meetings were going very well. The "public," of course, was comprised chiefly of homosexuals and primarily those of the female gender. The series of lectures by attorneys, psychologists, psychiatrists, employment and marriage counselors was planned to dispel some of the fears and anxieties of the Lesbian. We reasoned that at a "public" meeting you could hear about "those" people and not necessarily be so identified simply by being in the audience.

For those who doubted its legality or permanency, the Daughters of Bilitis became a full-fledged, nonprofit corporation under the laws of the State of California in January, 1957, on acceptance by the Secretary of State of the articles of incorporation, filed by attorney Kenneth C. Zwerin in our behalf. Later Mr. Zwerin was also to obtain for DOB its tax-exempt status with the federal government.

During that same month of January, sixteen women attended a get-acquainted DOB brunch in the English Room of the New Clark Hotel in Los Angeles in an effort to organize a second chapter. The meeting was held in conjunction with ONE's annual Mid-Winter Institute. It was not until 1958, after several false starts, that the Los Angeles chapter took hold under Val Vanderwood's leadership. Also in 1958, when we attended the Mattachine Society's convention in New York City two more chapters came into being—New York, headed by Barbara Gittings, who was later to become an editor of *The Ladder,* and Rhode Island, led by Frances LaSalle. Since then chapters of DOB have appeared, been active, lain dormant, revived or dissolved in such cities as Chicago, Boston, New Orleans, Reno, Portland, San Diego, Cleveland, Denver, Detroit, Philadelphia, and Melbourne, Australia.

At the outset, the founding Daughters had been completely unaware of the existence of Mattachine and ONE. Representatives and leaders of both organizations were extremely cooperative when we finally did meet them. Though their groups were open to both men and women, they had never been able to attract Lesbians in large number, and they offered encouragement and hope that we could manage to organize the women to swell the ranks of the homophile movement. Despite their show of generosity and help, for which we are forever grateful, there has always been the private (and sometimes not so private) resentment against the separatist and segregationist policies of DOB, which restricted its membership to women only.

ONE, in particular, took pride in having women actively involved from the first—one of whom "even had a vote on the board." Ann Carll Reid edited *ONE* magazine for a couple of years, and "The Feminine Viewpoint" was a regular feature of the magazine. Mattachine admitted to having only a couple of active women, now long since gone, and we were welcome to the few female stragglers we might find at their meetings. They would gladly run articles of interest to women in the *Mattachine Review,* if we would write them. But we had a magazine of our own to worry about.

Few of the foreign publications and organizations, which also generally maintained a co-ed policy, gave much time or thought to the Lesbian, though *Vennen* published in Denmark, and *Vriendschap* in Holland, regularly carried fiction, poetry and articles pertaining to the female homosexual. But *Der Kreis,* the oldest of them all, which had been published in Switzerland since 1932 and which had been edited solely by a woman from its inception through 1941, was strictly a man's publication. Mammina, its editor, was revered for her courage in the pioneering days, taking all the abuse and ridicule heaped upon her head, losing her job on three occasions, but never allowing herself to become discouraged. When the repeal of the laws against male homosexuals became effective in 1942, the men said, "Thank you, ma'am," took over, and have since then given the women, except for Mammina, short shrift.

From the beginning DOB was a self help organization. Certainly no one else was concerned about the Lesbian, not even the other homophile groups. DOB thus set about to redirect the self pity, self consciousness and self abasement that had always been the Lesbian's lot through the paths of self awareness, self knowledge and self observation toward another self—that of self acceptance, self confidence, and self esteem. The articles in *The Ladder,* the Gab 'n Javas, and the public discussion meetings served as consciousness raising vehicles for this process of re-education. The parties and other social gatherings provided the reinforcement, the camaraderie, the security, the humor and the warmth of group solidarity. Many women who had previously suffered as emotional cripples became whole. They realized at last that they were, in truth, worthy human beings.

Recognizing that it was in the self interest of the Lesbian to interact and help shape policy for the homophile movement as a whole, DOB regularly participated in and exchanged speakers at various conventions and conferences. In those days there were only three major groups—DOB, Mattachine Society and ONE (all based in California, though expanding with affiliated chapters across the country)—so communication was, of course, pretty easy to maintain.

Through such participation, DOB gained a great deal of information and data, learned from other's mistakes, and realized the profit (in time, energy and funds) that lay in not duplicating efforts or errors in judgment. DOB representatives, while attending homophile conventions in various cities, were also able to make contact with local Lesbians in order to form new chapters and thus expand the sphere of influence of the Daughters. But the DOBs always had another "hidden agenda" in mind: to find out what the male-oriented groups were up to. This was important because DOB felt a responsibility to temper the more rash or "far out" tactics of male organizations. They also wanted to be forewarned of eventualities they might be called upon to face. Whatever the policies of one organization, actions of others invariably affect the homophile movement as a whole.

We were there in the smoke-filled room at the Hotel Albany in Denver where Mattachine politics were being privately discussed prior to the next day's annual meeting of September, 1959. One William Patrick Brandhove, a well-heeled newcomer to the San

Francisco chapter and the appointed parliamentarian, was urging the passage of a resolution praising San Francisco Mayor George Christopher and Police Chief Thomas Cahill for an enlightened administration in "sociological problem areas." He claimed the resolution had been mailed to him in Denver by members of the San Francisco Police Department, who had requested its passage.

"Why?" we asked. "It doesn't make any sense. Of what earthly use would it be to the police or to Christopher to gain the endorsement of the Mattachine Society? If anything, it could be a detriment to them in an election year."

We knew there was something wrong with this picture. It just didn't add up. We were "honorary members" without vote, but we tried to dissuade our Mattachine brothers from taking this "request" seriously. However, they fell for Brandhove's money and supposed position "in the know," and with a few minor alterations, unwittingly passed his resolution. Brandhove also saw to it that a court reporter took the minutes of the meeting and that it was duly recorded. We were not long in learning why, and, despite our misgivings we were certainly not prepared for what happened.

Homosexuality was violently interjected into the mayoralty campaign in San Francisco on October 7, 1959. The exposé, which had been rejected by the three daily papers, broke in the weekly, *San Francisco Progress,* in a front page story headlined, "Sex Deviates Make S. F. Headquarters"—this by virtue of the fact that both Mattachine and DOB maintained their national offices in the city. Brandhove's resolution was duly noted by Christopher's opposition, Assessor Russell Wolden, to show the falsity of the incumbent's claim he had given the people a "clean city." The article went on to enumerate the bars, steam baths, cafes, hotels and after-hour spots frequented by homosexuals, emphasizing the "family aspects": i.e., that no child was safe, etc.

Christopher called the charges "the dying gasp of a desperate politician" and deplored his opponent's "dinner hour" radio broadcast on a subject Christopher could never bring himself to name. The *San Francisco Chronicle* revealed that Brandhove was "a plant by a behind-the-scenes operator in the Wolden campaign," and that he "was once a Communist, later a loud ex-Communist—and built up a long police record during both periods." Wolden supporters (ironically the homophile community had previously been in his camp) fell off the bandwagon in droves, among them candidates running on the Democratic ticket with him. His big financial backers agreed to continue their support, although they were not too happy with the campaign as it was being conducted.

In the meantime, the Mattachine Society filed a $1,103,500 slander suit against Wolden, declaring he "wrongfully and maliciously ... declared [the society] was organized homosexuals ... and exposed teenagers to contact with homosexuals." The Mattachine Society, while an avowed part of the homophile movement, had always billed itself as an organization "interested in the problems of homosexuality," but not a homosexual organization.

(As a matter of fact, when DOB held its first national convention in San Francisco in 1960, Hal Call, Mattachine's president, wrote us a letter criticizing us for calling it, in our publicity release, "the nation's first Lesbian convention." Under those circumstances he felt that most Mattachine members—99 percent male— might hesitate to attend our public functions. Jaye Bell, president of the San Francisco chapter of DOB, replied that "if the members of Mattachine were to dress properly and act with decorum, we are sure no one would take them to be Lesbians.")

Although DOB was mentioned in the first *Progress* election story, it was not mentioned at all in the daily press. But it was brought back into focus in a four-page letter-sized pamphlet, which was distributed door-to-door, with the following bold-face notation:

"And you parents of daughters—do not sit back complacently feeling that because you have no boys in your family, everything is all right as far as you are concerned. To enlighten you as to the existence of a Lesbian organization composed of homosexual women, whose purposes are the same as the Mattachine Society, the male counterpart, make yourselves acquainted with the name 'Daughters of Bilitis'!"

When the news first broke, Del, as national president, called an emergency meeting of DOB. The position of the Lesbian in society being what it was, we feared that the membership of DOB might dissolve out of fear. We had not, however, anticipated the psychological effect of a good crisis. To our surprise the meeting was heavily attended, and the sentiment was overwhelming to stand

our ground and to get a special edition of *The Ladder,* explaining
the facts, onto the newsstands post haste. Even the more timid
displayed grim determination to face the issue forthrightly. Panic
came from an unexpected source—the proverbial "big, brave"
butch type who insisted that we get the mailing and membership
lists out of the office. We complied with both requests. However,
having removed the lists and placed them in the back of our station wagon under a car robe, we didn't know what to do with
them. So, for the duration of the crisis, DOB operated out of our
car.

It was later reported to us by the manager of the building where
we rented offices that the police did indeed check us out. She
vouched for us as "nice girls" and good tenants who caused no
trouble and just conducted our business quietly. When we first
rented the offices in April, 1958 (the Daughters having ventured
forth on their own when they found themselves in the middle of
some Mattachine internal strife), Del had referred to DOB as a
women's organization "interested in sociological problems of
single women." To her chagrin the manager said she had a feminist
friend she just knew would be interested in our group. We
couldn't, of course, keep our cover for long, what with janitorial
services, delivery of packages, etc., which required access to the
premises. We never did hear from the manager's friend, but at least
we passed muster as far as the police were concerned.

The fireworks backfired on Wolden, and Christopher won the
election handily. Homosexuals, however, despite the Mattachine
resolution and the smear campaign, had previously vowed for
many reasons never again to vote for Christopher. It was, therefore, interesting to note that some nine thousand persons went to
the polls and voted for everything except for mayor.

This catapult into the realm of politics keynoted an awakening
interest in the homophile community which was to result some
years later in a strong voting bloc which politicians may question,
but hesitate to ignore. It also broke through what the movement
had previously termed the media's "conspiracy of silence" on
homosexual issues. It was this event more than anything else
which brought the Mattachine name to the forefront and gave it
national renown. The Daughters were unfortunately relegated to
being the "Mattachine women's auxiliary" by the chauvinist press—

a public label we were to suffer under for a number of years.

The DOB biennial conventions proved to be excellent vehicles for publicity focused on the Lesbian. The "first national Lesbian convention," held in San Francisco in 1960, received good press notices. During the second, in Los Angeles in 1962, Terry, president of the host chapter, who was self employed, attained nationwide coverage when she was interviewed by Paul Coates for television. By the third, in New York City in 1964, the *New York Times* had relented on its taboo on the subject and sent a reporter, though a scheduled interview with Del and Ginny Worth on the Les Crane show was canceled at the last minute because the subject was "too controversial." At the fourth, again in San Francisco in 1966, we pulled out all the stops.

When the San Francisco Convention and Visitors Bureau failed to include DOB in their weekly listing of conventions in the Sunday edition of the paper, Phyllis, as DOB's public relations director, wrote them a letter charging "discrimination" and demanding "a public statement of apology for this oversight"—with copies to the media, of course. She got her apology all right, and then some.

The *Chronicle* ran a four-column article headlined "S.F. Greets 'Daughters.' " Furthermore, the Convention Bureau provided help at the registration desk at no cost to DOB. And on-the-hour spot announcements were made on at least two radio stations—KEWB and KSFO. Reporters from Metromedia News taped some of the highlights of the program, and by afternoon Judge Joseph G. Kennedy's luncheon speech was on the air. Though cameras were barred at the convention itself to protect those registrants who might be vulnerable to publicity, television stations did give DOB some prepublicity through a taped interview with Phyllis. And the newspapers covered in depth the event which featured speakers from all branches of San Francisco's city government (including an official representative appointed by Mayor John Shelley, albeit the public health director).

In the meantime, Del Shearer, president of the Chicago chapter, braved the television cameras in the Midwest. There was a growing demand all across the country for radio and television appearances of "real live Lesbians," but only a few DOB members were free enough to risk personal identification. Interviews with the use of pseudonyms and without photos for newspapers, magazines, books and radio were one thing, but television was quite another. We devised a system whereby members were transported to areas outside their bailiwick for local shows where it wouldn't make any difference. But otherwise, all chapters handled requests for speakers (for universities, church groups and other civic organizations as well as for the media) in their own area.

Phyllis handled most of the West Coast television assignments for a number of years, until Rita Laporte was elected national president at the Denver convention in 1968. Prior to Rita's help in this direction, Phyllis had had trepidations. "I know we want to erase the stereotyped image of the Lesbian, but the next thing you know, there'll be a new stereotype—me!" Nowadays the subject has become quite commonplace, and with more Lesbians taking up the challenge of Gay Liberation to "Come Out," the difficulty of filling speaking and television engagements has abated somewhat.

DOB was originally formed as an alternate to the gay bars that were, up to that time, the sole meeting places for Lesbians. DOB nonetheless was very much concerned about homosexuals' rights to congregate in such public places, about unprovoked police raids and harassment, about entrapment procedures and about trumped-up charges used by Alcoholic Beverage Control agents to close bars. In the early days of DOB a great deal of energy was expended in apprising Lesbians of their legal rights, advising them of what to do in case of arrest, and obtaining legal counsel for victims of raids. *The Ladder* had the distinction of having its September and October, 1958 issues filed with the District Court of Appeals along with an *amicus curiae* brief by Lowenthal and Associates in the case of an Oakland Lesbian bar called Mary's First and Last Chance.

The "misconduct" in the state's case against owners Vallerga and Azar (besides the fact that some women were dressed in "masculine" attire, according to police testimony) consisted of such criminal and immoral activity as "a female with her arms around another female, or kissing themselves on the cheeks and necks" and a waitress calling an undercover policewoman a "cute little butch." But the case had to go all the way to the state supreme court (at no small expense to the taxpayers) before a decision was rendered that this conduct was hardly "inimical to the public welfare or morals," but was merely an indication that the clientele of the bar was indeed homosexual. The court reiterated its previous decision handed down in 1951 in the celebrated Black Cat case, also defended by the Lowenthals, that homosexuals have the same rights as other citizens to congregate in a public place, that an owner of a bar could not lose his license merely because his customers exercized that right, and that only "the commission of illegal or immoral acts on the premises" could constitute "good cause." The court made the additional observation in the Vallerga case that homosexuals should not be expected to exhibit a higher standard of conduct than that expected of other (heterosexual) citizens.

In the late 1960s New York DOB also played an active part in gaining support for Cooky's bar, which brought about a similar ruling from the New Jersey Supreme Court.

In the meantime, DOB, in addition to the libraries maintained by its various chapters, established a book service. It was devised with a twofold purpose: to bring in much-needed funds as well as to make available to the general public the best books and literature on Lesbianism. The Los Angeles chapter had a record cut with the DOB label featuring Lisa Ben, the first gay folk singer, who did a parody of "Frankie and Johnny" and another number called "Cruising Down the Boulevard." With the addition of the "Songs of Bilitis" recited by an anonymous Hollywood actress, the book service was extended to include certain selected records.

In recognition of their support and to honor those men who have made significant contributions to DOB and the homophile movement, the Daughters began to offer "honorary memberships" to the Sons of Bilitis. This "men's auxiliary" has only amounted to an honor roll of card-carrying SOBs, which awards were distributed amid much fanfare at the banquet of each DOB convention. Most SOBs covet their cards and ask for replacements if they are lost. We did get one complaint, though, from a psychologist who took affront at our "underlying, unconscious [?] motivations." Though the SOBs have never called a meeting, if they did so, they would find themselves in the company of many distinguished jurists, congressmen, attorneys, a mayor, clergymen, scientists, and police as well as professors, a carpenter, a retired railroad man and male leaders from the homophile community.

DOB also became aware of Lesbian organizations in Europe.

The Minorities Research Group was founded in London in 1963 by five women. Its purpose and program, both inner and outer directed, were much the same as DOB's. *Arena Three,* the organization's publication, edited by Esme Langley, reported that very familiar sorts of problems were experienced by Lesbians in Britain despite the fact that female homosexuals had never been proscribed by English Law. There was still the stigma—and there still is.

In 1965 two other English Lesbian groups sprang up: Kenric, in London, under the leadership of Cynthia Reid, and the New Group in Manchester. These were primarily social in character, the result of the same dissidence DOB had experienced: the rift between those who see the need for public relations and those who wish merely to socialize with their own kind.

Efforts to organize Lesbians on the continent have been unsuccessful for the most part. Most organizations there are male-oriented, like their counterparts in America. Some are open to both men and women, though few Lesbians are in evidence. COC (Cultuur-En Ontspanningscentrum) was founded in 1946 in Amsterdam and now has seven local branches in the Netherlands, each with its own center, usually with a bar and dancing. Like the early American homophile organizations COC took a name that was not readily identifiable and was originally known as the Shakespeare Club or Center for Culture and Recreation. During the fifties and sixties the women of COC joined together in an auxiliary called Vrouwenkern and had a separate page in COC's periodical.

"The group had pretty much only one responsibility: the organization of an annual occasion, Vrouwenlanddag, when only female members of COC came together—a 'now it is our turn' event," according to Joke Swiebel, who plays an active role in today's COC. "The program for the day which included lectures, discussions and a cabaret was less important than the amassing of no less than five hundred Lesbians in a gay women's funfare in a frenetic atmosphere." There was no question of attempting to make a significant contribution to a liberation movement on Vrouwenlanddag; nor was such the concern of Vrouwenkern. In those days the emancipation of women was an "old-fashioned" topic, according to Joke.

Today, however, COC does not encourage separatism of the

sexes. Of its seven thousand members one thousand are females, and its magazine *Seq* features articles and photographs of interest to Lesbians as well as to male homosexuals, there being female nudes included in addition to the male photos so prevalent in United States publications. Women visitors to COC who have DOB membership cards are accorded courtesy, short-term minimal rates with all the privileges of membership. The Vrouwenlanddag-ambience lingers on, however, in the sole commercial Lesbian bar in Amsterdam, Tabu. There no man, no matter his sexual persuasion, can enter. According to reports, there are now three Lesbian organizations on the continent: the Minerva Club in Geneva, Diana, in Stockholm, and Flamingo Brevklubb in Sverige, Sweden.

The Lesbians of Europe, though stigmatized socially, never came under the scrutiny of the law. Lesbians in America, however, were always keenly aware that their actions were illegal, even though they were seldom prosecuted. In a bid to change the sex laws, some of us from DOB and Mattachine discussed the possibility of introducing such legislation with Congressman Phillip Burton and Attorney John A. O'Connell, both of whom were then assemblymen in the California state legislature. Though cognizant of the inequities of the law and sympathetic to our plight, they gave us the stock answer of the politician: "To introduce such a bill at this time would be political suicide. It would be like being 'for' sin! But if you can get the church to support changing the law you might have a chance."

"That'll be the day!" we thought. "We have a better chance of getting to the legal profession where there's at least the Model Penal Code to build on. Or we can probably reach the psychologists and psychiatrists who believe in helping the homosexual to 'adjust' (though psychoanalysts are another breed). But the church—forget it! Christian brotherhood and love are nonexistent when it comes to the homosexual."

But challenge was not new to us. The church was at the core of all our problems, and there had to be some way, somehow to reach the church. In planning DOB's first convention in 1960, we noted that both Mattachine and ONE had previously counted among their speakers clergymen who recognized the needs of homosexuals. But they spoke unofficially, out of personal conviction, and never revealed what church they belonged to. Change could only come about if we could develop a dialogue with the church itself, and we were determined to have an official representative from some particular denomination.

To do that you had to start at the top. Since Rabbi Alvin Fine and the late Bishop James A. Pike had appeared on "The Rejected," the first documentary on homosexuality produced for the educational television network, we tackled them. They both quickly declined. Then we wrote to the San Francisco Council of Churches seeking their counsel on the problem. Some weeks later we received a reply from the executive director apologizing for the delay, but they had "never had a request of this nature before, and quite frankly, we didn't know how to deal with it." We had visions of the consternation our request had provoked within the city's church community, of those who scoffed at our audacity and of the others who had been forced to wrestle with their Christian conscience.

But we did get our speaker. The Reverend Fordyce Eastburn, chaplain at St. Luke's Hospital and official representative of the California Episcopal Diocese, addressed our luncheon. He said that certainly homosexuals would be accepted in the church, but once there, since homosexuality could not be considered other than as a sin, they would be expected to change—either that or embrace celibacy.

The wife of a psychiatrist was appalled at the note of doom the churchman brought to this first Lesbian convention. "Don't you feel that this will destroy all the good you have managed to build? Won't it set your members back?" she asked Del afterwards.

"No, it won't hurt them. After all, we're all used to it. We've already been called every name there is to call us," Del countered. "We look at it this way: we've opened a door to communication with the church. And that's what we were looking for."

The Los Angeles convention in 1962 featured a panel discussion on the role of the church in the mental health of the homosexual, this time with a hard-shell Baptist preacher from Beverly Hills who pronounced us "unclean vessels" and an Episcopal priest who thought the homophile community should really be a sort of Homosexuals Anonymous. Francis Cardinal McIntire had refused to allow a Catholic priest to participate because we were "broken reeds, not to be encouraged."

The big break came in 1964. The Reverend Ted McIlvenna, a Methodist whose specialty was in the youth ministry, discovered how many young homosexuals were alienated by and from the church. He sought out public agencies to find what counseling was available in this area. He found there was nothing in the church, nothing in any other social service agency—only DOB and Mattachine working within the homophile community. There he found the help he sought, and in him we found the understanding and Christian concern we had long looked for.

We were invited to participate in a "Live-In," a one-to-one confrontation over a three-day period with churchmen at White Memorial Retreat in Mill Valley. Facilities were limited, so there were to be fifteen from the homophile community and fifteen from the church. By screaming long and loud that there needed to be "more women" involved, DOB was finally allowed five representatives. The greatest accomplishment of the retreat was the breakdown of stereotypes on both sides and the recognition of a common humanity.

Out of this consultation came the Council on Religion and the Homosexual, established in San Francisco as the "test city"—and the "infamous" New Year's Ball on January 1, 1965, a date that will be long remembered in the history of the homophile movement. Its impact upon the religious community, on the police and the political scene, contributed indelibly to a "contract of accomodation" in the city. Its reverberations were also felt throughout the country, with sympathetic outrage in northern urban regions and with zealous condemnation in the southern states.

The day after the ball (which had been sponsored by DOB and five other San Francisco homophile organizations to raise funds for the newborn CRH) seven grim clergymen called a press conference to express their anger and dismay at the way the police had "broken faith" with the Council and for the "deliberate harassment" and intimidation of the guests attending the ball. Some fifty police officers (including at least one policewoman), in uniform and in plainclothes, had infiltrated California Hall and the area around it. Floodlights lit the entrance and photographs (both still and movie) were taken of everyone entering and leaving the hall. It was like the grand entrance made by the movie stars to the Academy Awards in Hollywood—only the implications were far more grim.

More than five hundred homosexuals crossed this picket line of cops to attend the ball. The clergymen of CRH and their wives awaited them in the receiving line inside the hall. If these people were willing to stick their necks out in the face of such harassment, then the homosexual community could do no less. We were taking the invitations at the door and watched our homosexual brothers and sisters file in, visibly shaken, silently, without protest. But somehow their backs seemed straighter, their heads held higher, and their eyes, though saddened, were determined.

For the clergymen and their wives it was a shocking revelation of police power directed against a minority group for no apparent reason other than that of harassment. ("We'll uphold God's law, if you won't!" one officer told the Reverend McIlvenna.) They were furious at the infringement of civil rights. None of them had seen any activity at the ball which was objectionable save that of the police.

Three attorneys and a woman, arrested at the ball, were charged with "blocking entry of the police to California Hall." The American Civil Liberties Union volunteered to defend them. On the fourth day of the trial the prosecution rested its case, at which time Judge Leo R. Friedman promptly directed the jury to bring in a verdict of not guilty. The defense had not even made an opening statement. But the judge pointed out that police testimony indicated that they had indeed "entered the hall," but had been detained in the foyer after routine "safety" inspections had been made. Unfortunately this victory on a technicality left all the civil rights questions unanswered. And the defendants, along with CRH, became plaintiffs in a $1,500,000 suit filed in federal court against the City and County of San Francisco and its employees. The case, which dragged on for years, was eventually dropped.

But the "conspiracy of silence" was at an end. Councils on Religion and the Homosexual began to spring up in other parts of the country. Major Protestant denominations began to wrestle with statements as to what the church's stance should be regarding homosexuality. The first to proclaim publicly its endorsement of CRH was the United Church of Christ, the only denomination which has consistently supported the Council financially as well as morally.

Actions of the United Church of Christ in Northern California in the spring of 1971 led us to question the "morality" involved in church decisions. Could it be that UCC was merely supporting the CRH out of guilt? When push came to shove over the question of ordaining a seminarian who was a declared homosexual the morality of the UCC commission involved vanished when it denied the young man's ordination because "it would rip the church apart." What then of morals? Of right and wrong? This particular young man had met all the qualifications set up. He was in the top of his class, the church with which he was working had endorsed his ordination, he had a call to a ministry from people who knew he was gay. It was only because of his sexual preference (and the fact that he had been open about that preference rather than lying as had so many of his predecessors in the ministry) that he was denied the culmination of seven years of schooling coupled with a strong desire to work within the church. But miracles do happen. On April 30, 1972, ninety-six clergy and lay delegates from Bay Area UCC churches met to review the case. After hours of deliberation, of soul-searching, of defining the true meaning of Christianity, sixty-two of the delegates voted for the ordination of William Johnson, a homosexual—a first in church history. Bill said to those who opposed his ordination, "I plead with you to do as I would have: remain committed to the church—where there should be no segregation or forced assimilation."

Along with Don Lucas of the Mattachine Society, Del was appointed by Bishop James A. Pike to represent DOB on a Joint Committee on Homosexuality. Bishop Pike, renowned for his forthrightness in facing controversial issues, saw to it that his blue ribbon committee from the Diocesan Departments of Ministry and Social Relations could not fall into the trap of simply talking *about* "those people," but must meet and *know* them as persons. (This last phrase is not to be mistranslated as it was in the story of Sodom.)

The Committee's recommendations included in some nine points: endorsement of homosexual law reform, denouncement of entrapment procedures used by police and ABC detectives against homosexuals, and the need for a broad sex education program for clergy and laity alike. They were approved by the Diocesan Council in 1967. Much to our disappointment, however, none of the points in the program has been carried out by Bishop C. Kilmer (Kim) Myers who succeeded Pike. This is particularly disconcerting considering the active part Kim Myers took at the original consultation in Mill Valley.

The changes coming about within many of the "name brand" Protestant denominations were neither widespread enough nor fast enough to meet the needs of the nation's awakening homosexual minority. In 1968 a young fundamentalist preacher from Alabama started the Metropolitan Community Church in Los Angeles. Troy Perry, blessed with a charismatic personality and the knowledge of how he, as a homosexual, had been treated by the church, reached out to his gay brothers and sisters. The need for such a church is spectacularly evidenced by the meteoric rise of MCC in its few years of life. Owner of its own church building, MCC/LA has become the "mother" church and spawned similar churches throughout the country. Unfortunately for the Lesbian, MCC is tradition-bound, meaning that it is male-dominated and male-oriented, and has, as usual, relegated the women to the "Ladies Auxiliary."

The CRH Ball made its impact on the political scene as well. The Young Democrats of California and Wisconsin passed resolutions calling for revision of sex laws. Elliott Blackstone of San Francisco's Police-Community Relations Unit was appointed liaison officer between the homophile community and the police department. Homosexual functions were no longer raided or harassed, but instead treated like any other public affair with police "protection" and direction of traffic. And politicians, including Roger Boas, former chairman of California's Democratic party, began to attend "Candidates' Nights" sponsored by CRH and the Society for Individual Rights (SIR).

One of the politicians who sought the vote of the homophile community in San Francisco was Willie Brown, Jr., a Black member of the state assembly. But Brown wasn't satisfied with merely coming around on Candidates' Night and telling homosexuals how he felt they were oppressed. He did something about it. In 1969, along with Assemblyman John Burton, also of San Francisco, he introduced a bill which would repeal all laws regulating sexual conduct between consenting adults in private. Brown's colleagues were alarmed. They didn't want to vote on such a controversial measure and demanded to know why he had introduced it. "So that what you and your wife do in bed will be legal!" he retorted.

Despite Brown's efforts to get the public to realize that his legislation applied to heterosexuals too, the media persisted in calling it Brown's "homosexual" bill. Yet, when hearings were held in Sacramento in 1969 there were no opponents who appeared to speak against it. Even the Northern California Council of Churches sent a speaker to appear *for* the bill. Pious Republican committee members who were in the majority outvoted Brown's fellow Democrats. In 1970, an election year, Brown reintroduced the measure. This time it was stalled by wary Republican committee members because they had not "heard any testimony from law enforcement agencies." By 1971 the Democrats had gained control of the California state legislature, and despite some protest from police, arranged by Republican dissidents, the bill was voted out of committee with a "do pass" recommendation and onto the assembly floor. Some legislators, sounding more like corner "Jesus freaks," turned theologians for the day, and the bill was defeated by a vote of thirty-eight to twenty-eight. In the meantime, other organizations like the National Organization for Women and the California Bar Association—not to be put off by the media's "lavender herring"—have endorsed sex law reform. Once passed by the assembly, however, Brown's legislation would have to go through committee to the floor of the senate and then to Republican Governor Ronald Reagan, who could still veto the bill. Brown has vowed that he will continue to reintroduce the bill year after year until it is eventually passed—even if it takes ten years, as in England.

In 1971 New York DOB and other homophile groups from throughout the state marched to the Capitol in Albany to demand that their representatives enact legislation similar to Willie Brown's in California. New York Assemblymen Stephen J. Solarz of Brooklyn and Antonio G. Olivieri of Manhattan have introduced two additional bills which would make it illegal for employers or landlords to discriminate against anyone on the basis of sexual preference. The homophile community seems to have come a long way since our conversation ten years ago with Congressman Burton and Assemblyman O'Connell. We don't see that the same kind of progress has been made in the attitudes of the majority of lawmakers, however.

Besides the areas of sin and crime, DOB was also aware of the dangers involved in the concept of mental illness. In order to change this concept the Daughters, like other homophile organizations, felt there needed to be more knowledge about the true nature of homosexuality. Knowledge they equated with research, and DOB's surveys of 1958 and 1960 were conducted merely to promote interest in studies on the Lesbian by reputable and responsible professional researchers. Many accepted the challenge, and DOB cooperated in numerous research projects, only to be sadly disillusioned by the results. Starting with the basic premise that heterosexuality is the only acceptable form of sexual behavior, most researchers limited the scope of their studies to a never ending search for possible causes. They concentrated primarily on family dynamics and early childhood or on sexual techniques; they rarely considered the Lesbian's adult adjustment. Because of their heterosexual bias most male researchers were unable to conceive of the possibility that a Lesbian might be happy in her chosen life style—without a male. Nor could they recognize any correlation between the distress a Lesbian may feel and the societal pressures to which she is subject. Furthermore, as points of view differed between professions, so did their findings, regardless of the similarity of their samples.

For example, DOB members participated in three different research projects in the 1960s with three different male researchers and, predictably, three differing results.

Drs. Saghir and Robins, in an extension of their study mentioned earlier, interviewed fifty-seven Lesbians from DOB and forty-three single heterosexual women as a control group. Briefly, they found that the chief differences between the two groups were in "the increased prevalence of alcoholism and of attempted suicide" on the part of the Lesbians. "Despite these difficulties, the homosexual women were able to achieve, adapt, and be productive citizens." The doctors conclude, "Being a homosexual seems to be compatible with functional and interpersonal productivity, although the risk of having a psychiatric disorder and of intrapersonal conflict seems to be greater in the homosexual than in the single heterosexual."

Nowhere (perhaps it wouldn't have been scientific) do the good doctors mention that the slight statistical difference between the two groups of women just might be a result of all the oppression to which the Lesbian is subject. Obviously during that phase in her life in which she must face and accept her homosexual identity in a self contained heterosexual world, she will display manifestations of her conflict. That most Lesbians have been able to achieve and be productive later in life, however, is an indication that they have overcome these obstacles and are as adjusted or as sane as anyone can be in a crippling society.

Dr. Harvey E. Kaye participated as an investigator on a Research Committee on Female Homosexuality established by the Society of Medical Psychoanalysts in New York City. He also co-authored the study. Although Dr. Kaye doesn't exactly call the Lesbian sick, he feels she is suffering from a "crippling inhibition of heterosexual development," and therefore she is "treatable." To come to this foregone conclusion the committee passed out questionnaires to 157 members of DOB/NY and studied the "exhaustive" case histories of twenty-four Lesbians in therapy plus an equal number of heterosexual women in therapy.

It seems to us that Dr. Kaye and his committee jumped to a number of amazing conclusions. For instance, because a high percentage of the Lesbians studied had had heterosexual sex relations he concludes that all Lesbians are really bisexual. Does this mean that one swallow *does* a summer make? He then continues his hypothesis through other nonsense to the conclusion that since all Lesbians are bisexual they can be reoriented to exclusive heterosexuality—through psychoanalysis, of course. We might add that Dr. Kaye finds that mother is not absolutely responsible for the creation of Lesbians. He has found the "close-binding, overly intimate father" to be the counterpart to the "close-binding, intimate mother" found in studies of male homosexuality. It is a switch, at least, and makes everything balance out neatly in case one wants to draw up a chart. And it does take mother off the hook, more or less, for once. Most other "experts" have blamed her for the Lesbian as well as the male homosexual (plus everything else that ails women and men).

Dr. Mark J. Freedman, a psychologist, gave a battery of psychological tests to DOB members and a heterosexual control group. He found there were no differences between the Lesbian and the control group in a "global measure of psychological adjustment. The members of the Lesbian group were no more neurotic than the members of the control group, and, in fact, the Lesbians looked significantly more self actualized than the controls" in half of the Personal Orientation Inventory tests given. He found Lesbians manifested a high degree of ability to live by one's own values, were able to acknowledge their own natural feelings of hostility and anger, were sensitive and responsive to their own needs and feelings, had the ability to react as the situation required without *rigid* adherence to principles, and were able to develop meaningful, contactful relationships with other human beings, unencumbered by expectations and obligations.

Dr. Freedman further found that homosexuality is not necessarily related to psychological disturbance, that it is possible for individuals who engage in homosexual relations to function effectively in our society, to have access to their potentialities and to actualize these potentialities. He added, "Hopefully, behavioral scientists will become more aware of studies like this on the psychological concomitants of homosexuality and will change their theoretical assumptions and personal attitudes on this topic as a consequence." To which we can only say, amen (but don't hold your breath).

The Lesbian made out pretty well in two out of three of the studies mentioned. But Dr. Kaye's study has received far more publicity. He is one of those who by virtue of being a prolific writer becomes an established authority. It is probable that many psychiatrists do not share his views and question his methodology and interpretation. But where are they? Nowhere has there been any public dialogue of which we are aware where one psychiatrist questions another. Even David Reuben has slid by scot free as the "conspiracy of silence" (professional ethics?) continues.

While the (in)sanity semanticists make the headlines, the "silent majority" of therapists in the quiet and privacy of their offices are in fact devoting their efforts not to trying to change their clients, but to helping them to "adjust to their homosexuality," to accept themselves and live out their lives as they are. We knew this, but the general public didn't. So Florence Conrad, DOB's research director, decided we needed to do another survey, this time to determine the actual or current trends in professional thought and practice.

One of the most revealing studies ever done on "Attitudes of Mental Health Professionals Towards Homosexuality and Its Treatment" was conducted in 1967-8 at Florence's instigation. Because of the nature of the research, a departure and reversal of the usual procedure (this time homosexuals wanted to study the professionals who usually study them), she felt the subjects probably wouldn't cooperate with the Daughters of Bilitis, a known Lesbian organization. So she took her idea to Dr. Joel Fort, the public health specialist who then was the director of the Center for Special Problems, an agency of San Francisco's Public Health Department. With the help of Drs. Fort and Claude M. Steiner a questionnaire was developed, printed at DOB expense, and sent out under the auspices of the Center to a random sample of 163 scientifically selected Bay Area psychiatrists, psychologists and social workers. The 147 who responded had practiced psychotherapy for an average of fourteen years, ranging up to forty-one years, and an overall 88 percent were in private practice and had treated homosexuals.

Nearly all (98 percent) felt it was possible for homosexuals to function in society effectively. Likewise, practically all (99 percent) opposed laws treating private homosexual acts between consenting adults as criminal. As to federal employment, 98 percent thought there should be no prohibition against homosexuals in civil service, 88 percent felt that homosexuality should not disqualify a person from serving in the armed forces, and 73 percent held that homosexuals should not even be barred from security-sensitive positions. Furthermore, 92 percent said that homosexuals should not be restricted from the teaching profession.

More than 90 percent felt that public misunderstanding arises from the terms "illness" or "disease" as applied to homosexuality, and 64 percent (almost two-thirds of the sample) said it should not be categorized as such. Also, 96 percent did not see any reason why the average homosexual should be required to undergo therapy. And 97 percent admitted that in dealing with a homosexual "patient" they would work with a goal other than change to a heterosexual orientation (the other goals: self acceptance, self assertiveness, and improved interpersonal relationships).

These results obtained from "expert" opinion are certainly in-consistent and at odds with those reports made public by the institutions which purport to represent them, the institutions (like the American Psychiatrists and the Psychoanalysts Associations) which have persistently spread the gospel of disease diagnosis. It also explains why the survey remained unpublished for about three years, until it was finally accepted by *Psychological Reports* in October, 1971. All the other professional journals to which it was submitted seemed to find the facts too "pro" homosexual.

That homosexuality "does not constitute a specific mental or emotional illness" was declared by the National Association for Mental Health at its annual meeting in New York City, according to *Psychiatric News* of February 3, 1971. The position statement, "Homosexuality and Mental Illness," traced briefly various theories about the etiology of homosexuality and ended with the summation that whatever its cause, homosexuality "appears to be as deeply motivated as normal heterosexual behavior." Further-more, the statement pointed out, in any event "there is no evi-dence either in empirical research or in the experience of other countries that homosexual behavior in itself endangers the health of the individual or of society," and called for elimination of criminal penalties for homosexual acts committed in private.

Needless to say, this bit of news caused some flack among those psychiatrists who regard themselves as the sole arbiters of what constitutes mental illness. At the same time we, as representatives of DOB, were serving on a Task Force on Homosexuality for the San Francisco Mental Health Association and attempting to get the local chapter to adopt a similar statement. We had met reluc-tance from some of the lay members who deferred to the psychi-atric profession. However, their Professional Advisory Committee showed no hesitation in stating that "homosexuality can no longer be equated with sickness, but may properly be considered as a preference, orientation or propensity for a certain life style."

While individual psychiatrists in their practice may allow that anxiety experienced by homosexuals may be due largely to societal pressures and stigma, while they may help the homosexual to accept herself or himself and learn to cope with the givens of a hostile society, they seldom speak out in public or confront their professional colleagues with whom they may disagree. Papers bent on converting the homosexual to heterosexuality through traditional psychotherapy or conditioned-reflex aversion therapy (use of severe electric shocks, nauseating drugs or fear-guilt fantasies to eliminate homosexual behavior) are the only ones that are presented at Association meetings.

Tired of being scapegoats and guinea pigs for brainwashing techniques (which red-blooded Americans deplored in the case of war prisoners during the Korean War), members of Gay Women's Liberation and Gay Liberation disrupted such a session at the American Psychiatric Association convention in San Francisco in May of 1970. Most of the six hundred psychiatrists present lost their cool and indignantly stomped out of the meeting which was hastily adjourned. But a few, shocked into seeing new issues and recognizing that the intruders might indeed be expressing legitimate grievances, stayed behind to listen and engage in dialogue. As a result the homophile community was invited to present a panel on "Life Styles of Nonpatient Homosexuals" at the APA meeting in Washington, D.C., the next year.

Invited to participate by Dr. Kent Robinson, Baltimore psychiatrist and coordinator of the panel, were: Frank Kameny, of Washington Mattachine; Jack Baker, newly elected president of the University of Minnesota student body; Larry Littlejohn, past president of the Society for Individual Rights, the nation's largest homophile organization; Lilli Vincenz, who had worked with various Lesbian groups on the East coast; and Del, representing DOB and the Council on Religion and the Homosexual. During the presentation of the panel there were inevitable and heated denunciations of Dr. Irving Bieber and Dr. Charles Socarides, the two most currently outspoken and self proclaimed authorities on homosexuality. The first respondent from the audience declared angrily that he resented being harangued by the panelists for the conclusions drawn by these two men, that they were not representative of most psychiatric thought, and certainly not of his.

"Then why aren't you and the others writing the papers and the books or making appearances on radio and television? Why aren't your differing views being made available to the public? That is what we are talking about!" Kameny retorted.

Later when we broke up into small groups for discussion, one psychiatrist said, "Most of us don't want to, or have time to, write papers or make public appearances. It takes a certain type of guy to get hung up on that." All of the psychiatrists we talked to claimed they were not out to change all homosexuals, only those who expressed a desire to change. It was on this basis that they defended their attention to methods of bringing about behavioral change.

The accent is always on "behavior," on whether or not the individual can "perform" heterosexually, which, of course, the Lesbian can more easily fake than can the male homosexual. What the "change artists" fail to realize is that there is so much more to homosexuality than displayed performance, which is only the outward expression of a much deeper, emotional and psychic inner life. What of the emotional and social adjustment of the male-homosexual-turned-heterosexual who fantasizes homosexually in order to win his heterosexual Oscar? What does that do to his relationship with his wife? Many "cured" homosexuals have told us that, while they can have adequate sex relations with their wives, they still look to men to fulfill their other needs. "Under these circumstances, would *you* want your daughter to marry one?" Del asked a psychiatrist. The doctor could not, or would not, answer.

Ramsey Clark, former United States attorney general, was the keynote speaker at the annual awards ceremonies of this same APA Convention. He challenged the psychiatrists to become "involved," to come to grips with the "over-criminalization" of our citizens who are poor, who may be addicted to drugs or alcohol, who may have a different life style or sexual preference. He was given a standing ovation by the same audience who an hour previously had heaped abuse upon the male and female homosexuals who had stormed the podium to say much the same thing. It is doubtful that many of the psychiatrists present could see the correlation. They do not yet fully understand that "Gay Liberation," which they perceive as only a small group of radicals, is the full force of a minority that will no longer allow itself to be "researched" or defined, labeled and criminalized simply for being different.

From the mid-sixties and into the seventies the homophile movement took on a new dimension. New organizations mushroomed in every major city and college campus in the nation. As the women's movement took hold, new DOB chapters, Gay Women's Liberation and Radical Lesbian groups also sprang up. In the meantime the East Coast Homophile Organizations (ECHO), with which New York DOB had long been affiliated, expanded into a North American Conference of Homophile Organizations (NACHO). And the homophile community of San Francisco joined forces with other minority groups to form Citizens Alert as a watchdog twenty-four-hour answering service for complaints of police brutality and malpractice perpetrated against minority citizens.

This new thrust into the public eye, into dialogue with the church, into politics, into a national awareness of the homophile community, brought with it many problems of policy and personnel in the Daughters of Bilitis. Some members felt they had been lost in the shuffle, that DOB had become so caught up in these various "causes" that it no longer cared about the individual. They split off from the San Francisco chapter and started their own club, Nova, which placed emphasis on social events and group therapy rather than involvement in the homophile movement.

At about the same time the Philadelphia Chapter of DOB withdrew from its parent and formed the Homophile Action League. HAL is practically the only group still functioning which has managed to achieve an even membership of men and women, all working together to forward the goals of the homophile movement. We suspect this balance has been possible because it was a group started by women: they were the majority and *then* the men were let in.

The rapid changes occurring throughout the nation in the awareness of the homosexual had much effect on DOB. With the chartering of the Los Angeles and New York chapters in 1960 DOB had become a national organization with a National Governing Board at whose head was the National President. Members of the Board were scattered throughout the country in an attempt to give equal representation to all areas and all points of view. Del was DOB's first national president, succeeded by Jaye Bell, Cleo Glenn, Shirley Willer and Rita Laporte, all extremely able women. But the problems inherent in running an organization from such an unwieldy structure inevitably brought about dissension, distrust and accusations that the president was "power hungry" and/or "dictatorial."

It was a combination of these problems and the current trend toward decentralization and local autonomy which led the organization to change its structure radically at the 1970 National Convention in New York City. At that time the National Governing Board was done away with as were all the "national" rules and regulations governing chapters. Instead the organization reaffirmed its policy that DOB was open to all women regardless of race, religion or ethnic background. Chapters were given total autonomy to "do their thing" in the way best suited to their area. Retention of DOB as a national organization was desired by all, and so a new national board was set up comprised of the presidents of each local unit. This board's primary function is to maintain contact between chapters, to authorize new ones, and to arrange a national meeting every other year.

The Ladder, subtitled "A Lesbian Review," had also gone through many changes since its beginning as a mimeographed "newsletter" in 1956. Phyllis, the first editor, was followed by Del, Barbara Gittings, Helen Sanders and Gene Damon. Each of these talented women made changes in format and content and the magazine improved steadily over the years.

At one point DOB spent a lot of time, energy and money in an attempt to put *The Ladder* on the newsstands and thus make it a truly large-selling national magazine. That attempt taught us one thing: Lesbians do not go into newsstands and buy anything that says Lesbian on it. Reports that came back to us indicated that with few exceptions the magazine was bought by men—either for their Lesbian friends or because, as heterosexuals, they thought it might be sexy. It wasn't.

From its inception *The Ladder* was a monthly magazine (with but a few combined issues when we got caught in a time or money bind). In 1968, however, the decision was made to print the magazine on slick paper, increase the number of pages and publish every other month.

As time went on it was evident that the winds of change were affecting *The Ladder* as well as DOB, its publisher. Gene Damon and Rita Laporte felt strongly that DOB should align itself solely with the women's movement. They felt that the homophile movement was too male oriented and that the Lesbian's salvation lay in working for equal rights for women. *The Ladder* began to print more and more news about the women's movement and early in 1970 dropped the subtitle "A Lesbian Review." As the 1970 National Convention approached it became obvious that there was disaffection between, on the one hand, the national president and *The Ladder* editor, and on the other, the rest of the organization. The culmination came when the entire physical production and mailing of the magazine was moved to Reno, Nevada, and placed in the hands of the chapter there.

Faced with this *fait accompli* at the National Convention the organization decided to let *The Ladder* go. A legal fight to retain it would have taken too much of the organization's time and money and probably would have effectively killed the magazine. The Laporte-Damon combination now publishes *The Ladder* independently. In the meantime, various chapters have begun their own magazines *(Sisters* in San Francisco and *The Lesbian Tide* in Los Angeles) which reflect the immediate concerns of their own city and state rather than the overview necessary for a national magazine published every other month.

In 1968, for the first time in thirteen years, we held no office at either a national or local level in DOB. Through the years DOB has attracted many dedicated women who have given of their time, talents and money to keep the organization going. Without these women the group would never have lasted. Despite all this other talent, however, we often found ourselves in a position of leadership willy-nilly. Because we were founders, old timers, always there, we were often looked to to solve problems which really should have, and could have been solved by others. People kept saying, "I remember in 1957 you said. . . ." It was probably true, but times change and situations change. And people grow—hopefully. We got pretty tired of being pinned down by what we had once said but did not now believe. We felt that the Daughters needed to stand unsupported by its two "mammas." If it couldn't, then maybe it hadn't been such a hot idea after all.

We are happy to report that DOB is doing well. The increase in membership and the number of chapters has been significant and, under the new structure, we envision chapters springing up in every large city in every state. It is indeed an "idea whose time has come." The New York and Los Angeles chapters have established centers in their cities—a goal for other groups to aim at—although there have been problems. In New York the problems stemmed from police harassment and lack of money. In Los Angeles, too, there was a shortage of funds, and DOB/SF has yet to raise enough in its building fund to move from its small offices into larger quarters needed for growth.

In 1971 it seemed strange that suddenly the New York police would begin to harass a group like DOB. Perhaps the growing strength of the organization became a threat. Whatever the reason, DOB/NY was visited by the cops at three different headquarters, and a number of DOB officers were arrested on trumped up charges, which were later dismissed. In the meantime, reports have been coming in from various parts of the country that police have stepped up action against gay people—apparently a backlash to the growing militancy of Gay Liberationists.

But now, in a nation on fire with "liberation" spirit, there is no turning back. DOB is only one of several alternatives for the Lesbian. The change has come in many gay people: from "fear" to "fight." Probably the biggest "shot in the arm" for the new aggression in the movement was the momentous march down Sixth Avenue in New York celebrating Homosexual Liberation Day 1970, the end of Gay Pride Week. An estimated twenty thousand gay brothers and sisters (with a smattering of straight supporters) marched "out of the closet and into the streets." There were banners, flags and signs. Lavender Menace T-shirts were in evidence along with some couples wearing "Femme" and "Butch" sweatshirts (they switched them every so often). DOB/NY was there with its banner and there were men and women from all over the East Coast. The New York march ended with a rally in Central Park. On the West Coast, Californians also marched in Los Angeles in what Morris Kight called a "joyful, folksy, funky, happy street parade." Reaction on both coasts to the marches was good, both from the public watching and from the media. It was surely an indication that the homosexual was on the move. Shouts of "Say it loud, gay and proud," "Two-four-six-eight, gay is just as good as straight!" and "Gay Power" have set the tone for a drive to freedom which will not be denied.

Occasion for the marches was the first anniversary of the Chris-

topher Street riots, the first time in modern history when homosexual men and women fought back against their oppressors in a
face to face confrontation. It began with a visit by the New York
police to the Stonewall Inn, a gay bar on Christopher Street in
Greenwich Village, on June 28, 1969. Apparently the tavern had
some license irregularity which the cops were checking out. They
could not refrain, however, from hassling the patrons, calling them
"faggots" and "fruits." The rage within the homosexuals rose to
the surface. They went outside and tried to lock the owners and
the cops inside. Bottles and matches were thrown and a parking
meter was wrenched from the sidewalk. A riot began which was
joined by others. Barricades were set up and manned, bonfires
flamed and there were three days of street action—at one time the
gays had "liberated" an area two blocks wide and three blocks
long.

This marked the beginning of open and overt physical battle by
the homosexual against the forces of society which have for so
long kept her/him from true humanhood. No more polite discussions, no more secret societies, no more concern about the
"image." Gay is Good! Once the bottle containing the genie is
open, it is not easy to get the genie back into the bottle. The
homosexual is out of the bottle—you will not get her/him back in!

9. Lesbian / Woman

"The Lesbian has agreed (with reservations) to join in common cause with the male homosexual, but her role in the homophile movement to date has largely been one of mediator between the male homosexual and society." So stated Shirley Willer, National president of DOB at the 1966 North American Conference of Homophile Organizations (NACHO) in San Francisco. She cited as an example the program of the DOB Convention, held the previous weekend, at which officials from all branches of city government were drawn into serious discussion of "police harassment, unequal law enforcement, legal proscription of sexual practices, and the problem of disproportionate penalties for solicitations, wash-room sex acts and female impersonation." In contrast, she pointed out, these problems rarely touch the Lesbian, since job security, career advancement and family relationships are of primary concern to her. "The important difference between the male and the female homosexual is that the Lesbian is discriminated against, not only because she is a homosexual, but because she is a woman."

Shirley then asked that the male-oriented homophile organizations show common cause with the Lesbian and DOB by affirming as a goal of the conference "to be as concerned about women's civil rights as male homosexuals' civil liberties" and suggested that "homosexual men attempt to appreciate the value of Lesbians as *people* in the movement, respect them and their abilities as individuals, not seek them out as simple 'showpieces.' "

Some men in the homophile community, we must admit, responded to the Lesbian challenge of 1966. Members of the

Lincoln-Omaha Council on Religion and the Homosexual picketed "Sister George" as being derogatory and untypical of the Lesbian. A few joined the picket line in front of the Hearst Building when the National Organization for Women protested the failure of San Francisco newspapers to comply with the mandate of the Equal Employment Opportunity Commission to "de-sexegrate" their "help wanted" ads. Others in Los Angeles picketed a gay bar which discriminated against Lesbians. Frank Kameny gave counsel to women caught up in the "purge" of an army camp. Larry Littlejohn took on the San Francisco Human Rights Commission, urging its members to extend their purview to include job discrimination on the basis of sex and/or sexual orientation. And CRH made it a policy to include both men and women in all speaking engagements. But these were isolated instances over a period of four years and were the acts of a few dedicated men. For the movement as a whole it was business as usual, and that meant male-dominated, male-oriented, male-chauvinistic policies and attitudes.

Shirley Willer's challenge went unanswered until the 1970 NACHO Conference, again in San Francisco, when on August 26, Women's National Strike Day, seven Lesbians from DOB, Nova, and Gay Women's Liberation disrupted the meeting once again to call attention to the irrelevance of the homophile movement to the needs of the women within its ranks. It was only then, under duress, that a resolution in support of women's rights was passed. But resolutions, like president's commission reports, are easily drawn up and even more easily forgotten. By the next evening, at a political dinner feting Assemblyman Willie Brown, the Lesbian was again "invisible."

Recognizing that their struggle was twofold, the leaders of DOB turned their attention to the issues of the women's movement. By her very nature the Lesbian is cast in the role of breadwinner and will be a member of society's working force most of her life, since there is no male in her life to support her. Because of traditionally low pay for "woman's work" the Lesbian is very much concerned with equal job opportunities for women and with "equal pay for equal work" laws. Because of her anticipated longevity in the working force she is vitally concerned with equal opportunity for education and professional careers for women. Because she is taxed as a single person at the highest available rate regardless of her commitments she is also concerned with the tax deductions for head of household espoused by many women's rights groups. Because she may be a working mother she has a definite stake in proposals for child care centers. Because of societal pressures against her Lesbian commitment she may find herself involved with men and therefore might very well have need of birth control information and/or abortion.

"This is all true. But what makes you think the Lesbian will be any more welcome or any more accepted in the women's movement than in the homophile movement?" asked Meredith Grey, a long term leader in the New York chapter who had frequently played the role of devil's advocate.

"Does that mean we support the women's movement as 'silent partners'? Do we once again put on the 'mask' and pretend to be heterosexuals so that we don't rock the boat or frighten the ladies? Or do we join with them openly and honestly, as Lesbians, committed to a common cause? If we do that, what kind of reception do you think we'll get? And if they shun us, what then?"

These were very crucial questions. Their answers have proved to be hilarious and heart-warming on some occasions, dire and sinister in others. Some women in the women's movement have wrestled with their own emotions, overcoming their fears and accepting Lesbians as sisters in a common struggle. Others, feeling threatened by what they call the "Lavender Menace," have indulged in whispering campaigns and tried to lock the closet door.

DOB's leaders did not find immediate response for the women's movement even from Lesbians themselves. Their historical alignment with the homophile movement seemed much more natural. They were not so sure about the wisdom of branching out into the women's movement which represented the straight world, more often than not: the enemy.

Valerie Taylor, author of several Lesbian novels, took DOB and *The Ladder* to task in the October, 1969, *Mattachine Midwest Newsletter:* "Of course, the Armed Forces and the government are discriminatory. Like the women's liberation movement, they're fifty years behind the times. A Lesbian who opts for either ought to have her motivation examined (see Freud, et al., on self defeat). . . ."

Six months later Valerie was writing about "People Power" and asking, "Is there a connection between the homophile movement and women's liberation?" She pointed out, "Women are not a minority, statistically speaking, but they're treated as though they were, and some of them display a minority mentality. Job discrimination, lower pay and a multitude of social slights are imposed by our socio-economic culture, and that's male dominated (not because men are sadists, but because of social lag). Self denigration is learned from mothers, female teachers and the peer group."

She wound up this time with a plug for DOB: "It's no accident that Lesbians are in the forefront of the feminist movement. In fact, one way to know what's happening in women's liberation is to read *The Ladder.*"

Long-term DOB members and advocates of the homophile movement, Barbara Gittings and Kay Tobin, found themselves strained between the dichotomy of the homophile and the women's movements. Barbara, who had long worked diligently with Frank Kameny on federal discrimination cases against homosexuals, finally opted for the Homophile Action League, the co-ed group in Philadelphia. And Kay, co-author of *The Gay Crusaders,* who has put her efforts into the Gay Activists Alliance in New York, admits she feels an innate loyalty to both movements, but still is "not quite comfortable in either of them."

More recently Barbara has been named 1971-2 coordinator of the Task Force on Gay Liberation, established by the American Library Association as part of its Social Responsibilities Round Table to combat discrimination in service to and employment of homosexuals. She has called for an all-out attack on "the lies in the libraries about gay people." One target is the library classification and subject-heading systems which place books on homosexuality under "sexual aberration" or "perversion." Barbara has also prepared an extensive bibliography of serious nonfiction books and periodicals on homosexuality and made it available to librarians.

Of particular interest to us as Lesbians and women is that writers in the women's liberation movement are now saying the very same things regarding religion and psychiatry that have been expounded in the homophile movement for the last twenty years. This is exemplified in *Sisterhood Is Powerful,* an anthology edited by Robin Morgan.

Dr. Naomi Weisstein, assistant professor of psychology at Loyola University, questions the acceptance of theory without evidence by psychiatrists and clinical psychologists who theorize about the "causal nature of the inner dynamic" without taking into consideration the social context in which individuals live, the influence of the bias of experimenters on the results of their research, and the arbitrary societal definitions of what is masculine and feminine.

Dr. Natalie Shainess, diplomate of the American Board of Psychiatry and Neurology, observes that *Sex and the College Student,* a 1965 report of the Group for the Advancement of Psychiatry, contains several examples of sexual involvement between male teachers and female students, in every instance of which the onus was placed upon the student. The only case where the responsibility was laid at the door of the teacher was in the case of a female instructor, who was, of course, a Lesbian.

Though she is really speaking about women, Dr. Mary Daly (who holds doctorates in religion, sacred theology and philosophy and is the author of *The Church and the Second Sex*) also registers the complaint of the homophile community when she protests against "the imposition of alienating sexual stereotypes and roles upon human beings."

Betty Rollin, *Look* magazine senior editor, wrote a provocative report on "The Motherhood Myth," which appeared in the September 22, 1970, issue. "The notion that the maternal wish and the activity of mothering are instinctive or biologically destined is baloney," she declared. Her thesis was supported by hundreds of sociologists, psychologists, psychoanalysts and biologists. The most vivid and cogent observation was made by Dr. Richard Rabkin, New York psychiatrist, who said, "Women don't need to be mothers any more than they need spaghetti. But if you're in a world where everyone is eating spaghetti, thinking they need it and want it, you will think so too." And Dr. Frederick Wyatt, president of the American Sociological Association, also observed, "There is no innate drive for children. Otherwise, the enormous cultural pressures there are to reproduce wouldn't exist." These pressures have, of course, been successfully used to perpetuate prejudice against the Lesbian because of the "sterility" of her relationship and to *confuse* her into believing that she could not be a "complete" woman unless her body fulfilled its reproductive function and until she satisfied the Madonna metonymy misnomered as her "maternal instinct."

In the May 29, 1970, issue of *Everywoman,* a newspaper published in Los Angeles, Sylvia Hartman, a self proclaimed *ex*-psychologist, exposed what she calls "shrinkthink." She particularly focused her wrath upon the Draw-A-Person test, in which the subject is asked to draw figures (no stick figures allowed) of parents, siblings, et al. for the psychologist to interpret. This, she claims, is invalid, unscientific, and subject to the whim, bias and prejudicial interpretation of psychologists who have long since lost all touch with common sense. She defined "intensive clinical experience" on which psychiatrists base their judgments as "doing the same thing for years, as they were taught, without thinking it through and without changing." They are "still dancing in the outdated Freudian Follies," Sylvia claimed, when it comes to sex differences and sex roles.

These were certainly familiar grievances and arguments to old-timers in the homophile movement. It was indeed encouraging to find that women were adding their voices and their protests against the same oppressive institutions, against the same stifling conformist roles, against the myth that they must bear children in order to be "fulfilled," and against laws and employers discriminating against women. But it was in the latter area that the women's movement effectively made the Lesbian realize how really oppressed she was—not as a homosexual, but as a woman.

The Lesbian's involvement in the feminist movement, however, is in direct ratio to her acceptance of herself in the various identities and roles she is forced to play in our society. It has a great deal to do with her world view, her ability to see beyond the particular niche in which she finds herself. Sometimes she is trapped in her identity as a Lesbian; because of fear of discovery and society's consequent reprisals she is unable to identify at all with heterosexual women. She finds security and safety in working with female—or even male—homosexuals who know and understand.

But with the momentum engendered in the women's movement in recent years Lesbians have been forced to face their own womanhood. Many are coming to realize that the so-called sexual revolution must also include an entire reshaping of the role of woman in our society. Just as some Blacks have dropped out of the homophile movement to re-identify themselves and work for racial equality, so are many Lesbians beginning to branch out into various women's organizations.

We chose to align ourselves with the National Organization for Women. When we first joined, we noted that the membership application blank designated a special rate for couples. That forced us to come to our first decision—to join as a Lesbian couple. We wrote to the late Inka O'Hanrahan, then national secretary-treasurer, saying that as a couple, together for years, and subject to all sorts of economic discrimination, we would hope that NOW would give us our first break. Inka honored our membership, so advised the Executive Board, and when we first met her in person, greeted us warmly, "It's so good to have you with us. Surely there are more of you. I hope you'll bring them around."

Later that year, 1968, Inka instigated an Ad Hoc Committee on the Status of Women and invited the presidents of various women's organizations (including DOB) to participate in efforts to get the city administration to appoint a Commission on the Status of Women for San Francisco. Such commissions had been established at the national and state level, but Inka felt that one was also needed at the local level and that it must include a wide representation of women from all segments of the community.

One real bonus which we shall always treasure from our involvement with NOW was the privilege of knowing and loving Inka. She was a lifelong feminist. The list of her credentials seemed endless, but what was most impressive about her was her genuineness, her warmth and humor. Her devotion to the cause of women was boundless—she called it "enlightened self interest"—and it cut across all barriers of class, economic status, education, race, religion and sexual orientation.

Del called the hospital after Inka's first heart attack to find out how she was doing. Though she was not allowed either phone calls or visitors at the time, the call somehow got through. It was the first word Inka had had from the outside world since her confinement. She was so delighted, so eager and enthusiastic that she lifted Del's spirits—as though Del were the patient instead of Inka. Her chief concern was that Del convey apologies to DOB because her illness prevented her from filling her scheduled speaking engagement. "I didn't want to speak to them just about N.O.W." (She always spelled out the initials rather than pronouncing them as a word). "There was so much more I wanted to say to them." More than a year later, during Phyllis's last conversation with her, Inka again showed her concern for the Lesbian: "How are they treating you in N.O.W?"

After her death we realized that we had only seen or talked to Inka about a dozen times. Yet we felt her loss as we would have had she been a very dear friend of twenty years' standing.

Upon Del's election as secretary of SF/NOW, she made it a point to level with her board at their very first meeting. The two of us have always been open with NOW's leadership about our personal relationship, though it may not have been common knowledge among the general membership. We have suffered no repercussions. We have not been hampered in our participation, nor has NOW been hurt by the fact we are "up front" Lesbians.

The leadership was all too willing to have Del assume the responsibility of setting up the first Bay Area Women's Coalition meeting in September of 1969, a meeting which was to bring together representatives from all the women's organizations we could reach. Quite naturally DOB was invited, but was not, because of time limitations, given a specific spot on the morning program. Only a few of the twenty-three participating groups were allowed time to speak of their goals and activities in relation to the women's movement. After the lunch break, however, Women's Liberation members requested an opportunity to hear from DOB. Rita Laporte, the national president, then gave a short rap on the Lesbian's role in the women's movement. There was an apparent demonstration of acceptance, even warmth, from the predominantly heterosexual assembly of some 150 women.

By the second coalition meeting of February, 1970, Gay Women's Liberation had come into being, and a special panel discussion on the Lesbian was presented. Pat, from DOB, opened with the observation, "One of the reasons for holding this panel today is to discuss a charge that is rather frightening for us all, namely, that the Lesbian movement is being infiltrated by feminists."

That broke the ice and led to a healthy discussion of the issue, which for most women in the audience was a very new experience. At the end, Alice, from Gay Women's Liberation, posed this question to her listeners, "Will you really be honest? Will any of you who have ever felt any sort of physical attraction towards another woman please stand up?"

It was a blockbuster her fellow panelists had previously vetoed in planning the meeting, but Alice couldn't resist. The response was something to behold. Some Lesbians who have themselves "together" jumped up immediately. Other Lesbians, who had never before admitted it publicly, slowly arose. Some heterosexual women stood up as a gesture of support and in acknowledgement of the educational program they had just been treated to. Others, more thoughtfully, rose because, "Yes, there was that time when I was a teenager. . . ." More joined in because they accepted the fact we were all women working for a common cause—until finally about three-quarters of the three hundred women from forty-four organizations were standing up in the auditorium.

Unfortunately the hold-outs didn't really understand what was taking place and undoubtedly went home thinking they had been duped into attending a Lesbian meeting. These were the more conservative women, who were only tentatively beginning to take note of the sweeping ramifications of the women's movement, though they had belonged to this or that women's group for years. They have yet to experience the togetherness that women are beginning to find—women who have been brainwashed in the past into thinking they must always be competitive, isolated, and defined by "their" man.

Hot on the heels of these positive responses, Del enthusiastically wrote to Betty Friedan suggesting that NOW's national conference in March take a stand on the Lesbian issue and put this "lavender herring" in its proper perspective once and for all. She received no response. She then wrote to Dr. Kathryn F. Clarenbach, chairman of the board, who considered such an idea sheer disaster. It would, she felt, offer the opposition ammunition which could destroy the advances that had been made in the women's movement. Other leaders further expressed fear that dealing with the Lesbian issue would dilute or diffuse the priorities that NOW was already committed to, that a chapter could be taken over by Lesbians who would address themselves only to this single issue. But even if such an unlikely thing should happen, Lesbian members of NOW are as deeply committed to women's rights and to all of NOW's goals as any other women members.

All that Del had asked were two small revisions: one, that NOW, which had already taken a stand on a woman's right to control her reproductive life, extend the statement to include her "sexual life"; the second, that NOW's call for repeal of all laws concerning abortion be extended to include repeal of all laws restricting "sexual activity between consenting adults in private." Unfortunately, the latter phrase is to most people a euphemism for homosexual law reform. What they fail to realize is that such laws also pertain to heterosexual men and women and that, until women are liberated sexually, no one will be free. The "double standard" must be eliminated and sex roles (what is masculine and what is feminine) redefined, if the perennial "battle of the sexes" is ever to come to an end. We presumed this is what NOW was all about in its avowal to establish a "truly equal partnership with men."

As one (heterosexual) NOW member put it to us, "I believe deeply that female sexuality is a key issue in the women's movement. Until every woman is able to say, 'Okay, so you think I'm a Lesbian. Fuck you—I will neither confirm nor deny it,' the women's movement will go nowhere. You see, I want liberation, not just equality."

Del still chuckles over the time when she, as chairman of SF/NOW's political committee, accompanied Victoria Selmier, then president, to City Hall. They went ostensibly to find out what had happened to the proposal for the Commission on the Status of Women. In their conversation with Mike McCone, aide to Mayor Joseph Alioto, they got into the area of job discrimination. McCone insisted, "We don't discriminate against women in our Civil Service system—why, we don't even discriminate against homosexuals!"

Vickie viewed him quizzically and said, "NOW is primarily a straight organization which is open to both men and women, though we have no doubt that there are Lesbians among our members."

"Oh, I didn't mean to imply—" McCone floundered. He was immediately on the defensive, gasping for words—and air.

This is the point Del had tried to get over to Betty Friedan and Kathryn Clarenbach. Instead of being constantly on the defensive NOW must accept and admit the fact that it has Lesbian members. So what? Accusations can invalidate the women's movement only if women allow them to. Fear breeds fear. We learned that a long time ago in DOB. We learned too, that as leaders, no matter how we felt personally, we could not display fear. In the process we overcame our own fears.

However, Ms. Friedan, who is obviously still caught up in her own "feminine mystique," saw to it that NOW's "couple" membership was eliminated and that any resolutions from the "Lavender Menace" were scotched before they ever reached the floor for consideration. In the process, NOW became vulnerable to unnecessary internal strife for failure to deal forthrightly with one issue that properly belongs among the many women's issues. By not facing it, it became in a sense *the* issue Ms. Friedan had hoped to avoid.

The first Congress to Unite Women called by NOW in New York City in November of 1969 left DOB off the list. As a result some members of NOW's New York Chapter in a "1970 Manifesto" accused NOW of "sexism," of using women to oppress a whole class of women—namely the Lesbian, "the one word that can cause the Executive Committee a collective heart attack." They cited the gap between leadership and membership: the subject had been broached at a general meeting and members had expressed a willingness to consider the problem in relation to their own personal reactions and in relation to NOW. But still Lesbians were ignored by the leadership.

The second Congress, the following May, was disrupted by the "Lavender Menace" and the issue brought out in spite of Ms. Friedan, who can be credited with creating the "monster" she feared. The band of women who descended on the meeting wearing their lavender T-shirts and carrying signs, "Take a Lesbian to Lunch" or "Women's Liberation Is a Lesbian Plot," went on to found the Radicalesbians, forcing the New York women's movement to recognize and come to terms with their Lesbian sisters.

NOW has often been the target or whipping girl of most women's groups. The conservatives claim picketing and demonstrations are radical; the liberation groups feel reform of the existing system is far too conservative. NOW, for the most part, has tried to maintain a policy of *not* running down other groups that are committed to a common cause. Certainly we need more exercises in affirmation and unity and certainly NOW missed its chance to affirm and unify in the case of the Lesbian.

While NOW nationally was wrestling with the Lesbian issue behind closet doors, DOB and NOW chapters were exchanging speakers in New York, Los Angeles, Chicago, and San Francisco. When the issue of Lesbianism became part of the public domain after the furor over Kate Millett's book *Sexual Politics,* members of NOW and other feminist groups joined Kate in a press conference in New York City on December 17, 1970. These women stood in sisterhood to "deplore *Time* magazine's malicious attack on the movement, operating from the premise that it could malign or invalidate us by associating us with Lesbianism." They pointed out the natural alliance between Women's and Homosexual Liberation, since both are struggling towards a common goal: a society free from defining and categorizing people by virtue of gender and/or sexual preference.

"Lesbian is a label used as a psychic weapon to keep women locked into their male-defined 'feminine role.' The essence of that role is that a woman is defined in terms of her relationship to men. A woman is called a Lesbian when she functions autonomously. Women's autonomy is what Women's Liberation is all about," they concluded.

"Betty Friedan, high priestess of the women's liberation movement and conservative on the Lesbian issue, did not attend," the *New York Times* noted, though some fifty other supporters with signs such as "Is the Statue of Liberty a Lesbian?" cheered their sisters on.

We on the West Coast rejoiced that NOW/NY had finally taken a positive step toward resolving its Lesbian hangup. We dusted off Del's previous resolution, which had been turned down by the national board, and presented a panel discussion on "The Lesbian in the Women's Movement" before the San Fancisco and Berkeley chapters. Both groups passed the resolution without fanfare, though a few did grumble that the statement was "innocuous" and others expressed resentment that there was even any question about accepting Lesbians in the women's movement. The resolution was then submitted to the Western Regional Conference (comprised of delegates from thirteen states) where it was again accepted without any ado. But controversy in New York had not subsided, as we had thought. To our dismay a new regime had taken over the chapter and was conducting a "purge" of all known Lesbians and their sympathizers.

Lesbian-baiting is, of course, a favorite masculine ploy in putting down feminists. Members of Women's Liberation, in earlier days, were known to take all sorts of insults at the hands of their antagonists, but dissolved into tears when called a "dyke." But after the invasion of the "Lavender Menace," the New York Radical Feminists and Women's Liberation (on both coasts) in their "consciousness-raising" small groups began to examine their feelings, their emotional reactions not only to the words but to the real live people who provoked them. They found that Lesbians were likable women, not unlike themselves. They realized that prejudice against Lesbians was a male concept which they had simply accepted without question. They began to see the Lesbian as a symbol of protest against male domination, against the ill-fitting, inhibitive sex roles designated to women. And they tentatively embraced her as a sister.

Mickey Jacudo, of the New York Feminists, described her feelings as total relief when she was finally able to open up to her sisters in her small group. "Before that they weren't really relating to me as a person, but, of course, they couldn't because I was still afraid to be honest with them. But after six months, I confronted them with my Lesbianism. Their initial reaction was one of fear. They were afraid they might be labeled 'gay,' and they were afraid of their own Lesbian feelings. But they came to realize that we could be friends and that we could relate to each other without the sexual component interfering."

We offer this observation to those women who feel threatened by Lesbians and who therefore feel they must affirm their heterosexuality in our presence: From the time you were a young girl, you were taught to say no to unwanted sexual advances from men. We have often pointed out that there might be less emotional violence had little boys been taught the same lesson. It is also possible for women to say no to other women—if they choose to.

Mickey Jacudo's experience in her small group is not unique. Many (if not most) Lesbians found less than total acceptance by their sisters in Women's Liberation. The consciousness-raising process has been slow, but it does seem to be working. In "A Letter from Mary" printed in *It Ain't Me, Babe* in 1970, one woman had this to say to her sisters:

"We have all said it in our leaflets, to our friends, in our screams in the night: what we want is equal, open, loving relationships where each person can see the other as an individual human being, not a member of some mythic group, where each person loves and wants the other instead of needing her for some quality he does not himself possess. So why when I affirm all this do you see me with strange eyes? Why when I love my sisters wholly do I make you uneasy? Why, if I talk of my feelings, do you look away or, if you listen, at the end relax as if to say: 'Well, I guess you had to do that ... it's probably very healthy that you brought your secret out into the open ... but now that's over and we don't, thank God, have to talk about it anymore.' And, after that, every remark I make is filtered through the label 'Lesbian.'

"The irony of it all is that I probably never would have discovered my homosexuality without Women's Liberation. ... Why does my body, which you claim should not be alienated from me, make my love for my sisters suddenly something furtive, something lower, something which is somehow wrong? Would that be too much of a separation from straight society, from men?

"The accusation of being a movement of Lesbians will always be powerful if we cannot say, 'Being a Lesbian is good.' Nothing short of that will suffice as an answer. ... Women's Liberation needs Lesbianism. Lesbians need Women's Liberation. We are all sisters.

"My love for my sister, for my sisters, was and is good and beautiful. I don't see how it can be ignored if women are to talk about liberation. This does not mean we all have to leap into bed with each other, now or ever. It does mean we can't make homosexuality the one thing we won't talk about honestly. It means we must really accept such love as a positive good, which I think we can do by dealing honestly with our feelings about it and each other. We can't afford to be afraid of these feelings or of our sisters."

As Mary indicated, in the small group process there is, of course, the possibility that latent Lesbian tendencies will be unleashed, that women will find they not only can identify with other women, but they can also love them. While in New York, we met two women who had been instrumental in getting eight Women's Liberation groups going in a small town in South Carolina. During their pioneering efforts they discovered their love for each other, but they were fearful that knowledge of their new personal relationship would undo the work they had done. When the situation became unbearable—the hypocrisy of the dual life— they migrated to the big city where they could live more openly.

Both Radicalesbians on the East Coast and Gay Women's Liberation in the west have identified almost wholly with the women's movement and have only an indirect alliance with the homophile movement. Their radical political stance and their leaderless, non-structured small groups have been taken from Women's Liberation. A few of them are ex-DOBs, but mostly they are women who became radicalized by their associations with NOW or with the male-oriented Gay Liberation. Some started out in small Women's Liberation groups, but were turned off by the inability of their sisters to accept them openly as Lesbians.

As Alice put it, "Gay Women's Liberation is not an organization, but a state of mind—a group of women who are for 'liberation' in every sense of the word." They are through with hiding. They are uncompromising in their demand to be accepted as they are for what they are—Lesbians. Though threatening and confusing to some of their straight sisters who are for the "live and let live" policy (as long as you keep your private life "private"), these groups have been more instrumental than any others in forcing women to face up to the realities of life. As long as women are allowed to oppress other women, as long as women ignore or deny their own sexuality and that of other women, as long as women can be divided against each other by race or class or sexual orientation, then the women's movement cannot be successful. They might gain a few "rights" perhaps, but their gains will be limited to legalities that benefit a few women in more privileged positions, and could still allow for the subjugation of some women. The message of the radical Lesbians, if it can be put in a single sentence, is, "*All* women must be freed."

Lesbian-baiting unfortunately is not confined to those opposing the women's movement. Some women, locked in a political power play within their own organizations, have found it a convenient tool. A heterosexual woman, the victim of a whispering campaign, told us, "I was deeply wounded and emotionally upset for some months. But their lies forced me to face certain fears in myself and the issue of Lesbianism as a whole. And, by God, I think I've finally got my head on straight!" Today she is one of our staunch supporters. She *knows* what it means to be thought a Lesbian.

While we deplore these tactics, and while we have empathy for the women who are their victims, we cannot help but secretly applaud those who use them; for in the name-calling they have forced many women to face themselves and to face us as Lesbians. And what was meant to be divisive ultimately brings us together in a common struggle for our humanity. A prime example is the San Francisco Mime Troupe's play *The Independent Female,* which was reviewed by a Women's Liberation group and sent back to the drawing boards because the women complained that the Lesbian character was too stereotyped and was not depicted as a person.

The literature—the anthologies of writings from the women's movement, the many newsletters, newspapers and magazines that have sprung up all over the country—all include articles in reference to the Lesbian. At both the rallies in New York and San Francisco on National Women's Strike Day Lesbians spoke from the platform. The tide has turned, Betty Friedan notwithstanding.

But with this turn of events has come a recognition by the more radical feminists that "Lesbianism is a political statement." They see sexuality itself as the essence of the women's struggle. They claim they can no longer have sex with men who denigrate them, who look upon them merely as sexual partners, who deny their personhood. And they seek Lesbian liaisons as an alternative to celibacy or demeaning sexual relations with men. To them a Lesbian relationship may be a stopgap until such time as men wake up to the fact that they, too, are oppressed by cultural conditioning, until men come to terms with what it means to be a man in our society, until men free themselves to interact with women on a human par.

"Shades of Lysistrata!" people scoff. "How utterly ridiculous!"

But the irrefutable fact still remains. Some excellent articles on the subject, "classics" of the underground press, include: Judy Grahn's "Lesbians As Women," the Radicalesbian collective's "Woman-Identified Woman," Martha Shelley's "Stepin Fetchit Woman," Sally Gearhart's "Lesbianism as a Political Statement," and Rita Mae Brown's "Say It Isn't So."

The point is that as women become woman-identified rather than male-defined, they are opening themselves up to the discovery of the many options available to them. No longer are they constrained to the limitations of the nuclear family and husband or the alternative of "going it alone." Some are experimenting with communal living—either same sex or mixed groups. Others are what we have called "instant" Lesbians, making a conscious choice for relationships with other women rather than the unconscious choice typical of the Lesbians we described earlier in the book. These women, no longer trapped in the Freudian hoax of the vaginal versus the clitoral orgasm, know that they can find sexual satisfaction, emotional and spiritual fulfillment, and human understanding with a woman; and they know that at this time in history they cannot find these things with a man.

As Dean recalled, "I made a public declaration in my Women's Liberation group that I would no longer relate to men in any kind of emotional relationship. I had come to believe that the only potentially 'healthy' relationship could take place with women. I call this my bisexual stage. The short affair I had with one woman ended not entirely as I would have liked. I wasn't able to deal to my satisfaction with the problems that opened up. It's different now. I've managed to transform all the 'male-heterosexual' hangups I had. When I went to the All Women's Dance given by the women of the Gay Liberation Front, when I danced close to another woman, the feeling of her closeness filled me with new and deep emotion. I know now that I have reopened myself, without restriction, to women."

Lesbians we had known and dealt with before usually became aware of their homosexual tendencies gradually during their growing-up process. To them it was a sexual identification as well as a preference. For these women there was no alternative. Their identification with a group was with other Lesbians or with the total homosexual community. They saw their *oppression* as stemming from their being gay. The "nouveau" Lesbian, on the other hand, like Dean, finds her *liberation* as a woman by making the conscious choice of opening herself up to "making *love* to women rather than having *sex* with men."

As we encountered more and more "instant" Lesbians in Women's Liberation and saw other women feeling pressured to make this radical switch, we perceived some inherent dangers in such experimentation and discussed our concerns with Robin Morgan. We found her to be a very dynamic, yet extremely sensitive young woman. While Robin firmly believes in the Sisterhood, which must be all-inclusive, she nonetheless shared our fears that some sisters will be hurt during this period of transition.

"It could be quite damaging to the Lesbian. She is having difficulty enough accepting herself, and she is naturally vulnerable to any responsive woman. She could be very badly hurt by a heterosexual woman who isn't serious, who is only waiting for her man to come to his senses," Phyllis pointed out.

"On the other hand," Del added, "some predatory butch could have a field day and take advantage of some very naive women."

But what bothered Robin was the thought of women *using* other women—the straight woman for the "kicks" or "experience" and the gay woman for a "lay."

Change is always painful and dangerous. Some women will not find happiness and fulfillment with another woman; others will. But hopefully none will be the poorer for the experience and the new insights and understanding reached. We hope that the "predatory butch," modeling her actions on those of the male, will be helped to a new consciousness of sisterhood and become aware of her own male chauvinism. We also hope that women who are seeking new female relationships will remember their own feelings of having been used and will, in their "new consciousness," be open and honest. And we also hope that any change in life style would be brought about by the individual's reasoned choice, not by pressure from the group.

Obviously not all women in the movement are going to turn gay. Lee said, of the same dance Dean attended, "I was moved, but experienced no great upheaval. It was not anything like a religious conversion. The idea of women loving each other just became more palpable and natural to me."

Since this first dance in April of 1970 in New York, All Women's Dances have become popular wherever Women's Liberation is in full sway. "A dance has sexual connotations to most men. For us it's an expression of solidarity. We work and plan together—why not play and dance together?" the women say.

We went to an All Women's Dance in San Francisco. It was great to find that women—gay or straight—could relate to each other, could relax and enjoy themselves in such a social setting. Our only problem was with the music. Rock and roll isn't our forte. But we like to talk, and there were lots of women to talk to. When a slow number finally was played, Phyl grabbed Del's arm. "Come on, here's our chance!"

And so we danced our old DOB style, holding each other close. Back in the early days Marie had taught Del to lead. The next thing we knew some of the young women had stopped and were watching us, intrigued by this "new step" which they began to imitate. We have high hopes that, perhaps under a new name, the old-fashioned two-step may come back into popularity. For you old-timers, if you hear of a new craze called the "Sex Step," you'll know what it really is!

Although many Lesbians have joined the European counterparts of Women's Liberation and NOW, they are usually "silent partners" in that they do not reveal their sexual orientation. In the Netherlands, the liberation of women has been a lively issue since 1966. The two main groups are Man Vrouw/Maatschappij (Man/Woman/Society), which is similar to NOW, and Dolle Mina, which rose from the student movement and is comparable to Women's Liberation. According to Joke Swiebel, however, Lesbians who joined these organizations did so mainly because of discrimination against them as women. "Only secondarily have they made it known during discussions within the movement that they are homosexual and the victims of a social suppression similar to that accorded women. A number of gay women from the homophile student movement have participated more or less under these colors, primarily as members of Dolle Mina. . . . They feared the reaction of the other women and so they have concentrated their efforts against the oppression of women in general."

The fear of the Lesbian by heterosexual members of Holland's women's movement also parallels the U.S. experience. As Joke explained, it is "fear of identification with Lesbians! Liberated women wish to do away with traditional roles without the risk that people will cease to recognize them as *female*." In the *Haagse Post* in March, 1970, members of Dolle Mina said, "We were prepared to be written off as strappers, she-men and Lesbians."

Joke feels that the leadership of the women's movement is well aware of, and sympathetic to the problems of the Lesbian and the homosexual, yet hesitates to form too close an alliance lest some of their members be alienated. The world certainly has become a "global village."

The idea that the women's movement in America or Europe has been overrun by Lesbians is, of course, patently ridiculous. Many Lesbians have made no attempt whatever to relate to women's liberation, some because their priorities are with the homophile or the Black movements, some because they are still struggling with an uncomfortable Lesbian identity and have not yet reached the status of Woman, some because they have been irretrievably lost to the womb of the closet, and some because they are only involved with themselves.

For those of us who recognize ourselves as Woman as well as Lesbian, the emotional furor our presence has wrought in the women's movement has been both comic and tragic. It has been much like an obstacle race to see who feared whom the most. And those of us who chose to be "up front" Lesbians stood stupefied in the middle of the course as symbols of fear to both sides (heterosexual *and* homosexual). Yet to those women who think of themselves as "woman-identified" we have become, possibly, symbols of unity.

The reality of sisterhood was reinforced when some 750 delegates to the 1971 national conference of the National Organization for Women held in Los Angeles voted overwhelmingly that "a woman's right to her own person includes the right to define and express her own sexuality and to choose her own life style" and that "the oppression of Lesbians is a legitimate concern of feminism." Members of NOW have indeed undergone some con-

sciousness raising. In this demonstration of solidarity they proclaimed that women as a class cannot be divided into Lesbian and
non-Lesbian, and that the women's movement is for the rights of
all women.

10. Not Toleration —
Lesbian Liberation

These are your daughters, sisters, wives and mothers. They are real live people, not just characters in a book, and there are millions of them. They are ridiculed, hunted, raped, fired, put down, prayed over and spit upon. Hardly anywhere are they being supported— even by you who are so intimately bound to them. It is time you began to listen to them, and to your consciences and hearts. Millions of lives have been and are being destroyed by sheer nonsense, by politics and semantic games. It is time you understood that.

We Lesbians do not want your sympathy nor your pity; we want your love and respect. We are not looking for society's toleration, a "let live" policy which would simply relegate us to a second best kind of life; we want to partake of the richness of life and be a part of the mainstream of society. We are not looking for a minister who will take us into the fold as pitiable sinners to be "saved" by the grace of God; ours is a God of Love embracing all Creation. We Lesbians are not seeking changes in the law that will only protect us in the "privacy" of our bedrooms; we want our full citizenship with all its privileges and responsibilities. Nor do we see the value of counseling which will help us to "adjust" to our homosexuality only that we might better cope with the hazards of living in a heterosexual society; we want a society that will recognize and adjust to the diversity and the humanness of all its citizens.

It is true that in today's tumultuous times of confrontation and change many institutions, like the church and professional associations, have been forced to make statements declaring that Lesbians and male homosexuals should no longer be condemned, prosecuted or discriminated against. But they are statements tentatively made and they smack of tokenism. It is what they *don't* say which is of far more importance, which exposes their hypocrisy. What is the fear, the insecurity, which keeps them from stating what is really true? Why can't they admit that homosexuality is a variation in sexual life styles equal in all respects with heterosexual life styles? Equality is the concept on which our country was founded; it is also the concept on which our country is floundering today. Its absence in practice is the root cause of the various liberation movements which call for freedom and equality for Blacks, for all Third World peoples, for women and for homosexuals. It is appalling that civil rights legislation is even needed to cover these people who comprise the majority of our citizens. It is even more appalling that when such laws are passed they are difficult to enforce.

By the same token, leaders of institutions, when backed to the wall, reluctantly make declarations about changing the status of homosexuals, but their statements are very carefully hedged by subtleties that effectively undo any positive effect they might possibly have had. They are not affirmations; they are still denials. Consequently they only serve to perpetuate the lies and the myths of prejudice and bigotry.

Certainly there have been changes for the better over the past twenty years, and especially in the last five years. But change is a slow process, and homosexuals of both sexes are getting impatient.

Many churchmen are showing a growing concern for the rehabilitation of Christian thinking in regard to human sexuality in general and homosexuality in particular. Likewise, there is widespread endorsement from unexpected sources for repeal of laws which criminalize citizens for their private sexual practices. Discriminatory policies in employment and elsewhere are being denounced by civil rights advocates. Some court decisions have backed their contention. More and more professional persons are exposing the foibles of their disciplines, admitting that previously held conclusions about human subjective experience, which is not readily translatable into empirical evidence, are really inconclusive and therefore reversible. Libraries are beginning to catalog books on homosexuality in its own separate category, removing volumes from locked cabinets and from the lists of "sexual aberrations." The American Psychiatric Association's Nomenclature Committee has taken under advisement the removal of the word "homosexuality" entirely from its *Diagnostic and Statistical Manual of Psychiatric Disorders.* San Francisco's grand jury in its 1971 report urged closer "communication and liaison with the city's gay community," adding that "these active and concerned citizens . . . deserve a voice in government." Lesbians and male homosexuals together have attained the dubious "status" of being accepted as a minority and now comprise a voting bloc which politicians dare not ignore. And Gay Liberation is in effect a forthright, outspoken, ever active Homosexual Anti-Defamation League which suddenly appears from nowhere at the crack of a sexist joke or at the crackle of electric shock therapy.

Despite all the seeming progress, liberation for the Lesbian is virtually nonexistent; it is still just an ideal or goal, a fleeting experience, an idea, a feeling, an awareness. It is the pride of standing up and being counted, of marching in the "Gay Liberation" parade, of recognizing one's self worth and defying the world to deny it. It is wanting to be open and honest—to be able to tell one's family, to be open with friends, to be honest with one's employer and coworkers. Liberation means leading one life, not the dual life: coming out of hiding, being part of the world instead of running from it.

Unfortunately many Lesbians who have tried to step out of the closet—who have tried to be open and honest with you—have found the price is martyrdom. Their honesty may give them a sense of self respect and personal dignity, which is heady stuff for the downtrodden. But their openness also makes them more vulnerable. Other people aren't always ready to relate to them as human beings, let alone equal human beings. Though change in social attitudes has accelerated in the last five years, it has not gone far enough and certainly not fast enough.

Such a martyr was Jean, of Wichita, Kansas. She made the mistake of revealing herself as a Lesbian to this small uptight American community that had bought lock, stock and barrel the "sin-crime-sickness" syndrome. Jean's family disowned her. Her girl friend left her, and the homophile community likewise shunned her. Neither she nor they could afford to associate with a "known" Lesbian. Jean couldn't find employment either, needless to say. She had no one to turn to for support, economically or emotionally. Somehow two sympathetic reporters learned of her plight. One wrote up her story in the newspaper hoping that some compassionate employer would at least come forward and offer her a job. The other gave her ninety minutes on a local television show. But there was no response from the "good" people of Wichita. The Reverend Troy Perry happened to be traveling in the area. He heard about Jean and made a special trip to Wichita to see if he couldn't help. But the day before Troy arrived Jean committed suicide.

Society's energies have been hung up for too long in trying to stamp out homosexuality. Such efforts have been and will continue to be useless as well as cruel. Homosexuality is a fact of life which can neither be refuted nor denied. On the contrary, it has been proven by history. Lesbians do not, as a rule, reproduce and therefore do not perpetuate themselves. (They are wholly dependent upon heterosexuals for that!) Yet through century after century and in generation after generation a small minority of women has turned to Lesbianism. Furthermore, all the wringing of hands or wagging of tongues or pointing of fingers has had no effect on the incidence of homosexuality. It simply *is*. The fact that heterosexuality is necessary to perpetuate the human race does not obviate and cannot obliterate the existence of homosexuality. Conversely, acceptance of homosexuality does not mean that there won't be any more babies.

What happens to the Lesbian from here on is up to you—you as a Lesbian, you as parents and relatives of Lesbians, you who are friends or work on the job with Lesbians, you who call yourselves feminists, you who are human beings. We would remind you that the Lesbian is first of all a person; secondly, a woman; and only thirdly, a Lesbian. That the third often becomes first is because of societal pressures which you have the power to lift.

For the Lesbian herself we have this particular advice. Know yourself, accept who and what you are, and then take charge of your own destiny. Your beingness does not depend upon other persons or rules for legitimizing or defining. You are you, no matter what others may say or think. It's what you think that counts. You are competent to deal with your own life as a Lesbian given the chance, but don't expect anybody to give you the chance—you'll have to take it. True, you will be taking certain calculated risks, but you do that every time you cross the street these days. Whatever else you do, quit sniveling and blaming others for your plight, even if it's true. Otherwise you can drown in your own self pity. If you are scared (and we all are in the beginning) remember that those whom you fear are probably even more afraid of you. They don't know any better, and at least you have the advantage of knowing the difference between the lies and the truth. Don't cut yourself off—be sociable, communicate, get to know other people and let them know you. Don't jeopardize your position or career needlessly, but don't be too uptight either. For your own mental health it may be better to lose the former than to fall into the traps of the latter. If you do feel free enough, by all means speak out. Vicious circular thinking that has always surrounded and victimized the Lesbian cannot be broken unless more of us come out into the open to disprove the myths and dispel the lies.

Aside from what has already been said in the chapter on the teenage Lesbian, we would remind parents that they, too, have been victimized by professional "historicism" or rationalizations based upon case histories of "disturbed" patients in therapy. What may be true in some cases obviously cannot be applied generally. While some Lesbians do come from broken homes or have felt rejected, others recall their childhood as having been happy and felt their parents were very supportive. Do not take on the guilt that society would heap upon you either. And quit worrying about what the neighbors or your friends might think—they need to be enlightened anyway. What should be more important to you is your relationship with your daughter. She may not give you grandchildren, but she can act as a catalyst in broadening your awareness of other existent human qualities and endeavors. Besides, more than ever before, she will need your love, understanding and support. And probably, if you can admit it, you need hers, too.

During one of the sessions on homosexuality at the 1971

American Psychiatric Association's annual meeting, one psychiatrist stated, "It is society that defines disease and social problems.
We only treat those who come to us for help and who call themselves sick." Dr. Charles Socarides, a proponent of the sickness
theory, once said that if it was true that homosexuals could really
love, then he might have to re-evaluate his position. And Dr.
Harvey Kaye has been quoted as saying, "If a Lesbian is happy, let
her alone. There is little enough of happiness in this world today."
These "men of science" continually talk out of both sides of their
mouths. If they really mean what they say, why do they keep
thinking of homosexuals in clinical terms?

Every one of you who reads this must realize your own role,
too, in determining the Lesbian's mental health, her freedom to
live and to develop the whole person she really is. As part of the
society that defines "disease" and "social problems," you need to
ask yourself some very pertinent questions: Why is it so important
to these men, and to you, who people go to bed with? Is it really
any of your damned business? What is it that threatens you personally because a woman happens to love and prefer living with
another woman instead of a man? Why is your ego so involved in
such personal relationships? Does such a relationship harm you or
society? What is it that is bugging you? In the final analysis, homosexuality is not so much the Lesbian's problem as yours. It would
be no problem to her if you could only understand that homosexuality is as natural to her as heterosexuality may be to you and
that her problems in dealing with her sexuality do not stem from
her homosexuality but are the manifestations of your oppressive
attitudes.

It is indeed time that society redefines and re-evaluates homosexuality as a preference, an orientation and a propensity for a
certain life style which is equal to and on a par with heterosexuality—with all that entails. It isn't enough just to call the cops
and the docs off, "to let them alone." That's like placing prisoners
on an "honor farm" where there is minimum security as opposed
to placing them in a penitentiary where there is maximum security. They are still prisoners.

Please, please don't say, "We don't know enough about homosexuality yet. There needs to be more research done before we can
possibly draw such a conclusion." Countless "studies" have al-

ready been made, and they are meaningless. At this point in history the "quality" of the homosexual life style cannot possibly be measured or evaluated. Such studies, if made, can only show if the Lesbian has been completely beaten down or if she has managed somehow to rise above the petty and the vicious restrictions society has placed upon her. Until such time as these barriers are lifted what else can they prove? The Lesbian's potential has not yet been realized. And it can't be under present conditions of repression, suppression and oppression.

The homophile community of fifteen years ago might have settled for "tolerance." But not today: no halfway measures will do. In our several identities (as citizens, as women and as Lesbians) we want equal rights and full citizenship—whether in relation to marriage, joint income tax returns, inheritance, property, adoption of children, job opportunity, education or security clearances.

In *The Well of Loneliness* Radclyffe Hall wrote: "We are coming . . . we are still coming on, and our name is legion—you dare not disown us! We have asked for bread, will you give us a stone? You, God, in Whom we, the outcast, believe; you, world, into which we are pitilessly born; you, who have drained our cup to the dregs—we have asked for bread; will you give us a stone? . . . Give us also the right to our existence."

That was back in 1928. It was a plea. Today there are no pleas nor pleases—there are only demands. And they come not from the minority of our population, but from the majority; not just from homosexuals, but from women and from Blacks and all Third World peoples. The Great Society can only be as great as its people, and the people can only be great as they know, appreciate, love, understand and express their diversity and individuality.

No longer is toleration acceptable. The Lesbians, along with all oppressed people, want freedom—and we want it *now*!

Lesbian/Woman Update, 1991

We started out to write an epilogue, but somehow that takes on the conno-
tation of an ending—and Lesbians are nowhere near the end of their struggle
in this society. Despite phenomenal strides made in civil rights for Gays of both
sexes since Lesbian/Woman *was first published—changes that we never*
dreamed would happen in our lifetime—what you have just read remains ba-
sically true for many Lesbian women today. The following pages represent a
very brief, and necessarily selective, view of what has happened—the gains and
the setbacks—in the 20 years since 1972.

For Lesbians the early 1970s were a time for introspection and
consciousness raising. A time to challenge the emerging Gay and
Women's Liberation movements. Were Gay men ready to grant
Lesbians equal status in planning strategy and leadership? Were
members of the National Organization for Women (NOW) willing
to accept Lesbians in common cause?

It didn't take a lot of consciousness raising to determine that
Gay men were mostly in a one-track movement. It wasn't until the
beginning of the 80s that organizations began to be called "Lesbian
and Gay." The New York chapter of NOW continued to be fearful
of a takeover by the "Lavender Menace." But grassroots members
in other parts of the country were way ahead of NOW's conservative national leadership under Betty Friedan. They welcomed
Lesbians as members and by 1973 had elected Del the first up-
front Lesbian member of NOW's national board.

In the meantime individual Lesbians were facing blatant discrimination in employment. Some of them began to stand up for

their rights. Following are stories of Lesbians which illustrate the fortitude, stubbornness, commitment, and heartache it takes to fight the system. They faced hostility, scorn, and threats because they believed in themselves. They had their privacy invaded and their souls bared publicly because they adhered to certain principles and ideals. Their greatest crime was honesty.

Peggy

Peggy Burton was a second-year science and math teacher at Cascade High School in Turner, Oregon, in 1971. When questioned by the principal about rumors, she admitted she was a Lesbian. He urged her to resign "for personal reasons." There was no question about her performance as a teacher or that her private life had in any way impaired her ability to teach. She asked for a hearing, but once the members of the school board extracted an admission from Peggy that she was a Lesbian they refused to let her speak further. They voted to terminate her contract because of her "immorality."

Peggy decided to sue, and the American Civil Liberties Union (ACLU) took her case and raised a pure legal issue: whether homosexuality in and of itself is a proper ground for exclusion from teaching in public schools. Peggy's attorney, Charles E. Hinkle, pointed out that Oregon had ceased to regulate the private consensual sexual behavior of adult citizens.

The court concluded that the school board had based its action on a statute which did not define "immorality," which "means different things to different people." The judge ordered the school district to give Peggy back pay plus another half-year's salary, but fell short of ordering her reinstatement.

Peggy refused to settle. She wanted to get her job back and to establish rights for Gay teachers. In 1975 the Ninth Circuit Court of Appeals, in a 2–1 decision, upheld the lower court, saying an award limited to monetary damages was adequate for wrongful dismissal of a nontenured teacher. Dissenting Justice C.J. Lumbard argued that reinstatement is the only appropriate remedy for removal from a job in violation of the constitution. Neither court addressed the sexual privacy issue raised by Hinkle.

Although hers was only a partial victory, Peggy says it is worthwhile to take risks. "I think it's people's fears that keep them where they are. We need to overcome that fear—reality is never as bad as our worst fears."

Sandra and Madeleine

The case of Sandra Schuster and Madeleine Isaacson, while unique, is of particular interest because it encompasses just about all the elements that may be encountered in a Lesbian mother custody suit. The two Seattle women met at a Pentecostal church and felt an immediate "spiritual communion," which soon blossomed into Lesbian love. After several months of wrestling with certain passages in the Bible and the "liturgy" of psychiatry, Sandy and Maddy came to terms with their love and its acceptance by God. In 1971 they took their six children and fled to California. Their husbands caught up with them, and they returned to Seattle to face their husbands' charges that they were unfit mothers because they were Lesbians and religious fanatics.

The closely intertwined relationship between the couples led Superior Court Judge James A. Noe to hear both divorce/custody suits together. The family court investigator, a psychiatrist, and a psychologist visited Sandy and Maddy's home. "This is a most happy, well organized, creative family. All three of us were impressed by both women's ability to provide structure, set limits, yet allow the children to be creative and develop inquisitive minds and demonstrate affection," reported Nancy Kaplan, the court investigator. "The children are well cared for physically, emotionally and intellectually ... The rigidity with which many fundamentalist church members view the world did not seem to be present in either of these women." Kaplan concluded that the women were warmer and more open than their husbands and recommended they retain custody of the children.

The judge awarded custody to both mothers but ordered them to live apart. Considering the high rate of divorce, it is not unusual to have no male model in the home, he reasoned, but having *two* mothers was highly unusual. He was not willing to risk such a step even though the women had already merged their families and separate residences would be a financial burden. Sandy and Maddy were crushed. The children felt the same way. The mothers decided to appeal and sought help from the Gay community.

It was 1972, and there was little information on Lesbian mothers except for a case that had been decided in favor of the mother a few months earlier in San Jose, California. The Mitchell decision, believed to be the country's first in favor of an acknowledged Lesbian in a contested divorce action, was more "a hollow victory," according to attorney Joan K. Bradford. Superior Court Judge Gerald S. Chargin placed so many restrictions on the mother's relationship to her lover that he seemed to be saying it was all right for her to be a Lesbian and a mother as long as she didn't practice Lesbianism and devoted herself almost solely to mothering. She was not allowed to live with her lover nor to permit her lover inside her home, nor visit her outside the home during the evening "in order that the children have adequate supervision in their own home." The only times the two women could see each other without being in contempt of court would be when the children were in school (they both worked) or when the children were visiting their father (two weekends per month).

Sandy, who was completing her M.A. in psychiatric nursing at the University of Washington at the time, began research on Gay parenting for her thesis. It was later published as *Love Is for All*, by Schuster-Isaacson Family Productions. She interested Karl Ullis, M.D., of the university's Department of Pediatrics, in producing a 30-minute documentary, *Sandy and Madeleine's Family*. A federal grant for the film was obtained by the Department of Visual Arts, and Dr. Ullis became its director.

The film crew went to the five-bedroom home where the family had lived happily for a year and a half. They photographed its setting on Lake Washington with lots of open space for the children to play. The camera caught the interaction between family members, the candidness and the love they expressed for one another. Among the experts interviewed for the film was anthropologist Margaret Mead, who said, "Anyone is in trouble with society when they don't conform, no matter in what way they don't conform . . . it is my personal feeling that it's a lot better for children to have 'two mothers' than none."

In 1973, armed with the film and the book, the family went public. Schuster-Isaacson Family Productions traveled up and down the West Coast. They were interviewed for newspapers, television, and radio. They spoke to professional and church groups. Only the most callous or prejudiced could remain unaffected by the joy and humor of this glorious family troop.

In 1974 Sandy qualified as an expert witness in a Tacoma, Washington, trial involving two Lesbian mothers who also had six children between them and who had been together "for ages." Sandy's and Maddy's film was entered into evidence as a research project and shown in the courtroom. "Praise the Lord, this may be the big one. When the judge saw Margaret Mead he just about fell off the bench," Sandy told us.

Shortly thereafter Sandy and Maddy were back in court. Their ex-husbands claimed "changed circumstances," since they had both remarried and could now provide homes with both a male and female model for the children. They also charged that Sandy and Maddy had violated their divorce decrees by living together (having taken two two-bedroom apartments across the hall from each other), taking the children out of the state without permission, flaunting their relationship, subjecting the children to public notoriety, and entering into a marriage ceremony. Sandy and Maddy counter-petitioned the court to modify their divorce decrees to delete the requirement that they live apart, and they sought damages and attorney's fees for "bad faith" on the part of their former husbands and an increase in child support from Schuster commensurate with his new income status.

This time the case was heard before Superior Court Judge Norman Ackley, Jr. The ACLU represented Sandy and Maddy, and NOW submitted a "friend of the court" brief. Testimony was heard from six psychiatrists and four psychologists. Three of them said they believed children raised by Lesbian mothers would be more likely to become homosexual than children raised by heterosexual mothers. The other seven held that there was no scientific evidence to support such a belief. Dr. S. Howard Kaufman, the court-appointed specialist who had examined the children during the first trial, said that after two years in the custody of the mothers the children were still "basically healthy" and "well within the standards of normalcy." Even Dr. John Lavalee, a witness for the fathers, had to agree.

Clay Nixon, attorney for the fathers, who had based his case on the *future* welfare of the children, tried another tack. He decided to make Sandy the heavy, the seducer, the one who exercised control over poor innocent Madeleine, and he implied that their film was pornographic. When Madeleine's mother was on the stand he tried to draw her into this scenario. She *had* noted a decided change in Madeleine's behavior since she met Sandy—a change for the better. Madeleine seemed so much happier than when she had been married to Isaacson, she said.

Then Nixon went after Sandy. Since the state of Washington still had laws on the books governing certain sexual acts (they have since been repealed), he decided to zero in on the women's sex life. In a day-long grilling on the stand, Nixon badgered Sandy, demanding that she describe the sex acts she and Maddy engaged in. Sandy beat around the bush and answered his questions in very vague terms. She did not want to plead the Fifth Amendment, since to do so would be tantamount to admitting guilt. Finally Nixon pulled out a copy of the penal code and read the Washington sex laws to her. Then he asked if she had ever performed any of these illegal acts. Sandy replied, "I guess I really did break the law! I certainly didn't know it at the time. But I suppose I broke the law when I was married—to my husband." The attorney dropped this line of questioning.

The women's attorney presented evidence that Sandy and Maddy had indeed discussed their lives in presenting educational programs based on psychological, sociological, and theological writings and studies on Lesbianism. Witnesses stated that they were informative public service programs guaranteed by the First Amendment and that there was no apparent detrimental effect on the children. Having heard the testimony of 21 witnesses during the five-and-a-half-day trial, Richard Yarmuth, the court-appointed attorney for the children, recommended that the earlier order be modified to permit the women and their children to live together.

Judge Ackley came to the same conclusion. However, he warned them that if they continued to "put the children on exhibition for the cause of homosexuality or if they spend too much time on that cause to the neglect of the children," they could jeopardize future custody. He also increased support for Sandy's four children from $35 per month per child to $100 each.

The fathers appealed the decision. In 1976 opposing attorneys argued before the Washington State Supreme Court over the merits and speculative demerits of Lesbian mothers having custody of their children. More than a year passed with no decision. A rare second hearing of oral arguments was held—and still no decision. We began to believe that the whole question would be moot, that the children would all be grown up by the time the high court came to a conclusion. Finally, in 1978, after seven years of legal wrangling, the state supreme court ruled in a 6–3 decision that Sandy and Maddy could retain custody.

"We won it all!" exclaimed Roselle Pekelis, the attorney who represented Sandy and Maddy. Unfortunately, the court took care to point out that this decision did not extend to other Lesbian families. But it couldn't stop the publicity. *People* ran a photo story on Sandy's and Maddy's family. One delightful photograph featured the family band, with Madeleine playing banjo, Sandy on accordion, and the six youngsters (by then 10 to 15 years old) playing the flute, clarinet, French horn, cornet and saxophone. Somehow debate on points of law and conjecture about the future miss the human quality of Lesbian families.

Miriam

When Miriam Ben-Shalom enlisted in the U.S. Army Reserves in Wisconsin in 1974 she answered "no" to the question about homosexual tendencies, adding, "I don't have tendencies. I am one." To the query about her community involvement she listed her membership in Milwaukee's Gay People's Union and the New York Radical Lesbians. Surprisingly, the army accepted her.

Miriam declared her Lesbianism in a basic training class on race and minority relations at Fort McClellan, Alabama, and demanded that homosexuality in the military be included in class discussions. Later she told the army newspaper at Fort Leonard Wood, Missouri, that she was "a radical Lesbian feminist." Her remarks never appeared in print. A general censored them "because she would be kicked out of the army if they were published." He wanted her to stay in.

In December, 1975, Miriam was graduated as the first woman drill instructor with the 84th Training Division of Milwaukee. A television station interviewed her and three male classmates who unanimously agreed that Miriam's Lesbianism didn't matter because she did her job more competently than most. A few days later, however, Sergeant Ben-Shalom was notified that discharge proceedings were being initiated against her for "publicly admitting" her Lesbianism.

Miriam appealed her discharge. In 1976 she and her eight-year-old daughter stumped the country to publicize the military's discriminatory policies and to gain support for her legal defense. She spoke at rallies and at Lesbian/Gay and women's meetings, pointing out that our civil rights were at stake as well as hers. "I won't back down, back out, give up, or give in," she vowed, passing her army hat for donations.

It was not until 1980 that U.S. District Judge Terence Evans ruled unconstitutional the army regulation requiring discharge of soldiers who exhibit "homosexual tendencies, desire or interest," even if they do not engage in overt homosexual behavior. The rule violated the First, Fifth, and Ninth Amendments to the Constitution, the court said, and ordered Miriam's immediate reinstatement.

The verdict was, at that time, the broadest interpretation of constitutional rights for Lesbians and Gays. The court said that Miriam's "sexual preference had as much relevance to her military skills as did her gender or the color of her skin." The court also said that it would be up to the army to show proof of actual deviant conduct and proof of a connection between sexual preference and a soldier's military capabilities. "The army, in this case, has not even tried to show that such a nexus exists."

Evans' ruling also referred to army regulations as "a readily available tool for intimidation and harassment. . . . No soldier would dare be caught reading anything that might be construed as a homosexually oriented book or magazine. Most importantly, no soldier would ever want to make any statements that might be interpreted as supporting homosexuality." The army, of course, appealed the court's decision.

The army stalled until 1987 when it was again ordered to reinstate Miriam by the Seventh Circuit Court in Chicago. She then served the final year of her three-year enlistment, but the army refused to allow her to reenlist. She sued again and a district court ordered the army to allow her to reenlist. The army appealed.

In 1989 the Seventh Circuit Court ruled for the army, stating that by identifying herself as a Lesbian Miriam had declared herself prone to "criminal" behavior and that evidence of same sex behavior was not needed. The court also declared that the army regulations were not necessarily unconstitutional.

Miriam appealed to the U.S. Supreme Court, which in 1990 refused to consider the case, leaving the prior decision for the army as the last word in Ben-Shalom's 16-year battle. "I feel devastated," Ben-Shalom said. "I feel outrage. I feel angry. What in the name of God do I need to do to be a citizen of this country and be fit to serve her?"

In a letter to us Miriam said she was officially kicked out in March, 1990. "Treated as an 'erroneous enlistment,' no discharge granted—merely a 'release from the custody of the U.S. Army.' This after being honor graduate of the Primary Leadership Development Course, NBC school graduate, nomination for Soldier of the Year in my battalion. And having been ranked in the top five percent of all soldiers in the 84th Division. Top instructor at the Drill Sergeants' School/Leadership Academy, 84th Division."

"Don't count any of us vets down and out yet," says Miriam, "the best is yet to come." She believes the high court is waiting for a large-scale class action suit and she is eager to initiate one. She feels the court has not addressed issues of citizenship and First Amendment rights for homosexuals.

Miriam is now a founder and president of the Gay, Lesbian and Bisexual Veterans of America which will continue the struggle with the Department of Defense (DOD). In November, 1990, speaking for the new organization, Ben-Shalom called for the DOD to suspend the rules excluding homosexuals from the military because of the Persian Gulf crisis and to establish a segregated brigade, which should ease fears about Gays in the service. The group, headquartered in Milwaukee, Wisconsin, called for the reactivation of the 54th Massachusetts Volunteer Regiment (MVR) in an open letter to President Bush, the secretary of DOD, Congress and the American people. "The 54th MVR was a segregated regiment of African-American men, freed slaves who were also told that they were unfit to serve, unfit for combat and a detriment to morale, good order and security, just as Lesbians and Gay men are being told today," she said.

Ben-Shalom is still fighting. "I'm not sorry—can still raise hell and shall continue to do so until no need or [the] day I die, whichever comes first. . . ." She is suing the Wisconsin Army National

Guard for having a discriminatory policy at odds with the state's nondiscrimination law. "I volunteered for front line duty in the Gulf because I speak Arabic and Hebrew and have familiarity with the culture and customs in that area," she explained. "They refused to enlist me as a combat MP."

Currently Miriam is working as a high school teacher of, as she puts it, "at risk students (gang members, truants, substance abusers, etc., all conduct disordered) . . . Odd, I'm trusted to **teach** but not to be in the military."

Although there appear to be great similarities between Ben-Shalom's case and that of Perry Watkins, except that he won and she lost, legal experts explain that Watkins' case was decided on a very narrow basis and the determining case of Lesbians and Gays in the military has yet to be heard. We assume it will happen very soon. Miriam Ben-Shalom's determination cannot be overlooked.

Josette

Reelection jitters no doubt motivated California Governor Jerry Brown to order the firing of Dr. Josette Mondanaro from her post as director of the Division of Substance Abuse of the state Department of Health on October 25, 1977—one day before her one-year civil service probationary period expired. The governor charged that a letter Josette had written on state stationery to Dr. Judianne Densen-Gerber, head of the Odyssey Institute in New York City, contained vulgarities that could discredit him and his administration. Josette contended that the letter was private, written to a friend in angry protest of an article in *Behavior Today* that seemingly condoned child sexual abuse and child pornography. She claimed the copy had been taken from her personal files and used as an excuse to fire her because she is a Lesbian. Four months after her supervisors had rated her outstanding in nine of nine categories on her job performance, the letter conveniently surfaced when anti-Gay, conservative Senator John Briggs announced he would run against Brown in 1978.

With the backing of her parents, her immediate supervisor Ray Procunier, and Health Department Director Dr. Jerome Lachner, Josette appealed her case to the State Personnel Board. She hired civil rights attorney Ephraim Margolin to represent her and generated community support for her case. Letters of outrage poured into Sacramento from other professionals, women's organizations, substance abuse programs, the Lesbian and Gay communities, and former patients and politicians, calling for reinstatement and/or public hearings. Josette Mondanaro got her hearing—five grueling days of it. Her boosters packed the hearing room. Lachner said he had fired Josette only after pressure and the threat of losing his own job to someone who would carry out the order.

Hearing Officer James Waller in his decision complimented the governor "for attempting to set a high moral standard for state service," but held that a one-time error by an otherwise outstanding employee did not warrant rejection during probation. The Personnel Board concurred and reinstated Josette.

Waller also stated that no "substantial evidence" showed that the governor had fired Josette because "he considered her Lesbianism a liability to his reelection campaign." Nonetheless, because of her courage in standing by her convictions and standing up to a powerful governor, Josette emerged as a symbol of strength, commitment, and hope for Lesbians everywhere. Brown learned the hard way that Lesbians, like other women, must be reckoned with as employees and as a constituency.

During his bid for a second term, Brown issued an executive order prohibiting employment discrimination on the basis of sexual orientation by all state agencies. Gay attorney Leroy Walker was named by the Personnel Board to implement the order. Brown also authorized a Commission on Personal Privacy and appointed several Lesbians and Gay men to state commissions. Although he received a lot of flak for naming Southern Californian Stephen Lachs the first openly Gay man to be a judge, he also appointed San Franciscans Herbert Donaldson and Mary Morgan to the municipal court. The only opposition to Brown's appointment of a Lesbian judge surfaced in the campaign literature of Barry Goldwater, Jr., in his losing bid for the Republican nomination for the United States Senate. The piece was quickly withdrawn as the "unauthorized" work of an aide. In California, at least, it is not always politically advantageous to use Lesbians or Gays to smear political opponents.

Denise

Denise Kreps had worked for the Contra Costa Sheriff's Department for more than two years as a dispatcher when she took the written, oral, and physical tests to become a deputy sheriff in February, 1979. She scored 16th out of 181 applicants. In October she was called back to fill out more forms and was scheduled for a lie-detector test.

During the polygraph test the examiner asked if Denise had ever engaged in sexual activity with a member of the same sex. She said "Yes." He asked her when had been the last time. She replied, "Last night."

Sheriff Richard Rainey later advised Denise that she was disqualified because he was concerned about possible liability to the county (should Denise and a prisoner commit a homosexual act), because of state law (prohibiting males from guarding females without a female guard present), and because he did not want to set the precedent of hiring a homosexual deputy. At that time approximately 20 Lesbians and Gay men already served as deputy sheriffs in San Francisco.

Denise retained Donna Hitchens, then directing attorney of the Lesbian Rights Project (now a San Francisco Superior Court judge), and appealed to the Contra Costa Civil Service Commission for a hearing. In February, 1980, an evidentiary hearing convened before an administrative law judge. Sheriff Rainey testified to his concerns that Denise might have sex with women prisoners and that she might not report, as required, incidents of homosexual acts between prisoners. Other employees in the sheriff's department testified to Denise's excellent performance on the job, that they hadn't known she was a Lesbian, that she had never done anything inappropriate, and that they were willing to work with her.

Sergeant (now Lieutenant) Connie O'Connor of the San Francisco Sheriff's Department, testified that she herself was a known Lesbian when hired, and had been with the department five years. She knew of no complaints by prisoners about homosexual guards, no blackmail by prisoners due to a guard's sexual orientation, no reports of homosexual guards using their positions to gain sexual favors from prisoners, and no failure by homosexual guards to report homosexual activity among prisoners.

The sheriff's "big gun" was Dr. Alfred Coodley, a psychiatrist who, in 35 years of practice, had seen many homosexuals and had evaluated various detention facilities in Southern California. With this background, Dr. Coodley proceeded to make some amazing statements as to why it would be unwise to hire a Lesbian. He agreed with Sheriff Rainey that a homosexual sheriff was likely to "act out" in a homosexual manner when under stress.

Coodley noted that Denise admitted a "homosexual episode" the night before taking the polygraph test. Because the prospect of taking the test had "a considerably stressful quality," it was "significant that the way in which she chose to cope with her anxiety and stress" was to have sex. He indicated that Denise's honesty about her same sex experiences (during a lie-detector test) showed a "certain intrinsic, unconscious, self defeating quality."

During cross-examination, Donna asked the doctor to clarify whether he thought Denise's truthful answers on the polygraph test showed signs of abnormality. The doctor replied, "I would say it did." Asked if it would be "abnormal" for a heterosexual to have sex before taking such a test, he answered "No." Donna questioned whether a Lesbian would be more likely to have sex with a prisoner than would a male heterosexual. Dr. Coodley admitted that under stress heterosexual guards might act out sexually with prisoners, but added, "Statistically it probably would not occur, for the simple reason no mature person is going to have a sexual relationship with a prisoner under any circumstances." Asked Donna, "So that is your assumption, that homosexuals by nature are less mature than heterosexuals?" "No question about it, despite their feelings to the contrary."

Donna asked Coodley if he had read scientific literature concluding that, other than choice of partner, virtually no difference exists between homosexuals and heterosexuals. She cited studies published in psychological journals. The doctor replied that he was a psychiatrist and did not read journals for psychologists.

Coodley said that prisoners would know Denise was a Lesbian. When asked how, the doctor gave the court a five-minute course on "dyke detection." He pointed out that Lesbians wore pants or pantsuits. Referring to Denise, he said, "She has at times the body stance of a homosexual woman rather than a heterosexual woman." Asked to explain, he said, ". . . when she was seated she was sitting with her two feet flat on the ground and her legs spread apart approximately 18 inches or so. Percentage-wise, the number of heterosexual women who sit in that position, dressed as she is (in a pantsuit) would be quite small. The number of homosexual women who, dressed as she is, sit that way is fairly high." He added that "short hair is intrinsically a fairly common phenomenon in homosexual women," a statement he said was based on research, and that with short hair the "individual looks masculine." His final, telling point was that Lesbians wear no, or minimal, makeup. In summary Coodley said, "All those things put together suggest an individual has a more masculine appearance." His testimony created a stir in the courtroom since virtually every woman there fit his "dyke" description.

Administrative Law Judge Michael C. Cohen found that none of Rainey's concerns "were anything more than speculation . . ." and that his action in disqualifying Denise "violated her right to equal protection under the law . . ." Further, he found that the sheriff had failed to show that Denise's Lesbianism made her unfit to serve as a deputy sheriff and, in granting her appeal, he ordered the sheriff to allow her to complete the employment process and to consider her for a deputy sheriff's appointment regardless of her sexual orientation.

Sheriff Rainey appealed to the Superior Court where Judge Richard P. Calhoun upheld the findings of the hearing, adding that the sheriff's refusal to hire homosexuals "is discrimination on the basis of sexual orientation, has no rational basis and violates the equal protection clauses of the California and United States Constitutions."

Rainey asked for reconsideration. It was denied. Finally, in January, 1981, almost two years from the time Denise had applied for the job, the case was closed by the signing of a stipulation that Contra Costa County would pay court costs and attorneys' fees and grant Denise seniority within the department "as if she had been the second person appointed as deputy sheriff" the previous January. She was sent to the police academy for training and graduated *first* in her class of 40 men and women.

Lesbian Movement

Individually these women achieved a fairly high degree of visibility and helped make changes in the way Lesbians are perceived by the public. As a movement, however, Lesbians have had low visibility because their energies are so diffused. Some are developing a Lesbian/woman culture, others are separatists building a Lesbian nation counterculture, and many relate primarily to the women's movement, while others relate to the Gay movement. There is no readily identifiable Lesbian liberation movement. Yet it does exist—in various, often conflicting, forms—with an unrelenting advocacy for change.

In the 70s many Lesbians experimented with collectivism as a way of life as well as in their business ventures. They rejected hierarchical structure (leader, secondary leaders, and followers) as perpetuating authoritarianism and inequality. They experimented with leaderless groups, encouraged each woman to speak up and to share experience and responsibility, and made their decisions by consensus. Meetings seemed interminable—and more articulate women emerged as leaders anyway. To circumvent this, some groups gave each woman ten matchsticks. Each time a woman spoke she threw a matchstick into the pot. When they were gone she was not permitted to speak again. This system allowed for more equality, eliminated class divisions, and helped reach a more "real" consensus. Other groups, finding need for coordination of tasks between meetings, rotated leaders and spokeswomen every few months. Another system was a quasi-executive board selected by lot.

Lesbians were preoccupied with redefining self. They experimented with alternate relationships to avoid perceived controlling and dependency factors in monogamous couplings. These included celibacy, multiple relationships, and "open marriages." Some joined communes and moved to the country to find their own womanspace and womanspirit. Some drew strength and nurturance just from being with other Lesbians. It was a form of renewal, of recouping positive energy—a retreat from the sexism and heterosexism they encountered in the everyday world and a chance to express the rage those encounters engendered.

Out of experiences emerged a new Lesbian culture and a "personal is political" Lesbian separatist counterculture. A new interest

in Lesbian "herstory" developed. With it came new creativity—
Lesbian music, poetry, plays, fiction, photography, painting, and
crafts. Lesbian publications proliferated as did Lesbian publishing
houses, recording companies, film and theater productions.

The Lesbian feminist separatist movement flourished in the
early 70s. Growing out of a total rejection of the establishment, the
building of an independent Lesbian nation counterculture was a
political statement. A new value system based on Lesbian/woman
experience evolved to validate the primacy of women and give them
individual and collective power. For many women, coming out in
the Lesbian feminist separatist movement was a very positive
experience.

Unfortunately, what began as a means of centering and of getting strength from one another in the struggle for social change
became rigid in its political orthodoxy. New values meant rejecting
old ones and forming new taboos: association with the "enemy"
(men and male children) or with women who consorted with the
enemy; middle-class values; achieving "star" status; involvement
with sexist institutions or electoral politics. Women who broke the
rules were branded "politically incorrect" and rejected. This new
form of tyranny effectively destroyed existing service-oriented "re-
formist" Lesbian organizations, such as the Daughters of Bilitis
(DOB).

We never could understand the animosity some separatist
Lesbians displayed toward heterosexual women. We all grew up in
heterosexual homes and experienced the same early training and
oppression as women. That is our common bond. We are bothered,
too, by the contradictions of Lesbian separatists who reject conformity to women's roles in the larger society but impose on
Lesbians another conformity in dress, thought, and behavior. To
us it is trading one form of tyranny and oppression for another.
We had always envisioned Lesbians coming together to find solidarity and strength in numbers, yet respecting our diversity. We
never expected any one philosophy or lifestyle to become the
"ideal." Nor do we believe that different political approaches to
social change need divide us. We have always thought in terms of
opening up options for Lesbians to choose freely whatever they find
personally most fitting to them.

Radical Lesbians took over the New York chapter and the center DOB had struggled to acquire and maintain for Lesbians regardless of their state of consciousness or political persuasion. What these radical women failed to understand was that DOB was a "coming out" place, a self help organization and a safety net for women who were struggling with their new identity, hoping to meet other Lesbians and learn survival skills. Women at that point in their lives need a chance to express and sort out their feelings and fears. Radical politics scare them away. Separatist economics—everything should be open to *all* women and should therefore be free—soon bankrupted the organization and New York DOB folded.

Because of the conflicts and because women's centers began to provide space and resources for Lesbians, DOB chapters across the country gradually disappeared. The demise in 1970 of DOB as a national organization was precipitated by the actions of the editor of *The Ladder,* Barbara Grier (Gene Damon), and Rita LaPorte, DOB national president, when they took the magazine from the organization and began to publish it privately. At the 1970 national convention DOB delegates decided that their time, energy and money could be better spent than on a long and costly federal lawsuit to regain the magazine. *The Ladder* was DOB's vehicle of communication and also its national tie. Since it was gone, the delegates decided to dissolve the national structure in favor of a loose network of autonomous chapters. Grier and LaPorte learned the hard way that the magazine could not be sustained without the financial support of the organization that had spawned it. After almost 16 years of continuous publication *The Ladder* went defunct in 1972.

San Francisco DOB, which had maintained the organization's national headquarters for almost two decades, managed to hang on until the late 70s. As in earlier times, what kept the volunteer staff going were the letters from Lesbians in faraway places looking for help or a way to plug in to Lesbian activities. The group also published *Sisters,* a monthly magazine, for several years. To our knowledge, only Boston DOB remains.

Lesbian Tide, which began in 1971 as the newsletter of Los Angeles DOB, went independent at about the time *The Ladder* folded, and replaced it as the national Lesbian publication. The staff of *Lesbian Tide* fluctuated over the years, but its success for nine years was due

largely to the work and energy of Jeanne Cordova. Unlike its prede-
cessor, which was strictly volunteer, *Lesbian Tide* was run as a
business—it carried advertising and paid its photographers, writers,
and editors. Editorially the paper flowed with the times, from its Gay
liberation perspective in the early days, to Lesbian feminism, to Lesbian and Gay rights in the late 70s.

Lesbian Music

Lesbian culture went through stages similar to those of *Lesbian Tide*.
The early 70s brought new talent and a new Lesbian music recording industry. Concerts were zealously limited to "women only"
audiences. Singers Alix Dobkin and Linda Shear would only sing
for women-identified women. Shear's record albums had a FOR
LESBIANS ONLY imprint. In the early days concerts had a predominantly Lesbian audience, which the latter wanted to keep that
way. But the artists began to realize that while a private political
statement gave individual Lesbians hope and pride in themselves,
a more public statement also needed to be made.

In 1976 California Women on Wheels (Margie Adam, Meg
Christian, Holly Near, and Cris Williamson) went on tour to bring
the power and joy of women's music to thousands of women.
Margie (Pleiades Records), sponsored by the National Women's
Political Caucus, stumped the country singing and playing her
heart out for the Equal Rights Amendment. Meg and Cris (Olivia
Records) made Lesbian history with their sold-out performance at
Carnegie Hall in 1982. Holly (Redwood Records) specializes in
"Music that Rocks the Boat," not only for Lesbians but for oppressed people of other cultures and countries. She also brought
folk singer Ronnie Gilbert (Abbe Alice Music) out of retirement.
Ronnie sang with The Weavers 40 years ago. McCarthyism drove
them off the stage because they sang about unionism, world peace
and disarmament. Ronnie's "work in progress" is a musical,
"Mother Jones." Black artists, two in particular, also emerged in
the 70s. Mary Watkins, composer-musician, received national ac-
claim for her "Winds of Change" recording with a full jazz orches-
tra. Linda Tillery, a powerful rhythm and blues vocalist, has her
own band. Instrumental music and improvisation is her trademark.

These are some of the pioneers of women's music. Today talented
Lesbian artists are innumerable. In the past 15 years women's music

festivals have established themselves as annual events in all parts of the country. The largest, Michigan Womyn's Music Festival, draws as many as 7,000 women to a rugged, woodsy camping area. The National Women's Festival, held indoors at Bloomington, Indiana, is the oldest. Others are Southern and West Coast Women's Music and Comedy Festivals near Atlanta, Georgia, and in Yosemite, California, Sisterfire near Washington, D.C., and Northeast near Providence, Rhode Island. The newest is the East Coast Lesbians' Festival established in 1989, the first to come out of the closet.

Lesbian Writers

In 1970 when Barbara Gittings began preparing bibliographies to acquaint the American Library Association (ALA) with Lesbian/Gay literature, it consisted mostly of nonfiction and periodicals. Today we have Lesbian novelists, poets, and playwrights galore. Jane Rule was already a major novelist. Her first, *The Desert of the Heart,* and her latest, *Memory Board,* are classics. All of her works are now back in print. Rita Mae Brown started out with political prose and poetry, but turned to novels with her irreverent and still popular *Rubyfruit Jungle. A Place for Us* by Isabel Miller was self published but later "discovered" and reprinted as the legendary *Patience and Sarah.* Beloved and prolific author-poet May Sarton has written her first really *out* Lesbian novel, *The Education of Harriet Hatfield.* Anita Cornwell, one of the early Black Lesbian activists, combines fiction, autobiography, and essays in *Black Lesbian in White America.* Ann Allen Schockley is the author of *Loving Her,* one of the first novels with a Black Lesbian protagonist. She received an award from the OUT/LOOK Foundation for her outstanding pioneering contribution to Lesbian writing.

A few of the Lesbian novelists who won awards in the 80s include Sarah Schulman *(After Delores),* Nisa Donnelly *(Bar Stories: A Novel After All)* and Dorothy Allison *(Trash).*

Sara Levi Calderson is the pen name of a Jewish, Latina Lesbian grandmother and native of Mexico City. Her first novel, *Dos Mujeres,* on the Mexicab best seller list, is being translated into English. Lesbian feminist Rosa Maria Roffiel also had her first novel *Amora* published in Mexico.

Lesbian writers have also delved into the science fiction and fantasy genres. Sally Gearhart's renowned book *The Wanderground:*

Stories of the Hill Women explores the extension of feminism into a visionary world of women. Elizabeth Lynn's trilogy, *Chronicles of Torner,* received the 1980 World Fantasy Award. The cover of Sandi Hall's book *Wingwomen of Hera* promises that it is the first of the Cosmic Botanists Trilogy.

There has been an explosion of mystery writers who feature Lesbian detectives or amateur sleuths. In *Murder in the Collective* and *The Dog Collar Murders* Barbara Wilson weaves a little feminism into her murder plot unraveled by amateur sleuth Pam Nilsen. In Katherine Forrest's *Murder at the Nightwood Bar,* clues lead police detective Kate Delafield into the "Gay City" of West Hollywood.

Three novels aimed at teenagers are *Annie on My Mind* by Nancy Garden, *Happy Endings Are All Alike* by Sandra Scoppetone, and *Crush* by Jane Futcher. These are sensitively written stories about teenage Lesbian relationships and the bigotry and misunderstanding the young women face.

Poet Elsa Gidlow's autobiography *Elsa: I Come With My Songs* was released shortly before her death in 1986. Elsa was always a poet first. She dared to celebrate woman love openly and erotically in her collection *On a Grey Thread* published in 1923.

Writing as a Black Lesbian in the early 70s, SDiane Bogus could not find a publisher and received no support from the Black community. She started Women in the Moon Press (WIM) initially to produce her own poetry and essays. Among her works is *Dyke Hands and Sutras Erotic and Lyric.*

Susan Griffin started out in 1971 with a collection of poetry, *Dear Sky,* published by Shameless Hussy Press. In *Women and Nature: The Roaring Inside Her* she finds a new lyrical form in exploring the connection between feminism and ecology.

Pat Parker's *Child of Myself* was also first published in 1971 by Shameless Hussy Press. Pat, Judy Grahn, and Willyce Kim used to do poetry readings together. When Pat read at Scott's, a Lesbian bar in San Francisco, the place was packed—wall-to-wall women. Pat died of cancer in 1989, leaving us a legacy of powerful words. WIM has set up a Pat Parker Poetry Award to an outstanding Black Lesbian feminist poet.

In the early 70s Judy Grahn began the Women's Press Collective in Oakland, California, to publish her early works: *The Common Woman* poems, *A Woman Is Talking to Death* and the *She Who* poems.

The Queen of Wands in 1982 was the first in a series of books called *A Chronicle of Queens.*

Adrienne Rich was an established writer long before her 70s volumes of poems, *Diving into the Wreck,* and *The Dream of a Common Language.* In one of her more recent poems "Dreamwood" she wrote, "Poetry isn't revolution, but a way of knowing why it must come."

Minnie Bruce Pratt received the prestigious Lamont Award from the Academy of American Poets for her autobiographical collection of poems, *Crime Against Nature,* in 1989 . Much to the consternation of the Academy chancellors she made a passionate acceptance speech about all the women in the feminist, Lesbian, and Gay movements "who made the political and cultural realities that helped me to survive." Since then Pratt has received a National Endowment for the Arts (NEA) fellowship to finish her verse narrative *Walking Back Up to Depot Street* and the 1991 Lesbian book award from the ALA's Gay/Lesbian Task Force.

Theater, Films, and Video

Jane Chambers became America's most renowned Lesbian playwright before her death in 1983. She had been appointed a Eugene O'Neill Playwright in 1972 and had nine plays produced. She received a Writers Guild Award for her work on the TV series "Search for Tomorrow." But she really came into her own when she addressed her Lesbian identity in plays like *My Blue Heaven* and *A Late Snow.* Jean Smart, Susan Sullivan, and Lee Meriwether have played the lead role, Lil, in *Last Summer at Blue Fish Cove.* The story is about a young woman dying of cancer and her chosen Lesbian family. After Chambers found that she had cancer she learned how true her play was. *The Quintessential Image,* a one-act comedy, was Chambers' last play. *Kudzu* was unfinished when she died and her lover, Beth Allen, and writer Marsha Sheiness finished it.

Cycles, a theater piece by Carol Grosberg, Muriel Miguel, and Laura Foner, grew out of the New York Womanspace Theater Workshop in 1973. Carol is a Lesbian, Muriel is Indian and Laura is a Weatherwoman. The three women conceived, developed, directed, produced, and played themselves. Their separate and collective experiences are woven into a beautiful and intricate structure in which the personal and political are synthesized.

One of Terry Baum's best known works is *Dos Lesbos,* which she co-authored with Carolyn Myers and in which she played a lead role. *Immediate Family,* a one-woman play Terry wrote in 1983, concerns Virginia as she confronts the reality that her lover of 20 years is dying, and the homophobia she encounters from Rosie's family and hospital attendants. It has been performed throughout the United States and internationally, translated into Dutch, French, Hebrew, and German, and filmed for Dutch television.

Terry's most outrageous comedy is *ONE FOOL or How I Learned to Stop Worrying & Love the Dutch or The Astonishing & Terrifying Adventures of a Yankee Dyke in the Land of Dikes and Tulips or How She Found Love & Lost Love & Found Love, Etc.*

When Cherrie Moraga made the transition from poet to playwright her first play, *Giving up the Ghost,* spoke with the first real voice of the Chicana Lesbian on stage. Major funding for her second play, *Shadow of a Man,* came from the Fund for New American Plays and the Rockefeller Foundation's Multi-Arts Production Fund. The play is a blending of Spanish and English into "teatropoesia," the powerful poetic theater of the Chicana. *Shadow of a Man* is the story of a young Chicana's coming of age and of the women of the family. The men are literally in the shadow, showing how machismo causes estrangement from the women.

Going to Seed by Eve Powell is a play about Black Lesbians. It is a domestic comedy-drama on how three generations of women relate to the youngest's affair with a local female radio DJ.

Lesbian playwright Holly Hughes received a NEA grant in 1991 for *No Trace of the Blond,* a work on which she and playwright/director Ellen Sebastian will collaborate. Hughes is best known for her irreverent *Horniness.*

In 1980 Adele Prandini was co-author, director, and performer in *The Mountain Is Stirring.* Her play *A Safe Night* was presented by San Francisco's Theatre Rhinoceros. She collaborated with Sue Zemel on a musical comedy in 1987. *Pulp and Circumstance* is a take-off on the Lesbian pulp novels of the 50s set to song and dance.

Oranges Are Not the Only Fruit, a 90s film based on the autobiographical novel by Lesbian author Jeanette Winterson, got rave reviews and appeared to have the same impact on the Lesbian community as *Desert Hearts* had in the 80s. Beeban Kidron is the British filmmaker who directed the work, originally filmed in three one-hour episodes for airing on prime time BBC television. *Oranges* shows a harrowing response of a religious fanatic mother to her daughter's Lesbian tendencies.

Award-winning filmmaker Barbara Hammer has made more than 50 experimental films and videos. "The Body Politic: Recent Video Art by Bay Area Women 1987–1990" included "Two Bad Daughters" by Barbara in collaboration with Paula Levine.

Michelle Parkerson, nationally acclaimed filmmaker, uses the medium to reflect the experience of Black Lesbians. *Storme, the Lady of the Jewel Box,* is the story of a male impersonator in New York. Parkerson showed a clip of her film-in-progress about Audre Lorde at a 1990 event in Washington, D.C., sponsored by Black Women Together to honor the Lesbian poet.

The Love Songs of Hilary Stevens, a movie starring Glenda Jackson, is being produced by writer-director Linda Thornburg. It is based on May Sarton's novel *Mrs. Stevens Hears the Mermaids Sing* and has her blessings. Linda's play *Leap of Faith* won an Applause Award in Provincetown and a Cable Car nomination in San Francisco.

Lesbians have produced many videotapes that can be purchased or rented for VCR home viewing. Videomaker Pam Walton's "Out in Suburbia" won Best Documentary at the 1989 Lesbian and Gay Film Festival in San Francisco. Her next project is on Gay youth. She is concerned about the isolation of young Lesbians and Gays and the high rate of suicide among sexual minority youth. She wants to do a positive video, letting them know that being Gay does not mean you are doomed for life.

Our own soap opera, "Two in Twenty," follows the adventures of seven diverse women, blending romance, comedy, and serious issues like coming out and Lesbian parenting. It's complete with hilarious commercials.

Pictures and Crafts

In our day, photographs of Lesbians were scarce—mostly very private snapshots friends took of each other that were hidden in a shoe box in the closet. For publication they were in shadow or the head was turned so as not to be recognized. To our knowledge, the first collection of photographs of real live Lesbians (who were not famous writers) appeared in the 1973 edition of *Lesbian Love and Liberation* for which we wrote the text.

By 1979, Lesbian subjects were much bolder. Joan E. Biren (Jeb) came out with *Eye to Eye: Portraits of Lesbians.* Her second volume (1987), *Making a Way: Lesbians Out Front,* was dedicated to Audre Lorde who wrote, "We fear the visibility without which we cannot truly live . . . And that visibility which makes us most vulnerable is that which is also the source of our greatest strength."

Cathy Cade put together a marvelous *Lesbian Photo Album* (1987) which covers the lives of seven Lesbian feminists. She brings visibility to the intimacy of Lesbian family life.

Lesbian artist Lenore Chinn's realistic acrylics on large canvases are meticulous in detail, texture, color and light. In 1981 she received the Ligoa Duncan Award in Paris and one of her paintings is on permanent display at the San Francisco International Airport. During Gay Pride festivities in 1990, she helped organize a Lesbian and Gay Fine Arts exhibition in City Hall.

Cori Couture, president of the Association of California Ceramic Artists, is an out Lesbian. She says that with craft fairs and galleries there are many more artists than space for their work. Even though the majority of those applying are women, men still get precedence.

Lesbian crafts for the most part are exhibited at women's conferences. Caroline Whitehorn of Feminist Forge would like to see experienced writers help crafts artists display their wares, perhaps in a book.

Lesbian Humor

Stand-up comedy is another art form. Robin Tyler had been in show business, first as a singer and then as half of the comedy team of Harrison and Tyler. In 1979 she branched out on her own when Olivia Records produced her *Always a Bridesmaid—Never a Groom.*

We have a couple of 70s vintage 45 records: Ivy Bottini's *Women's Lip* which has a "Lesbians!" segment and Maxine Feldman's *Angry Athis* on the Harrison & Tyler label. Then Kate Clinton came along in the 80s with wisecracking feminist humor. Her fourth album, *Babes in Joyland,* was recorded in 1991.

Marga Gomez and Karen Williams, both from the San Francisco area, are at the top of the new crop of Lesbian comedians. Marga, a Hispanic Lesbian female comic, began stand up in 1982 after a

career as an actress. She won San Francisco's Cabaret Gold Award
for solo female comedy performer in 1986, '87, and '88. Karen, a
writer, poet, and Lesbian mom, was a finalist in the Bay Area Black
Comedy Competition for three years and was nominated for a 1989
Cable Car Award for Outstanding Comic of the Year.

The comic strip, *Dykes To Watch Out For*, by Alison Bechdel is
extremely popular nationwide. *The Lesbian Wear Weekly* is a take off
on *Women's Wear Daily*. Lesbians can learn about "Strategies for
Facing the Haircut Police" or "Makeup Jobs for Beginners." Kris
Kovick's cartoon of *The Amazon Army Knife* carries such necessary
items as a dental dam, handgun, dildo, condom, lipstick, labyris,
tarot cards, crystal, mascara, mace, remote control, and vibrator.

Then there are self help books for the 1990s like *Telling Your Inner
Child to Shut Up* by Jerry Lee Slobotnic Melody Ross.

Laura "Lucky" Baker has a Lesbian greeting card company.
Sample birthday card: Three Lesbians stand over the candle-lit
birthday cake. One says of the cone-shaped party hat, "I refuse to
wear these phallic hats!" Second says, "I think it should be called
re-birthday cake." Third says, "I think you're both projecting."
Card opens to the message, "Have fun processing your birthday."

Towards Understanding Lesbian Sexuality

Lesbians didn't talk much about their sexuality in the 50s and 60s.
Since then an explosion of discussions, workshops, articles, books,
and research has helped Lesbians to understand that sexuality is a
basic part of our being. Exploring our sexuality with partners or
with ourselves nourishes and nurtures us. Understanding our sexuality and the sexuality of others enables us to feel good about
ourselves and to view the diversity of sexuality in a nonjudgmental way.

The National Sex Forum of which Phyllis was co-director for
many years, made two Lesbian sex films in the early 70s: *Holding*
and *In Winterlight*. In 1976 the Forum retained Lesbian Ann Hershey
to film *We Are Ourselves* starring Tee Corinne and Honey Lee
Cottrell. The three films were distributed nationally but only to
professionals for use in sex education or therapy.

Now Lesbians can find videotapes meeting their particular interests. Tigress Productions offers *Hay Fever* and *Erotic in Nature;* Fatale

Video's fare includes *Private Pleasures* and *Shadows*. Audio tapes and 900 numbers feature "hot talk" for women.

The Nomadic Sisters published the first "how to" book on sex in the early 70s. It was followed by *The Joy of Lesbian Sex* (which set another performance standard by stating Lesbians *always* had orgasms), and more recently by the wise and witty *A Lesbian Love Advisor* by Celeste West.

Research by and about Lesbians has added another dimension to our understanding. *The Gay Report* by Karla Jay (the Lesbian section), was one of the first. *Sapphistry: The Book of Lesbian Sexuality* by Pat Califia has gone through several printings and revisions, attesting to its worth, in spite of shipments being destroyed by British customs. Pat also published *Macho Sluts*, a collection of erotic fiction which was confiscated by Canadian Customs, and she edited *The Lesbian S/M Safety Manual.*

JoAnn Loulan's *Lesbian Sex* in the mid-80s established her as one of Lesbianism's brightest sex stars and researchers. It was followed by *Lesbian Passion* and *The Lesbian Erotic Dance.*

In 1986 Little Sister's Books in Vancouver, B.C., reported unprecedented seizures of books by Canadian Customs, including *The Joy of Lesbian Sex*, translations of ancient Greek poetry, and *Lesbian Sex.*

The market today is full of Lesbian erotica. Tee Corinne was one of the pioneers with her *Cunt Coloring Book* in 1975. Since then she has published numerous books but, may be best known for *Lovers* and *Dreams of the Woman Who Loved Sex*. Tee also edited *Intricate Passions,* a collection of short fiction.

Novelists like Katherine V. Forrest write very hot love scenes. Erotic magazines have made their way into our community, but not without controversy. *On Our Backs* is probably the best known followed by *Bad Attitude.* Susie Bright, founder and editor of *On Our Backs,* is also the author of *Susie Sexpert's Lesbian Sex World.*

Erotic photography is another Lesbian art form. An example both outstanding and controversial was the "Drawing the Line" exhibit by the Canadian Lesbian art collective, Kiss and Tell. The collective was started to explore the pornography and censorship debate. Their exhibit is "part of a discussion in Lesbian and feminist communities about sexual imagery, sexism, censorship, pleasure, violence, power and empowerment." The photographs, explicitly sexual and some sadomasochistic, were shown in Vancouver and Toronto, Canada; Melbourne, Australia; and San Francisco.

So what does all this material say about us Lesbians?

Data on Lesbians collected from the 60s to the 80s, shows little difference in actual sexual activity over the years. The majority find sex and emotional involvement with their partner an important part of their lives. Although some would prefer to have more sex than they are currently having, Lesbians for the most part are highly satisfied with their sex lives and our rate of orgasm is way ahead of that for women during intercourse. A note of caution here, all Lesbians are not orgasmic every time, and being non-orgasmic does **not** mean you are not a real Lesbian.

The way most Lesbians achieve orgasm is manual stimulation, although oral sex (the most preferred method) is a close second. Tribadism, though still third in our affections, was stronger in more recent studies. Most Lesbians indicated they use some or all of the above during sexual activity.

A very high percentage of Lesbians masturbate to a vast variety of fantasies and with very positive feelings. In both partnered and masturbatory sex, the majority still don't use dildos or penis substitutes. Vibrators are used more than in the past and a substantial number use erotica/pornography as a turn-on. Response to sex toys appears to be more positive now. JoAnn Loulan's survey of 1,500 Lesbians indicated no significant difference between any age group in how much they masturbated, had sex, or enjoyed sex.

Lesbian sadomasochism is a disturbing subject for many. In the Gay 90s, however, S/M has been joined with the discussion/debate over butch/femme and Lesbians "sleeping" with men. On all three of these subjects Lesbians hold various and diverse opinions which fall everywhere between "politically correct" and "politically incorrect."

Proclamations by S/M spokeswomen that they are feminists produce outraged howls from those who cannot reconcile dominance/submission behavior patterns with feminism. Assurances by proponents about the consensual power exchanges of S/M, its cathartic effects, and sexual freedom, do not impress Lesbian feminists who cannot understand oppressive role play. They view S/M as eroticized violence and powerlessness.

S/M defenders complain that their treatment by other Lesbians is the same kind of discrimination all Lesbians have experienced from heterosexuals. Women who appear to be into S/M, or who are friends of women who are, also experience rejection. Authors like Pat Califia and Gayle Rubin draw particular criticism because they write about S/M in positive ways.

When S/M between women first came to our attention, the talk was of silken bonds and playing occasional fantasy scenes to add variety to one's sex life. As the years have passed, however, it appears that whips, ropes, handcuffs, nipple clips, and slave collars are in the ascendant. We still wonder about young Lesbians who, dazzled by the aura of glamour surrounding S/M, get into the practice unwittingly and then don't know how to leave their "support" group, which may be the only friends they have. And seeing a woman leading another woman on a leash is a gut-wrenching experience for us.

Against Sadomasochism, A Radical Feminist Analysis, edited by Robin Ruth Linden, Darlene R. Pagano, Diana E.H. Russell, and Susan Leigh Star, presents a varied selection of essays. Not all of the contributors agree with all of each other's views and politics. They believe in a woman's right to choose how she expresses her sexuality, but question the ideological concepts used in defense of S/M as a feminist practice.

Many feminists believe that the barrage of images depicting women as victims of violence contributes to the acting out of rape and other assaults on women. The emergence of groups such as Women Against Pornography and Feminists Against Censorship politicized the issue and the sometimes strident voices of spokeswomen left the impression that erotica and sex itself were under attack. Most important, neither side appears to listen to the other, making it impossible to have a dialogue on their differing positions as a means of coming to an understanding.

The controversy came to a head at the 1982 Feminist and the Scholar Conference, "Toward a Politics of Sexuality," at Barnard College. The Barnard Women's Center and the planning committee had designed the conference to focus on "sexual pleasure, choice, and autonomy, acknowledging that sexuality is simultaneously a domain of restriction, repression, and danger as well as a domain of exploration, pleasure and agency." Before the conference began it was "trashed" by a coalition of feminists associated with various antipornography organizations for inviting proponents of "antifeminist" sexuality to speak.

The Barnard administration reacted by confiscating all copies of the conference *Diary,* a 60-page booklet that included planning committee minutes, workshop abstracts, bibliographies, and graphics, and was part of the conference packet. The college did reprint *Diary of a Conference on Sexuality,* minus the Barnard name. It is a superb booklet and raises questions about sexuality and feminism that will inform discussion for years to come. In 1984 Carole Vance edited *Pleasure and Danger: Exploring Female Sexuality* which includes the papers and talks from the Barnard conference.

Our community needs to rediscover our tolerance. We are still objects of hatred and discrimination. We must not turn our own anger at the larger community against our sisters who dance to a different drummer than we do. Whatever Lesbians do sexually it is the right thing for them as long as it is consensual and no one is harmed.

Attitudes toward butch/femme couples have changed over the last ten years. In the 70s the practice appeared to be dying out, but today the butch/femme persona is strong and healthy.

JoAnn Loulan's *The Lesbian Erotic Dance* delves deeply into the butch/femme concept as an inherent part of Lesbianism. Her 1989–90 survey of 589 Lesbians from across the country showed that 19 percent identified as butch, 25 percent as femme, 46 percent as androgynous, and 12 percent as none of the above. Joan Nestle in *Restricted Country* raises the butch/femme banner to help us recognize how important they are in our herstory.

Many attacks in the 80s by the religious right were directed at women's studies programs, sexuality courses, and anything remotely suspected of being connected to Lesbianism. For example, in 1982, a small group of women religious extremists and Eagle Forum members zeroed in on Dr. Betty Brooks and her course "Women and Their Bodies" at California State University in Long Beach. They charged promotion of Lesbianism and denigration of the family. The university's administration dropped Betty's classes, drastically altered the women's studies program, and removed other instructors as it caved in to the right-wing witch hunt to purge radical feminists and Lesbians from the campus.

The ACLU filed a class action suit, Sondra Hale, et al, v. Board of Trustees of the California State University, et al, on the basis of violations of rights of free speech, freedom of association, due process, and equal protection. Hale had been the women's studies director. The "et al" refers to Betty and four other women. But the case, which dragged on until 1990, really centered on Lesbianism. The women, who had stood their ground, agreed to a six-figure settlement because they knew they wouldn't have a chance with the United States Supreme Court.

The irony is that Betty still teaches in the university's continuing education program. She received the well-earned Gay and Lesbian Community Activist Award in 1989.

Interference with academic freedom and First Amendment rights is with us in the 90s. Although attacks in recent years have been sporadic, faculty in many women's studies and sexuality programs were scared. Programs are generally more conservative and discussion of Lesbianism is limited.

Bisexuality

Bisexuality has been around for a long time but as a sexual minority movement it really didn't get off the ground until the mid 70s. The Bisexual Forum of New York began in 1975. By 1980 it had 200 active members with a mailing list of several thousand, but met last in 1983. San Francisco's Bisexual Center was founded in 1976 by Maggi Rubenstein and Harriet Levy, and at one point boasted 550 members. It was followed by BiPOL, a Bisexual, Lesbian and Gay political action group in 1983. BiPOL continues to this day. Chicago's Bi-Ways held its first meeting in 1978, and spawned the feminist-oriented Action Bi-Women in the early 80s. Both groups are still active. The movement is growing both in this country and globally.

According to the *Bay Area Reporter,* June, 1990, was the "Bisexuals' Stonewall" as 415 women and men gathered together for the First National Bisexual Conference in San Francisco. Approximately 250 marched in the largest ever Bisexual contingent in the Lesbian/Gay Freedom Day Parade. Registrants at the BiPOL-sponsored conference came from all over the United States and from

Canada, Britain and Australia. Greta Christina, writing in the July issue of *San Francisco Bay Times,* said:

". . . one of the most positive and promising aspects of the conference was its overwhelmingly feminist character. . . . there was an overriding sentiment that one of the best things about the bisexual movement was that it inherently challenges traditional attitudes about sex roles and relations between men and women."

At the end of the conference, Co-Chair Lani Kaahumanu summed up the feelings of the elated crowd by saying "I feel like I've clicked my heels three times and come home." It was not just the conference that buoyed Lani's spirits, but the knowledge that a book on bisexuality she and Lorraine Hutchins were editing, *Bi Any Other Name: Bisexual People Speak Out,* would be published in 1991. It joined another book on bisexuality, Thomas Geller's *Bisexuality: A Reader and Sourcebook.* Due in late 1991 from Seal Press is *The Bisexual Feminist: Essays on Feminism and Sexual Identity,* edited by Beth Reba Weise.

Triumphs of Bi conferences and books were matched by a rising interest in the subject by Lesbians and Gay men. The interest, however, was not always Bi-positive. Some of the attitudes are delineated in these lines of Lani Kaahumanu's poem about her life in *Bi Any Other Name:*

"I am sick and tired of lesbians who love lesbians, not women.
I will not allow lesbian chauvinism to silence me one more
    time.
I am angered by unexamined and unacknowledged
    internalized misogyny, homophobia, biphobia and
    heterophobia wherever it exists, but especially in my
    lesbian, gay, and bisexual communities.
I am pissed at politically conscious people
    who do the work of liberation but don't recognize
    sexism, racism, and classism as the tap root of all
    oppressions."

When we did the ten-year update of *Lesbian/Woman* in 1983, the issue of Lesbians relating sexually to men was just surfacing in the women's press. It has stayed aboveground since that time. In a survey of 1,000 women by the Lesbian organization Southern California Women for Understanding (SCWU) in 1980, 6.7 percent of 960 responding to the question of how they referred to themselves, said "Bisexual." *OUT/LOOK: National Lesbian & Gay Quarterly* in its Spring 1991 issue published the results of a survey with 638 people responding: 54 percent women and 46 percent men, using the Kinsey scale, reported almost exclusively homosexual experiences. More women (14 percent) than men (9 percent) identified themselves as Bisexual, and women had slightly more heterosexual fantasies than men.

Despite the progress Bisexual activists have made in terms of their movement's relationship with Lesbians and Gay men, not everyone is convinced that Bisexuals really exist. It seems to us that people have a right to self define their sexual orientation, and that orientation can change over the years. Using the Kinsey scale as a measuring tool, with zero as totally heterosexual and six as totally homosexual, most people fall in between, from one to five. If you concede the one to hets and five to homos, aren't the two through four folk rather Bisexually oriented?

Columnist Louise Sloan of the *San Francisco Bay Guardian*, wrote of an activist woman friend who had the legend "bisexual by luck, queer by choice" on the back of her jacket. Sloan noted her own place on the Kinsey scale as a four which meant to her she was sexually attracted to men and women but, for various reasons, "more apt to end up with a female partner."

In 1991 Lesbian Agenda for Action (LAFA), Women's Radical Multicultural Bisexual Alliance, and BiPol sponsored a conference on "A New Direction for the Decade: Lesbian and Bisexual Women's Dialogue." And the Bay Area Bisexual Network announced publication of a quarterly magazine titled *Anything That Moves: Beyond the Myths of Bisexuality.*

Changes in Attitudes of Health Professionals

The trustees of the American Psychiatric Association (APA) gave us a clean bill of health in 1973 when they voted to remove homosexuality from the organizations' *Diagnostic and Statistical Manual of Psychiatric Disorders* (DSM). The resolution, later ratified by the membership, stated that "homosexuality per se implies no impairment in judgment, stability, reliability, or general social or vocational capabilities"—the exact wording later adopted by the American Psychological Association.

The APA retained a category on "sexual orientation disturbance" for individuals "whose sexual interests are directed primarily toward people of the same sex and who are either disturbed by, in conflict with, or wish to change their sexual orientation."

Even so, this category would still keep homosexuals in a holding pattern of mental illness, since every Lesbian and Gay man, in the process of self acceptance and coming out, must deal with the reactions of the heterosexuals in our lives. They are the ones who are disturbed by, in conflict with, or wish to change our sexual orientation. It's really a heterosexual disorder.

Psychiatrists came up with a new category in 1978—"ego-dystonic homosexuality"—the desire of a homosexually behaving person to acquire or increase heterosexual arousal. Ironically, the Lesbian or Gay man who succumbs to the hard sell of heterosexual bias is immediately labeled mentally ill.

In 1980, seven years after homosexuality per se was removed from the APA's list of disorders, Dr. Terri Levy tested 106 graduate clinical psychology interns on their attitudes toward Lesbians. Two groups of interns viewed a 20-minute videotape of a therapy session with a woman who had just ended an intimate relationship. One group was told the woman had broken up with a woman and identified her as a Lesbian, and the other group was allowed to assume that the relationship was heterosexual. Interns who thought the client was heterosexual rated her "way above normal" and were impressed with the way in which she handled the stress of breaking up. Those who thought she was a Lesbian rated her as having a low personal adjustment, negative personality characteristics, poor sexual identity, poor self control, and negative attitudes toward men.

What we perceived as a major breakthrough in psychological theory and practice has had little effect on what students are being taught. The observations of these interns reflect the negative stereotypes that the psychological professions have held historically, despite numerous research studies to the contrary, and despite a declared change in diagnostic policy.

Lesbians and Gay men who feel good about themselves, have self esteem and are well adjusted, are healthy and should no longer be a concern of psychiatry. Removing the "sickness" label and the stigma attached to it is the best "cure" yet. We only wish the "change" advocates could understand how they are responsible for making people sick.

The suspicion their daughter was having a Lesbian relationship drove the parents of Stephanie Riethmiller to the extreme of hiring cult "deprogrammers" to change her lifestyle. They kidnapped and raped her. Homosexuality is not the sickness. Society's "sexual orientation disturbance" is.

That the APA's change in mental health policy depended upon a *vote* of its board and membership did not escape us. There was no commitment to change in public or institutional education.

"The Politics of Diagnosis" was further revealed by Michael Botkin in *Gay Community News*. While Gays were still trying to remove "ego-dystonic homosexuality" from DSM III, the Nomenclature Committee in early 1986 announced two new disorders: "Sadistic personality disorder" (battered women) and "perilutal phase dysphoric disorder" (premenstrual syndrome). Outraged feminist psychologists formed a "Ms. Diagnosis" coalition. Lesbian and Gay mental health professionals joined forces to remove all three labels from the manual.

A meeting between coalition members and the Nomenclature Committee resulted in deletion of "ego-dystonic homosexuality." The category "sadistic personality disorder" was changed to "self-defeating personality disorder," but the committee retained both of the classifications that pertained only to women. Botkin observed, "The psychiatrists' sudden decision to de-pathologize homosexuality may have been an attempt to break the alliance— to pacify lesbians and gay men who appeared to be winning anyway, and thereby isolate the feminists."

The coalition remained intact and the "cause" was heatedly debated at the psychologists' annual convention that summer in Washington, D.C. Dr. Lenore Walker, renowned researcher and national authority on battered women, and other speakers questioned scientific methods of the psychiatrists, decried the victim-blaming implicit in the diagnosis applied to battered women, and warned of the effects of such a classification.

In the latest version of the APA's DSM, as of early 1991, the phrase "ego-dystonic homosexuality" has been deleted, but the holding pattern is still in effect under the heading of "Sexual Disorders not Specified." It still has to do with sexual orientation discomfort because of internalized homophobia due to the stigma imposed by society. As to the two new categories affecting women, both are listed as "needing further study."

Fortunately for Lesbians the last 20 years have produced a quantity of excellent Lesbian therapists. A crop of books analyze our problems, explain us to non-Gay therapists, and give us the "how" to do our own analysis. And to start us on the right path, Dr. Marny Hall wrote *The Lavender Couch: A Consumer's Guide to Psychotherapy for Lesbians and Gay Men.* In 1990 the Los Angeles Gay and Lesbian Community Services Center offered a 10-week 1½ hour therapy group for Black Lesbians to explore how their identity is affected by racism, sexism, and homophobia.

Pat Norman and the San Francisco Public Health Department

Pat Norman, Black Lesbian activist, listed in *Ms.* magazine as one of the "Women to Watch in the 80s," is a pioneer in the field of Lesbian and Gay health. She began her civil service career in San Francisco as a community health worker for the Public Health Department's Center for Special Problems.

In 1978, through Pat's persistent efforts, 400 employees, by mandate of San Francisco's Community Mental Health Services, attended the in-service training workshop, "Gay Male, Lesbian and Bisexual Lifestyles." The City contracted the services of the National Sex Forum of which Phyllis was co-director. The workshop included films and presentations by a wide spectrum of Lesbians, Gays, and Bisexuals who were young, older, parents, and people of color. Attendees were physicians, psychiatrists, psychologists, social workers, nurses, administrators, and receptionists—anyone who might come in contact with sexual minority clients. Some doctors who resented the mandate and came reluctantly later admitted how much they had gained from the experience. Black, Hispanic, and Asian therapists, who had thought homosexuality was only a white/Anglo phenomenon, had to face and respond to Lesbians and Gay men of their own race and national origin. The workshops— eight of them with 50 mental health workers participating at a time—were highly successful in breaking down these and other stereotypes.

Pat carved out a new position for herself as Coordinator of Lesbian and Gay Health Services within the department. She conducted workshops for medical personnel at San Francisco General Hospital and other branches of the department and monitored city contracts with community agencies that provide services for Lesbian and Gay clients.

Through Pat's efforts, San Francisco became the first city to establish the position of Gay Health Specialist in its mental health system. Currently the specialty has been expanded to cover regular health care. It requires 500 hours of supervised counseling or direct services with Lesbians, Gays, and Bisexuals, who are now guaranteed "Gay-sensitive" treatment.

Pat also chaired the California Task Force on Lesbian/Gay Wellness which became involved with a project of the Office of Prevention, State Department of Mental Health. "Friends Can Be Good Medicine" was a campaign to develop public awareness by producing television spots designed to reach six communities: Elderly, Blacks, Asians, Latinos, American Indians, and Gays/Lesbians. The commercials were ordered in 1981 and, with the exception of the Lesbian/Gay tapes, were completed and given free air time. B.T. Collins, Governor Jerry Brown's chief of staff, suppressed the Lesbian/Gay commercials because they were "too pro-Gay."

In the late 80s Pat Norman and the task force undertook another project with the Office of Prevention—this time Public Service Announcements on AIDS to reach the Gay/Lesbian audience. The task force had input on content and recommended Peter Adair (*Word Is Out*) as the filmmaker. The mental health chief agreed, but the next month he changed his mind, or someone in Governor Deukmejian's administration changed it for him. The job went instead to someone hopelessly out of touch with the Gay/Lesbian community. The tapes, at a cost in six figures, were useless.

The AIDS Epidemic

Pat first learned from the Centers for Disease Control (CDC) in 1981 that an epidemic of a very rare disease, to be known later as Acquired Immune Deficiency Syndrome (AIDS), was turning up largely in the Gay male population. The cause was not clear, but the disease appeared to be sexually transmitted. At high risk were intravenous (IV) drug users and those who had multiple sex partners.

Pat immediately formed a citywide coordinating commmittee to respond to the crisis. From the beginning she emphasized, "This is *not* a Gay disease. We need to be clear about the disease without being moralistic in our judgments." She knew that unless information was handled sensitively and reasonably there would be panic in the streets. Heaping blame on the Gay community could only lead to homophobic persecution, psychological and physical Gay bashing.

Her committee put together press releases for the Gay media which were not taken too seriously at first—the facts about AIDS were so sketchy then. The committee also prepared information to be distributed in the baths, bars, and other places where Gays were apt to meet. They stressed precautionary use of condoms, and their distribution in bath houses.

Of course the media came out with headlines about the "Gay Plague," and all the things Pat had predicted came true. In 1983 *California Magazine* published an article called "California Whitewash" with a subheading, "While the number of AIDS victims doubles every six months gay leaders in California have obscured information about how the deadly disease is spread endangering thousands of lives . . . ."

Pat was on the hot seat for a while. In San Francisco conflict in the Gay community centered around a study by researchers at the University of California Medical Center. They concluded that one of every 333 single men in the Castro area of San Francisco had been diagnosed with AIDS. The statistics had not been released lest they be taken out of context and be misinterpreted. When the statisticts were leaked to the press accusations were made, many of which were politically motivated. When the emotional blood bath died down, Pat received more cooperation than ever before from the community at large. A network of services was already in place. The fact that San Francisco's systems approach to AIDS has become a model for the nation is due in large part to Pat Norman.

She resigned from the health department in 1986 when the department was going through some organizational changes, but she is still involved in AIDS education. She has a contract with the California AIDS Intervention Training Center, and is overseer for a San Francisco contract training people to provide emotional and practical support for African Americans with AIDS.

Lesbian Health Issues

The concept of "Lesbian Health" as an issue is a relatively new one, brought into prominence as the AIDS epidemic has focused the Lesbian/Gay communities more and more on medicine, sickness, and health.

In 1979 some Lesbian physicians and health workers in San Francisco, headed by Dr. Patricia Robertson, did a study of Lesbian health needs. They found that because of social, institutional, and medical prejudice, Lesbians were far less likely to seek medical intervention than were non-Lesbian women. A one-day-a-week clinic for Lesbians was started at San Francisco General Hospital and immediately had a long waiting list.

As a result, in 1980 Dr. Robertson, Nurse Practitioner Sherron Mills, and others began a nonprofit clinic for Lesbians. They honored us by naming it Lyon-Martin Women's Health Services. Sherron was the first director, and for a while they held evening hours at one of the Health Department's centers in the Castro district. Then they shared offices with another physician who had extra space, and finally moved to a medical building in the Mission district where they had their own premises. In 1991 they again moved, this time to Market Street and much larger quarters allowing for more personnel and clients, meetings and workshops, and additional services such as safe-sex counseling, HIV-positive support groups, and acupuncture.

In other cities, Lesbian health programs tended to focus more on mental than physical health. Celebrating its tenth anniversary in 1990, Whitman-Walker Clinic, Inc., in Washington, D.C., instituted new Lesbian services: Lesbian Resource and Counseling Center, Lesbians Choosing Children, Black Lesbian Support Group, and Lesbian Wellness. An anonymous Lesbian donated $50,000 to fund the services. Amelie Zurn was named director.

The 80s saw the publication of *The New Our Bodies; Ourselves;* and *Ourselves, Growing Older: Women Aging with Knowledge and Power.* In 1990 *The Black Women's Health Book: Speaking for Ourselves,* came out. Evelyn C. White edited the anthology which includes articles by Pat Parker and Audre Lorde and one entitled "Taking the Home Out of Homophobia: Black Lesbian Health" by Jewelle Gomez and Barbara Smith, which discusses how sexism and homophobia affect the mental health of both Lesbian and non-Lesbian women.

Silent Crisis in
Women's Health Care

When AIDS appeared on the scene at the beginning of the 80s an appalled Lesbian/Gay community rallied to fight the epidemic. Many Lesbians got involved with AIDS health care either as health workers, volunteers, or employees. And Lesbians grieved over the deaths of their Gay friends.

As the 80s and the AIDS epidemic progressed, however, another factor entered Lesbian awareness. That was the death or illness from cancer of many of our Lesbian friends and lovers. We lost DOB members Cleo Bonner, Helen Sandoz, Evelyn Whitworth, Marion Glass, and Adrianne Mericone. Terminally ill Lesbians found they were not welcome at, or eligible for, the medical and support programs set up for people with AIDS. The question began to be raised, "If AIDS was primarily a women's disease would Gay men support us the way we have them?" A 1989 study showed 42,000 women die from breast cancer each year—almost as many as the total number of people who have died from AIDS since 1981.

Jackie Winnow, founder of the Women's Cancer Resource Center (WCRC) and coordinator of the Lesbian, Gay, and AIDS unit of the San Francisco Human Rights Commission, was the opening speaker at the 1989 Lesbian Caregivers and AIDS conference in San Francisco. She centered her speech on the demand that Lesbians look at what it means to be focusing on AIDS in the middle of the silent crisis in women's health care.

Jackie pointed out, "In 1988 there were 40,000 women in San Francisco and Oakland living with cancer; at least 4,000 of them are Lesbians; 4,000 will die this year. Only 1.5 percent of the San Francisco health department budget went to women-specific services in 1988. There are so many women in our community with health problems, be they cancer, environmental illness, Epstein-Barr (renamed Chronic Fatigue Syndrome), or multiple sclerosis, but they are not seen as having anything serious enough to be taken care of . . . Why aren't we screaming that sexism kills us?"

San Francisco's budget for women's services is less than 3 percent in 1991, despite organizing by women and promises from the health department. Budget problems citywide are given as the reason. AIDS funding, however, has gone up although not as much as is needed. This appears to be true throughout the United States.

Lesbians face a number of health issues. Central to the problem is failure to obtain adequate preventive care either because of the homophobia and sexism of a majority of medical professionals, lack of funds or health insurance, or lack of information about needs. Lesbians are at risk for cancer, environmental illness, sexually transmitted diseases, and Chronic Fatigue Immune Dysfunction Syndrome. None of these are Lesbian-only diseases, but for some of the reasons mentioned above Lesbians may be more at risk than other populations.

Although WCRC is for all women, about half of those who contact it are Lesbians. In other parts of the country there are Lesbian-specific groups. In 1987 Lesbians with cancer and other life-threatening illnesses began meeting weekly in West Hollywood. There was a separate group for domestic partners.

The Mautner Project for Lesbians with Cancer was formed in 1990 in Washington, D.C. Named after Mary-Helen Mautner who died of cancer, the project offers support groups for Lesbians with cancer and their families. The Charlotte Maxwell Complementary Clinic began in Oakland in 1989 to provide low or no cost medical care for women with cancer. Their staff is made up of men and women, Lesbian and non-Lesbian. They are working cooperatively with WCRC.

Environmental Illness (EI), also known as Multiple Chemical Sensitivity (MCS), is another health problem which impacts heavily on women, and therefore on Lesbians. A majority of physicians are following tradition by calling this women's medical concern "psychosomatic." Since it is not seen as a "real" disease there is little or no funding for research, medical care, support organizations, or outreach services.

Chronic Fatigue Immune Dysfunction Syndrome (CFIDS)

In 1984 CDC reported that a strange illness with symptoms similar to flu had infected almost 200 people in Incline Village near Lake Tahoe. Twice as many women as men were affected. The disease causes severe debilitating exhaustion along with a variety of other symptoms. Its resemblance to AIDS is "frightening" although it is not as lethal. Currently an estimated 3.5 million Americans are affected, most of them women—which means that about 350,000 Lesbians are affected.

In 1984 Jan Montgomery, a Lesbian community organizer, formed the Chronic Epstein-Barr Foundation in San Francisco. She had been ill with the disease which was then thought to be caused by the Epstein-Barr virus. Through the foundation she asked the San Francisco Health Commission to hold hearings on the illness. Following voluminous testimony in 1985, the commission directed the Department of Public Health to continue investigation of Epstein-Barr and to provide patient support. It turned out the Epstein-Barr virus was not the causative agent of the illness, which was renamed Chronic Fatigue Syndrome (CFS). The Chronic Epstein-Barr Foundation changed its name to Chronic Fatigue Immune Dysfunction Syndrome Foundation, and the acronym CFIDS has become widely used.

What causes CFIDS is not clear, although something causes the immune system to overreact. Research is being done by CDC and other institutions. Lesbian physicians have been particularly impacted by the epidemic. Dr. Carol Jessop, formerly Lyon-Martin Clinic's medical director and now in private practice, at one time identified 1,000 women patients with CFIDS. She has become one of the experts on the disease.

Lyon-Martin Clinic, LAFA, and several other organizations sponsored a day-long conference on CFIDS in March, 1991. Marya Grambs, executive director of the CFIDS Foundation, said her organization was applying for a grant which would allow them to train physicians to diagnose and treat the disease. Currently there is no "official test" for CFIDS. "Its a diagnosis of exclusion," Marya said. "You test for and rule out everything else. It is treatable but not curable," she added. "I don't know anyone who has recovered 100 percent."

A new group, CFIDS Action Campaign for the U.S. (CACTUS) is a "national coalition of CFIDS leaders formed to wage a campaign of advocacy and activism by and for people with CFIDS."

Women and AIDS
Women are the fastest growing segment of the population becoming HIV-positive. In April, 1991, CDC advised that more than 16,000

United States women have contracted AIDS since the epidemic began. The number of cases appears to be increasing faster in women
than in men. The results of blood tests on newborns in 38 states and
the District of Columbia between January, 1988, and September,
1990, indicate that about 80,000 American women of childbearing age
are infected with HIV. It is most common among women who live
along the Atlantic Coast or who are Black or Hispanic. So far, there
are no confirmed cases where woman-to-woman sexual transmission
of HIV was the only risk factor. Lesbians have been infected through
IV drug use, transfusions, and intercourse with infected men.

Lisa M. Keen, in *The Washington Blade,* came up with the following
information. A CDC report, "Epidemiology of Reported Cases of
AIDS in Lesbians, United States 1980–89," states that out of 9,717
recorded cases of AIDS in women, 79 cases were women who had
only female sex partners and 103 were women who had sex with
both women and men. Of the 79 women, 75 were IV drug users
and four had received transfusions when blood had probably been
infected. Ergo, no confirmed cases of sexual transmission of HIV
infection by a woman to another woman.

Dr. Susan Chu, the lead researcher on the report, notes two
instances of female-to-female transmission of HIV infection which
were reported but not confirmed. One was a New York Lesbian,
26, with AIDS. The only identified method of transmission was sex
with a female intravenous drug user who was HIV infected. The
second case was a 24-year-old Lesbian in the Philippines. She had
sex only with women, didn't use IV drugs, and had never had a
blood transfusion.

Dr. Chu concluded that although woman-to-woman sexual
transmission of the HIV virus appears to be rare, "the occurrence
of AIDS among lesbian and bisexual women indicates that women
who engage in sex with other women can be exposed to HIV." She
notes that vaginal secretions, menstrual blood, and mucous mem-
brane are potentially infectious.

A 1988 survey of more than 400 Lesbian and Bisexual women in
Minneapolis and St. Paul, Minnesota, indicated that three-fourths
of them felt they didn't have enough information about AIDS, and
nearly one-third said they had decreased their sexual activity because of fear of AIDS. The group was almost 94 percent white and
85 percent Lesbian.

No study of oral sex between women as a method of transmission exists. CDC's records of infected individuals show that "no identified means of transmission" is two-and-one-half times greater for women than for men and children. Thus many Lesbians continue to feel they are immune to HIV infection since they have been considered to have the lowest risk rate of any group. Safer sex guidelines for Lesbians have been drawn up, but most of the information and resources available for women is aimed at those having sex with men. According to Marsha Blachman, Women's Services Coordinator at the San Francisco AIDS Health Project, Lesbians who have AIDS or ARC or are HIV-positive fear hostility and ostracism from the Lesbian community, since sleeping with men and IV drug use are not seen as being "politically correct."

Lesbian communities are beginning to set up support groups for Lesbian and non-Lesbian women. More are agitating to get CDC to change the list of symptoms that denote AIDS to include those which are woman-specific so that women can be eligible for Social Security benefits and other services available to persons with AIDS. CDC is finally moving slowly on this.

Several books are helpful in learning more about women and AIDS, including: *AIDS: The Women* edited by Ines Rieder and Patricia Ruppelt, *Women and the AIDS Crisis* by Diane Richardson, *Making It: A Woman's Guide to Sex in the Age of Aids* by Cindy Patton and Janis Kelly, with Spanish translation by Papusa Molina. Also available is a videotape, "Fighting for Our Lives: Women Confronting AIDS" from the Center for Women Policy Studies in Washington, D.C. It focuses on women of color, who are 70 percent of the women with HIV infection.

Fears about Homosexual Teachers

Lesbians and Gays have a vested interest in the school system, not only as teachers and administrators but as parents and students. In 1972 the Board of Education of the District of Columbia barred discrimination against Gay schoolteachers. Four years later the *Washington Post* reported, "There is no shred of evidence that this formal affirmation of citizens' rights to equal protection under the law has fostered moral decay among the city's young people." School officials in San Francisco, Minneapolis, New York City,

Santa Barbara and other cities have similar policies with similar results.

Dr. Benjamin Spock, noted pediatrician and author of *Baby and Child Care,* at a family conference in New York City, said that homosexual teachers are being scapegoated although "the overwhelming majority of seductions and molestations of children are carried out by heterosexuals—and mostly by members of the family circle. Yet we would not recommend the firing of all heterosexual teachers because a few heterosexuals are unprincipled, nor the breakup of all families because of the culpability of an occasional family member."

Statistics from Seattle (93 percent), Boise, Idaho (95 percent), San Francisco (100 percent) and Multnomah County, Oregon (85 percent) support Spock's statement that child molestation involves mostly adult heterosexual males and young girls. Hank Giaretto, director of the Child Sexual Abuse Treatment Program in San Jose, California, says, "We have handled less than half a dozen cases of a homosexual nature out of a total seven hundred in the last six years." By our math that's less than 1 percent.

At least one PTA group got the message. Shortly after the Dade County, Florida, election which repealed its Gay rights ordinance, the West Palm Beach PTA distributed brochures on their children's summer movie series. It stated no adult males would be admitted. Fathers, who had never cared about sexism before, rose up in righteous indignation because they would not be allowed to accompany their children. PTA President Lottie Gaffney stood firm. "We want to avoid child molesting. Statistics prove that a child molester is almost 100 percent male. We're trying to make our program as safe as possible."

Support for Lesbian and Gay Youth

Adolescence is often a difficult transition period of budding sexuality, little information, and lots of misinformation. Parents who find it difficult to talk about sex with their children are often the ones who protest attempts to include sex education in school curricula. They also vehemently protest any mention of homosexuality which, if presented sensitively, can prevent some of the problems that develop because of ignorance and prejudice.

Joyce Hunter, director of social services at the Hetrick-Martin Institute for the Preservation of Lesbian/Gay Youth, is a founder (1985) of the Harvey Milk High School in New York City. Lesbian and Gay students who have been harassed or assaulted at other schools can transfer to this alternative program run by the city school district.

In 1984 a young man transferred to Fairfax High School in Los Angeles because he had been harassed out of his previous school for being Gay. The same thing happened to him at Fairfax where Dr. Virginia Uribe, a closeted Lesbian, had taught for 34 years. She was so moved by what occurred that she came out and persuaded school authorities to let her set up Project 10, so named because it is estimated that 10 percent of the population is Gay. A major component of Project 10 is educating staff, counselors, and teachers; demystifying homosexuality; and increasing tolerance and respect for differences. For students, Project 10 provides a supportive and safe place to talk about homosexuality and receive nonjudgmental counseling.

Dr. Uribe is firm in her belief that Lesbian and Gay teenagers should be able to attend school free of verbal and physical harassment, have access to accurate information from trained adults, and be included in support programs to help deal with the difficulties of adolescence. Her program has been so successful that other school districts are adopting similar programs.

A Lesbian/Gay Resource Center for students was adopted by the San Francisco Board of Education in 1990, in spite of opposition from School Superintendent Ramon Cortines.

Long before high school, Lesbian and Gay families need to be recognized by the school system. A group of mothers whose children go to an elementary school in San Francisco has been meeting to discuss ways in which to counter homophobia at their children's school. The group seeks to overturn deeply rooted and far-reaching assumptions about the kinds of families that are taught and subtly validated in the classroom and school system. Mother-father family assumptions are found in printed forms such as who to call in case of emergency and in verbal instructions to take a report home to your "mother and father." The mothers made up a bibliography for the school library with a broad focus on multicultural families and values, including *Heather Has Two Mommies*.

Project 21 was initiated by Bay Area Network of Gay and Lesbian Educators with the goal of a fair and accurate representation of Lesbians and Gays in public school materials by the year 2000. Speakers testified at a hearing of the Curriculum Commission of the California Board of Education on content of history and social science textbooks. They deplored the omission of any reference to some of the famous people who were Lesbian or Gay.

At its 1990 convention, the American Federation of Teachers, an international teachers' union, adopted resolutions giving Lesbian and Gay students and teachers equity with heterosexual peers. Some 3,300 delegates agreed by voice vote to include sexual orientation in anti-discrimination protections, bargain for bereavement leave for domestic partners, condemn harassment or violence against Lesbian/Gay students, and protect the rights of those who are HIV-positive.

Ignored and sometimes exploited, sexual minority youth is now receiving some of the attention so long needed. Besides the steps taken by some school districts, there are now organizations which are run by or for young Lesbians, Gays, and Bisexuals.

In San Francisco, Lavender Youth Recreation and Information Center (LYRIC) was started to empower young people to coordinate events such as dances and LYRIC's annual pancake feed. An adult coordinator raises money and is supportive, but youth are part of the entire decision-making process. New York City has a similar program, Sexual Minority Youth Assistance League, which focuses on rap sessions. Lambda Youth Group which meets in Sacramento, California, also places emphasis on rap sessions facilitated by adult Gays and Lesbians. Youth groups can be found at many colleges and in many communities.

In 1990 the Seattle (Washington) Commission on Children and Youth held a full-day conference for Gay, Lesbian, and Bisexual youth with more than 140 people attending. Jenie Hall is co-clerk of the American Friends Service Committee's (AFSC) Gay/Lesbian/Bisexual Youth Program in Seattle. She wrote us in 1991, "I'm amazed at what we've done in the last year and a half. Besides developing the youth phoneline we've started a Youth of Color Support Group and started doing trainings with local school and health care providers so they can identify and meet the needs specific to the youth." Jenie also works with the Lesbian Resource

Center's young Lesbian group, which includes social activities with rap sessions. The AFSC has published *Bridges of Respect: Creating Support for Lesbian and Gay Youth.* The resource guide, written by Kay Whitlock, former chair of NOW's Lesbian Task Force, is aimed at parents, educators—all who work with youth. It presents a powerful analysis of the effects of homophobia on youth and creative ideas for effecting change.

At the beginning of 1991, the Child Welfare League of America staged its first colloquium on serving Gay and Lesbian youth in child welfare agencies. Never before had the League, with its membership of over 650 executive directors of youth assistance projects nationwide, addressed Lesbian/Gay youth issues so visibly. Teresa DeCrescenzo, executive director of Gay and Lesbian Adolescent Social Services in Los Angeles, stated, "With this conference the most respected and powerful children's advocacy agency in the country—if not the world—[is] taking a leadership role in ensuring good service, very good social and public policy, and good advocacy on the part of Gay and Lesbian youth."

Pivotal to the League's decision to hold the conference was the report commissioned by the Department of Health and Human Services in 1990, examining the issue of youth suicide. The report said that Lesbian and Gay teenagers are two to three times more likely to attempt suicide than their heterosexual counterparts, and may comprise up to 30 percent of completed youth suicides annually. Confronting homophobia, not homosexuality, was the solution to the problem, the report concluded.

That statement prompted the right wing to urge President Bush to denounce the study. Secretary of Health and Human Services Louis Sullivan repudiated the report, saying, "The views in the paper run contrary to [the aim] of advancing traditional family values."

Perhaps if everyone in the country were forced to watch "Growing Up and Coming Out," a television special aired by Channel 4 in the San Francisco Bay Area in March, 1991, Secretary Sullivan might change his mind. Shown in prime time, it was the top-rated program. Out of more than 100 phone calls immediately after the program all but three were favorable or seeking help.

Included in the program of the fourth annual Texas Lesbian Conference in Austin in 1991 was the workshop "Out Youth: Baby

Dykes; the Facts behind the Fiction." The panel of young Lesbians age 17–21 talked about their lives and isolation. They look to older Lesbians for information, our history, socializing, and mentorship. They want to be included in the Lesbian movement.

It isn't just United States youngsters who have problems. A Gay organization in Tokyo has filed suit against the city's government for barring open Gay youth from meeting at the Tokyo Youth Activities Center. The group had been meeting at the center for four years. The Tasmanian (Australia) Gay and Lesbian Rights Group has joined with the local Young Gay Association to launch a "come out" print advertising campaign. Their aim is to bring the support of the established Gay community to young Lesbians and Gays.

Issues on Campus

Dr. Lois Flynne pioneered Gay studies at San Francisco State University. Her social science course "Homosexuality as a Social Issue," first offered in 1972, examined Lesbianism, male homosexuality, and the Gay Rights Movement. Students were exposed to a range of scientific, legal, political, and moral/ethical positions on homosexuality and asked to evaluate each position within its own framework. Instruction combined lectures, guest speakers, and class discussion.

A 1982 concert by feminist musician/songwriter Margie Adam on the campus of Colorado Women's College was cancelled by College President Sherry Manning when she learned that tickets were on sale at the Denver Lesbian Center. "We don't have any Lesbians here," she said, adding that it was against college policy to rent facilities "for any event which promotes the Gay and Lesbian movements."

A heterosexual Colorado instructor, Sue Brown, invited three women from the Denver Lesbian Center to address her class, "Psychology of Women," at Aims Community College. The students responded so enthusiastically to the discussion that what ordinarily would have been a 90-minute class developed into a four-hour session. Dean Rex Craig fired Brown despite faculty protests about academic freedom and the appropriateness of the session in a psychology course.

On the other hand, Edra Bogle, associate professor of English, who had been "out" on the campus of North Texas State University for five years, not only suffered no reprisals, she was elected secretary of the Faculty Senate. Bogle had even gone public, which is the worst taboo. She wrote for the campus paper, spoke on television, and served as director of the Gay/Lesbian Association of Denton. Instead of being called on the carpet for her activities she drew admiration from her colleagues for being willing to stand up for her own rights and those of others.

Handing homosexuals one of their rare victories in the nation's highest court, justices of the U.S. Supreme Court in 1978 let stand a decision that forced the University of Missouri to recognize Gay Liberation as a campus student organization. The Eighth U.S. Circuit Court of Appeals had ruled that the university's refusal violated the rights of members to free speech, freedom of association, and equal protection under the law.

When the Florida legislature tried a new tack in 1981—cutting off state funds to universities that recognized groups advocating sex between unmarried people—the Florida Supreme Court unanimously declared the law unconstitutional. The chancellor of the University of Tennessee granted official campus status to Students for Gay Awareness in 1982 to avert a possible lawsuit.

Merle Woo's troubles began in 1981–82 during a political struggle in the Asian American Studies Department at the University of California, Berkeley. She was fired under a controversial rule that called for non-renewal of untenured lecturers after four years. She claimed she was dismissed because she was outspoken in the classroom and in public on race and sex equality and because she is a Lesbian feminist, a trade unionist, and socialist. In 1984 a "no-fault settlement" was reached in which Woo received a two-year contract, a year's back pay, and fees for her lawyer, Mary Dunlap.

Woo was assigned to teach field studies in the Graduate School of Education. When her contract ended in 1986, the university said goodbye to her again—this time on the basis that her field studies post wasn't important enough to warrant a rehire. Woo filed a grievance with the university, which usually takes 90 days or less to process. She was represented by the University Council of the American Federation of Teachers. The university stalled for 2½ years before the case finally went to arbitration in 1989. Under the arbitration agreement Woo was to be reinstated with full back pay, benefits, and seniority. The arbitrator, Professor Leo Kanowitz, found that the university had acted "unreasonably" in refusing Woo continued employment, but failed to call it "discrimination."

The university offered her two unacceptable jobs in the English Department, one of them being Subject A (remedial English). They refused to employ her in ethnic studies because requirements had changed. She was no longer qualified because she didn't have a Ph.D. Then U.C. attorneys filed a motion in court to compel Woo to undergo a psychiatric examination because she had claimed emotional damages in her 1986 grievance. Judge Dawn Girard called the university's action "abusive and frivolous." But that still didn't get her a job at U.C.

In 1990, after eight years of wrangling with the university and winning judgments that were not implemented, Merle Woo announced her candidacy for governor of California on the Peace and Freedom Party ticket. Although she lost, she got her message out, noting that as governor she would became an ex officio member of the university's Board of Regents.

She now teaches "Literature of Women of Color in the United States" at San Francisco State University.

Lesbian Studies

Margaret Cruikshank, editor of *The Lesbian Path* and *Lesbian Studies Present and Future*, has written a creed for the Lesbian Studies Movement: "We will no longer accept anthologies on women in literature which neglect lesbian writers, courses in women and society which ignore lesbian culture, sexuality courses which do not consider *our* sexuality, or any course which presumes to be about *human* experience but merely covers heterosexual experience."

Margaret, who was a pioneer in Women's Studies in the Midwest before coming to San Francisco to champion Lesbian Studies, is now a tenured member of the English faculty at San Francisco City College. (City College is one of the first to have a Gay and Lesbian Studies Department.) For her supplemental reading list on Lesbian literature she refers students to the Harvey Milk branch library in the Castro area. Florence Mitchell, an out Lesbian who manages the library, has developed an extensive Lesbian/Gay collection of books and periodicals.

In 1988 Mildred Dickemann, professor of anthropology at Sonoma State University (Calif.), began drafting a new course on anthropology and homosexuality on the backs of fliers announcing National Coming Out Day. To her knowledge the course is the first of its kind.

Judith Schuyf is the first Lesbian in The Netherlands to receive tenure in Gay and Lesbian Studies at the University of Utrecht. The group which created Homostudies in 1983 consisted of four men and Schuyf. Today there are 25 people on staff, paid by the university, outside institutions, and government to conduct research. Schuyf visited California to look at Gay/Lesbian Studies American style. She was surprised to see the rift between "academe" and "community," which is nonexistent in Holland. Communication between these groups is very valuable, she said.

We agree. Historians who are removed from the grassroots have difficulty in describing and interpreting the flavor of what was (and is) actually happening as the Lesbian/Gay movement emerged and developed after World War II. What we need is to record "living" history as it occurs.

W. Dorr Legg, a founder of ONE, Inc., and Gay activist since 1952, serves as dean of ONE Institute of Homophile Studies which received official authorization from the State of California in 1980 to confer M.A. and Ph.D. degrees. Deborah Ann Coates, whose thesis was on Lesbian representations in cinema, was the first Lesbian to earn a Ph.D. from the Los Angeles based graduate school.

Lesbian Mothers and Their Children

Aside from the lack of recognition of Lesbian heads of households by the school system, there is the court system to contend with. Attorneys who have studied judicial decisions in Lesbian mother custody cases say there is no rhyme nor reason to them. Cases they would expect the mother to win, lost, and those they thought would lose, won. Co-authors Gillian Hanscombe and Jackie Forster of the British book *Rocking the Cradle* refer to "Courts of Flaw."

Research in the United States and England shows there are no differences between children of Lesbian and heterosexual mothers

in social and emotional development. Yet in 1987 the Missouri
Appeals Court refused to overturn a lower court's decision granting
the father custody of four children (three daughters and a son) and
the family home solely on the basis that the mother is a Lesbian.
Both courts were so deeply concerned with *her* morals they ignored
allegations that the father sexually abused the children and is an
alcoholic.

The Lesbian Rights Project (LRP) based in San Francisco,
founded by Attorney Donna Hitchens in 1977 as the ACLU for
Lesbians, took on cases of discrimination and fought for rights of
Lesbian mothers to custody of their children. A big breakthrough
came when LRP received a grant from the Rosenberg Foundation
(which deals exclusively with children) so Donna could hire a psychologist to do crisis counseling with the Lesbian mother and her
family while she handled the legal work. In 1982 LRP published
the *Lesbian Mother Litigation Manual,* a tool for lawyers representing
Lesbian mothers. Another first was the mainstream legal treatise
Sexual Orientation and the Law edited by LRP Attorney Roberta
Achtenberg. LRP has expanded its scope and is now the National
Center for Lesbian Rights (NCLR). In order for the one organization which primarily represents the legal rights of Lesbians to retain its independent voice in the 90s, Lesbians around the country
should join as members and support NCLR.

When we were in Paris participating in the 1974 National Sex
Forum workshop "Sexual Attitude Restructuring," we spoke of
Lesbian mothers. A man in the audience jumped up, identified
himself as the head of France's sperm bank, and exclaimed, "No
Lesbian is going to get any of *my* sperm!" Lesbians don't need his
sperm. They can and do find their own donors.

In London, Jackie Forster, editor of the British Lesbian magazine *Sappho,* told us that Lesbians had tried to adopt children but
agencies "freaked out." Then they turned to artificial insemination
by donor (AID). The women found willing donors among Gay
males, and a gynecologist with a private clinic to impregnate them
with the donated sperm. Because of negative publicity, the doctor
stopped taking Lesbian clients. Defenders of Lesbian births staged
a sit-in at the *London Evening News* and threw stink bombs into the
newsroom until the editor agreed to print their views.

After an emotional debate the British Medical Association decided it was not unethical for doctors to administer AID to Lesbians, which is now legal in Britain. AID allows Lesbians to attain the feminist goal for reproductive rights—the "right to choose."

Lesbians today become aware of their sexual orientation earlier and are not as apt to marry and get embroiled in husband/wife divorce/custody battles. Today there are some cases, however, involving conflict between Lesbian birth mothers and their former lovers who had functioned as co-parents. Courts have consistently denied any rights to the nonbiological parent, even though she may have shared responsibilities and care for the child over a period of years.

Using the same process as a stepparent adoption, Lesbians have been successful in the states of California and Washington in establishing themselves as legal co-moms. Shelly Cohen, Seattle attorney, pointed out that one fundamental of family law is that a child has the right to two parents.

In a 21-page decision, Florida Circuit Court Judge M. Ignatius Lester ruled in 1991 that a state law which barred Lesbians and Gays from adopting children was "blatantly unconstitutional."

After a five-year battle, Massachusetts foster care policy was amended in 1990 allowing Lesbians and Gays to be foster parents. Conservative attempts to reopen the issue have been blocked. Placement decisions are back in the hands of social workers.

Today many books, films, and seminars on Lesbian families are available. Cheri Pies' book *Considering Parenthood: A Workbook for Lesbians* helps Lesbians make informed choices. *Heather Has Two Mommies,* written by Leslea Newman and illustrated by Diana Soreeza, is recommended "for children ages 3 to 103." The documentary film of six families, *Not All People Are Straight,* allows children to speak candidly of their lives.

The first organizations to acknowledge, bring together, and assist Lesbian mothers and their children were the Lesbian Mothers Union in San Francisco and Dykes and Tykes in New York City. That was in the early 70s. Today we have Maybe Baby in Fairfax, Virginia, for Lesbians considering parenting, and Lesbian Mothers with Young Children (under six) in Washington, D.C. Lesbian Mothers National Defense Fund in Seattle, Washington, publishes

Mom's Apple Pie which keeps us up-to-date on custody cases and other parental concerns.

Parents of Lesbians and Gays

In 1974 Betty Fairchild, who had come to terms with her son being Gay, did something about it. She talked to Lesbian/Gay groups in Washington, D.C., about forming the Parents of Gays support group. The *Gay Blade* newspaper and "Friends," a local Gay radio show, advertised the new group. Only four parents—all women—showed up at the first meeting. Today the Federation of Parents and Friends of Lesbians and Gays, Inc., (P-FLAG) is a national organization with chapters in most major cities. Each year thousands of parents are counseled by other parents who have affirmed their love for their Gay children.

P-FLAG chapters join in Gay Pride Parades, always with thunderous applause from onlookers. Members also speak at PTAs, to elected officials, in newspaper and magazine interviews, on radio and television, and to many government, university, school, and church groups.

In June of 1989 Paulette Goodman, president of P-FLAG, wrote to First Lady Barbara Bush, requesting that she "speak kind words to some 24 million gay Americans and their families, to help heal the wounds, and to keep these families in loving relationships." Paulette mailed the letter but later hand-delivered it to the White House. Mrs. Bush responded in a letter on White House stationery dated May 10, 1990:

"Thank you so much for your letter and for sharing your work with the Federation of Parents and Friends of Lesbians and Gays, Inc. You sound like a caring parent and a compassionate citizen.

"I firmly believe that we cannot tolerate discrimination against any individuals or groups in our country. Such treatment always brings with it pain and perpetuates hate and intolerance. I appreciate so much your sharing the information about your organization and your encouraging me to help change attitudes. Your words speak eloquently of your love for your child and your compassion for all gay Americans and their families.

"With all best wishes, Warmly, Barbara Bush"

The First Lady's letter was hailed by Lesbians and Gays every-where but caused consternation in the ranks of the religious right. Mrs. Bush did not apologize.

P-FLAG took several steps in 1990 to make their organization more powerful in advocating for the sons and daughters of its mem-bers. An extensive program was launched in Orange County, Cal-ifornia, a stronghold of anti-Gay bigots, to stem the flood of Gay teenage suicides. The program has the backing of a major Episco-palian agency. The organization also expanded its programs of support for families of people with AIDS. And for the first time P-FLAG hired an executive director, Tom Sauerman, a Lutheran minister with 20 years of top-level administrative experience with national church agencies. Reverend Sauerman says his vision for P-FLAG is that it will "reach into every county in the nation, and beyond," and its name will become "as well known as the Red Cross or Girl Scouts."

The Clergy and Homosexuality

The Metropolitan Community Church founded by Reverend Troy Perry was from its beginning in 1968 as sexist as other Christian churches. After waging a fierce battle to gain equality for women in MCC's by-laws, Freda Smith was elected an elder by 60 Gay white males at the 1973 General Conference. She opened the door for other Lesbians and, by her estimate, today's MCC leadership is more than one-third women. Freda took over River City MCC in Sacramento in 1973. By 1979, as vice moderator of the Board of Elders, she had become second in command to Troy.

Many Lesbians/feminists abandoned patriarchal religions alto-gether. These "spiritual expatriates," as Mary Daly called them in *Beyond God the Father* (1973), found a new sense of Be-ing, a "cosmic covenant" of sisterhood. In 1971 Zsuzsanna (Z) Budapest founded the first feminist coven, a model for thousands of other spiritual groups spreading across the nation. Z's *The Feminist Book of Lights and Shadows* (1975) was the first hands-on book to lead women into their own spiritual/Goddess heritage.

Wave after wave of fundamentalist groups waged a "moral" war on homosexuals throughout the 80s. Some wanted to put us to

death, others to overturn hard-won local ordinances banning discrimination against Gays. The tactics of fundamentalists are more
flamboyant, but the attitudes and actions of mainstream denominations are not much different.

Reverend Jane Spahr was forced to resign her post as executive
director of the Council of Oakland (California) Presbyterian
Churches when it was learned she is Lesbian. Had she not resigned, the council was prepared to dissolve itself. Janie, as she is
affectionately called, now conducts the Ministry of Light in Marin
County, California, as an open Lesbian.

When Bishop Paul Moore, Jr., of the Episcopal Diocese of New
York, ordained Ellen Barrett in 1977, she became the focus of controversy both as a woman priest and as a Lesbian. Moore gave her
unqualified support, stating, "Her personal life has never been
under criticism. Many persons with homosexual tendencies are
presently in the ordained ministry. Ellen Barrett's candor in this
regard is not considered a barrier to ordination. She is highly qualified intellectually, morally and spiritually to be a priest."

The House of Bishops disagreed. They made no attempt to overturn the decision to ordain women, but indicated an Episcopalian
would not be considered "disloyal if he or she resisted the decision." The bishops declared it "inadmissible for the Church to
authorize the ordination of anyone who advocates and/or willfully
and habitually practices homosexuality." They added the usual
qualifier that homosexuals as children of God have "equal claim"
upon the love, acceptance, concern, and pastoral care of the
Church and should be "entitled to equal protection under the law."
They deplored "the tragedy of humiliation, persecution and violence" to which many homosexuals are subjected. Unfortunately
the bishops failed to recognize their own culpability in creating the
climate in which this occurs.

Despite continued debates, many Lesbians and Gays still are
graduated from seminaries and are ordained. In 1978 three Lesbian
feminist graduates of the Pacific School of Religion in Berkeley,
California, were ordained by the United Church of Christ.

Chris Madson, reporter for the *Christian Science Monitor* for seven
years, was fired when the manager learned she is a Lesbian. He
called her "evil" and "immoral" and handed her a termination

memorandum from the Mother Church. Ironically, in 1977, several years prior to Chris's firing, an editorial in the *Monitor* stated: "There can be no justification for mistreatment of homosexuals [who] often suffer blatant discrimination in housing, employment and such areas as bank loans." Chris filed suit against the church for discrimination—and lost. Recently because of pressure from Lesbians, Gays, and their supporters over broadcast of the "Monitor Reports" radio show, the *Monitor* changed its hiring policy.

Howard University Professor James S. Tinney, in a guest editorial in *Insight,* broke the silence about the "cowardly and denigrating treatment" of homosexuals in Black churches. He asserted that Black Lesbians and Gay men "have as much right and authority to speak for the Black church as do heterosexual Christians." Tinney said that homosexuality is "both a part of African cultures and unalterably God's own will." The editorial was as much an appeal to Black Lesbians and Gay men to come out of the closet as an admonishment to the churches to change their attitudes. "We stand as a proud new generation of persons who are unashamedly Lesbian and Gay as we are Christian," Tinney declared.

His appeal drew supporting statements from ten national leaders including Coretta Scott King; Reverend Clarence Joseph Rivers, a Black Catholic priest-composer; H. Carl McCall, former United Nations ambassador and a minister of the United Church of Christ; Gilbert H. Caldwell of the United Methodist Commission on Religion and Race; and Dr. Thomas Kilgore, president of the Progressive National Baptist Convention, among the largest Black denominations in the world.

Reverend La Paula Turner, an African-American who has been with MCC for 21 years, is now executive director of its Department of People of Color. She has vowed to overcome racism and has been conducting workshops and worship services at various local MCC churches.

The National Council of Churches was challenged when the Universal Fellowship of Metropolitan Community Churches, which now boasts some 200 congregations worldwide, was endorsed for membership by a unanimous vote of the membership committee. The second step for certification requires a two-thirds vote of the governing board and final approval from two-thirds of the member denominations. Reverend Nancy Wilson of Los Angeles said she wanted to make it perfectly clear "that we are not asking the National Council to legitimize our ministry." Our own feeling is that it's the other way around. MCC's membership would legitimize the National Council of Churches. But it hasn't happened—yet.

The book *Lesbian Nuns: Breaking Silence* prompted a media circus and angry response from Roman Catholic authorities who tried to suppress television shows and news stories—and sometimes succeeded. Co-editors Rosemary Curb and Nancy Manahan, both former nuns, were right in the middle of it as they toured the United States, Canada, Europe, and Australia. They proved to be excellent spokeswomen in dealing with the role of Lesbians in the church.

Jeanne Cordova describes her experience in the convent before she became a Lesbian activist in her book *Kicking the Habit.* Two other national Lesbian leaders, Virginia Apuzzo and Jean O'Leary, are also ex-nuns.

Reverend Rose Mary Denman's book *Let My People In,* published in 1990, tells of her struggle in the United Methodist Church when her friendship with Winnie grew into deep love. She thought she could solve her conflict with the Methodist Church as an admitted Lesbian by having her ministerial credentials sent to the Unitarian Universalist Church. She was refused. Rather than resign, she forced an ecclesiastical trial. She was found to be "in violation" of Methodist church law but allowed to transfer her credentials to the Unitarians.

The New Hope United Church of Christ hired an open Lesbian pastor, Margarita Suarez, in Milwaukee, Wisconsin. The search committee of the 200-member congregation of mainly low-income families was impressed with her views of urban ministry and her interest in reaching out to the Hispanic community. This action caused no problem since U.C.C. was the first mainstream denomination to ordain a Gay man, William Johnson, in 1972.

Two San Francisco congregations of the Evangelical Lutheran Church in America defied institutionalized discrimination when they ordained and hired two Lesbians and a Gay man who had refused to take the oath of celibacy. The Lesbians, Ruth Frost and Phyllis Zillhart, are domestic partners and are assistant pastors at St. Francis Lutheran Church, a predominantly heterosexual congregation. Jeff Johnson is assistant pastor at First United Lutheran Church which has a large Gay congregation. The ordinations are not recognized by the Lutheran church as a whole, and the congregations have been suspended for five years. In 1995 they face expulsion unless they change their ways or the denomination changes its policy.

Largely because Lesbians and Gays have organized within their denominations, various Protestant churches are forming all-inclusive congregations. The Presbyterians have "ministries of light," the Methodists "reconciling congregations," the Lutherans "reconciled in Christ" congregations, United Church of Christ "open and affirming churches."

After a four-year study, a committee of Reform Judaism recommended the ordination of Lesbian and Gay rabbis. The 1990 conference of reform congregations held in Seattle overwhelmingly endorsed the statement of religious equality. The inevitable "but" was the reaffirmation of "heterosexual, monogamous, procreative marriage" as the ideal relationship.

The Vatican in 1990 warned wayward theologians that they had no right to dissent publicly from official Roman Catholic teaching on sex and morals. The National Conference of Catholic Bishops met a few months later to clarify what this meant. They said Gays are not sinful per se because their sexual orientation is not freely chosen. However, the picture changes if they do not lead chaste lives. The practice of homosexuality is still evil. Accordingly, Chapters of Dignity, the organization of American and Canadian Lesbian and Gay Catholics, which had been holding mass in various Catholic churches, have been ousted and are meeting now in Protestant churches. In New York City they have gathered on the steps of St. Patrick's Cathedral in protest.

The Dignity chapter which was kicked out of the Newman Center at the University of Minnesota took its case to the Minneapolis Commission on Civil Rights. The commission ruled that the Catholic Archdiocese of St. Paul and Minneapolis had violated the city's law which bans discrimination in housing based on sexual orientation. The Archdiocese was ordered to pay nearly $20,000 to Dignity and a $15,000 civil fine to the city. The Archdiocese plans to appeal on the basis that "freedom of religion" exempts the church from having to comply with civil or human rights.

Interdenominational Lesbian clergy 300 strong met in New York City to draw up a statement of commitment. According to Jann

344   LESBIAN/WOMAN

Weaver in a 1991 newsletter of the Bay Area Career Women
(BACW), a national coalition called Christian Lesbians Out Together (CLOUT) is in formative stages. The call is for Lesbian
Christians to come out in an interdenominational, multiracial solidarity coalition. A network with Christian and Jewish Lesbians
and other religious and secular groups is also anticipated.

Evidence that we have made homophobic sexual attitudes part
of the agenda that faces religious institutions is a report of the
Committee on Human Sexuality of the Presbyterian church. By an
11–6 vote the committee suggests that sex is a God-given gift to
be enjoyed by everyone including single women and men, Lesbians
and Gays, and responsible adolescents. The report affirms masturbation and petting among teenagers, endorses new family structures including same-sex couples with children. Homosexuals
should be ordained into the ministry, it says, and Lesbian and Gay
couples should enjoy the same rights as heterosexuals. Since the
report was released in February, 1991, it has become a Presbyterian
best seller. In two months it sold 10,000 copies at $5 each and
requests continued at the rate of 1,000 a week. Not surprisingly
the report was soundly rejected by the General Assembly by a vote
of 534–31.

Media Coverage

According to *Forum*, "Lesbianism may be out of the closet, but it's
still on the back of the bus in mainstream women's magazines."
Redbook admitted that its policy was to ignore the subject. At
McCall's there is "no editorial policy against it," but the magazine
is geared to a *married* audience. At *Mademoiselle*, "We don't ignore
it, but we just don't have much reason to cover it." How much
importance female homosexuality is due, *Forum* says, is 20 percent.
"Cosmo Reports found that one out of five American women has
had a Lesbian experience. *Cosmopolitan* is the one mainstream wom-
en's magazine that is unafraid to print articles about Lesbians."

The news media seldom bother with women's conferences unless
there is a controversial angle. Lesbian presence or a resolution on
Gay rights usually draws headlines. When coverage of the "Lesbian
issue" overshadows other issues equally important to women, it
undermines some of our support.

Heading into the National Women's Conference (NWC) in Houston in 1977, feminists feared media attention would focus on the controversial sexual preference plank and overshadow the key issue that affected all women—the Equal Rights Amendment. Sure enough, on arrival an ad in both Houston papers showed an innocent little girl holding a bouquet of flowers and asking, "Mommy, when I grow up, can I be a Lesbian?" The ad was a come-on for Phyllis Schlafly's Pro-Family Coalition rally scheduled at the same time the NWC opened debate on its National Plan of Action.

Our silver anniversary (Valentine's Day 1978) became a media event because of controversy over Supervisor Carol Ruth Silver's request that the San Francisco Board of Supervisors issue a certificate of honor on the occasion of our 25th anniversary and for our "years of devoted service to San Francisco."

"Twenty-five years of what?" shouted Supervisor Quentin Kopp. "Some citizens have moral reservations about such relationships," Supervisor Lee Dolson said. Several supervisors expressed outrage at these comments. Kopp summed up his feelings: "Toleration, yes—glorification, no!" The certificate was approved by an 8–2 vote.

With cameras flashing and much fanfare, Supervisors Silver, Ella Hill Hutch, and Harvey Milk presented us the certificate. We were interviewed by both of The City's dailies and were on television and radio.

"Gay Power, Gay Politics," a documentary that grossly misrepresented both Gay power and the politics of San Francisco, was shown nationally on CBS in 1980. To Lesbians it was a blessing to be omitted. The few who had been approached by co-producer Grace Diekhaus declined to be interviewed. They suspected CBS was out to do a hatchet job. Sally Gearhart consented to an interview in New York. It lasted three hours and seven film packs. Sally protested George Crile's manipulative questions and guarded against saying anything that could be taken out of context. When CBS failed to include her in the documentary she was ecstatic. Diekhaus confessed later that Lesbians were not presented because they were "not disturbing enough."

Mayor Dianne Feinstein, however, found their display of yellow journalism disturbing enough. She asked for three minutes of air time to reply to the hour-long show. CBS refused. The San Francisco Board of Supervisors and the Human Rights Commission filed complaints with the National News Council, and the National Gay Task Force (NGTF) took our grievance to the CBS home office in New York City. Gay journalist Randy Alfred documented more than 40 counts of deliberate misrepresentation and distortion. He testified in person before the News Council, which found that the program concentrated "on certain flamboyant examples of homosexual behavior" that tended to reinforce stereotypes, "exaggerated political concessions" to Gays that made them appear "to threaten public morals and decency," and failed to make it clear that the purpose of the homosexual demystification program in the schools was to reduce "the danger of harassment and violence by heterosexuals against homosexuals."

By contrast Deborah Gee of San Francisco's ABC station produced a nonhomophobic documentary, "Lesbians: The Invisible Minority," which was shown on prime time. She contacted some 40 Lesbians for background and shot scenes of such Lesbian "hangouts" as The Women's Building, the Artemis Society coffee house and restaurant, Old Wives' Tales bookstore and Amelia's bar. To illustrate the diversity of Lesbians she interviewed six women on camera: Comedian Pat Bond, who had served in the military; a couple who were in business together; Lesbian mother Margaret Sloan, who had been a contributing editor for *Ms.* and founder of the National Black Feminist Organization; Sally Gearhart, then chair of the Speech Department at San Francisco State University; and an unidentified woman who described what it was like to be "locked in the closet." Deborah Gee renewed our faith that one can produce a truthful, informative, and sensitive documentary.

So did the television movie *A Question of Love,* adapted from the book *By Her Own Admission,* written by reporter Gifford Guy Gibson because he was so deeply affected by the Texas jury trial in which Mary Jo Risher lost custody of her two sons. The film, starring Jane Alexander and Gena Rowlands, was true to life, and the courtroom scenes accurately reflected the testimony of witnesses and arguments by opposing attorneys regarding Lesbians as mothers. Hollywood reviewer Cecil Smith was struck by the "ordinariness of the principals" in the story.

Ginny Vida, who edited the excellent resource book *Our Right To Love,* pioneered efforts by NGTF to establish a relationship with the media. She alerted groups across the country about upcoming films or broadcasts that were atypical and derogatory. (Ginny is presently editing another edition of *Our Right To Love.*)

Word came in 1980 that United Artists was about to release two homophobic films, *Cruising* and *Windows,* in 600 theaters across the United States and Canada. The late Charles Morris, publisher of San Francisco's *Sentinel,* twice defended *Cruising* on First Amendment grounds, despite NGTF's warning. Following a screening, however, he sought its withdrawal, saying, *"Cruising* is an incitement to violence . . . It is a snuff film." Lesbians and Gays protested to Transamerica and its subsidiary United Artists, picketed the latter's local theaters, and distributed leaflets.

When the equally bizarre anti-Lesbian *Windows* was released, movie houses throughout Northern California refused to show it. Runs in other parts of the country were short-lived. Picket lines effectively turned patrons away. In 1982 the films *Personal Best* and *Making Love* dealt with homosexuality in a more positive light.

That same year Rita Mae Brown broke into Hollywood TV as a writer for Norman Lear's special, "I love Liberty," the liberal patriotic extravaganza in response to the Moral Majority. In 1986 she and Reginald Rose collaborated on the screenplay *My Two Loves* starring Lynn Redgrave and Mariette Hartley. Redgrave, who played a closeted Lesbian, said she accepted the role because the character was real, not like the stereotypes in exploitive films.

An almost unbelievable journalistic achievement, a 16-part special report "Gay in America," appeared in the *San Francisco Examiner* during June, 1989. An army of reporters, photographers, and researchers (many of whom were Gay) interviewed, photographed, and unearthed historical information on Lesbians and Gay men, not only in San Francisco but throughout America. Carol Ness was project editor of the series, which was honored by the Meritorious Achievement Award from Media Alliance, a San Francisco Cable Car Award, a Pax et Bonum award from San Francisco Dignity, and an award from the University of Missouri School of Journalism.

The *Arkansas Gazette* in Little Rock followed suit with a three-part series "Searching for Acceptance: Homosexuals in Arkansas" in July "to go beyond stereotypes and offer an accurate profile of an often-misunderstood group." In October, 1990, *The Des Moines Register* joined in with "Gay Iowa: The Untold Story," a five-parter with reporter Melinda Voss as the project head. The paper was honored in April, 1991, by the New York, Los Angeles, and San Francisco chapters of the Gay and Lesbian Alliance Against Defamation (GLAAD).

Imagine picking up the *San Francisco Examiner's* Sunday magazine *Image* and seeing Lesbian Supervisors Roberta Achtenberg and Carole Migden staring at you from the cover. They are standing beside a headline "Lesbian Power." Then the story inside, "Painting the Town Lavender: San Francisco's lesbians have more visibility and clout than ever . . ." We waited 36 years for this treasured moment. It actually happened!

The National Women's Conference of 1977

It was very different in November, 1977, during the National Women's Conference in Houston. In the recommendations from the National Commission on the Observance of International Women's Year (IWY) to meetings held in all 50 states and six territories, there was a glaring omission: no mention of Lesbians and their concerns. Lesbians were also left out of the original IWY report *To Form a More Perfect Union.* The fear persisted that acknowledging Lesbians would mark defeat for the ERA. Not until April, 1977, when President Jimmy Carter appointed Jean O'Leary to the commission, did Lesbian power begin to move. Jean, then co-executive director of the National Gay Task Force, urged Lesbians in states that had not already had their conferences to get themselves elected as delegates. She later identified 60 up-front Lesbian delegates (the number was probably doubled by those in the closet) and urged them to make alliances within their state delegations. Jean worked on strategies with leaders of national women's and minority organizations.

Antifeminist forces had captured the entire delegations of at least eight states and had made inroads into other state delegations. They were a loose coalition of Mormons, Catholics, and religious fundamentalists opposed to abortion and Lesbian/Gay rights, joined with the Eagle Forum, the John Birch Society, the

Ku Klux Klan, and various conservative caucuses opposed to the ERA.

The 25-point National Plan of Action, put together by the IWY Commission from resolutions passed by at least ten states, was the agenda on which delegates were to vote. Pro-Lesbian resolutions had been passed by 30 states—hardly a safe margin since individual delegates were not bound to support *all* resolutions passed in their state.

Lesbians organizing before the conference brought hundreds of nondelegate Lesbians to Houston. On the streets they traveled in bunches for protection. Religious fanatics shouted that Lesbians were doomed to hell unless they repented. Klansmen threatened and followed them when they crossed the street to avoid confrontation. One Lesbian, directing her group to keep silent and move on, was punched by a Klan member.

Despite threats of physical violence, Lesbians held speakouts, conducted educational workshops, and staffed hospitality rooms at the mini-convention held during the official women's conference. They ran errands and brought food for distraught delegates who didn't dare leave the conference floor. Lesbian singers, musicians, and comics provided entertainment.

The sexual preference plank called for legislation to ban discrimination against Lesbians and Gays in areas including, but not limited to, employment, housing, public accommodations, credit, public facilities, government funding, military, child custody, or parental visitation rights. It also called for repeal of laws that restrict private sexual behavior between consenting adults.

The resolution was 23rd in line to be voted on. Tension began to rise with passage of the 21st (reproductive freedom) and swelled as a floor fight developed over the rural women's resolution. Finally Lesbians and their supporters, most wearing orange armbands and orange "happy face" buttons, lined up at the microphones. The chair announced a pro and con debate, and Jeanne Cordova, California delegate, took the microphone with a procedural question, to insert the word *Lesbian* into the resolution instead of the more oblique *sexual preference*. The chair ruled her out of order.

Patricia Benavides, a Washington delegate, spoke movingly on behalf of Third World Lesbians who are victims of triple oppression in our society. Eleanor Smeal, then president of NOW, gave an impassioned plea for the right of women to choose their sexual lifestyle. Charlotte Bunch, delegate from Washington, D.C., said, "This is not only for Lesbians, it's for all women, for those who fear being called a Lesbian." Con debaters voiced fears that support of Lesbian rights would jeopardize ratification of the ERA, and that God was against such immoral practices that would destroy the family.

As Betty Friedan, one of the founders of NOW, took the microphone tension among Lesbians rose to a new height. "I am known to be violently opposed to the Lesbian issue in the women's movement," she said. "It has been used to divide us. I know and you know that nothing in the ERA will protect homosexuals. I believe that we must give Lesbians protection in their own right. Join me in voting for this."

As the chair announced that the resolution had passed, hundreds of multicolored balloons inscribed "We Are Everywhere" rose to the ceiling of the vast hall. Women of all sexual preferences and racial backgrounds hugged and kissed one another, many in tears. Sisterhood was present everywhere except in those delegations that were anti everything. Outside the hall, Lesbians and their supporters from all over the country lit candles in an emotional response to the long-awaited victory.

Lesbians had come by the droves from all parts of the country as delegates and nondelegates, as a force that could not be ignored or intimidated. We were visible, we were vocal, we were strong.

The entire conference was a powerful consciousness-raiser. American women—from every state and territory, from all racial and ethnic groups, from every walk of life, from different generations and backgrounds—came together, supported one another, and established a common bond and purpose.

We came closest to a Lesbian sisterhood, solidarity, and movement at Houston. Lesbians put aside personal and ideological differences and demonstrated the power of unity. We also came closest to a fully integrated, all inclusive women's movement. Women who had never identified with feminists before found that their concerns did not differ from feminist objectives. It all came together in Houston. When it was over, women of every type and description hugged and kissed, sang, danced together in the aisles of the convention hall as Margie Adam played "We Shall Go

Forth." The memory of that experience will forever sustain us during times of discouragement.

The Los Angeles Meeting of 1978

With the momentum gained from the Houston experience, a group of Lesbian feminists in Los Angeles called a meeting in 1978 to give Lesbians a continuing voice and presence on the national scene. If ever we needed solidarity as Lesbians we needed it then. But the conveners were attacked as elitists, and the delegates were hamstrung by concepts of stardom and the dictates of "politically correct" ideology.

The quantum leap from an inner-directed, quasi-separatist Lesbian culture to national political organizing seemed to be too much. Fear and distrust prevailed as the delegates struggled with issues of process, accountability, regionalism, representation of Lesbians of color, the pros and cons of a national network as opposed to an organizational structure, and grassroots autonomy versus national spokeswomen. After two-and-a-half days, the delegates declared themselves a founding convention for the National Lesbian Feminist Organization (NLFO).

Having run out of time, they spelled out a statement of purpose: "to enable Lesbians to meet challenges collectively and individually, to provide for survival, and to create social, political, cultural and economic change through empowerment on four levels—mental, emotional, spiritual and physical." A steering committee was formed and another convention proposed in 1979 in Minneapolis to ratify the organization. The steering committee had several meetings, a few newsletters were published, and ten chapters were formed—mostly in the Midwest and Southwest. But NLFO never got off the ground as a national Lesbian organization.

Ethnic Homosexuals Organize

During a national conference of charitable foundations in San Francisco in the 70s, nonprofit organizations were invited to have a booth in the exhibit area. We had some copies of *The Ladder* on display. The issue with a Black Lesbian on the cover drew the most attention, mostly from Black exhibitors who were shocked into the realization that homosexuality was not just a white phenomenon.

In 1979 the National Coalition of Black Lesbians and Gays (NCBLG) was formed at the Howard Inn owned by Howard University. The founding group was reinforced by chapters across the country. The object was to bring about social change in the Black community and recognition of the NCBLG as a force in the Lesbian/Gay movement. Issues of concern were integrating Black heritage, developing a dialogue with traditional Black institutions, addressing homophobia in the church, unlearning sexism and role trips, registering people to vote, and getting them to the polls.

Leaders of NCBLG made two requests of those planning the 1983 March on Washington to commemorate the 20th anniversary of the historic march led by Martin Luther King, Jr. The Gays wanted to march openly as a contingent and have a speaker at the rally. That caused a big ruckus which wasn't resolved until the last minute when Audre Lorde was allowed to speak.

The Black Gay and Lesbian Leadership Forum (BGLLF) was founded in 1988. Two years later some members of the Forum met with a group of Black leaders at the King Center in Atlanta. Dr. Marjorie Hill, director of New York City's Office for the Lesbian and Gay Community and liaison to Mayor David Dinkins, helped convince the assembled Black leaders they shouldn't shut out 10 percent of the Black population. They agreed that recognition and use of Lesbian/Gay expertise and resources should be a priority.

Dr. Hill was the keynote speaker at the Forum's Conference in Los Angeles in 1991. Since taking up residence in City Hall, she said, she had received death threats and had a cinder block thrown through her car door. Yet she stressed coming out as the key to our freedom. Her boss Mayor Dinkins won the hearts of Lesbians and Gays across the nation when he gave up his traditional spot at the beginning of the St. Patrick's Day Parade to march at its end with Irish Lesbians and Gays.

In May, 1991, the first ever Black Gay and Lesbian Pride Day was held in Washington, D.C. An estimated 800 people turned out on an extremely hot day. Plans are in the works for another such event in 1992.

For the first time in its 14-year history the Atlanta Association of Black Journalists honored an out Gay person. Sabrina Sojourner received an award for her editorial "Accepting Difference" published July, 1990, by *BLK*, national monthly for African-American

Lesbians and Gays. Sabrina is now Racial Diversity Program director for NOW in Washington, D.C. When she was offered the job she asked, "You do know that I have been very critical of NOW?" The answer was, "Yes, but we've decided to put our money where our mouth is." Sabrina will be revising NOW's literature to be all-inclusive and to reflect women in all their diversity.

The concerns of Latina and Asian Pacific Lesbians are more international in nature. Many are recent immigrants who came to the United States in fear for their lives and still have ties with their native countries. Amaranto is a San Francisco Bay Area Lesbian/ Gay organization whose goal is to keep communications open with like groups in Latin America.

Recognizing the scarcity of mental health practitioners who are knowledgeable and sensitive to the needs of bilingual, bicultural Lesbians, CONNEXXUS Women's Center/Centro de Mujeres co-sponsored a conference in Los Angeles, "Cross Cultural Therapy Training for Human Services Providers Working with Latina Lesbians." The Latina Lesbian Support Group is in East Los Angeles.

Thyme Siegel, self-identified Lesbian feminist networker, reported in *Bay Area Women's News* on her 1987 trip to Mexico City for Mujer a Mujer Intercambo, a ten-day exchange of experiences for grassroots United States feminists and Mexican and Latin American women. Booklets were handwritten and drawn by Guatemalan refugees. The schedule included visiting a tent camp of the costuraras (seamstresses) who were trying to start a union; a Lesbian dance; visiting Cuarto Creciente, a women's cafe/library/ workshop/performance space; lectures on Mexican history and economics; sharing personal stories at social events; and speaking with media women, educators, artists and political activists.

In 1990 Ola Gay, a Spanish-speaking Lesbian/Gay hotline, was established by ENLACE, a Gay Latino group in Washington, D.C. Yolanda Santiago, vice-president, said the hotline would also field calls about domestic violence, whether Gay-related or not.

Another first—Kaarina Ornelas, Hispanic Lesbian, was elected president of the student body at Macalester College, Minnesota.

Asian/Pacific Lesbians held a national retreat on the University of California Santa Cruz campus in 1989. The event represented the continued coming out and coming together process of Asian

Lesbian groups from New York to Honolulu, according to organizer Cristy Chung.

The government of Hong Kong in April, 1991, rescinded all laws
which criminalized Lesbians and Gay men.

Dung-Zoon Nguyen, who left Vietnam two days before the fall
of Saigon, is a founder of Asian Pacific Sisters in San Francisco.
"The movement can't include us as tokens anymore. We have to
be heard and be taken seriously. . . . We have to be part of the
decision-making process."

Co-chair Linda Boyd proudly reported that the 1983 Lesbian/
Gay Freedom Day Committee in San Francisco had met its goal
for parity in its membership: Third World (30 percent), disabled
(20 percent), youth (10 percent) and 50–50 women and men. Documentation of the process is available for future organizers.

This Bridge Called My Back: Writings by Radical Women of Color, edited
by Cherrie Moraga and Gloria Anzaldua, was one of the first books
to speak out about racism in the women's movement. The anthology used prose, poetry, personal narrative, and analysis by a variety
of women of color to reflect their definition of United States
feminism.

International Activities
Lesbian/Gay groups have been part of a global movement for their
civil and human rights, but lacked cohesiveness because of communication problems. The U.N.'s Decade for Women, which
spawned international women's conferences, brought a measure of
communication between Lesbians. Of great help has been the international Lesbian and Gay news service provided by Rex
Wockner of Chicago which has acted as a catalyst for worldwide
coordinated action.

Loretta Ross, of the International Council of African Women,
reported in *off our backs* that the diversity of workshops and attendees at the non-Governmental (NGO) International Women's Conference in Nairobi in 1985 was record-breaking. Women of color
were in the majority, putting the conference more in touch with
reality. Lesbians had been uncertain about their reception in a
society as anti-Lesbian as Kenya. They were warmly welcomed by
African non-Lesbians, who outnumbered Lesbians at the latter's
workshops. Information about Lesbians had been suppressed in

their countries. Separatists who claimed they were not willing to work with heterosexual women until they were no longer homophobic were told these women wouldn't get over their homophobia unless they had contact with Lesbians. Some African Lesbians came out at the conference. They said it was the first time they could do so without fear of repercussions. Most were working and independent of men.

The 8th International Lesbian Conference held in Geneva in 1986 brought together 600 Lesbians from Europe, the Caribbean, Latin America, Asia, Africa, and the United States. The International Lesbian Information Service based in Geneva had organized the three-day event which included workshops and a high-spirited march through the streets of Geneva. Its theme was "The Right to Political Asylum for Lesbians of All Countries."

As Mayumi Tomihara traveled through the United States just before the 1987 March on Washington, she was an enthusiastic ambassador for a new Lesbian organization in Japan, Regumi Studio Tokyo. It had just surfaced in March after two years as an underground organization. While male homosexuality is accepted in Japan, Lesbianism is considered a real threat to family and society. Feminists are afraid to acknowledge Lesbians. Aware of its vulnerability, the Studio is publishing a newsletter in hopes of creating a Lesbian counterculture.

In response to the arrest of two Lesbians in Madrid in 1987 for kissing in public, several hundred Lesbians showed their outrage by chanting slogans against anti-Gay Spanish government policies. They conducted a "Kiss-In" to show that "it is a normal thing to do."

At the International Lesbian and Gay People of Color Conference in Los Angeles in 1986, Dawn Thomas and Araba Mercer reported on the fate of the Black Lesbian and Gay Centre Project in London. It was originally funded by the Greater London Council to pay for four part-time workers to maintain the office and do research on how the Council could best serve Lesbians, Gays, and children. But Parliament abolished the GLC.

During the summer of 1988 two international Lesbian/Gay conferences were held in Toronto. The first was "CelebrAsian" to synthesize conflicting identities and loyalties in their own lives as Lesbians and Gays—and as East and South Asians living in North

America. An important discussion led by Olivia Chow, Chinatown School Board member, covered strategies for reaching out to non-Gay Asian communities. Emphasis was on the need for constant advocacy to ensure that Asian Gays and Bisexuals are not ignored in AIDS prevention education.

The second was the Fifth International Lesbian and Gay People of Color Conference. Plenary speakers from New Zealand (Maori), Mexico, England, Canada, and the United States spoke of their struggles as Gay people of color. Guatemala and West Germany were also represented. At the closing plenary session the participants agreed upon self determination for aboriginal peoples, a comprehensive statement on fighting AIDS, and a commitment to take home and work on the ideas that came from workshops and caucuses.

Hadar Namir came to the United States as a delegate of Israel's Society for the Protection of Personal Rights (SPPR) to the 1989 World Congress of Gay and Lesbian Jewish Organizations. In an interview with Rose Appleman for *Coming Up!* she said that the rabbinical establishment controls your life in Israel. "You can't register an organization for Gays and Lesbians—it's illegal. So we had a legal organization for an illegal issue . . ." It took SPPR ten years to get the law against homosexual relationships repealed by the Knesset in 1988.

The most active Lesbian group in Austria is the Woman's Section of Homosexuelle Initiativo (HOSI) in Vienna. Austria's laws do not criminalize Lesbian behavior, but publicizing Lesbian/Gay lifestyles is prohibited, making HOSI, which celebrated its 10th anniversary in 1989, illegal.

Lesbian AIDS activist Rita Arauz, formerly from San Francisco and now living in Managua, reports that Nicaragua's new government under President Violeta Chamorro has dismantled most of the reforms instituted by the Sandinista regime. In Managua there is a crackdown on homosexuals. Sex education in the schools which had provided information on birth control and safe sex has been scrapped. Sex education in Nicaragua now has to be within the canons of the Catholic Church.

The second conference of Latin American and Caribbean Lesbian Feminists was switched from Peru to San Jose, Costa Rica, in 1990.

Increasing violence from the left and the right compelled the Peruvian organizing committee to cancel. Consuelo Garcia, a feminist campanera, had been assassinated and others had received death threats. Many Gay men had been massacred by revolutionaries.

In 1990, Graziella Bertozzo was elected by a sweeping vote to be the first Lesbian national secretary of Arci Gay in its 10-year history as Italy's 10,000-member national Lesbian/Gay club. The Italian Lesbian League, a separatist group, promptly denounced Bertozzo, saying Lesbians should reject men, even Gay men.

Lambda was formed in 1990 in Czechoslovakia to push for decriminalizing homosexual activity. The laws are such, one Lesbian pointed out, that if my lover lived in my flat and was unemployed and I shared my pay with her it would be a criminal act. Likewise if a neighbor found out we were lovers and made a fuss about it.

In Warsaw some Lesbians belong to a mixed Lesbian/Gay group also called Lambda. They would rather have their own group, but they are too few. They hope to increase their numbers by publishing a paper to serve and attract other Lesbians.

The International Lesbian and Gay Association (ILGA) which is based in Stockholm, Sweden, represents Gay rights and AIDS activist groups in 50 countries and all continents. This international network labors for elimination of legal, social, cultural, and economic discrimination against Lesbians and Gay men in countries throughout the world. Member groups of the network support each other by confronting foreign embassies in their own countries, writing letters, and sending delegations supportive of Lesbians and Gays who live in abusive countries.

Human Rights Violations
Tolerated by Governments

A major concern is the violence perpetrated against Lesbians and Gays. A Gay holocaust is going on in Peru. Assassins have been infiltrating Lesbian and Gay bars and discos in Venezuela, brutally beating and murdering homosexuals. Turkey's police have raided bars, beaten customers, shaved their heads, and forced them to take compulsory tests for sexually transmitted diseases. Federal police in Argentina engage in psychological torture. Gays arrested are forced to undress, threatened with guns, verbally abused, deprived of anything to drink or eat, humiliated, and sexually assaulted. Arrests on trumped-up charges of prostitution are allowed under "police edicts" which circumvent the courts.

Mystery surrounds the murder of a Gay activist in Moscow whose body was found burning on a stack of books in his apartment. Roman Kalinin, founder of the Moscow Gay and Lesbian Union and editor of *Tema,* believes the KGB was behind the murder because of the dirty and cruel way the press focused on the victim's Gay lifestyle. Kalinin sued a Moscow paper for libel and won. He now plans to file an identical suit against *Pravda,* which also insinuated that Gays promote necrophilia and pedophilia.

Lesbian activist Olga Zhuk, founder of the Tchaikovsky Foundation for the Cultural Initiatives and Defense of Sexual Minorities, was arrested on false charges and detained while KGB agents stole her keys, ransacked her apartment, and made off with foundation documents.

The International Gay and Lesbian Human Rights Commission (IGLHRC) was founded as a result of American tourist Julie Dorf's clandestine meeting with Lesbians and Gays in Moscow in 1988. Dorf is co-chair of the commission which funded the United States tours of Kalinin and Zhuk. A Sister Cities relationship was established by Mayor Art Agnos between Lesbians and Gays in San Francisco and Moscow during Kalinin's visit to San Francisco. IGLHRC's first goal is to repeal Article 121 of the Soviet Penal Code which imposes a five-year prison sentence on men convicted of homosexual acts. This law keeps Gays underground.

For more than ten years ILGA has been trying to get Amnesty International (AI) to support Lesbian/Gay people who are imprisoned because of their sexual orientation. Curt Goering, deputy director of AI USA, says its chapter is willing to change AI's policy but does not want to "impose its own morality on the world." Chapters in Latin America, Africa, the Middle East, and Asia have been adamantly opposed. Western Europe and North American chapters have supported inclusion of Gays.

As a new approach, AI USA voted overwhelmingly at a regional meeting in Boston in 1990 to create a task force to compile information about human rights violations against Lesbians, Gay men, and people with AIDS. Compelling evidence of human rights abuse against Gays might convince the international membership to expand AI's mandate.

Tom Williams, director of the Country Human Rights Reports Team of the United States Department of State which reports on human rights abuses around the world, agreed in 1991 to include anti-Gay incidents. Margaret Cantrell of Gay and Lesbian Watch was a participant in the meeting with Williams, who said anti-Gay incidents merely need to fit into existent categories such as disappearance, torture, and arbitrary arrest. Activists from around the world should file verifiable reports with the political counselor at the United States Embassy in the nation where the incident occurred. Carbon copies should go to the Washington "desk officer" for that particular country and to Williams, Bureau of Human Rights, Department of State, Washington, D.C., 20520.

ILGA also submitted an application for admission to the United Nations (UN) as an official nongovernmental organization. Lisa Power of London and Joan Clark of Vienna, co-secretary-generals of ILGA, and Susan Allee, board member of the National Gay and Lesbian Task Force (NGLTF), presented documentation of the human rights struggle of Lesbians and Gay men to the UN's NGO committee.

Delegates from various countries serve on the committee which deferred a decision on ILGA's admission to 1993. Any opposition, even from one country, is enough to veto or defer admission. Dissent came from the Philippines and Arab countries—Libya, Oman, and Sudan—where homosexual acts are crimes punishable by death. Vocal support during committee debate came from Ethiopia and Lesotho, an African state formerly part of South Africa. They praised ILGA's strong position on apartheid and said that protection of the rights of minorities is what the UN stood for. Other supporters who spoke up were from Ireland, Burundi, France, Sweden, and—surprisingly—Nicaragua, considering the new government's anti-Gay stand. The Soviet Union, Cuba, and Iraq abstained. The United States is not a member of the NGO committee.

The mayor of Guadalajara, Mexico, denounced ILGA's 13th Annual Conference scheduled for June 30-July 6, 1991, in his city. He said he could not authorize such an event because custom and religion would not permit it. On the other hand, he acknowledged that Gay Pride Liberation groups had the right under Mexico's constitution to host the conference. Several weeks before the conference date the mayor changed his tune. He forced the hotel to cancel and said he would withhold police protection and would arrest delegates for "immoral behavior." With assistance from the Mexican government the conference was moved to Acapulco.

Immigration Policies

Policies of the Immigration and Naturalization Service (INS) barring admittance of Lesbians and Gay men to the United States came to a head when a rash of denials occurred in 1979. California Senator Alan Cranston interceded on behalf of a Lesbian Filipina who had tried to enter the country to join her family. He told his colleagues in Washington that United States immigration law was "out of touch with reality," that equating homosexuality with "psychopathic personality" was no longer valid.

Gay Rights Advocates obtained a restraining order against the United States Public Health Service from Federal District Court Judge Stanley Wiegel after London reporter Carl Hill was stopped at San Francisco International Airport for wearing a Gay Pride button. Surgeon General Julius Richmond issued a directive to Public Health Service officers to discontinue examining or certifying aliens suspected of homosexuality because the medical profession no longer considered it a mental disorder. INS likewise issued a temporary directive to the border patrol to cease turning suspected homosexuals away until United States immigration policy was clarified. Canadian women on their way to the Michigan Women's Music Festival were nonetheless harassed, detained, or denied entry at the border.

John H. Harmon, assistant attorney general in the Justice Department, upheld the statutory ban, the surgeon general held steadfast by his directive, and appeals were made to the Congress to change the law and to President Carter to solve the problem by executive order. In the meantime immigration inspectors continued to stop and harass foreign Gay visitors.

Comic relief came in January, 1980, when American tourists landing at Amsterdam airport were quizzed by uniformed officers as to whether they were heterosexual or homosexual. Members of the Dutch Association for the Integration of Homosexuality, calling themselves the Homosquad, had borrowed police uniforms and were conducting these interrogations to dramatize their protest against United States immigration policy. Dutch Gay activists later persuaded their government to make a formal protest to the United Nations.

Finally, in 1982, after almost three years of legal and political finagling over the issue, Lesbian attorney Mary Dunlap successfully persuaded U.S. District Court Judge Robert Aguilar to issue a *national* injunction barring the attorney general and the INS from enforcing the government's 30-year ban on Lesbian and Gay foreign visitors. The injunction became effective six weeks before the commencement of the first International Gay Olympic Games in San Francisco.

Unlike gossip, the news of the policy change was slow to reach East Coast immigration authorities. Wenche Lowzow, Lesbian member of Norway's Parliament, and her domestic partner, Kim Friele, were detained on their way to a 1983 ILGA convention in Washington, D.C. After they were admitted Wenche gave some members of Congress, including the late Phillip Burton, a briefing of her experience with United States immigration.

The next scramble over barring of visitors to America came when San Francisco hosted the International AIDS Conference in 1989. Federal authorities declared they would not admit foreign visitors who had AIDS or were HIV-positive. The medical profession was astounded and San Francisco Lesbians and Gays who had worked so hard to develop model education programs about AIDS/ ARC were furious. When a large contingent of conferees threatened to boycott the conference the Feds relented—too late for some to make travel plans.

We learned later that Jesse Helms had attached a rider to a Congressional bill stipulating that persons with AIDS/ARC or who were HIV-positive be automatically denied entry to the United States. That was official INS policy at the time of the conference. In 1990 Congress lifted this prohibition and the homosexual exclusion clause. It was left to the secretary of Health and Human Services to provide a list of communicable diseases. The secretary, Louis Sullivan, issued such a list without HIV infection. As of April, 1991, however, it appeared that HIV infection might be placed back on the list as a bar to immigration but not to tourists and other visitors. By July, 1991, the entire issue was up in the air. We keep having to fight the same fights over and over again.

Gay Olympics and International Games

The Gay Olympics were the dream of the late Dr. Tom Waddell, who placed sixth in the decathalon at the 1968 Olympics in Mexico City. The first Games were held in 1982 in San Francisco and delighted and entranced thousands of Lesbians and Gay men despite the cloud cast by the United States Olympic Committee. Just 19 days before the games were to begin, a federal court ordered Waddell and his committee to refrain from using the O word. Congress had given the Olympic committee sole rights to the word. That meant scratching the word Olympics off thousands of tickets, medals, flags, banners, posters, and T-shirts. Other groups held all kinds of Olympics—crab, dog, diaper—without objection. Why this exception? Attorney Mary Dunlap tried to get an emergency stay until an appeal could be heard. It was denied, leaving us with the Gay (Bleep) Games.

The Games torch, lit at Stonewall Inn in New York City and carried by runners across the country, was carried by Sue Walker across the Golden Gate Bridge. Susan McGreivey, who swam in the 1956 Olympics in Melbourne, and George Frenn, a track and field competitor in the 1972 Olympics in Munich, concluded the torch run into Kezar Stadium for the opening.

On the field to greet them were 1,500 athletes—almost half of them women—from 12 countries, 28 states, and 149 cities, the Gay Marching Bands and Twirling Corps of Los Angeles and San Francisco, the Sistah Boom Women's Salsa Band, color guards with flags and banners of participating countries and states, and 250 journalists covering the event. Both Emcee Rita Mae Brown and Tom Waddell stressed that love rather than competition was the real message of the Games. "We are all winners." Everyone at the ceremonies was moved emotionally by the pride of belonging to a Lesbian/Gay extended family that encompasses the planet.

The hope was that by 1986 when the Games would again be held in San Francisco they would be Olympic. Not until 1987 did the U.S. Supreme Court hear arguments over the use of the word and the decision, when given, upheld the court order. Gay Games II was the last for Tom Waddell, who died in 1988, but his dream of games open to everyone regardless of sexual orientation, color, gender, or physical ability lives on.

Gay Games III and Cultural Festival was held in Vancouver, British Columbia. More than 8,500 people took part in 29 sporting and 14 cultural events. At the opening ceremonies Emcee Robin Tyler said, "This is the largest sporting event in the year 1990, and it belongs to us! Here we are in the Gay 90s with an entire decade named after us."

Among the many highlights in Vancouver was Sarah Davis, 67, who won eight medals in the swimming events. In 1994 Gay Games IV will be held in New York. Among those working to make sure that all goes well again with the Games will undoubtedly be Sara Lewinstein, whose daughter, Jessica, was fathered by Tom Waddell. Sara served on the first Gay Games committee. In 1986 she was national sports director and on the board of directors of Games II. In 1990 she was on the board of the Federation of the Gay Games and co-chair of the committee for the Tom Waddell Cup. She also participated in all three games as an athlete.

Sex Laws in the United States

The Gay "Olympics" was not the only case we took to the U.S. Supreme Court in the 80s. Michael Hardwick was arrested in his own bedroom in Georgia and charged with committing the crime of sodomy in 1982. Local authorities realized this was a perfect test case and didn't pursue criminal charges. Hardwick went to the federal court and was joined by a heterosexual couple because Georgia law, like most sodomy statutes, applies to just about any sexual act that isn't the missionary position. The court dropped the heterosexual couple from the case and dismissed Hardwick's complaint since he had not been charged with an offense.

The state pursued the case to the U.S. Supreme Court hoping to confirm the constitutionality of Georgia's sodomy statute. Hardwick and his ACLU attorneys contended that an individual's right to conduct intimate sexual relations in the privacy of one's own home is at the core of the Constitution's protection of privacy.

In 1986 a bitterly divided court decided 5–4 to uphold the Georgia sodomy law. The majority opinion focused on homosexuality and relied heavily upon moral, historical, and religious tradition of condemning and criminalizing homosexual activity. While the Georgia law did not differentiate among Gay, non-Gay or married people, the court upheld the law only as it applied to homosexuals.

The minority opinion, written by Justice Harry Blackmun, criticized the majority's obsessive focus on homosexual activity and argued that the right of adults to choose whether to engage in private, consensual sexual activity is akin to other constitutional spheres of privacy, such as the right to contraception, procreation, marriage, and child-bearing decisions.

Ironically, Justice Lewis Powell, who cast the critical fifth vote in upholding Georgia's sodomy law, three years later acknowledged he had made a mistake. He added that the case was "frivolous"— a stinging remark considering how *Bowers* v. *Hardwick* has been cited to justify numerous civil rights injustices. In half of the states Lesbians and Gays remain "unapprehended felons." This has been used in court to deny Lesbian mothers custody of their children, to justify firing Lesbian employees, to refuse professional licenses, and to withhold security clearances.

NGLTF decided to prioritize its Privacy Project and hired Sue Hyde, researcher and project manager at Harvard University's Kennedy School of Government, as director. She facilitated a meeting of activists during the Southeastern Conference for Lesbians and Gay men in Raleigh, North Carolina, in early 1990, to form a new "Sod Squad." Members of the Squad were committed to repeal of sodomy laws and received training from leading experts on such subjects as the impact of sodomy laws on AIDS prevention, criminal code recodification, state court challenges, legislative repeal, and statewide grassroots organizing.

Maryland was perceived as the most likely to repeal its sodomy laws. But the state's Court of Appeals interpreted Maryland's law against "unnatural or perverted sexual practices" as prohibiting oral sex for everyone *except* for noncommercial, consenting, heterosexual couples, married or not.

The 1990 campaign, however, had two successes. A criminal court in Kentucky ruled on appeal that the state's sodomy law violated both the state constitution's right to privacy and its equal protection clause. Michigan's sodomy law was also overturned. The ruling came in a test case brought by a 75-year-old Lesbian, a Gay couple, an unmarried non-Gay man, a married non-Gay man, a Bisexual woman, and a non-Gay disabled woman. All the plaintiffs testified that the state "sodomy" and so-called "gross indecency" laws had a chilling effect on their behavior because the language was vague and provided law enforcement officers unlimited discretion. Wayne County Circuit Judge John A. Murphy agreed.

Other states that are being targeted by the Sod Squad are Oklahoma, Tennessee, Missouri, and Florida. In the District of Columbia a new bill, District of Columbia Criminal Code, Right to Privacy Amendment Act of 1991, was introduced by council member Jim Nathanson. Dr. Melvin Sabshin, executive director of the American Psychiatric Association, endorsed the bill. In a letter to the City Council Dr. Sabshin said it has been the position of the APA since 1973 that laws criminalizing sex acts between consenting adults in private should be repealed. He offered to testify at a public hearing. It's about time, after 18 years, that the APA take an active role for social change.

Many states which have legalized private homosexual activity still retain laws on the books that prohibit solicitation. In other words, it is all right to have sex, but don't ask anyone. In *State* v. *Fault,* the Ohio First District Court of Appeals declared that the state's homosexual solicitation law violated the Equal Protection statute and was therefore unconstitutional. The court ruled that authorities cannot prohibit homosexual solicitation while allowing heterosexual solicitation. The Massachusetts Supreme Court, in an unanimous decision, ruled it illegal for police to arrest an individual for solicitation of a sexual act to take place in a private residence, that the law pertained only to public sexual conduct.

Integrity, the Lesbian and Gay justice ministry of the Episcopal Church, has called upon the denomination as a whole to stop holding conventions in states which still have sodomy laws. Integrity claims the Church should "honor its commitment to Lesbian and Gay Rights by opposing heterosexism" in states where sex laws have exempted heterosexuals and criminalized homosexuals. If an act is illegal it should pertain to anyone who performs it. Or the law should be repealed.

At the behest of Queer Nation, San Francisco's three Gay supervisors introduced for discussion a 1991 resolution to make The City a sanctuary for sexual minorities facing prosecution in their home states or persecution in their home countries. According to the preliminary draft, San Francisco police would be forbidden to assist any agency in locating or extraditing members of the military facing prosecution or discharge on grounds of homosexual behavior. Police and other city personnel would not be allowed to help any agency in deporting non-citizens who are domestic partners of United States citizens. The resolution also condemns Amnesty International for its continued refusal to deal with sexual minorities (Lesbian, Gay, Bisexual and transgender individuals) who are imprisoned and tortured around the world. Hearings were held in June, 1991, but no action has been taken.

Sex Laws Abroad

Lesbians and Gays from other countries are also confronting their governments' sex prohibitions. They point to the 1988 social issues report of the United Nations recommending legalization of sexual practices between consenting adults in private.

Israel's Knesset repealed their anti-Gay sex law by a unanimous vote in 1988. No members of the religious parties were present.

In October, 1990, 6,000 homosexuals marched through Berlin, in one of the largest German Gay demonstrations ever, to make the age of consent for Gay male sex the same as that for Lesbians or heterosexuals. In 1991 the new German Parliament deleted anti-Gay Paragraph 175 of the former West German penal code.

The Parliament of the Australian state of Queensland, by a vote of 51–31 in 1990, decriminalized anal sex between any two people, setting the age of consent at 18. Tasmania is now the only Australian state retaining a sodomy law. Upon learning that a legislative draft was in the works to repeal the law that pertained only to Gay males, the Free Presbyterian Church called instead for a law to criminalize Lesbian sex. The church maintained that erotic acts between persons of the same sex are condemned by the Bible and the cause of social decay.

Gay sex is not explicitly illegal in China, but Lesbians and Gays have been jailed under laws against "immorality" and "indecency." In Tientsin in 1987 a 40-year-old Lesbian was put in a reeducation camp for having a sexual relationship with another woman.

Civil Rights for Lesbians and Gays

Because passing federal or state antidiscrimination laws protecting Lesbian and Gay rights seemed so remote at the time, moves were made to try to pass ordinances at the local level. Almost simultaneously East Lansing, Michigan, and San Francisco became the first to do so in 1972.

In 1982, after tallying the wins and losses following Anita Bryant's anti-Gay crusades in the late 70s, we reported that prohibition against discrimination on the basis of sexual orientation was law in 53 cities and 12 counties of the United States. In November, 1990, *The Washington Blade* reported that at least 100 cities and/or counties had passed local ordinances outlawing discrimination against Lesbians and Gays.

Looking at reports we had collected about such decisions, during the year 1990 alone we found that we won new laws in 15 cities and five counties while seven cities and one county turned us down Our guess would be that the *Blade's* estimate is conservative.

In 1990 Salvador, the fourth largest city in Brazil, banned discrimination against Gays, according to Grupo Gay Da Bahia, one of Brazil's oldest and most active Gay organizations. Shortly thereafter the county of Rio de Janeiro did the same.

The city of Ghent, Belgium (one of Europe's most conservative countries), also passed a Gay equity law. Police there are now actively trying to recruit Lesbian and Gay officers.

United States courts, whether considered liberal or conservative, continue to chip away at institutional and personal prejudice exhibited against Lesbians and Gay men. In 1975 the U.S. Civil Service Commission finally changed its guidelines on employment because so many court decisions and injunctions forced them to. A person can no longer be disqualified solely on the basis of sexual orientation or unsubstantiated conclusions concerning possible embarrassment to the federal service. To dismiss or disqualify a Lesbian or Gay, the government must establish a relationship to ability to function in the job or to the agency's ability to discharge its responsibilities.

Former Congresswoman Bella Abzug and Steve Endean, of the National Gay Rights Lobby (now defunct), were pioneers in the movement to gain passage of federal legislation banning discrimination against Lesbians and Gays. The Civil Rights Amendment

Act would prohibit discrimination on the basis of affectional or sexual orientation in housing, employment, credit, public accommodations, and federally funded programs. Passage of the bill would specifically amend Title II of the Civil Rights Act of 1964 which prohibits discrimination on the basis of race, color, religion, national origin, or sex. Courts have interpreted sex as meaning gender, not orientation.

By 1981, despite the negative and conservative political climate of the Reagan administration, Steve reported a record high of 59 co-sponsors in the House. He credited the late Congressman Phillip Burton with lobbying help.

Today we have two organizations based in Washington, D.C., to educate the public and lobby for our rights: NGLTF and the Human Rights Campaign Fund (HRCF). The 15th anniversary of the Gay rights bill in 1990 was celebrated by NGLTF with a series of commemorative events designed to increase momentum and awareness of the Act. A reception was held to honor Bella Abzug and current lead sponsors Representative Ted Weiss and Senator Alan Cranston.

As of March 21, 1991, the Civil Rights Amendments Act which would prohibit discrimination on the basis of affectional or sexual orientation had 81 co-sponsors in the House and nine in the Senate, the highest number of co-sponsors ever registered. These are official figures, but by June, HRCF reported 91 House and 13 Senate co-signers.

Civil Rights Problems in England

England's notorious anti-Gay law, Clause 28 of the 1988 Local Government Act, reads: "A local authority shall not (a) intentionally promote homosexuality or publish material with the intention of promoting homosexuality, (b) promote the teaching in any maintained school of the acceptability of homosexuality as a pretended family relationship, (c) give financial assistance to any person for either of the purposes referred to in paragraphs (a) and (b) above."

Familiar words, we thought, and sure enough Section 108 of the United States "Family Protection Act" of 1982 stated: "No Federal funds may be made available under any provision of Federal law to any public or private individual, group, foundation, commission, corporation, association, or other entity for the purpose of advocating, promoting, or suggesting homosexuality, male or female, as a life style."

These laws grew out of the Margaret Thatcher and Ronald Reagan governments. Unfortunately our sisters and brothers in England have to live with the Thatcher legacy. Fortunately for us, the Family Protection Act failed. It was a dud in many ways.

As we have always found in time of crisis, more Lesbians and Gays come out and unite forces to, in this case, protest. During debate on the Clause several creative Amazons swooped down on ropes, Tarzan style, from the gallery to the floor of Parliament to make their point. Four Lesbian demonstrators burst in on the live broadcast of the BBC Six O'Clock TV News. They chained themselves to cameras and to anchorwoman Sue Lawley's desk. Co-anchor Nicholas Witchell swiftly sat on the demonstrator chained to the desk and clapped his hand over her mouth to stifle her shouts. Lawley calmly announced to viewers, "We have rather been invaded." The women were eventually removed by police but no charges were filed.

Right after passage of the Clause about 100 rain-soaked Lesbians and Gays broke into raucous cat-calls and jeers as Big Ben struck midnight. Outside Parliament they roared, "We're out, we're angry, and we aren't going back!" Labor unions and 350 volunteer organizations (from arts projects to groups of seniors, Blacks, and ethnic minorities) added their voices to publicly condemn the new law, the first in Britain to legalize discrimination.

International Lesbians and Gays joined the protest. In Antwerp, Belgium, a group demonstrated outside the British-owned department store Marks and Spencer wearing Margaret Thatcher masks. According to Maureen Oliver of the Organization for Lesbian and Gay Action, 30 Italian senators "from across all parties" wrote to Thatcher denouncing Clause 28. The AIDS Coalition to Unleash Power (ACT UP) of Houston, Texas, staged a protest at the British consulate.

"Promotion of homosexuality" was not defined in the law, and the mere mention of homosexuality in a project might be interpreted as promotion. A number of cases surfaced almost immediately. A Lesbian lecturer at a London college of adult education was fired because she had discussed Clause 28 and came out to her class. In Scotland the Council of Strathclyde wrote to all Colleges of Further Education in the region advising that grants to student associations should be withheld unless they agreed to cease all Lesbian and Gay related activity. New foster-parenting guidelines from the Department of Health state that some adults "would not be able to provide a suitable environment for the care and nurture of a child. Equal rights and gay rights have no place in fostering services."

A move was made in East Sussex to ban a directory of 100 volunteer organizations because one asked for Lesbian and Gay volunteers. The city of Salford stopped the exhibit of an AIDS art show.

Sex between two men in private has not been illegal in Britain since 1967. A total of 2,780 men from England and Wales were arrested in 1989 under other statutes: "Indecency between men," "solicitation by a man," and "procuring others to commit a homosexual act." Police have been raiding Gay bars and discos—Gay bashing is on the rise.

Ironically, in this politically conservative anti-Gay climate, before she left office Prime Minister Thatcher nominated famed Shakespearean actor Ian McKellen, who came out in protest of Clause 28, to be knighted by Queen Elizabeth II on New Year's Eve 1990.

Clause 25, Paragraph 16, of the new British Criminal Justice Bill which surfaced in early 1991 would increase penalties for the crimes listed above. Homosexual sex offenses would be punished more severely than heterosexual ones. A group of 300 Lesbians and Gays demonstrated at the Bow Street police station, chosen for the action because it is where Oscar Wilde was booked for indecency in 1895. Ten couples turned themselves in, "confessing" their "crimes" of soliciting, procuring, and gross indecency. A few days later 7,000 Lesbians and Gays marched from London's Embankment to Hyde Park. Gays on the Continent also launched protests against the proposed law. In March the Government responded by letter to the British Stonewall group that the bill was never intended to discriminate against Lesbians and Gays, did not add any new offenses, and increased sentences only for certain sexual acts that threaten the public, particularly children.

In 1990 British Customs confiscated a special issue of *SEK*, a Dutch Lesbian/Gay magazine, which was devoted to Lesbian sexuality. Customs agents called it "immoral." The case was given to a lawyer representing Stonewall, the British Gay group, for appeal.

Canadian Status of Women groups, meeting in Edmonton in 1988, were "reminded" by the secretary of state that women's organizations supporting Lesbian or abortion projects are denied government funds. A letter drafted at the conference "reminded" the secretary that the Canadian Supreme Court had struck down abortion restrictions. Also that the ban on projects involving sexual orientation contradicts women's equality, a stated goal of the secretary of state. Furthermore, the letter said, "It's up to our organizations to define the status of women."

Gay Rights Bills

Hawaii became the third state to pass a Gay rights bill which prohibits discrimination in employment on the basis of sexual orientation. The bill passed the Senate 22–2 and the House 34–17. It had the support of the Hawaii Council of Churches, the Catholic Diocese of Honolulu, the Episcopal Diocese of Hawaii, the state Civil Rights Commission, the Governor's Committee on AIDS, the State Department of Health, Hawaii State Teachers Association, and the ACLU. Lesbian and Gay activists who had lobbied the legislature for 17 years were ecstatic when Governor John Waihee signed the bill into law on March 21, 1991. His office had received several thousand calls in opposition, but he noted, "The rights of a religious organization to carry out its religious principles are unchanged by this amendment."

Similar bills have been introduced in California, Connecticut, and Maine. The California legislature passed the bill in 1984 but it was vetoed by Governor George Deukmejian. It is expected that the new governor, Pete Wilson, will sign it when it reaches his desk, in which case Reverend Lou Sheldon of the Traditional Values Coalition will attempt to overturn it by an initiative put before the electorate.

In an historic breakthrough after a dozen years of trying to win passage of Gay Civil Rights bills in at least 24 states, Representative David Clarenbach successfully steered a bill through the legislature of Wisconsin. Conservative Republican Governor Lee Dreyfus signed the bill into law in 1982, making Wisconsin

the first state to ban discrimination on the basis of sexual preference. Clarenbach attributed the bill's passage to defining the
issue as one of human rights and pinning opposition to it with
condoning bigotry. He also cited strong support from mainstream religious groups. The Wisconsin law prohibits discrimination based on sexual orientation in housing, employment, and
public accommodations.

When Gannett, publisher of *Bay Press-Gazette,* refused to print ads
containing the words "Lesbian" or "Gay" a court appeal was
made. In 1991 the court ruled that newspapers were not covered
by Wisconsin's "Gay Rights Bill" because they do not offer the
public "accommodations" in the sense the term is usually
understood.

After a 17-year legislative struggle, in 1989 Massachusetts became the second state to ban discrimination against homosexuals.
But there was a price to pay to gain its passage: an exemption for
religious institutions and a disclaimer that Massachusetts does not
endorse homosexuality or recognize homosexual partnerships.

Even so, Citizens for Family First collected enough certified signatures to place a repeal question on the ballot. The attorney general ruled the measure ineligible for the ballot question because of
the religious exemption. His ruling was challenged, brought before
the Supreme Judicial Court, and upheld by a 5–1 vote. The Gay
and Lesbian Advocates and Defenders, a legal group, argued successfully that the law's opponents defeated their own cause when
they insisted that religious institutions be exempted from compli-
ance. The Massachusetts Constitution specifies that "religious
practices or religious institutions" cannot be the subject of
referenda.

Where legislatures have failed to pass Gay rights bills another
strategy is to get the governor to issue an executive order to prohibit discrimination in state government. The trouble is that the
order is not permanent since it depends on each governor's stance
on Gay rights.

Rhode Island Governor Edward Di Prete signed an executive
order in 1985 which was in effect while efforts were being made to
pass Gay rights in the legislature. The bill won in the House in
1988 and 1989, but failed in the Senate. In 1990 it passed the
Senate in a close 13–11 vote and lost in the House by a 45–45 tie.

Opposition had been mobilized by Phyllis Schlafly's Eagle Forum and the Coalition to Preserve Traditional Values. In the meantime, the New England Synod of the Evangelical Lutheran Church in America approved a resolution at its 1990 meeting in Kingstown to support and lobby for inclusion of Lesbians and Gays in human rights legislation.

In 1987 Governor Neil Goldschmidt signed an executive order forbidding most Oregon state agencies to discriminate against Lesbians, Gays, and Bisexuals. The state's right wing banded together in an organization called the Oregon Citizens Alliance to gather signatures to place the issue to rescind the Governor's order on the 1988 ballot. They called themselves the "No Special Rights Committee" on the petitions they distributed. Cathy Siemens of Oregonians for Fairness (OFF) complained, "This is a misrepresentation in itself, because the executive order doesn't give Gays more rights, just the same rights." The lies prevailed and Ballot Measure 8 was approved by a margin of 53 to 47 percent.

The Oregon referendum went one step further, however, than just repealing the executive order. It specifically allowed state officials to fire employees solely on the basis of sexual orientation. Harriet Merrick, a Lesbian who is a manager in the University of Oregon business office, filed a suit against the state in 1990 challenging the law created by the referendum. The State Board of Education, prior to passage of the referendum, passed a policy which prohibits employment discrimination based on sexual orientation. In her suit Merrick argues that the education board's policy and the referendum "impose inconsistent and mutually exclusive requirements on her as a supervisor of state employees." The Oregon Court of Appeals ruled that there are adequate grounds for the suit.

The New Jersey Supreme Court in 1990 announced changes to the state's judicial professional codes to prohibit lawyers and judges from discriminating on the basis of sexual orientation.

States in Australia (New South Wales and South Australia) and provinces in Canada (Quebec and Ontario) have passed Gay rights laws. The Coalition for Gay Rights in Ontario, which includes 22 member groups in 17 cities, waged the campaign for law reform for almost 12 years.

Virginians for Justice have included in their 1991 legislative
agenda the repeal of the Alcoholic Beverage Control statutes which
prohibit serving alcohol to Gay people. The ABC provision is seldom enforced and most people are unaware of its existence. Surely
it is time to rescind this absurd, antiquated law. Enough is enough
is enough, as Gertrude Stein might have said.

Lesbians and Gays in the Military Services

In our original edition of *Lesbian/Woman* (1972) mention of the Lesbian and the military centered on witch hunts and/or purges of
Lesbians from the services. Unfortunately, this is still going on.
Following is the (DOD) directive, reformulated in 1982, used as
the basis for keeping homosexuals out of the armed forces:

"Homosexuality is incompatible with military service. The presence in the military environment of persons who engage in homosexual conduct or who, by their statements, demonstrate a
propensity to engage in homosexual conduct, seriously impairs the
accomplishment of the military mission. The presence of such
members adversely affects the ability of the Military Services to
maintain discipline, good order, and morale; to foster mutual trust
and confidence among servicemembers, to ensure the integrity of
the system of rank and command; to facilitate assignment and
worldwide deployment of servicemembers who frequently must live
and work under close conditions affording minimal privacy; to recruit and retain members of the Military Services; to maintain the
public acceptability of military service; and to prevent breaches of
security."

Now homosexuals of both sexes are fighting back, and powerful
forces are allied with us. Studies by the military in 1945, 1952, and
1957 all found that Lesbians and Gays are fit for military duty.

Two more current studies on the military's anti-Gay policy had
been suppressed by the DOD until leaked to members of Congress.
Representative Gerry E. Studds, one of the two open Gays in Congress, and Representative Patricia Schroeder released findings to
the press. Both reports were done by the DOD's Personnel Security
Research and Education Center in Monterey, California. "Noncon-
forming Sexual Orientations and Military Suitability" was completed in December, 1988, but didn't see the light of day until Fall,

1989. Asked to determine if homosexuals were high security risks, the center found they were not and should be permitted in the military. The report likened the military's exclusionary policy to the manner in which women and Blacks were previously discriminated against.

The second report was finished in January, 1989, but was not submitted to the DOD because of the reception accorded the first report. This research studied suitability for the service and for security clearance. Lesbians and Gays were found to be as good or better than the average heterosexual.

DOD statistics in 1989 showed that each year five of every 10,000 men and 16 of every 10,000 women on active duty are discharged for being Gay or Lesbian. A total of 14,311 members of the military were discharged for homosexuality between 1973 and 1983. The General Accounting Office (GAO) said the cost of training and then discharging them was $180 million. The monetary cost, alone, is unconscionable; the human cost is incalculable. We question why the ratio of discharged Lesbians to Gay men is so much higher.

Kate Dyer, editor of *Gays in Uniform: The Pentagon's Secret Reports,* said the military is not only the last bastion of institutionalized homophobia, but also the nation's largest single employer. Apparently it has no intention of giving up its vendetta against homosexuals without a fight. However, Congresswoman Schroeder says, "The real question is how long the military can maintain a personnel policy based solely on prejudice."

Ongoing witch hunts against homosexuals in the military have been documented back to World War I. They appear to be more numerous during peacetime, but the number of lives ruined by these practices will never be totally known. For more information we recommend Alan Berube's *Coming Out Under Fire: The History of Gay Men and Women in World War Two* and Mary Ann Humphrey's *My Country, My Right To Serve: Experiences of Gay Men and Women in the Military, World War II to the Present.*

In 1975 two members of the Daughters of Bilitis, Shirley Willer, former national president, and Marion Glass, started Gay Assistance League for Servicewomen (GALS) to aid women who were being harassed in Florida. Eight servicewomen at the Key West Naval Air Station were being separated from the service for being

Lesbians. GALS, NOW, and the ACLU protested the methods used in investigating the women. They were not told of their rights, were followed by agents, their homes bugged, and mail opened. Information that they were entitled to individual service or civilian legal counsel and/or public hearings was not given to them. One of the women stated that she had been investigated five or more times during her 5½ years of naval service. For most of that time she was heterosexual. If you are accused often enough you take the hint. GALS helped the women raise funds and publicize the situation, and gave them housing and moral support. All were eventually discharged honorably from the service.

Secretary of the Navy John Lehman in 1981 intervened in the case of Petty Officer Joan Dowling. A navy panel had ruled, after hearing four days of testimony, that Dowling had not been involved in a Lesbian affair with another sailor, and recommended she be retained in the service. Lehman overturned the ruling and Dowling, after eight years in the navy, was given an honorable discharge "for the convenience of the government."

In 1980 the actions of Capt. James Seebirt of the USS *Norton Sound* exemplified the navy's thrust to remove women from its ranks by charging them with being Lesbian. On the *Norton Sound* 24 women were charged with committing Lesbian acts as a result of a questionnaire distributed to all the women sailors asking them to list any woman they "thought" was Lesbian. Susan McGreivy, then attorney for the ACLU of Southern California, threatened the navy with going to federal court on the lack of due process since the women were to be discharged without hearings. As a result, charges against all but eight of the women were dropped.

Eight weeks of hearings followed on four of the women. Because of bad press the navy dropped charges against the other four. During the hearings the women's sex lives were discussed freely and outrageously. Charges against two were dropped and the other two received general discharges under honorable conditions.

In December of 1987 Naval Intelligence began to investigate Lesbianism at the Marine Corps' Parris Island, North Carolina, base. By September, 1988, 14 women had been discharged and three were imprisoned. At one point the investigators had a list of alleged Lesbians ten pages long, so enthusiastically put together that it included the name of one woman's cat. Up to 65 women left the Corps as a result of the witch hunt. DOD records show that in the Marine Corps eight times more women than men are discharged for homosexuality.

In 1988 a court martial convicted Marine Corporal Barbara Baum of sodomy, obstruction of justice, and indecent acts with women and sent her to prison for one year. After she served seven months, her conviction was voided because her trial had been constitutionally flawed. She was later given clemency but was reduced to the rank of private and forfeited all pay and allowances. Sergeant Cheryl Jameson, who was betrayed by her lover, spent nearly a year in prison and suffered the loss of a ten-year career.

In 1988 Sergeant Christine Hilinski testified in the trial of Sgt. Jameson that she "did a fine job" and her sexual orientation didn't affect her work. Following that testimony Hilinski was demoted and her pay cut $220 a month because her superiors didn't like her attitude. In 1989 she left the service after 11 years, and in 1990 the ACLU got her back pay and good service record restored.

Captain Judy Meade, stationed at Camp LeJeune, N.C., was to be honorably discharged from the Marines because she visited a civilian friend who was a Lesbian. A Military Board of Review reversed the lower board's recommendation.

We have won some good decisions in lower courts only to have them reversed on appeal. Sergeant Perry Watkins' victory, however, gives us new hope. When he was drafted in 1967 he indicated he was Gay on his application. The army apparently didn't care, as Watkins was an exemplary soldier rising to the rank of sergeant. Didn't care until 1982, that is, when the army changed its regulations to oust known Gays and Lesbians with or without sexual acts being involved. Watkins sued the army to allow him to reenlist, and with the help of the ACLU he won and the army kept him until 1984 when an appeals court ruled against him.

In 1988 the case was heard by a three-judge panel of the 9th Circuit Court of the U.S. Court of Appeals. By a 2–1 vote the court ruled against the army on the constitutional issue that discharging people solely on the basis of having a homosexual orientation was a violation of equality before the law. However, a federal appeals court granted an unusual rehearing of the case before 11 judges of the 9th Circuit Court. Again the army lost. The court ordered Watkins reinstated to serve until he was eligible for retirement.

Again the DOD appealed, this time to the U.S. Supreme Court. On November 5, 1990, the justices refused to hear the appeal and the previous court decision prevailed. After almost ten years of litigation Perry Watkins was the winner. Subsequently Watkins settled with the army for back pay, an honorable discharge, and full retirement benefits.

In September, 1990, a memo from Vice Adm. Joseph S. Donnell to the commanding officers in charge of nearly 200 ships and 40 shore installations of the Naval Surface Forces of the U.S. Atlantic Fleet, was leaked to NOW and to Representative Studds. The memo said that Lesbians should be rooted out of the service and acknowledged that officers might pursue investigations "halfheartedly" because Lesbian sailors are generally "hard-working, career-oriented, willing to put in long hours on the job and among the command's top performers." Studds, Molly Yard, president of NOW, and countless others decried this new evidence of homophobia.

The military often complains that it should not have to move faster than public sentiment about Lesbians and Gays. Evidence shows that the public is way ahead of the Pentagon. A 1990 *Newsweek* study showed 60 percent of civilians polled believed Lesbians and Gays should be able to serve in the military.

Dissatisfaction at many educational institutions over discriminatory practices has fueled the move to get rid of the Reserve Officer Training Corps (ROTC). In 1990 a number of bright young men were dismissed from ROTC because they were Gay. The men were ordered to repay scholarships they had received. Later the orders were rescinded.

Started during the Vietnam war, the fight to remove ROTC from college campuses has gradually expanded. As more and more universities add sexual orientation to their nondiscrimination rules, the harder it becomes for those same schools to host a discriminatory ROTC. Law schools have played an important role in banning ROTC and other military recruiters from campuses.

In 1982 the army threatened law schools at Harvard, Yale, UCLA, Columbia, New York University, and Wayne State University that officers and civilian army attorneys might be forbidden to attend the schools and "no Defense Department contracts [would] be awarded to your universities as long as our officers are denied the ability to recruit on campus."

However, in the early 90s all seven law schools in the Chicago area terminated use of their placement facilities by the United States military. Northwestern, University of Chicago, DePaul, Loyola, IIT Chicago-Kent College, Northern Illinois, and John Marshall law schools are complying with new amendments to by-laws of the Association of American Law Schools. These require member schools to "pursue a policy of providing . . . students and graduates with equal opportunity to obtain employment, without discrimination," on the basis of sexual orientation and other factors.

University officials still fear that the DOD will carry out its threats. (In April, 1991, a bill was introduced in the House which would "deny funds to programs that do not allow the Secretary of Defense access to students on campuses or to certain student information for recruiting purposes.") Nevertheless, the movement against ROTC continues to grow. Demonstrations and press conferences were held on 26 campuses across the country on May 4, 1990. Some faculty resolutions called for dismissing ROTC from their campus on a certain date, such as by 1993, although students wanted more immediate action. University administrators and boards of regents, treading more lightly, tended to call for intensified lobbying of the military and Congress to change the discriminatory policy.

An estimated 70 to 80 percent of military officers come from ROTC. In response to all the letters and lobbying from academia the response from Secretary of Defense Richard Cheney's office was, "We do not plan to reassess the Department's policy," and "A meeting with the secretary to discuss the issue would not be productive at this time."

The advent of war in the Persian Gulf put additional stress on Lesbians and Gays serving in the armed forces. In January, 1991, several newspapers printed a story quoting Lieutenant Commander Kenneth Satterfield, a DOD spokesman, saying that although current regulations bar Gays and Lesbians from serving "the discharge of known Gay personnel may now be deferred until they are no longer needed for the Gulf operation." This, of course, raised a storm of condemnation from Lesbians, Gays, and our supporters that the armed forces would callously send us overseas to fight and die for our country and then throw us out of the services if we survived to return to the United States—the same thing that was done in past wars.

Paul DiDonato, legal director of National Gay Rights Advocates (NGRA), called for an immediate end to the anti-Gay military regulations. "If Gays and Lesbians are fit for military service during a war . . . they are equally as fit during peacetime." He added that letting them serve only during wartime was "dishonest, hypocritical and repugnant."

It may be that the statement by Satterfield was a DOD trial balloon to see how such an idea would be accepted. Satterfield swiftly told the *San Francisco Sentinel* he had been misquoted. "The regulations are still in place. If someone tells us that they are homosexual they would be discharged upon verification of their assertion."

Subsequently NGLTF started a letter-writing campaign asking President Bush to issue an executive order rescinding the military's ban on Lesbians and Gays, and 40 members of Congress signed a letter written by Gerry Studds urging the president to sign such an order. Support came from many sources, including the California State Senate majority caucus and two editorials in the *San Francisco Examiner*. Congresswoman Nancy Pelosi indicated that changing the DOD policy would be a high-priority item during the 1991 legislative session. In response, the White House wrote Studds that the matter "has been directed to the appropriate administration officials for their careful review and consideration." The congressman said he was "less than overwhelmed" by the reply.

Caught in the middle of the controversy was army reservist Medical Support Specialist Donna Lynn Jackson. Her unit was called up for duty in the Gulf, and before it was due to leave she told her superiors that she was a Lesbian, willing to serve, but wanting to join the regular army when she returned and afraid that her homosexuality would be used to prevent that. Donna Jackson was the first to come out over the Persian Gulf war, but not the last. She was swiftly severed from the service with an honorable discharge.

Lesbian/Gay legal groups, however, reported that they were working with more than a dozen Gay and Lesbian reservists who were being shipped out even though they made it known they were Gay. Miriam Ben-Shalom, chair of Gay, Lesbian and Bisexual Veterans of America said she had been contacted personally by seven women and three men who said their commanding officers knew they were homosexual but they were being shipped to Saudi Arabia anyway.

During the war with Iraq it was estimated by Paul Bray, public relations director of NGLTF, that at least 50,000 Lesbians and Gay men were in the war zone in all the various branches of the service. Some evidence of the Lesbian presence in Saudi Arabia is shown in the following excerpt from a letter published in the March/April 1991 issue of *Lesbian Connections.*

"I'm presently in Saudi Arabia leading a platoon of 53 soldiers (13 women) that deploys out to the desert for 35–40 days at a time. I'm very proud to be one of the many strong Lesbians over here doing my job and out-performing my male counterparts. I will tell you, from firsthand experience, that the women are holding up 100% better than the men. There are many Lesbians here, and we have our ways of finding each other—we get together once or twice a month to laugh and talk about 'family' things. My girl-friend of five years is also over here with a medical unit. I miss her dearly!"

The "intelligent" approach of the military to Lesbians and Gays is illuminated in the following bit of information from Paul Di-Donato of NGRA: A Lesbian Air Force Reserve officer in California told her commandant of her sexual orientation. The officer told her that she needed to provide "a marriage license stating that she was married to somebody of the same sex" or an affidavit "saying that she intended to marry someone of the same sex" in order to validate her claim.

With the end of the war, the problems didn't go away. Lesbian and Gay couples suffering from diminished income because one of them had been called to duty, because they could not marry, were not eligible under bills allowing reservists called up to defer payment of mortgages and other debts. Nor were they entitled to assistance from the American Red Cross and other organizations set up for aid to families of service members. Also, most homosexuals were afraid to use such facilities for fear the military would find out they were Gay.

Services were available in some Lesbian/Gay communities which geared up to help their homecoming soldiers and their families with support groups, hot lines, and legal services. San Francisco's Board of Supervisors, noting that The City has laws prohibiting discrimination on the basis of sexual orientation, passed a resolution that the city attorney act as a friend of the court for Lesbian and Gay San Franciscans "who served in the military during Desert Storm, and who are dismissed from the military subsequent to the termination of hostilities on the basis of their sexual orientation."

Unlike the United States military, the Council of Europe mandates that no member country may deny Gays the right to serve in the military. Spanish Gays have protested their country's defiance of the Council's requirement.

Pat Bond

Veteran Pat Bond was characterized as a comedian, a dramatist, and an activist, and was known for her Lesbian humor, charm, and intellect. She said of herself, "I'm not a monologist, I'm an oral historian." An impressive woman of much strength and of many fears. Pat Bond died of cancer on Christmas Eve in 1990 at age 65. She is missed by many.

A native of Iowa, Pat Bond enlisted in the U.S. Women's Army Corps (WAC) in early 1945 as a means of getting away from home and meeting other Lesbians. The move worked on both counts. Unfortunately not all of her experiences were gloriously happy. After basic training she was sent to Japan. It was there that Pat was caught up in a lesbophobic witch hunt which she talked about so movingly in the 1970s film and book entitled *Word Is Out*. Her experiences of Lesbian women turning in other Lesbians to the army intelligence ("It was **our** Lesbian officers who were conducting the summary court martials.") and the suicide of a 21-year-old friend of hers after being found out, had a profound and lifelong effect on Pat. "Her family will never know why she died," Pat wrote, "and then they gave her a military funeral." Subsequently some 500 Lesbians were dishonorably discharged and sent back to the states.

Because Pat had married a Gay man in San Francisco before she went to Japan, she got out of the service on that basis and was shipped back to The City. She made friends with other dykes, worked at dead end jobs for enough money to frequent the bars, and generally partied. For a while she owned and ran a bar, Bond Street, and then worked at other bars. Appearing in *Word Is Out* launched Pat in a new career. "I'd trained in theater and writing for 54 years before my moment came," she said. She took the plunge, quit her job, and began to act and write for a living.

Pat Bond's first one-woman show was *Gerty, Gerty, Gerty Stein Is Back, Back, Back.* In it she portrayed an amazing likeness to Stein, and in answering questions from the audience following the play she maintained that persona as if it were her own. She began *Stein* around 1977, and in 1980 it was aired on the Public Broadcasting System under the sponsorship of Maryland Public Television. The show covered the early years of Stein in Oakland, California, and Paris, France, with Alice B. Toklas. Evoked in the play were Stein's famous artistic friends such as Hemingway and Picasso, and always present was the love between Gertrude and Alice.

Pat toured the country with her one-woman shows. Doric Wilson called her "The First Lady of American Gay Theatre," and she was a 1982/83 recipient of a Jane Chambers-Billy Blackwell National Gay Theatre Award for acting and writing. She served on the board of directors of Theatre Rhinoceros, a Lesbian/Gay playhouse in San Francisco, during the mid 80s.

Stein was the first piece Pat Bond wrote and performed. It was followed by *Conversations with Pat Bond* which she first performed in a major night club. Pat would go on to do various versions of *Conversations* and the Stein piece throughout the country for colleges and universities, women's groups, and Lesbian/Gay gatherings.

We didn't see Pat in *Murder in the Women's Army Corps* which she performed only a few times. The horror of the witch hunts in Japan and the suicide of her friend so upset Pat that she finally stopped presenting it. In the book *Long Time Passing: Lives of Older Lesbians* edited by Marcy Adelman, she said "I still hate those women (the Lesbian officers who conducted the summary court martials). As I say at the end of that show I did, 'Mildred Burgess, I indict you for murder in the Women's Army Corps'."

To us the most exciting performances Pat did were *Stein* and her powerful paean to love, *Lorena Hickok and Eleanor Roosevelt: A Love Story.* Like us, Pat had grown up in the Roosevelt era and loved Eleanor. She was a role model for all of us. When Doris Faber's book *The Life of Lorena Hickok, E.R.'s Friend* was published in 1980, Pat, like many of us, was furious over Faber's assertion (as well as that of the Roosevelt family and friends) that the passionate letters passed between Eleanor and Hick were merely overblown expressions of deep friendship—certainly nothing to do with Lesbian love.

Pat journeyed to Hyde Park to see for herself some of the actual letters which Lorena Hickok had left to the F.D.R. Library. In an interview with *Our Paper* (San Jose, California's, Gay newspaper) in 1984, Pat said ". . . it's **wonderful** to get to be in love with her on the stage and go through everything that Hick went through. They went on a honeymoon!—six months after he was inaugurated—alone." As she did with Stein, Pat Bond **was** Lorena Hickok—Hick—in the show. Unfortunately it was never videotaped. In fact, Pat had difficulty booking the show on the East Coast because of the power of the Roosevelt family and others.

We ran into Pat on and off over the years but it wasn't until she started doing her shows that we saw much of her. In 1986 the three of us journeyed together to the West Coast Women's Music and Comedy Festival. Robin Tyler, who produces the festival every year, had asked us to do a workshop on aging and Pat to do Stein and Hickok. We drove up together and were housed in a small cabin with its own bathroom but one double bed and a very lumpy sofa which Pat got stuck with. It was the first music festival the three of us had been to, and we were impressed and awed by the organization which kept 2,000 Lesbians happy and healthy in a fun-filled weekend.

Most of Pat's close friends were Gay men, although she loved women. She never forgot her army experience and never got over her anger and bitterness. She mistrusted Lesbians and wouldn't let them get too close. But in the end, when she was bedridden, Terry Baum, Little Sun, and Gail Lynch, her former lover, became her support group. At her memorial service they recounted three different and moving stories of their individual and very special relationships with Pat.

Pat's beloved Gertrude Stein once said, "Dead is dead. But dead is not done. Not over." In Pat's memory, the Pat Bond Memorial Old Dyke Award has been formed to be presented annually to Lesbians over 60 whose contributions to our community have not been sufficiently acknowledged.

Denial of Security Clearances

The government's policy of denying security clearances to known Lesbians and Gays remains in force today in spite of more than a quarter of a century of litigation by homosexuals. Early in 1990 a federal appeals court ruled that the DOD can discriminate against Gays seeking security clearances by subjecting them to stricter scrutiny than other applicants. That ruling overturned an earlier one which granted us the same constitutional protection as other minorities. The newest ruling said that homosexuality is not a "suspect class" like race, gender, or religion, therefore we don't have the same right to equal protection as other groups.

Nevertheless, Lesbians and Gay men who contest denial or revocation of security clearances win every once in a while. Betty B. Anderson, a Lesbian employed by the Pentagon as a secretary, won a two-year battle in 1982 for a top secret clearance she needed for promotion to a better job. Army security had ordered her to undergo a psychiatric examination to see if she suffered from ego-dystonic homosexuality. Dr. Robert Spitzer, former president of the APA and author of the ego-dystonic diagnosis, wrote the army that the term pertains only to people unhappy with their homosexuality.

Another Lesbian wasn't so lucky. Julie Dubbs, a technical illustrator, received a top-secret clearance from the DOD for her job with a military contractor, but was turned down by the Central Intelligence Agency (CIA) which said homosexuality "may be exploitable" by those seeking secret information. This is the reason given by all government agencies, based on not one single shred of evidence. Dubbs filed suit in 1985, but it bogged down in pretrial proceedings over the extent to which CIA policies are subject to court review. Finally, in 1991, Dick Gayer, her attorney, and the CIA came to an agreement which was approved by U.S. District Court Judge Eugene Lynch: to reconsider Dubbs' application and treat homosexual conduct and associations in the same manner as heterosexual conduct and associations.

The government's method, it appears, is to take so long to act or go to court that the Lesbian or Gay involved will go away. In 1982 Dan Siminoski filed a request under the Freedom of Information Act to the Federal Bureau of Investigation (FBI) for documents collected on Lesbian and Gay organizations. When the FBI didn't respond the ACLU filed suit. Six years later a federal judge ordered the FBI to release thousands of pages of the records requested. DOB was among the organizations under surveillance. Names of informants were blacked out and reports were mostly inconsequential.

A class-action lawsuit challenging the FBI's employment discrimination against homosexuals has been filed by Frank Buttino, a counterespionage and organized crime expert with a 20-year career with the bureau as a special agent. The FBI revoked his security clearance and fired him when he admitted he was Gay. As of April, 1991, Buttino's attorney was taking depositions from FBI officials seeking to probe patterns of discrimination.

Progress in countering governmental discrimination over security clearances has been a long and expensive process. Some Lesbians and Gays won't fight back, others can't afford to. Lesbian and Gay public interest law firms do take test cases on constitutional grounds of discrimination, and some Gay attorneys specialize in cases against the government.

The Washington March of 1987

On Sunday, October 11, 1987, more than 500,000 women and men, Gay, Lesbian, Bisexual, and non-Gay, marched in Washington D.C. to underscore demands for Lesbian/Gay rights with the slogan, "For Love and For Life, We're Not Going Back!" The march, one of the largest civil rights demonstrations in the United States, was the climax of a week of activism which included a mass "wedding," civil disobedience at the Supreme Court, and showing of The Names Project Quilt. This was the second Lesbian/Gay march on Washington; the first, in the Fall of 1979, was dedicated to Harvey Milk who had been assassinated.

Demands of the 1987 march included: legal recognition of Lesbian and Gay relationships; repeal of sodomy laws; a presidential order banning anti-Gay discrimination by the federal government; passage of the Congressional Lesbian and Gay Rights Bill; an end to discrimination against people with AIDS, ARC, or HIV-Positive status and increased funding for AIDS education, research, and patient care; reproductive freedom; the right to control our own bodies; and an end to racism in this country and apartheid in South Africa.

Before the march there were two days of intensive lobbying of members of Congress. Representatives Barney Frank and Gerry Studds spoke about being Gay in the House of Representatives; Representative Nancy Pelosi spoke to the House about the march and its meaning.

On Saturday, at an emotional ceremony at historical Congressional Cemetery, some of Harvey Milk's ashes were interred along with a photograph, a piece of his ponytail, and other mementos. The site is one purchased by Leonard Matlovich who, with Ken McPherson, started the Never Forget Foundation to remember Gay and Lesbian heroes when they die. The grave site of Leonard Matlovich, who spoke that memorable day, is nearby. The headstone, already in place in 1987, reads "A Gay Vietnam Veteran: When I was in the military they gave me a medal for killing two men and a discharge for loving one."

(Leonard Matlovich died June 11, 1988, of complications of AIDS, just short of his 45th birthday. He was buried with full military honors, after which the Gay community offered its own tribute to the man who fought the Air Force for reinstatement and won in 1980, when the courts ordered him reinstated. He didn't rejoin but was given back pay, other compensation, and an honorable discharge. In December, 1990, Leonard's parents received a scroll, signed by President George Bush, honoring the sergeant for "devoted and selfless" military service.)

Two thousand Lesbian and Gay couples took part in The Wedding on Constitution Avenue in front of the Internal Revenue Service building. The celebration was a "recommitment ceremony" demanding legal equality and recognition of their bonding. The ceremony was arranged by Couples, Inc. It was moving and the love, joy, and excitement a palpable feeling. The Wedding demands included: Lesbian and Gay domestic partners to be entitled to the same rights as married heterosexual couples; equal treatment for our relationships and our self defined family structures; elimination of discrimination against same-sex couples with particular attention to taxes, insurance, medical care, survivor benefits, foster care, adoption, child custody and visitation rights; and recognition of same-sex unions by religious organizations.

At dawn, before the march began, The Quilt, with 1,920 squares, was unfurled on the elipse and remained, a moving, inspiring, sad reminder of the carnage AIDS is visiting on our community.

At the rally following the march Jesse Jackson, presidential candidate, spoke as did Whoopi Goldberg and Ellie Smeal, past president of the NOW. Many Lesbians and Gays also spoke, but the media focused on the non-Gay speakers, causing criticism from some that we allowed "them" to render "us" invisible.

On the final day of that incredible week, 5,000 Lesbians and Gays besieged the U.S. Supreme Court building to protest the court's 1986 decision to uphold the Georgia sodomy law. The first wave of civil disobedience was led by Lesbians, who had been a powerful force in planning the action, followed by countless waves. Over 800 were arrested by D.C. police, who wore yellow gloves in fear of AIDS contamination. Some of those arrested put up bail, others pleaded guilty to "failure to quit" protesting and paid a fine or spent three days in jail. The protest was nonviolent but some police officers were verbally and physically abusive.

Pat Norman, national co-chair of the march, said: "We have turned around the Lesbian and Gay movement with this march. . . . The coalitions we have built with Hispanics, Blacks, women and labor are unprecedented. Even Gay men are now saying Lesbian and Gay. I am thrilled to know that there is unity around the real issues that affect our community. This is just the beginning of a new wave of our movement."

Like the San Francisco New Year's Ball of 1965 and the New York Stonewall riots of 1969, the Washington march of 1987 was a turning point in the Gay and Lesbian movement. It marked a resurgence of energy and a renewed commitment to join nationally to achieve mutual goals.

The 1987 Conference of Lesbian Agenda for Action

In the mid 80s Lesbians had already decided we needed more visibility and an agenda of our own separate and distinct from that of Gay men and non-Lesbian women.

In early 1987, about 25 Lesbians met at San Francisco's Women's Building to discuss ways to involve more Lesbians in the social and political process. By July, 1987, LAFA had 200 members. In

November LAFA produced a conference attended by 500 women to build consensus on the Lesbian political agenda and devise strategies to make government more responsive to our issues. Workshops covered health services, domestic partners, child care, advancement in the work place, reproductive freedom, violence prevention, overcoming poverty, and racism. Rose Appleman, writing in *Coming Up!*, said the themes emerging "strikingly and consistently" were the urgency of visibility, diversity of concerns, and the significance of politics.

Carmen Vazquez, one of LAFA's founders, said, "I believe that the power to change our individual and collective social and political status requires that we be visible. I believe that the attempt to create rights for ourselves in the courts and in legislative halls can only succeed if we are successful at the work of mitigating our invisibility in the public's mind, in the lesbian/gay movement, in the women's movement, in the social services that we have been central to creating, in the educational systems that shape and mold the minds of every generation, in the literature of our age and the music of our time, on scaffolds, and train tracks and telephone poles, in hospitals and law firms, in all movements for peace and justice . . . in ma and pa's living room."

She pointed out that all the coalition work in the world won't be of any use to us unless we can make ourselves visible as Lesbians. "We can't expect our allies to support she whom they don't know." Nor can we lobby on behalf of an invisible constituency. "Empowerment through visibility is an indispensable tool for health and for change," she said. "That is true for individuals and it is true for movements."

Conference facilitators spent the night sorting out workshop summaries and came up with six priority areas: health, education, sexuality, family, legal discrimination, and consciousness raising. The latter because of Lesbians' general ignorance of the old and the differently abled. On Sunday, five workshops met to strategize on how the new agenda was to be carried out through a particular type of work: grassroots organizing, electoral/legislative process, social services, workplace organizing, and cultural/political art.

Further Actions on Our Issues
A week later in Washington, D.C., the National Womens Continuing Committee (NWCC) celebrated the passage of ten years since

the Houston conference adopted the Women's National Plan of Action. In 1986 an "update" of the plan was published indicating the progress (or lack thereof) which had been made on each of the planks.

In 1977, the "Sexual Preference" plank was adopted by the 2,000 delegates. By 1986 some city and state laws protected homosexuals against discrimination, half the states had revised their sex laws, yet some mothers were still losing their children because of their sexual orientation. One of the problems was a matter of semantics. The term sexual orientation more accurately describes homosexuality as a condition than does sexual preference. You don't just decide one day to become a Lesbian.

The Lesbian Agenda workshop at the NWCC conference centered on the need to redefine family to include Lesbian and Gay domestic partners, the need to make Lesbian concerns part of a global women's movement, the possibility of a national Lesbian organization, and the integration of Lesbian perspectives in workshops covering other planks of the Plan of Action.

"Power Through Action" was the theme of the National Lesbian Rights Conference sponsored by NOW in San Diego, California, in 1988, to develop a national Lesbian rights agenda. Addressing the 1,000 plus attendees, NOW President Molly Yard emphasized ". . . not a NOW agenda, but a full-scope national [Lesbian] agenda."

Lesbians spoke enthusiastically of strengthening alliances with the feminist movement and oppressed minority groups, developing a global perspective, Lesbian visibility, increased influence over legislation, and increased contact with establishment media.

Workshop resolutions were presented to the 1989 NOW national conference which officially supported the full Lesbian agenda and picked seven issues for priority attention: Set up Political Action Committees to earmark funds for Lesbian and Gay candidates; reestablish consciousness raising on Lesbian issues; protect Lesbian families through reform, networking, and support; promote Lesbian/Gay rights in the military through litigation, political action, and public education; endorse and help organize the 1991 National Lesbian Conference; endorse a national health care plan; and support legal protection of the rights of open Lesbian/Gay teachers.

Other items on the Lesbian agenda included developing skills training to increase activism and effectiveness in politics and

dealing with the media; establishing a network of hotlines and response alerts; working for passage of the Equal Rights Amendment
and urging the ERA campaign to initiate consciousness raising on
racism and homophobia; legalizing domestic partners; combatting
ageism and dealing with issues of Lesbian/Gay youth; providing
opportunities for women with different abilities to participate;
working to eradicate poverty; acknowledging Lesbian battering and
promoting services to deal with the problem. They also resolved to
promote support for Lesbian archives; support Lesbians for whom
religion is important; push for categories on reporting of AIDS to
include Lesbian, non-Lesbian and Bisexual women; and include
women's studies in educational curricula, K through 12.

Jeanne Cordova, who called herself a "dinosaur lesbian leader,"
originated the idea of the National Lesbian Mentorship Project at
the NOW Lesbian Conference. Some younger Lesbian leaders had
expressed a desire to develop their skills with direct assistance
from experienced leaders who built the Lesbian movement during
the 60s, 70s, and 80s. Jeanne signed up many old-timers on the
Mentor Roster. But later the matching process of mentor/mentee
broke down for lack of money and womanpower. We suggest that
upcoming Lesbian leaders take the initiative in approaching mentors of their choice.

Cleve Jones initiated a different approach. He and Luke Adams
co-founded New Pacific Academy to train young Lesbians and Gay
men in community service and activism. During the summer of
1990 more than 100 students from throughout the country went
through an intensive four-week basic training at San Francisco
State University. The Academy was funded by the Critical Literacy
Institute. Students were in the 18–30 age group, half female and
half male, and as diverse in background, race, and ethnicity as
possible. All but their travel expenses were covered.

The daily timetable went from 7:30 a.m. to 10 p.m. A comprehensive curriculum included Lesbian/Gay history, philosophy, and
psychology. Classes covered the diversity of the Lesbian/Gay community: various racial and ethnic groups, Bisexuals, youth, elders,
the disabled. Workshop topics ranged from confronting homophobia, AIDS, and Lesbian health to issues affecting Lesbian/Gay families. Students sharpened their skills in political organizing, using
the media, oratory and writing, coalition building, direct action,

lobbying, and fundraising. The faculty was comprised of Lesbian, Gay, and Bisexual activists from across the country.

Assaults and Police Behavior

San Francisco is often touted as the great Gay Mecca. According to Barbara Cameron, director of Community United Against Violence (CUAV), The City also has the distinction of reporting more hate-motivated assaults against homosexuals than any other city in the United States. During 1989, attacks against Lesbians and Gays increased by 67 percent. Attacks aimed at Lesbians more than doubled. About 10 percent of all attacks involved some reference to AIDS. While 27 percent of the incidents occurred in the Castro district, incidents in other parts of The City increased a whopping 231 percent. In the first quarter of 1990, CUAV reported 92 hate-motivated assaults: 47 percent resulted in physical injuries to the victim and 19 percent required medical attention. San Francisco may lead the nation in reporting because CUAV was organized long before NGLTF's Anti-Violence Project.

A total of 7,031 episodes of homophobic victimization were reported to NGLTF in 1989. The highest number of reported incidents were in North Carolina, Texas, California, Illinois, and Ohio. Other cities reporting high numbers of physical assaults included New York, Chicago, Boston, Fort Worth, Los Angeles, and Denver. The actual extent of anti-Gay violence nationwide is much greater than these figures indicate because of under-reporting and a lack of systematic data collection.

In 1991 a rash of anti-Lesbian/Gay incidents (physical attacks, telephone death threats, letters, and vandalism) was so bad that the University of Chicago offered a $3,000 reward for information. The FBI joined campus police in the investigation.

Lesbian-baiting is an all-American sport which often leads to violence. The Lesbian and Gay press has chronicled many incidents involving arson of Lesbian meeting places, vandalism of property, beatings, rape, and murder.

It is bad enough to be victimized physically by hate mongers, but mistreatment by police compounds the emotional stress and scars. When Joy arrived at the emergency room of St. Vincent's Hospital in Greenwich Village to be with her lover, Amy, who had been raped, security guards stopped her. She raised such a fuss that a woman police officer let her in. Amy had been in a room, hysterically crying, for four hours without any attention. After the doctor arrived and exams were over, Amy was allowed to wash the excrement from her face and body. But she and Joy were not given any privacy. When Joy tried to hold Amy to comfort her a nurse called security guards who dragged her outside and began beating and kicking her. When police arrived they spoke only to the guards, and hauled Joy off to the Sixth Precinct where *she* was charged with misdemeanor assault.

Latino Gay activists in San Diego and Tijuana have reported that 20 Lesbians in Guadalajara, Mexico, were arrested and raped by police officers after a raid on a local Gay disco.

In San Francisco witnesses saw about a dozen drunk and rowdy men get off a motorized cable car shouting, "Let's go to Peg's, let's get the dykes." Alene Levine locked the bar door to prevent them from entering. The men were carrying beer bottles and appeared too drunk to be served legally. Later, when Levine opened the door to admit some regular customers, the men shoved her aside and broke in. She threatened to call the police. They responded, "We are the police and we can do what we goddam well want to." In the melee several women were injured. The off-duty officers were brought up on charges by the police chief, and criminal charges were filed by the district attorney. The bar owner and women who sustained injuries sued the City and County of San Francisco for damages.

Lesbians and Gays have engaged police top brass across the country in problem-solving. In some cities, Lesbians and Gays are permitted to make presentations at roll call or at the academy. Kate Bykowski of Cincinnati said she approaches the police by stressing points of similarity since they are both from a stereotyped minority. A personal approach is nonthreatening, she believes, and will reduce hostility. Experience indicates that young officers are more receptive than old-line cops who are hardened and cynical.

San Francisco has a long history of Lesbian/Gay community input into recruiting and academy training. Open Lesbian and Gay officers on the force number about 170. An eight-hour crash-course covers the history of Gay politics, sexuality, alternative families, and the historically rocky relationship between police and the Gay community.

The incident at Peg's Place and another which occurred outside of Amelia's bar led to the formation of Lesbians Against Police Violence (LAPV). The organization rallied support for the women brutalized at Amelia's and Peg's Place.

For the final game of the Pioneers, San Francisco's team in the Women's Professional Basketball League, LAPV bought a block of tickets at a discount. Members and friends came 250 strong on Banner Day, the one time the game was televised. They unrolled a huge banner and placed it over the rail of the balcony. When the Pioneers' management saw LESBIANS AGAINST POLICE VIO-LENCE so prominently displayed, they had a fit. They asked the women to take down the banner, saying it was a political statement rather than the name of a group. The women insisted it was the name of their organization and that they had been invited to bring their banner, and refused to take it down. Others throughout the Civic Auditorium were alerted to what was going on. When women security guards came to take the banner down, they were blocked by 250 dykes who sat proudly behind it. Simultaneously, from throughout the auditorium, chants began: "Keep the banner up."

Frustrated by the impasse, management called the police. Two squad cars arrived. Four officers rushed in. When they learned that the trouble was a minor squabble over a banner the police looked annoyed. When they saw it, they exclaimed, "You want **us** to take down a banner that says *'Lesbians Against Police Violence'?* You've got to be kidding!" They left.

Having Lesbian and Gays in law enforcement is helpful. Some Lesbians have been police officers for more than 15 years. Lieutenant Connie O'Connor is the highest ranking Lesbian in San Francisco's Sheriff's Department.

In 1979 Mayor Dianne Feinstein appointed Jo Daly, long-time political activist, to the Police Commission—the first time an open Gay person had held such a position. Mayor Feinstein was fulfilling a promise made by Mayor George Moscone before his death. The fact that a Lesbian was chosen did not sit well with the Gay male community. They never supported Jo as they should have. Mayor Feinstein later replaced Jo with another Lesbian, Juanita Owens, who had chaired the Commission on the Status of Women. Juanita, who is of Native American heritage, found her background and profession as an educator useful in monitoring police training and curriculum. After his election, Mayor Art Agnos appointed Black Lesbian Gwenn Craig, also active in politics and with concerns of people of color. By law the Police Commission must have at least one woman on it.

With the rising crime rate against Lesbians and Gays, some activists have decided it is time to take up arms against their attackers. Training in self defense, the use of mace, blowing of whistles as an S.O.S. call, and patrols of Gay/Lesbian districts have been offered before. ACT UP/New York is arming and taking target practice. New York's Queer Nation, on the other hand, has taken to the streets with marches much like women's "Take Back the Night," going directly to the homes of the perpetrators of the violence. San Francisco voted in the 70s to ban handguns. When Lesbian/Gay activists suggested taking up arms in self defense there, no one took them up on it.

Domestic Violence

Sometimes the violence against Lesbians is an inside job. Domestic violence is not just a heterosexual phenomenon. It also happens in Lesbian homes. For many years this was kept hidden by the denial and minimizing that are endemic in battering relationships. It was feared that right wing antagonists would use Lesbian battering to the detriment of battered women's shelters.

Lesbians were founders and the backbone of the Battered Women's Movement in the 70s. They learned organizing skills, ran hotlines, developed training for police, and functioned in emergency treatment centers as advocates for rape victims. They set up a network of shelters for battered women based on women helping women, peer counseling, and empowerment of battered women to take over their own lives. They took on the criminal justice system and the so-called helping professions who were content to blame the victim and let the batterer go scot-free.

These Lesbians, who had made it safer for battered heterosexual women, had the tables turned on them. When fundraising corporate types were placed on shelter boards and "professionals" with academic degrees took over staff, Lesbian workers were pressured to be closeted and denied promotions. There was no room at the inn for battered Lesbians.

In the 1980s Lesbians "came out," formed a task force within the National Coalition Against Domestic Violence and addressed the needs of battered Lesbians and accountability of Lesbian batterers. They developed workshops on homophobia for domestic violence workers and on internalized homophobia for the Lesbian community. In 1986 they went public with *Naming the Violence: Speaking Out About Lesbian Battering,* an anthology edited by Kerry Lobel.

Lesbians on staff in San Francisco Bay Area shelters banded together for mutual support, mapped out a program on homophobia, and confronted the problem head-on. Today brochures from their shelters mention services available to battered Lesbians. Rosalie House, sponsored by the Catholic organization St. Vincent de Paul, even has an open Lesbian on its staff.

The movement also established domestic violence as a crime to be treated like any other crime of violence. When a woman commits a crime she is apt to get a heavier sentence than a man would. If a Lesbian is convicted of the same crime, she is likely to get the book thrown at her. In 1990 a Lesbian in Modesto, California, was sentenced to life in prison because her lover beat her son to death while she was away from home. She was convicted of murder for not *preventing* it. Would there have been a conviction or so stiff a sentence if a heterosexual woman or man had been in the same circumstances?

The California Alliance Against Domestic Violence has made several attempts to make domestic violence laws applicable to same-sex couples, to no avail. In 1991 an Ohio intermediate appeals court ruled such laws must be applied to same sex couples the same as they are applied to married couples. In the first domestic violence case involving a Lesbian couple in Los Angeles in 1991, the defendant was sentenced to three years probation and mandated to a batterer's treatment program after expert testimony on the "battered woman syndrome." In 1989 a Florida jury found a battered Lesbian guilty of second-degree murder, rejecting the "battered woman syndrome" as a defense in the fatal shooting of her abusive partner.

It is up to us, Lesbian and non-Lesbian alike, to put our full support behind the struggle to put an **end** to domestic violence. The Battered Women's Movement, like the Feminist Movement, must be all-inclusive if it is to succeed. And Lesbian batterers must be held accountable.

Hate Crimes Legislation

The first Hate Crimes bill mandating data collection on crimes motivated by prejudice based on race, religion, ethnicity, or sexual orientation passed in 1990. Chief sponsors were Paul Simon and Orrin Hatch in the Senate and John Conyers in the House of Representatives.

Senate Bill S419 passed 92–4. The House accepted Senate changes and passed it 402–18—the first federal law ever to address a Lesbian/Gay issue in a positive way. We were surprised to have Utah's conservative Senator Hatch on our side. The reason: declared support of "American family life" and statement that the bill does not promote or encourage homosexuality.

NGLTF and HRCF, both situated in Washington, D.C., lobbied tirelessly, joined coalitions, and promoted constituent letters and telegrams. For the first time representatives of Lesbian/Gay organizations were invited to the bill signing ceremony at the White House. Peri Jude Radecic, a forceful lobbyist, represented NGLTF (Director Urvashi Vaid was not invited because she had disrupted a speech on AIDS by Bush two weeks before). Lobbyist Karen Friedman and Operations Director Sheryl Harris were there from HRCF. Paulette Goodman, then president of P-FLAG, and Claudia Brenner, whose Lesbian lover was killed in an anti-Lesbian crime, were also present, as were the Illinois Gay/Lesbian Task Force and Log Cabin Republican Clubs. President Bush took the opportunity to announce a new toll-free number at the Justice Department to receive reports of hate crimes: 1–800–347-HATE. He also said the FBI would be gathering statistics on hate crimes for its annual unified crime reports.

Lesbian/Gay lobbyists also saw the president sign the Americans with Disabilities Act of 1990. An amendment that would have allowed food handlers with AIDS to be fired or moved to other types of jobs had been deleted.

Twelve states (New Jersey, California, Vermont, Connecticut, Wisconsin, Massachusetts, Illinois, Iowa, Minnesota, Nevada, New Hampshire, Oregon) have also passed hate crimes bills. They vary in form and most increase penalties for such crimes, but all include coverage of sexual orientation. Anti-Gay legislators blocked passage of such bills in Georgia, Maryland, and New York. Sexual orientation protections were deleted in Texas and Washington.

Hate crime bills have also been passed at the local level. The City Council of Wichita, Kansas, increased penalties for hate-motivated crimes against Gays and other groups. The legislation, however, included a disclaimer that the law did *not* "promote, encourage or condone any organization, group or religion." The Board of Aldermen in Louisville, Kentucky, increased penalties for crimes motivated by sexual orientation or health-related conditions. The bill also instructs city officials to collect hate crimes statistics, train police officers about the law, offer assistance to victims, and provide public education to reduce the number of hate crimes. A bill was passed unanimously in Chicago mandating increased penalties for attacks motivated by hatred even if the victim is not a member of specified oppressed groups.

In San Francisco the police and district attorney have made hate crimes a top priority, and both have formed hate crimes units. Deputy District Attorney Anna Bravo heads a special Hate Crimes Unit in Sacramento, California. The Alameda (California) County Board of Supervisors approved a Hate Violence Prevention Project setting up a $128,000-a-year hate crimes reduction agency. The proposal calls for a crisis hotline, coordination with law enforcement in reporting and response to hate crimes, and monitoring such incidents in the schools.

In Australia, the New South Wales Parliament passed a law in 1989 allowing Lesbians and Gays to initiate legal action against those who taunt or threaten them. Victims of harassment can secure a restraining order if the court finds reason to fear an act of violence or further harassment.

In 1991 NGLTF received a $50,000 grant from the Public Welfare Foundation to support the task force's Anti-Violence Project. The grant was the Foundation's first ever to a Gay organization.

The Importance of Coming Out
"Out of the closet and into the streets," became the slogan of Gay Liberation in the early 70s. After Harvey Milk was elected in 1977 as the first Gay on the San Francisco Board of Supervisors, he

became a national figure. He stressed the need for more of us to come out to show our numbers, give us more political clout, and provide Lesbian and Gay youth with role models.

As the AIDS epidemic grew in the 80s and the Reagan administration failed to respond, a "War Conference" of 200 Lesbian and Gay leaders was held in Virginia in February, 1988. "National Coming Out Day '88: Take Your Next Step" emerged as the slogan of a bold new national campaign. Jean O'Leary, then executive director of NGRA, and Rob Eichberg, founder of Experience Weekend, assumed leadership for enlisting active support from more than 8,000 local and state Lesbian/Gay groups across the country. People were encouraged to participate on Coming Out Day on October 11 by doing some of the following:

Wear an openly Gay symbol or button for an entire week, call a radio talk show and introduce a Gay/Lesbian topic, read a Gay paper on the bus or in a restaurant, confront your coworkers about a bigoted joke or comment, boycott a company or organization that discriminates, take a lover/partner home for the holidays, come out to your family—parents, brothers, and/or sisters—consider leaving *Lesbian/Woman* in your bookcase when Mom visits. Local organizations were encouraged to hold parties, rap groups, or community town hall meetings to share Coming Out Day stories.

Some came out on television on the Oprah Winfrey Show. It was so successful that Oprah has continued to observe Coming Out Day each year.

Coming Out Day 1988 inspired Donna Yutzy, president of Bay Area Career Women, to lead her organization and some of its 1,200 members out of the closet. BACW's membership is predominantly upwardly mobile career-oriented "Dykes on Spikes." BACW was the only Lesbian organization invited to participate in a San Francisco symposium on the Bay Area's economic future attended by the presidents of Fortune 500 companies. Having an organization the size of BACW out gives Lesbians more visibility and political clout. Its leadership can be outspoken and membership lists protected, allowing individuals to decide for themselves what risks they are willing to take.

In 1990 on Coming Out Day, the Rainbow Flag was raised at dawn above California's State Capitol, an historic first in the nation. Although the display had been approved, within hours

Governor George Deukmejian ordered the flag down. On Gay Pride Day in New York the same year, the top of the Empire State Building glistened with lavender lights.

When Wenche Lowzow, Lesbian member of the Norwegian Parliament, spoke at San Francisco's Pride rally in 1983, she emphasized the importance of elected officials coming out openly as Gay. "We have a certain status, and it is important for ordinary people to understand that Gays are everywhere—teachers, judges, clergy and politics."

Wenche and her lover Kim Friele told us their "coming out" story. They met when Wenche was first elected in 1977. Kim, who had been active in Norway's Lesbian/Gay liberation movement since 1963, won Norway's internationally renowned Free Speech Award in 1978 for her writing and public speaking on Gay Rights. That made it more difficult for Wenche to keep her relationship with Kim hidden. But it was not until 1979 after attending a meeting between Gays and a group of politicians that she decided to go public. "It was at that point I understood how little the Norwegian government understood about Gays."

Today Norway has a progressive Gay Rights law that prevents discrimination in housing, jobs, and social services. Gays cannot be denied rights/benefits such as full employment and generous welfare, medical and retirement. Kim is among 55 Norwegian citizens who have been awarded a pension for years of community service. How's that for coming out?

British filmmaker Derek Jarman, an openly Gay person with AIDS, criticized Sir Ian McKellen, in an article for the *Guardian*, for accepting knighthood from the Tory administration that had "stigmatized homosexuality." The next day 18 Lesbian and Gay actors, playwrights, producers, and directors came out en masse in an open letter. "Never again will public figures be able to claim that they have to keep secret their homosexuality in fear of it damaging their careers." McKellen is "an inspiration to us all . . . as an artist of extraordinary gifts, as a public figure of remarkable honesty and dignity." Lesbians among the letter signers were director Nancy Diusguid and actors Bryony Lavery and Pam St. Clement. Michael Leonard, painter of the Queen's official portrait, also signed.

In the wake of Clause 28 several dozen old British Lesbians braved the camera to tell of their struggles in creating a Lesbian identity, both privately and publicly, in the 1930s, 40s, and 50s. As Ruth, a participant in the 49-minute tape which was originally produced for London's Channel 4, said, "... as you get older you haven't got much more to lose." Some of the women in the film were pioneers of the British Lesbian movement: Diana Chapman of the Minorities Research Group in the 50s, Jackie Forster who founded *Sappho,* and Monica Still who is raising funds to refurbish the grave site of Radclyffe Hall. *Women Like Us,* is being distributed by Women Make Movies to groups and theaters in the U.S.

Frustrated by continued attacks of the "traditional values" movement and radicalized by the fight for funding for AIDS research and treatment programs, some Gay leaders began to discuss exposing politicians who are secretly Gay but publicly hostile to the goals of the Lesbian and Gay movement. Vic Basile, former director of HRCF, spoke bitterly in a 1989 article in *The Advocate,* a Gay publication: "Their duplicitous, devious, harmful behavior ought to be exposed."

Roberta Achtenberg, then directing attorney for NCLR, disagreed. "I don't want to see anyone punished for being Gay. I might want to punish them in other ways for being anti-human, and I pity them for being so self loathing. But it seems to me the punishment is not siccing a homophobic society on them and allowing them to be ravaged by that society."

Urvashi Vaid, executive director of the NGLTF, pointed out that "outing," as it came to be called, was "an underhanded way of using the charge of homosexuality (as a slur) to discredit someone."

The media, sensing a split in the Lesbian and Gay movement, jumped into the fray trying to pit militants against those who still upheld the traditional code of silence to protect the privacy of individuals. The debate became one of the big news items of 1990.

Bill Mandel, *San Francisco Examiner* columnist who became an advocate for Gay rights during the Gay Olympics struggle, wrote, "So now we have 'outing' a new violent trendy verb to go with 'wilding.' ... a desperate tactic for desperate times. It is an invasion of privacy, but privacy doesn't mean much during wartime. The danger, of course, is that outing will catch fire, become an anti-Gay witch hunt with Gays both the hunter and prey."

At its National Conference, NOW members recommitted themselves to an aggressive program of education on Lesbian/Gay
rights. "However," the resolution stated, "the rights to privacy, self
determination and self definition are basic feminist principles
which exclude such 'outing' as a feasible or acceptable strategy to
achieve our common goals of equality and liberty."

Three ACT UP/D.C. members held a press conference on the
steps of the Capitol and named allegedly closeted homosexual
members of Congress. ABC, *The New York Times, Washington Post,
USA Today,* and the arch-conservative *National Review* were all there.
But no newspaper or TV station or wire service ran the story they
so eagerly covered.

The shelf life of outing as a phenomenon was over by the end of
the year. Or so we thought. ACT UP/Portland, Oregon, came up
with a Postcards to the Stars campaign. Their slogan, "How can
we gain civil rights if we pretend we don't exist. **Come out of the
closet!**" The message on the cards is: "As a visible public figure
you have a tremendous ability to promote civil rights for lesbians
and gay men. Every time you hide the truth you perpetuate the
misconception that there is something wrong with being a gay man
or lesbian. Some people would like us to . . . keep our mouths shut.
I feel it's time for all lesbians and gay men to openly and proudly
speak out about our lives. By publicly identifying yourself as a
lesbian or gay man you can change the course of history and create
a positive image of who we are. I support your step out, I do not
support your silence."

To us sending a postcard is tantamount to outing. The message
is well stated but we would prefer to mail it in a sealed envelope.
We can state our case, but coming out is a personal choice.

Another way to be outed is to die. Eager Lesbian historians are
at the ready to cull biographical material on a "suspected" famous
woman. It was a non-Gay woman, however, who first gave us an
inkling of Eleanor Roosevelt's romantic love for a woman "friend."

The 30-year correspondence between Eleanor Roosevelt and reporter Lorena Hickok, reported in 1979 in *The Life of Lorena Hickok:
E.R.'s Friend* by Doris Faber, revealed the deep love the two women
had for each other. In one letter the First Lady wrote, "Hick, dar-
ling. Oh I want to put my arms around you, I ache to hold you
close. Your ring is a great comfort. I look at it and think she does

love me, or I wouldn't be wearing it." A letter from Hickok to her said, "Most clearly I remember your eyes, with a kind of reassuring smile in them, and the feeling of that spot just northeast of the corner of your mouth against my lips."

What this revelation started is best described by Ellen Goodman in her syndicated column. "Those who think her prose was purple are arguing with those who think her life was tinged with lavender. Across the tabletops and country, people are talking about her 'sexual preference' as if it were hair color: Did she or didn't she? Only her friend knew for sure."

Eleanor Roosevelt was a heroine to each of us as we grew up in the 30s. She taught us how to overcome fear, how to turn pain into strength and disappointment into purpose. She cared for the poor, supported the rights of women and minorities, and was the force behind the Human Rights Covenant of the U.N. We have a portrait of E.R. hanging on our living room wall—a pencil drawing by Jan U'Ren. When we first heard the news, we were glad to know there had been a measure of personal intimacy in her life. We also admit to a certain relish in knowing that our role model fits the definition of a Lesbian stated at the beginning of our book.

We were chagrined by the hysteria and denials of the family, historians and heterosexuals. Whether the two women had an intimate friendship or a mad love affair doesn't matter. Quibbling over whether they "did it" (we hope they did) denigrates the deep love they shared. Some people so fear intimacy between women they make *love* a four-letter word.

When Billie Jean King was outed by Marilyn Barnett, she bungled her moment of truth. She tried to lie her way out, ostensibly to save women's professional tennis. She collaborated with homophobic repressionists, demeaning her own sexuality and that of other women-loving-women. In her autobiography *Billie Jean* she described herself as a victim of circumstance. She didn't "feel homosexual," she felt "soft and feminine." It was the loneliness and the pressure of being on top of the tennis world that drove her into "another woman's bed." In her relationship with Marilyn, "I was the girl," Billie Jean said. Translated into homophobic idiom, that means Marilyn, the aggressive butch, took advantage of poor Billie Jean in a moment of weakness—a moment that lasted almost seven years.

In 1981 a sleazy reporter for the *New York Daily News* outed a very young and naive Martina Navratilova, who had a habit of being honest and straightforward. Steve Goldstein probed and got her to admit she was a Bisexual and had had Lesbian lovers. She added that she was afraid for that to get out, that she'd been told if one more top woman tennis player came out they would lose Avon as a sponsor.

That story has followed her throughout her career. In 1984 Glenn Dickey, *San Francisco Chronicle* columnist, observed, "She is everything a champion should be, but that's still not enough for those who are hung up on sexual stereotypes."

The clincher came when Martina won the Wimbledon singles title in 1990 for the ninth time, breaking Helen Wills Moody's record. Her moment of triumph was short-lived. Three days later "born again" Margaret Court held a press conference to berate Navratilova as unfit to be a role model for younger players because of her sexual preference. Sports writers called "foul!" Pat Hickey of the *Montreal Gazette* said, "She is intelligent and generous and her court demeanor—the only measuring stick that should be used to determine whether she qualifies as a role model for tennis players—is exemplary." An article in *Tennis* magazine indicated one would be hard pressed to find a woman who is a better model of determination, strength of character, and success. Art Spander of the *San Francisco Examiner* asked, "Who could hate Martina Navratilova? She's talented, intelligent, witty and, maybe most significantly in this era of insincerity, wonderfully honest. She never tried to be anyone except herself."

The Issues of Domestic Partners and New Kinds of Families

Ten years ago the concept of domestic partners emerged as a pay equity issue, an extension of the feminist movement's drive for comparable worth. Fringe benefits are part of the wage package. Heterosexually married employees have certain entitlements that are denied Lesbians and Gays who are legally "single." Married employees can place their spouses and dependents on group health insurance plans while the partners of Lesbians or Gays and those partners' children go unprotected. Other examples are bereavement leave, hospital visitation when one's partner is in intensive care, or jail visitation when a partner is detained. These are givens for married people, but Lesbians and Gays who have the same responsibilities for their loved ones cannot marry.

Local ordinances have been drawn up to obtain such benefits for city and county employees not covered under existing work agreements. Some city councils like Berkeley and West Hollywood in California passed such laws early on. But San Francisco hit a snag when Supervisor Harry Britt, a former Methodist minister, added to his 1982 legislation the registration and certification of domestic partners at the Marriage License Bureau. Equating Lesbian and Gay partnerships with marriage made pay equity a side issue.

The wrath of God came down on City Hall and the Gay community when the Board of Supervisors passed the measure. Mayor Dianne Feinstein said her office received more negative mail and telephone calls on this issue than any other in her 12-year political career, the majority from members of African-American churches and from Roman Catholics. She chastised Britt for not attempting to educate the public about domestic partners before springing this volatile legislation; she vetoed the bill.

A citywide debate ensued about the merits of including fringe benefits for unmarried heterosexual couples, who had the option of marrying, along with Lesbian/Gay couples who cannot marry. Many drafts later domestic partners legislation passed the board again, and Mayor Art Agnos signed it. Opponents gathered enough signatures to put it on the ballot in 1989. Voters rescinded the concept of domestic partners mainly because of perceived costs to taxpayers. Pundits had warned that the defeat of Proposition S would mean the loss of Lesbian/Gay political clout.

Nonetheless, Britt gave it one more try. A watered-down version with only the registration clause, was put to the voters in 1990. Under the leadership of Jean Harris, Britt's legislative aide, it passed. In April, 1991, The City's Health Services Retirement Board voted to adopt a plan which includes health benefits eligibility for domestic partners of city workers.

Other jurisdictions across the United States and Canada produced and debated plans for unmarried domestic partners, heterosexual or homosexual. Some were all-inclusive; others had only parts of the package like health insurance or bereavement leave or registration. Some were passed by city councils, others negotiated by labor unions or ordered by courts of law.

In 1991 Linjeflyg, Swedish domestic airlines, offered Lesbian and Gay partners the same reduced fares as heterosexual couples. Lesbian and Gay partners are now admitted to student housing previously reserved only for married couples at Stanford and New York Universities. New Zealand Immigration accepts residence applications for Lesbian/Gay partners of New Zealand citizens. The German Gay Union has made legal recognition of Lesbian/Gay relationships a top priority. Lesbian members of NOW, like the rest of the membership, can obtain health and other insurance plans for themselves and their domestic partners.

In 1990 the *Washington Blade* started an "Occasions" column to recognize ceremonies of commitment for Lesbian/Gay couples. Linda Warschoff and Ellen Weiser were the first Lesbian couple to use this means of announcing the birth of their son, Jeremy. Some mainstream papers are also running domestic partner notices. The *Everett Herald* (Washington) was the first, followed quickly by *Marin Independent Journal* (California) and *Brattleboro Reformer* (Vermont) with circulations under 75,000. In 1991 after recognition of domestic partners became law, the *Minneapolis Star-Tribune* became the first major daily to run the notices.

NGLTF took on the issue of the 1990 census. Ivy Young, director of the Lesbian and Gay Families Project, aggressively encouraged same-sex couples to check off the "unmarried partner" box. This count is vital to efforts to gain rights for Lesbian and Gay families. Social and economic policy is guided by census data, and legislative agendas and priorities are determined by numbers.

The Family Diversity Project in Los Angeles found a section in the California Corporation Code allowing families of different configurations to register and receive certification from Secretary of State March Fong Eu.

Lambda Legal Defense and Education Fund has a Family Relationships Project in New York. In San Francisco Roberta Achtenberg, chair of The City's Family Policy Task Force, said, "Families have redefined themselves, and we want to ensure that we are not providing services and benefits based on just one family model that doesn't apply to many city employees."

The status quo has got to go!

Celebrating Relationships

St. Valentine's Day has taken on a new significance for Lesbians and Gays. On February 14, 1990, HRCF began the National Family Registry to lay the groundwork for public recognition of Lesbian and Gay families. A survey of HRCF's women members by Kathleen Stoll, director of Lesbian Issues and Outreach, found that family and relationship issues were a high priority. "To pass legislation supporting our families, we must first educate the public," Kathleen said. The registry together with a Family Photo Album are educational tools in lobbying Congress. Numbers and "seeing" can be persuasive. We have endorsed and participated in both the Registry and Photo Album.

In 1991, St. Valentine's Day really turned out to be a Lesbian/Gay holiday. More than 275 Lesbian and Gay couples took over San Francisco's City Hall to register their relationships openly for the first time. Martha Cody and Susan Berry, both paramedics, were the first of many Lesbian couples to sign the domestic partners declaration. "It's more than a political statement," said Berry. "To us, this is a way to reaffirm our lifelong commitment and love for one another."

An interdenominational religious ceremony was held on the steps outside City Hall. The day's most moving event was the procession of newly-registered domestic partners down the ornate marble staircase to the floor of the rotunda as their names were called. Some carried babies, teddy bears, good-luck charms, flowers, or bottles of champagne. They held hands or walked arm-in-arm as they descended the 36 steps, and scores of cameras and reporters documented their joy.

The procession was followed by an "Affirmation of Partnership" ceremony at which Superior Court Judge Donna Hitchens presided. Speakers included Mayor Art Agnos; Supervisors Roberta Achtenberg, Harry Britt, and Carole Migden; School Board Commissioner Tom Ammiano; and Jean Harris. The Lesbian/Gay Chorus and City Jazz provided entertainment. An evening reception was sponsored by LAFA and nine other Lesbian/Gay organizations. There was a huge celebration cake and close dancing to romantic music.

We missed the whole thing! We had booked passage on the Olivia Valentine's Cruise to celebrate our 38th anniversary. On the Olivia "maiden" voyage the year before on SS *Dolphin IV,* one passenger said she would never forget the commitment ceremony the ship's captain performed for a Lesbian couple. He began, "Wondrous Amazons," and after the cheering died down conveyed that the lovers were joined not by the power vested in him, but the power within themselves and in nature. Judy Dlugacz, president of Olivia Records/Cruises, told us that before the cruise she had given the captain and his staff an orientation about what they could expect—600 women, at least 99 percent Lesbians. "Do you have any problem with that?" she asked. The captain asked Judy, "Who is the oldest known Lesbian?" Judy said, "Sappho?" "Where was she from?" Judy hesitated, wondering why this quiz. "The Isle of Lesbos," the captain replied. "I am from Lesbos. There is no problem." Later a passenger asked a crew member what he thought about having all these Lesbians aboard. He replied, "I am Greek. We invented you!"

Our Olivia Valentine cruise was indeed "a fairytale holiday" as Rand Hall and Nancy Valmus, editors of *The Gazette* of Tampa, Florida, described it. There were a host of activities around the clock, elegant dinners and extravagant buffets, nightly Olivia concerts, star quality entertainment, and stops at Key West and Nassau topped by a trip to Blue Lagoon on Paradise, a private island. And, of course, the Valentine's commitment ceremony by the ship's captain. Lesbian energy, hundreds-fold, was exhilarating and empowering—and fun.

Other events celebrating Lesbian/Gay/Bisexual love were held across the country. There were Kiss-Ins at San Jose, California, the University of Illinois at Chicago, and on the East Coast. In Washington, D.C., "Get a Heart On for Valentine's Day" was the slogan for a Tracks benefit for the Names Project. There was also a Bisexual Women's Valentine Dinner.

Legalization of Gay Marriages

Denmark made world history when 11 Gay male couples were legally married October 1, 1989, at the Town Hall in Copenhagen. An elder couple, Axel Axgil and Eigel Axgil, drew particular attention because Axel was a founder of the Danish Gay Rights movement in 1948. At that time he came out of the closet and was promptly fired from his job.

Members of the National Association for Gays and Lesbians (NAGL) had thought that 50 to 100 couples would show up and be married because of the historical significance. Why no women? Else Slange, president of NAGL, surmised it was a matter of media attention or privacy. She did not plan to marry because of distaste for the patriarchal model of marriage. Having a chance to choose is important, she added.

Denmark's new law gives homosexual couples the same rights and responsibilities as heterosexual married couples with two exceptions: Gays are barred from adopting children, and the state Lutheran Church has the option to refuse to officiate at homosexual weddings. Slange says NAGL will challenge both exceptions.

A routine check of marriage licenses by Danish officials revealed that one Lesbian in her rush to take advantage of the new marriage law forgot to get a divorce from her husband. Her failure resulted in a four-month jail term for bigamy and the first dissolution of a Lesbian marriage in Denmark.

It appears Czechoslovakia is considering Gay marriage as a result of the foreign minister's trip to Denmark. The media planted the idea in the Czech consciousness that equal rights for Gays and Lesbians go hand in hand with democracy and westernization, according to the French magazine *Gai Pied*. Czech Gay/Lesbian activists are delighted.

For a brief time in 1990 several cities in The Netherlands permitted same-sex couples to marry. Then the Dutch Supreme Court declared that marriage is reserved for heterosexuals by the laws of "nature." Almost 80 percent of the Dutch people, including Minister of Justice Hirach-Ballin, favor equal rights for Lesbian and Gay relationships. Leeuwarden's city Board of Supervisors is drafting an ordinance to allow Lesbian and Gay couples to marry. National governments of Holland, Sweden, and Norway are expected to follow Denmark's example. Sweden's parliament passed a measure, but it was vetoed by Secretary of Justice Leila Frievald.

In California at the height of Anita Bryant's anti-Gay crusade, the legislature made it clear that the state's marriage law applied only to man-woman couples. In 1989 feminist attorney Laura Goldin, who is not Gay, made the first move to redefine marriage as a "civil contract between two persons," gender unspecified. She sponsored a resolution to that effect that passed the San Francisco

LESBIAN/WOMAN

and California Bar Associations. The ACLU already had a national policy in favor of Gay marriage. The California Democratic Party joined the pro column. Newspapers such as the *San Francisco Examiner* and the *San Jose Mercury News* endorsed the idea. In 1990 the San Francisco Board of Supervisors became the first government body to call for legalization of Gay marriages. Assemblyman John Burton introduced a bill amending California's Civil Code. Burton said his legislation is fairer than the domestic partners measure, which is largely symbolic. Marriage law extends substantial legal and economic benefits and protects parenting rights as well as inheritance and pension benefits.

Another View on Marriage

Not everyone in the Lesbian/Gay community is overjoyed by the bill, especially its timing. The Lobby for Individual Freedom and Equality (LIFE) had already set passage of AB-101, adding sexual orientation to the state's antidiscrimination law, as a priority for 1991. Conventional wisdom is that AB-101 has a very good chance of passage now that George Deukmejian has vacated the state house. The marriage law is a long-term issue. LIFE would rather it be put on hold. Having public hearings on it might create a media circus that could result in the defeat of both bills.

Attorneys Thomas Stoddard and Paula Ettelbrick of Lambda Legal Defense and Education Fund took opposite sides of the Gay marriage question in *OUT/LOOK* magazine. Both deplored the "institution" of marriage as currently constructed and practiced. Stoddard admitted if given the "right" to marry he probably wouldn't. However, he offered three reasons why Gay marriage is a priority: (1) practical—instant spousal benefits; (2) political—as the centerpiece of our entire social structure it is the key to equality, and (3) philosophical—abolishing gender requirements can help divest the institution of its sexist trappings.

Ettelbrick argued that marriage runs contrary to two primary goals: the affirmation of Gay identity and culture, and validation of many forms of relationships. She emphasized, "We must combine the concept of both rights and justice and work toward goals of true alternatives to marriage and of radically reordering society's view of family."

Religious Ceremonies of Union

For some Lesbians there is a deep yearning for acceptance within their religious denominations and for holy union blessings. Contrary to church doctrine covenant ceremonies for Lesbian and Gay couples have been conducted by individual members of the clergy for decades. Ceremonies for homosexuals are similar to, but not the equivalent of, heterosexual marriage. Neither of them is legal without a state marriage license.

The Commission on Human Sexuality of the Episcopal Diocese of Massachusetts recommended in 1990 that Lesbians and Gay men in "committed and life-giving relationships" should be able to have the blessing of the church. The report was submitted to the parishes for a one-year period, after which the church has the option of taking formal action.

The 230-member congregation of the Dumbarton United Methodist Church in Washington, D.C., approved a policy of "holy unions" for Lesbian/Gay couples with the same seriousness and pastoral support that are afforded heterosexual couples. This action sets the congregation up for possible discipline by the denomination for defying official policy.

Reverend Carla Gorrell, who had been assigned by Presbyterian officials to provide services to the Gay community in Washington, D.C., went too far when she conducted holy union services for Gays. A complaint to the D.C. Presbytery accused her of "delinquency."

Troy Perry, founder of MCC, has conducted Lesbian/Gay "marriages" for over two decades. On Thanksgiving Day, 1990, he performed a holy union for Robin Tyler and Tracy Michaels aboard a cruise ship with 700 Lesbians headed for Mexico, a trip sponsored by Tyler Enterprises. Dozens of couples asked Troy to hold a ceremony for them, too. According to Keith Clark of the *Bay Area Reporter*, "the ever resourceful Tyler managed to transform the SS *Enchanted Isle* into the SS *Enchanted Aisle*."

No matter how we feel personally about domestic partnerships, Gay marriages, or alternative family groupings, as a movement we should not make a decision on which is "politically correct." Instead we should make every effort to see that these options are available to Lesbians and Gays.

The Tragic Case of
Sharon and Karen

Nan Hunter, former director of ACLU's Lesbian and Gay Rights
Project, wrote in *Gay Community News* that denying legal access to
marriage with its affirmation of bonding and material benefits "is
a fundamental violation of civil liberties." Nan referred to the
tragic case of Sharon Kowalski and Karen Thompson as an example of the cruel treatment by the courts and other institutions that
can befall a Lesbian couple in crisis when there is no legal documentation of their relationship. The story of Sharon and Karen has
been variously described as a tragedy, a nightmare, a bitter love
and legal triangle, and a powerful Lesbian love story.

The two women entered into a binding relationship in 1979.
They exchanged rings, bought a house and life insurance, and considered themselves "married," but not Gay. In 1983 Sharon was
critically injured in an automobile accident that radically changed
their lives. Today they are probably the most "out" Lesbian partners in the United States.

Sharon suffered head injuries and was rendered a quadriplegic.
Karen, a professor in the Physical Education Department at St.
Cloud State University, Minnesota, had been trained in occupa-
tional rehabilitation and factors that motivate learning. She was by
Sharon's side constantly helping her in the arduous fight to regain
basic life skills.

"I treated Sharon as if she could recover," Karen said. "Her
long-term memory was intact. She remembered everything before
the accident. Sharon could type words to communicate, swallow
and perform small tasks such as combing her hair. She could even
play checkers."

Sharon's father, however, treated Sharon as a hopeless case to
be put away in a nursing home. Karen wouldn't hear of it and filed
for guardianship. She revealed the nature of her relationship to
Sharon and found she had no legal rights. Though doctors acknowledged that Karen was key to Sharon's progress (Sharon only
responded to Karen), the court awarded guardianship to Donald
Kowalski. He denied his daughter was a Lesbian and claimed that
Sharon was in danger of being sexually abused by Karen. He
barred Karen from any contact with Sharon and moved her to a
nursing home more than 150 miles away.

"He'd rather have his daughter be a vegetable than admit she is a Lesbian," Karen said. From her professional experience she knew what could happen if Sharon didn't have immediate and continuous rehabilitative care. That was 1985—the beginning of a national crusade to bring Sharon home—the filing of countless legal appeals, organizing grass roots financial and emotional support from Lesbian-Gay-women's-disabled-patients rights groups, speaking at rallies and to the media, appealing to government and health agencies. Karen's travels crisscrossed the country. When she was home she spent her spare time collaborating on a book and consulting with attorneys about legal strategy.

Karen was thwarted at every turn. She had no proof she and Sharon had lived together in a relationship like marriage. "I spent four years trying to hide the relationship and four-and-a-half years trying to prove it." No one would listen to Sharon, who confirmed it and pleaded to be with Karen.

Sharon needed proper treatment or she would lose all she had gained when Karen had been working with her. The attorneys hit on a new strategy, getting the court to appoint legal counsel for Sharon to protect her rights. This led to a court ruling that Sharon should be formally tested for competency. Although previous court orders stipulated that her father must have his daughter tested annually, Sharon had not been tested since 1985. Testing was delayed by parental appeals, but Judge Robert Campbell ordered that Sharon be transferred to a rehabilitation center and be allowed to visit whomever she chose.

Finally, after three-and-a-half years of legal battles, Karen and Sharon had an emotional reunion filled with tears and laughter for a whole weekend in February, 1989. Thompson was distressed and angry, however, by the deterioration of Sharon's physical condition. But at this time she was allowed to attend all of Sharon's physical and mental therapy sessions.

Donald Kowalski backed off, saying he could no longer afford legal costs. Presumably the money from the accident insurance settlement was spent in denying Sharon her rights. The judge still refused to award legal guardianship to Karen, but gave her unlimited access to Sharon. She could even bring her home for visits.

In the meantime, Karen Tomberlin, a family friend, asked to be appointed guardian. In a ruling on April 26, 1991, Judge Campbell awarded her guardianship of Sharon and her estate. Fifteen expert witnesses testified that Thompson should be Sharon's guardian, but the judge refused to take the political risk of appointing an "avowed" Lesbian. Karen Thompson is brokenhearted. "If we had been in a legally recognized marriage this would not have happened to us," she said. She plans to appeal on grounds that the judge did not follow Minnesota's legal procedures in making his appointment.

This brief account doesn't begin to do justice to the transformation of Karen Thompson, a simple midwestern woman who was apolitical, religious, and extremely conservative. Circumstances propelled her to come out nationally before she had really come out to herself. During her courageous and unwavering struggle against overwhelming odds she became radicalized. Today she is an activist, an eloquent advocate for the rights of the disabled and for Lesbian/Gay domestic partners.

Even if you have seen news clippings or heard Karen speak, you should **buy** and read *Why Can't Sharon Kowalski Come Home?* by Julie Andrzcjewski and Karen. To us it is "the ultimate Lesbian love story." Royalties will help to defray the enormous legal costs Karen incurred in her quest for justice.

Gay Political Gains

In the political arena we have experienced many triumphs in the past two decades. In 1972 Madeline Davis of Buffalo, New York, and Jim Foster, founder of the Alice B. Toklas Memorial Democratic Club, San Francisco, presented the first Gay rights plank, albeit a minority report, in the wee hours of the morning at the Democratic National Convention. We were surprised and thrilled to hear Jim quoting *Lesbian/Woman* from the podium on national television. (Sadly, we heard Jim's presentation again in the Fall of 1990 at his memorial service.) In 1980, with many more Lesbian and Gay delegates and representation on the platform and other influential committees, Gay rights became part of the Democratic Party's platform.

In 1974 Elaine Noble was elected to the Massachusetts House of Representatives, the first open Lesbian to be elected to state office. Elaine, who was a member of the Boston Chapter of the Daughters of Bilitis, was elected to two terms. When she first came to the legislature several of her colleagues tried to block her from taking her seat. The move failed, but the verbal abuse continued. With disarming courage and hard work, Elaine gradually won them over. In her second term the three top Democrats—all male and all conservative—actively worked for passage of her 1977 Gay Rights bill. It still failed, but by a much narrower margin, 120 to 101. Elaine did manage to get a state ERA passed.

Her success as a Lesbian legislator prompted State Senator Allen Spears to come out in Minnesota. His disclosure did not prevent his reelection. In 1980, Representative Karen Clark, also of Minnesota, became the second open Lesbian to be elected to state office. Kathy Kozachenko, a 22-year-old Lesbian, was elected in 1975 to a seat on the Ann Arbor City Council in Michigan. Over the years Lesbians have been elected to city and state offices, including mayor, but they have not been "out."

Besides our lobbyists in Washington, D.C., there are Lesbian lobbyists in state capitols. Laurie McBride is the executive director of LIFE in California. Laura Zambardi was hired by Virginians for Justice as the first lobbyist for Gay concerns in Virginia. Betty Naylor served for many years as lobbyist for Lesbians and Gays in Texas. Betty Gallo is a lobbyist for the Connecticut Coalition for Lesbian and Gay Civil Rights. When California NOW's State Coordinator Shireen Mills gave up her post in 1989 after four years of service, she was honored by the state legislature as "Woman of the Year." Lynn D. Shepodd has held an important role as aide to California's Senate President Pro Tem David Roberti.

In the 70s many Lesbians and Gays began to organize political clubs within both the Democratic and Republican parties. Candidates soon learned that this voting bloc could deliver not only votes but financial support and workers. They began to seek endorsements from the clubs and Lesbian/Gay leaders. They also found that we are not just one-issue, self interest oriented, but are better informed on major issues than many other groups they encounter on the campaign trail.

Our political clubs are a good training ground for aspiring Lesbian and Gay candidates. In 1982 eight Lesbians and Gay men were elected out of 24 openings on San Francisco's County Democratic Council, a number that has held steady ever since. Today there are national associations of the Lesbian/Gay political clubs and elected officials. And there are countless numbers of us who have been appointed to city and state commissions as open Lesbians.

At the March on Washington, D.C., in 1979 we came 100,000 strong. About 40 percent more Lesbians marched than ever before. Lesbian feminist Arlie Scott said at the rally: "Look at us, America. You know us. You see us in your offices, you see us in your schools, your churches, in your government. . . . In the 80s we are moving from Gay Pride to Gay politics. No longer will we tolerate the violence of our enemies, nor the silence of our friends. . . . Listen, America. You are going to have to deal with us in the 80s."

Community agencies providing services for Lesbians had to become more politically savvy in the 80s. They had to learn the art of writing grant proposals and how to tap into community development government funds. They had to get away from the garage sale mentality and go for big bucks.

In San Francisco the Women's Foundation was started with Lesbian money and staffed by Lesbian co-directors Roma Guy and Marya Grambs. When the first ten grants were awarded one went to LRP (our 10 percent). That caused a lot of flak from the Foundation's supporters and prompted the development of an educational program on homophobia. Later Roma received the award for the Women's Foundation from the Girls' Clubs of America. In accepting she said the Foundation was set up to serve all women and girls, including Lesbians. No one appeared to have trouble with the L-word.

Organizations catering to upwardly mobile Lesbians flourished in the 80s. They started in California and spread to Oregon, Washington, and Arizona. BACW now has a charitable fund which is distributed to Lesbian service organizations. Lesbians who inherited wealth formed Resourceful Women to provide funding for worthy Lesbian projects. The Chicago Women's Resource Center has also been a funding source. Recently a new national grant-making program, the OUT Fund for Lesbian and Gay Liberation, started under the aegis of the Funding Exchange.

Lesbians began talking about the lack of Lesbian visibility and held conferences about empowerment, political clout, and the Lesbian agenda. In 1988 two Lesbians, Carole Migden, chair of the San Francisco Democratic Party, and Jean O'Leary, who served on

President Carter's Women's Committee, became members of the Democratic Party's National Committee.

Thus the groundwork had been laid for a Lesbian coup in the 1990 elections. In the June primary Donna Hitchens was elected to the Superior Court in San Francisco, defeating a white male incumbent. This triumph was followed by a "Lavender Sweep" in the November election. Two Lesbians, Roberta Achtenberg and Carole Migden, were elected to San Francisco's Board of Supervisors. This turn of events was reinforced when Tom Ammiano, Gay comic and teacher, received the most votes in the Board of Education race. And Proposition K, which provided for The City's domestic partners registry, passed.

When the new supervisors were inaugurated they both proudly introduced their domestic partners. Roberta added, "My son Benjie knows many kids from different families. He has met enough of them to know that two moms is not the only legitimate form of family." Roberta's lover is Judge Mary Morgan, appointed to the Municipal Court in 1981 by Governor Jerry Brown. Mayor Art Agnos later said, "They are probably the most powerful couple in The City."

Also in California, Santa Monica's city council unanimously elected its only woman member and out Lesbian, Judy Abdo, as mayor. And a Gay man who received the most votes in the election became the only man on the city's school board.

On the East Coast Deborah Glick, with 78 percent of the vote, won a seat in New York's General Assembly. When she took the oath of office she held one hand up and rested the other on a copy of *Sisterhood Is Powerful.* Already she has introduced a domestic partners bill. In Maine, Lesbian activist Dale McCormick won a seat in the state Senate with her victory over the Republican incumbent. McCormick's sexual orientation was an issue in letters to the editor, but most people were supportive because of her openness. In the Midwest Karen Clark was reelected to her sixth term in the Minnesota legislature, garnering 72 percent of the vote.

Also in the 1990 elections, HRCF tallied 113 Congressional victories including 19 brand new members of Congress, 15 of whom indicated they would sign on to the the Federal Gay Rights bill.

New York City Mayor Dinkins appointed three women and one man as judges early in 1990. Dinkins' press office identified two as

Lesbians: Rosalyn Richter, former director of Lambda Defense and Education Fund, and Paula Hepner, supervising attorney of New York City's Human Resources Administration. After the third woman, former state senator Karen Burstein, had been sworn in, she introduced her female life partner.

When a vacancy on the Contra Costa County, California, Human Relations Commission did not go to a Lesbian or Gay, community groups were highly critical. That prompted Commissioner Sherry-Ann Nichols to come out. In Oregon Gail Shibley was appointed to the Oregon State House to fill out the term of a legislator who had become secretary of state. Minutes later she came out publicly as a Lesbian.

We have more visibility and more political clout than ever before. These gains have been made in spite of homophobic bigots who have been hounding us for the past 15 years. The evidence shows that Lesbians need not be precluded from political careers. Lesbian activists agree that it is only through our visibility that we will gain any freedom, either individually or collectively. We are establishing our own agenda and we must be prepared to seize opportunities as they open up. As Carmen Vazquez put it at a LAFA conference, "There is an absolute necessity of creating and supporting networks, organizations, institutions and movements that don't stammer or equivocate the existence of Lesbians and the contributions of Lesbians to everything that can be called human."

Old Is In—Ageism Is Out

Lesbians of our generation spent most of our lives in the closet. A large number of the 160 attending the first Old Lesbian West Coast Conference and Celebration had waited until their children were grown and had left home before coming out. The conference, held at California State University/Dominguez Hills in 1987, was a time of meeting one's peers, of consciousness raising, finding a common voice, and defining our own turf.

Old is In. Ageism is Out. Forget words like older, elder, or senior. Lesbians over 60 are **old** as a matter of chronology, a biological fact. "You're in good shape for your age," or "That makes you look younger," are not compliments. They are ageist remarks. Illness, being confined to a wheelchair, loss of sight or hearing are not inherent risks of old age but rather risks of life. Old Lesbians are sisters, not mothers, of young Lesbians.

This was a recurring theme at the second Old Lesbian Conference and Celebration held two years later at San Francisco State University which zeroed in on expanding the network nationally. For the 1991 National Lesbian Conference in Atlanta, the Old Lesbian Organizing Committee (OLOC) put together a full day of activities and made sure that old Lesbians had a visible showing.

Monika

Monika Kehoe, Ph.D., who is now an authority on old Lesbians, lived in the closet until she arrived in San Francisco when she was 69 and rode with Win Cottrell and the Gray Panthers in the 1978 Lesbian/Gay Pride Parade. She told us of the time in the 30s when Gertrude Stein lectured at Ohio State. Monika, so naive, didn't know who Stein was. Stein was dressed in a long burlap skirt, a man's serge jacket and vest, had short hair and spoke in a deep voice. "I was so overwhelmed by her appearance I didn't hear a thing she said. My reaction astonishes me now." Monika never heard the word Lesbian until she was 40, never wore slacks in public until she came to San Francisco.

Monika, now in her 83rd year, serves as Research Associate at the Center for Research in Education and Sexuality and just (1991) retired from teaching in the Gerontology Institute at San Francisco State. Her book *Lesbians Over Sixty Speak for Themselves* was published in 1989. She serves on the boards of the Older Women's League and Gay and Lesbian Outreach to Elders, and is a member of Options for Women Over 40 and the Gray Panthers. Monika takes pets to nursing homes as a volunteer in the Pet Therapy Program of the SPCA. She still plays and coaches tennis. Her recipe for a healthy old age: exercise.

Lesbian Diversity

When announcements first go out about national or international conferences, expectations abound about the pride and strength in a gathering of dykes hundreds or even thousands strong. The expression "We are everywhere" that became a slogan after the Houston IWY conference conveys our diversity. We come from different racial, ethnic, religious, educational, generational, and class backgrounds. We are out, in the closet, institutionalized, disabled, single, or coupled. We are mothers, part of an extended family. We are political activists for whom "political" has many meanings—mainstream electoral politics, separatism ("the personal is political," woman-only culture), sexual freedom (sex education, S/M, anti-porn, anti-censorship).

We have different ways of organizing meetings: From Roberta's rules and majority vote to processing in a leaderless, structureless frame of reference to reach consensus. Like any group we have differences of opinion—not so much on what the issues are as how to attain our goals.

We have learned the hard way—from the disastrous 1973 National Lesbian Conference at the University of California, Los Angeles, when everyone came with her own expectations and agenda. Featured speakers got their cues mixed up: Poet Robin Morgan (now editor of the new *Ms.* magazine) gave a political speech and Kate Millet waxed poetical instead of talking about *Sexual Politics.* And we have learned from NOW-sponsored national Lesbian conferences (Milwaukee in 1984 and San Diego in 1988), which for many may have been too structured.

The 1991 National Lesbian Conference

In all the history of Lesbian conferences there had not been the scale of outreach and inclusiveness as at the 1991 NLC in Atlanta. The theme, "Diversity, Solidarity, Empowerment," reflects the organizers' pledge to fight racism and other forms of oppression. An expansive affirmative action goal showed this commitment: 50 percent of the planning committees, entertainers, and workshop leaders would be Lesbians of color; 20 percent of the seats on the steering committee were reserved for Lesbians with disabilities, and 5 percent for old Lesbians. Planners attended to special needs such as: housing, diets, child care, signing for the hearing impaired, wheelchair access, low income scholarships, and a clean and sober environment with 12-step programs available. Use of camera flashes and wearing of scents were banned for health reasons.

Every effort was made by the planners to build trust, provide a safe place, and encourage participation from all segments of the Lesbian population. They succeeded. Almost 3,000 Lesbians came together at the conference, the first of its kind dedicated to the inclusion of *all* Lesbians. The vast span of our diversity was shown in the official conference poster by artist Pat Wiles.

In addition to workshops aimed at the various isms of oppression, speakers at the plenary sessions reflected our diversity and reinforced the need to do away with institutional and personal prejudices which sometimes separate us. Issues of disabled persons were dealt with more extensively than at any other event. Old Lesbians had their day, and Lesbian youth took exception to the word "ageism" as applied only to the old. Lesbian veterans and those still in the military evoked a strong emotional response from anti-war Lesbians. One plenary session dealt with Lesbians in poverty and with inherited wealth. If burning subjects had been omitted time was allotted for plenary speakouts.

The five-day program was so all-inclusive that it ran nonstop from 9 a.m. to as late as 2 a.m. Taking time out to eat could mean missing something important. The Market Place was a vast space for art, crafts, books, and the familiar buttons and tee shirts. There were dances, afternoon performances in the "showcase," and a grand concert.

There were glitches as could be expected in the best of all worlds and perhaps were inevitable considering the size of the conference. Processing in a leaderless structure may work on a small scale at a local level, but is nigh unto impossible on a national scale. About 200 attended one or more meetings of the steering committee. Planning lacked continuity because of sporadic attendance due to lack of travel funds. The operation had only three paid staff. Just getting us all together was a miracle in itself. And togetherness is empowering.

At the Queer Nation workshop we learned Connecticut had become the fourth state to pass a Gay rights bill. A woman said that Lesbian feminists, frustrated by 18 years of struggle for such a bill, formed their own Queer Nation group and took a more militant stance. *The Washington Blade's* report credited the Connecticut Coalition for Lesbian and Gay Civil Rights and the "coming out" speech of state legislator Joe Grabarz.

Probably all three approaches worked. Our experience shows militant groups like Queer Nation and ACT UP that "stretch the limits" capture media attention, allowing others to grab the moment to press their case—a sort of one-two jab to get the job done.

The last plenary session on Sunday afternoon was poorly attended because many had to leave to get back in time for work Monday. No vote was taken on the possibility of a national Lesbian organization or another conference. Sentiment leaned toward using the empowering energy of the conference to strengthen Lesbian organizing at the grassroots level, to use skills learned in workshops to resolve differences, and to build statewide and regional coalitions.

To our knowledge Texas is the only state thus far with organized annual Lesbian meetings. Del attended the fourth Texas Lesbian Conference (TLC) prior to the Atlanta meeting. TLC, she found, also meant "tender loving care." A plenary session called "Lesbians of Color Speak Out" was set up as a modified fishbowl. Hispanic and African-American speakers first introduced themselves and talked about their people. In the second round they expressed feelings such as, "I don't want to hear . . ." And finally, "As my ally I expect you to . . ." After each round the audience was asked to report what they heard. At the end the coordinator said she was pleased that people actually listened. "We know you will still make some mistakes, but we will forgive you and still love you." This nonconfrontational emotional and educational approach resulted in new understanding and sense of togetherness—and a lot of hugging.

Toward the end of the NLC, Urvashi Vaid charged our batteries when she looked forward to the "new world order" when Lesbians pull together as one and no longer need splinter group representatives on an unwieldly steering committee. A New World Order of changed priorities in which a reduced Pentagon budget would allow institution of national health care. No more money for warfare, more money for well fare. "The Lesbian agenda," she said, "is making social change, eliminating discrimination within our own movement and in the **New World Order.**"

Lesbian Leadership and Leadership Styles

Urvashi also touched on a subject that has been bothering us— Lesbian leadership. She was excited, as we were, to see and meet so many Lesbian leaders at the conference. She remarked, "We need to honor them, not trash them."

For two decades Lesbians have been striving to find a way to organize that will not mimic patriarchal structure—a way to be as inclusive and democratic as possible and yet function and move ahead. Consensus has proved to be painstakingly slow at times when quick decisions need to be made. And the concept of leaders as "elitists" inhibited efforts to form NLFO in 1978. If the delegates and nondelegates who had experienced triumph and empowerment at the IWY conference had been able to stay over for another week we probably would have come up with a national organization. We did wind up with a national network which has sustained us as a national Lesbian movement.

Lesbian Agenda for the 90s

The 90s have brought us to another plateau. More of us are coming out, giving voice and visibility to Lesbians distinct from the Gay and women's movements. We can see articulate, committed Lesbian leaders emerging among our youth, from so-called leaderless groups, among Lesbians of color, from caucuses within professional and religious institutions, among the old who have recently come out, within political parties, among the disabled, in cities and rural areas across the nation. We are delighted to see this happening. It proves that coming out is empowering individually and collectively.

It behooves us to develop and treasure our new leaders. They need a grounding in our herstory (perhaps a mentorship program), a handle on our rapidly changing society (from the horse and buggy to the space age in one lifetime), and a global vision for the future (emphasizing connections, alliances, coalitions).

Family issues are at the top of the Lesbian agenda of the 90s. *Our Paper*, San Jose, California, calls itself "The Gay Family Paper of the Santa Clara Valley," reminding us of the days when mention of homosexuality was not fit for family newspapers. The traditional patriarchal family has been on the decline for decades and comprises only 26 percent of all American households. Most people fall into alternative family groups: single-parent, adoptive, or foster; unmarried couples and Lesbian or Gay couples with or without children; homesharing by old or disabled people. These are critically important social units deserving of respect and protection.

From 1979 to the present various presidential, state, and local task forces on the family have had to recognize family diversity. But government/media/business have yet to catch up to social change. They still accord majority status and privilege to the 26 percent minority. The time has come to deal with reality. Families affected by this tyranny of the minority need to coalesce politically to redefine families by function rather than structure, recognize the wide range of existing committed relationships, and demand that their legitimate needs be met in an equitable fashion.

England's Clause 28 refers to Lesbian/Gay relationships as "pretended" families. Representatives of Brighton Area Action Against Section 28 and Outrage! interrupted the opening speech by Princess Diana at the 1990 International Congress for the Family in London. They walked on stage and handed her a flyer while carrying a sign, "Lesbian Mothers Are Not Pretending."

Initial plans by the National Conferences on Parenting of Santa Clara, California, for its "Family 2000" conference held in San Francisco in February, 1991, failed to include Lesbian and Gay families. GLAAD and Queer Nation activists pointed out this omission and were offered the one remaining display booth, a workshop, and inclusion of Lesbian/Gay spokespersons in several existing workshops.

Two video documentaries on Lesbian herstory will be forthcoming in the early 90s. "Last Call at Maud's," produced by Paris Poirier, is about the longest surviving Lesbian bar in the United States. Maud's, in San Francisco's Haight-Ashbury district, closed its doors in 1989 after 23 years as a haven for thousands of women from all over the world. The "Daughters of Bilitis Video" produced by Sara Yager, Manuela Soares, and Morgan Gwenwald will be available through the Lesbian Herstory Archives in New York City.

With the help of IGLHRC and in recognition of our sister city relationship, a delegation of Lesbians and Gays from San Francisco traveled to Moscow in July, 1991, to join in the first Lesbian/Gay Pride Celebration in Russia.

The 90s Lesbian/Gay calendar of events promises to be exciting. In 1992 the National Health Care March on Washington organized by Gays and non-Gays will push for sweeping reform of the entire United States health care system. Attention in the 90s will also center on electing Lesbian/Gay delegates to the Democratic and

Republican conventions and getting appointments to key commit-tees. Plans are in the works for another Lesbian/Gay March on Washington in April, 1993.

The major event of the decade, "Stonewall 25," calls for a massive global celebration of Lesbian/Gay Pride and Protest in New York City. June, 1994, will mark the 25th anniversary of the Stonewall riots and the 30th anniversary of the Civil Rights Act. That year the annual human and civil rights march and entertainment rally, and the Gay Pride Parade, on the weekend of June 25–26 will be supplemented by many major events: Gay Games IV/Unity '94 with over 12,000 athletes and 60,000 spectators from more than 40 countries; the ILGA conference representing 170 organizations from 55 countries; joint concert of Lesbian/Gay Bands of America featuring 500 musi-cians from around the world; chorus of 1,000 voices assembled by the Gay/Lesbian Choral Association; national conferences of Men of All Colors Together/Black and White Men Together, and P-FLAG; the largest worship service of Lesbians and Gays ever hosted by MCC; and major activities directed toward the U.N.

Today's world is in a state of upheaval. The Berlin Wall has been torn down. By 1992 Western Europe expects to become United Eu-rope. The Eastern Bloc is in a state of transition. The struggle be-tween Black Africans and the South African white government is changing ever so slowly. The arms race between superpowers Russia and the United States has bankrupted both countries. Russian people are struggling to get the bare necessities of life. The United States national debt is more than $3 trillion. The Reagan and Bush admin-istrations made the rich richer and the poor homeless during more than a decade of indifference and neglect.

In this state of flux and uncertainty, of turmoil and tyranny, Lesbians and Gays around the planet have decided there is no better time than now to organize and stand up for their rights. Some have declared the last decade of the 20th century "The Gay 90s." But the increasing visibility of Lesbians, their election and appointment to city and state office as open Lesbians, the expan-sion of the National Center for Lesbian Rights, and the success of the 1991 National Lesbian Conference to gather together every conceivable group within the group, lead us to believe the 90s is the Decade of the Lesbians.

List of Acronyms in Text

ACLU—American Civil Liberties Union
ACT UP—AIDS Coalition to Unleash Power
AFSC—American Friends Service Committee
AI—Amnesty International
AID—Artificial Insemination by Donor
AIDS—Acquired Immunodeficiency Syndrome
ALA—American Library Association
APA—American Psychiatric Association
ARC—AIDS Related Conditions
BACW—Bay Area Career Women
BGLLF—Black Gay and Lesbian Leadership Forum
CACTUS—CFIDS Action Campaign for the United States
CDC—Centers for Disease Control
CFS—Chronic Fatigue Syndrome
CFIDS—Chronic Fatigue Immune Dysfunction Syndrome
CIA—Central Intelligence Agency
CLOUT—Christian Lesbians Out Together
CUAV—Community United Against Violence
DOB—Daughters of Bilitis
DOD—Department of Defense
DSM—Diagnostic and Statistical Manual of Psychiatric Disorders
EI—Environmental Illness
ERA—Equal Rights Amendment
FBI—Federal Bureau of Investigation
GALS—Gay Assistance League for Servicewomen
GAO—General Accounting Office

GLAAD—Gay and Lesbian Alliance Against Defamation
GLC—Greater London Council
HIV—Human Immunodeficiency Virus
HOSI—Homosexuelle Initiative Wien in Vienna, Austria
HRCF—Human Rights Campaign Fund
IGLHRC—International Gay and Lesbian Human Rights
  Committee
ILGA—International Lesbian and Gay Association
INS—Immigration and Naturalization Service
IWY—International Women's Year
LAFA—Lesbian Agenda for Action
LAPV—Lesbians Against Police Violence
LIFE—Lobby for Individual Freedom and Equality
LRP—Lesbian Rights Project
LYRIC—Lavender Youth Recreation and Information Center
MCC—Metropolitan Community Church
MVR—Massachusetts Volunteer Regiment
NAGL—National Association for Gays and Lesbians in Denmark
NCBLG—National Coalition of Black Lesbians and Gays
NCLR—National Center for Lesbian Rights
NEA—National Endowment for the Arts
NGLTF—National Gay and Lesbian Task Force
NGO—Non Governmental Organization
NGRA—National Gay Rights Advocates
NGTF—National Gay Task Force
NLC—National Lesbian Conference
NLFO—National Lesbian Feminist Organization
NOW—National Organization for Women
NWC—National Women's Conference
NWCC—National Women's Continuing Committee
OLOC—Old Lesbian Organizing Committee
P-FLAG—Parents and Friends of Lesbians and Gays
ROTC—Reserve Officer Training Corps
SPPR—Society for the Protection of Personal Rights in Israel
TLC—Texas Lesbian Conference
UN—United Nations
WAC—Women's Army Corps
WCRC—Women's Cancer Resource Center